THE SEATON FAMILY

WITH

GENEALOGY AND BIOGRAPHIES

BY

OREN ANDREW SEATON, Editor.

Topeka, Kansas:
CRANE & COMPANY,
1906.

Copyright 1906, by O. A. Seaton.

CRANE & COMPANY.

TO

ALL THE PRESENT AND FUTURE

GENERATIONS OF SEATONS,

especially

To all of the writer's relatives,

THIS GENEALOGY OF THE SEATON FAMILY

IS AFFECTIONATELY DEDICATED,

*As a matter of pleasure and duty, with the hope that some one of them will continue
the subject as existing conditions require; that no one of them will ever commit an act that might cause a blush of shame on the face of any
member of the family, or that he and they would not willingly see published with their names by future
writers of the family history.*

PREFACE.

THE work of preparing this book has been done almost entirely in the idle moments, rainy days, and other odd spells of a busy man's working hours in his grain office, when there was no other regular work unperformed.

The typewriter stood on its desk, capable, ready and convenient, and was made use of as opportunity offered; the work being dropped, even in the middle of a word, to wait upon a present, prospective customer, and not approached again sometimes for days at a time when business was flourishing.

This work has been the fad or pastime of the writer, for all ambitious business men must have some relaxation from their regular work and worry. It has also been a work of love in which this Scripture injunction has been heeded:

" Remember the days of old, consider the years of many generations; ask thy father and he will shew thee; thy elders and they will tell thee."—Deuteronomy xxxii. 7.

It might have been pardonable had we spelled the name of each member of the family S-e-a-t-o-n, but in deference to the different writers on the subject and to some members of the different branches of the family, their spelling of the name has been retained, except possibly in a moment of preoccupation, when the name may have been written mechanically, as it were, from force of habit.

At the request of friends for information as to where we connect with the great family whose heroic deeds have been set forth in

Archbishop Robert Seton's inimitable work, "An Old Family, The Setons of Scotland and America," the copyright of that book has been purchased and enough material has been gleaned from that magnificent memorial of a pious, learned, and indefatigable man to show the connection. And we take this opportunity to recommend the above genealogy as the best in existence without regard to cost, and as well worth the price asked, to anyone interested in the history of our ancient family.

This book is intended as a continuation of "An Old Family" along some lines not brought down to date in the former. There are also some added statements from other authorities, in regard to some persons whose names appear in the earlier work.

It is with regret the work must be presented in its present imperfect condition, in many instances resembling the bare skeleton of a deciduous tree in springtime before the new-born leaves and lovely blossoms have clothed it with living verdure, making it "a thing of beauty and a joy forever." But, where the necessary facts to make each individual life sketch as complete as desired, could not be ascertained from outside sources, and the subject of the sketch could not, or would not, render the desired assistance, we have been compelled to console ourselves with the old saying which declares that "What cannot be cured must be endured."

It is feared some errors may have crept unnoticed into the statements made herein, but the best possible efforts have been made to prevent anything of the kind happening, and it is hoped that anyone finding any such slips of the fingers on the typewriter, or misinformation, will kindly advise the writer, so corrections may be made before a revision is attempted. And if any possible mistake of the writer's should happen to touch you, dear reader, in a tender place, you will please be generous enough to remember that errors have appeared in very much more pretentious volumes. In this connection be pleased to read what is said in the Bible, the greatest and best of all books, as to the sons of Benjamin: First Chronicles, vii. 6, 7; then in chapter viii. 1, 2; and again in Numbers, xxvi. 38, and in Genesis xlvi. 21; or where the descendants of Bela are given, in First Chronicles, vii. 7, and viii. 3 and 5; and in Numbers xxvi. 40. And still further, kindly remember that the writer was not on the spot when each incident mentioned is reported to have happened, but has been obliged to take some one's word for the fact and the date thereof. Also, that the writer of this page makes no pretensions to being the author of the book, but compares himself, in this connection, to a fisherman who frequently passes his office with a considerable string of fish. After much search the fisher finds the proper place to cast his hook, baits it the best he knows how, and then strings the catch together, just as the several biographies are being strung together here. This genealogy is really a book of quotations, very little herein being original with us. In the words of the poet,

> "We have gathered posies from other men's flowers,
> And nothing but the string that binds them is ours."

With kindest regards to every one mentioned in the body of the work, and all their kith and kin, I remain, as ever and forever, your humble servant and well-wisher,

OREN ANDREW SEATON.

ACKNOWLEDGMENTS.

OUR grateful acknowledgments are due to all who have assisted in gathering material for this work, and their names are many. But especially are we indebted for assistance in tracing the earlier generations, to Monsignor Seton's matchless work, "An Old Family. The Setons in Scotland and America"; to Leonard Seaton, Jr., of Henderson, New York; to John Seaton, of Greenup, Kentucky, who in the kindness of his heart has turned over to us the gleanings of his father and himself, for a period of seventy-five years, in the genealogical field; to "A Biographical Sketch of William Winston Seaton," Editor of the *National Intelligencer* of Washington, D. C., and for ten years Mayor of that city; and last, but not least, to Samuel T. Seaton, Editor of the Olathe *Register*, of Olathe, Kansas, a lawyer of experience, our friend and co-worker, the most enthusiastic and successful searcher of recent years in the field of genealogy.

We have found some one or more of the family mentioned in, or assisting with, the following works, or we have made quotations from them. No apology is offered for the length of the list; it is by no means complete, and would have been much longer if more time had been allowed to the search.

Abbott's Life of Mary Queen of Scots, mentioned on pages 39, 84, 85.
Abilene Chronicle, 340.
A Biographical Sketch of William Winston Seaton, 96, 106, 107, 109, 113, 114, 118.
Alan of Winton and the Heiress of Seton, 55, 114, 118.
Abstracts of Virginia Land Patents, 103.
Academia Ecclesiastic, 99.
Advocates Library of Edinburgh, Scotland, 64.
A Group of College Stories, 39.
A Jacobite Family, 90.
An Old Family, 8, 49, 50, 67, 77, 82, 93, 95, 97, 99, 100, 103, 387.
Antiquities of Edinburgh, 64.
A Recantation, 37.
Bible, 7, 9, 35, 39, 44, 108, 115, 313, 375.

Birds of Manitoba, 100.
Blue Laws of Connecticut, 116.
Bridge's Northamptonshire, 390.
Brief Notices of Families (Arnot's), 390.
British Museum, 34, 57, 83.
Brown Book, The, 11, 15.
Buchanan's History of Scotland, 37, 53, 55, 73, 75, 85, 86, 88, 103.
Burke's Landed Gentry and Peerage and Baronetage, 45, 387.
Caledonian, The, 47.
Camden's Works, 11.
California Law Reports, 390.
Cedar Rapids Republican, 139.
Century Dictionary, 100.
Century Magazine, 113.
Chambers's Encyclopædia, 71, 76, 151.
Chambers's Family of Gordon, 58.
Chart of the Descendants of John and Elizabeth Seton, 14.
Cincinnati Commercial Tribune, 97, 182.
Clan Ferguson, The, 237.
Clark's Heraldry, 30.
Continental Encyclopædia, 111.
Courier, The 339.
Cram's Atlas, 33.
Descendants of Comfort Sands, 14.
Descendants of John Ogden, 14.
Descendants of Martinus Hoffman, 14.
Detective, The, 137.
Dictionary of English Literature, 11.
Dictionary of National Biography, 36, 387.
Dignity of Labor, The, 99.
Doomsday Book, 11.
Dugdale's Works, 11, 32.
Eminent Men of Kansas, 216, 319.
Encyclopædia Britannica, 37, 48, 50, 113, 389.
Family of Seton, The, 93.
Family of Seyton, The, 37, 38, 71, 72, 76, 77, 78, 80, 82, 390.
Farmer's History of Amherst, New Hampshire, 241.
Ferguson's Handbook of Architecture, 151.
Fitzhugh's Valleys of Virginia, 105.
Fordun's History, 55.
Freeman's History of the Goths, 42.
Freeman's Norman Conquest, 11.
Froissart's Works, 57.
Galesburg Free Democrat, 339.
Genealogist's Guide, 11.
Genealogy by Pierce, 388.
Genesis of the United States, 104.
Gibson's Works, 42.
Gordon's Genealogical History, 58.
Gravestones, 255, 322.
Gray Days and Gold (Winter's), 70.
Gray's Elegy, 243.
Greek Politics, Utopian and Practical, 364.
Green Book, The, 11, 15.
Hatfield's Historical Notes of Doncaster, 390.

Rangers of the Frontier, 388.
Records of Cities, Churches, and Courts, 106, 111, 240, 247, 257, 392
Record of the Bayley Family in America, 14.
Register of the Privy Seal, 68.
Richmond Journal, A, 110.
Robertson's History, 107.
Ruins of Seton Chapel, The, 67.
Salina Herald. The, 221.
Scotch Guards in France, The, 68.
Scotch History, 37, 39, 40, 48, 53, 73, 103.
Scottish Chiefs, 50.
Scott's Works, 35, 36, 37, 39, 47, 50, 60, 71, 72, 76, 78, 79, 80, 84, 90, 102.
Seaton's Manual of Marine Engineering, 321.
Seecomb's History of Amherst, 236, 240, 242, 244.
Seton of Parbroath in Scotland and America, 14.
Seton's Law and Practice of Heraldry, 27.
Some Account of the Family of Prime, etc., 14.
Student's Herald, The, 226.
Swinburn's Works, 48.
Taylor's Works, 55.
The Olirestob Hamiltons, 14.
Thermodynamics of the Steam Engine, 321.
Tytler's History, 49.
Valleys of Virginia, 105.
Virginia Historical Magazine, The, 103, 104, 38'.
Virginia Land Patents, 103.
Warranties of Land, 366, 389.
Webster's (Daniel) Writings, 113, 134, 290.
Webster's (Noah) International Dictionary, 134.
Western Watchman, The, 99.
Who's Who, 39.
Who's Who in America, 39.
Wild Animals I have known, 101.
William Winston Seaton, A Biographical Sketch, 96, 106, 107, 109, 113, 114, 118.
Wood's Memoirs of Walter Pringle, 390.
Wyman's Record of Families, 245

BIBLIOGRAPHY.

I. THE HISTORY OF THE HOUSE OF SEYTOUN TO THE YEAR MDLIX. By Sir Richard Maitland of Lethington, Knight, with a continuation, by Alexander Viscount Kingston, to MDCLXXXVII. Printed at Glasgow, MDCCCXXIX.

II. A HISTORY OF THE FAMILY OF SETON DURING EIGHT CENTURIES. By George Seton, Advocate, M. A. Oxon., etc. Two volumes. Edinburgh, 1896.

III. SETON OF PARBROATH IN SCOTLAND AND AMERICA. Printed for private circulation. 12 mo, pp. 28. 1890.

IV. THE OLIVESTOB HAMILTONS. By Rev. Arthur Wentworth Hamilton Eaton, B. A., New York. Privately printed, 1893.

V. CHART OF THE DESCENDANTS OF JOHN AND ELIZABETH SETON.

VI. RECORD OF THE BAYLEY FAMILY IN AMERICA. By Guy Carleton Bayley, M. D., Poughkeepsie. N. Y.

VII. DESCENDANTS OF JOHN OGDEN. 1640. By Henry Ogden, Esquire, of New York.

VIII. DESCENDANTS OF MARTINUS HOFFMAN. B. 1640. D. 1671. With Notes. By Lindley Murray Hoffman, Esquire, of New York.

IX. SOME ACCOUNT OF THE FAMILY OF PRIME OF ROWLEY, MASS. With Notes on the Families Platts and Jewett. By Temple Prime. Second edition (illustrated), New York. 1897.

X. DESCENT OF COMFORT SANDS AND HIS CHILDREN. With Notes on the Families of Ray, Thomas, Guthrie, Alcock, Palgrave, Cornell, Dodge, Hunt, and Jessup. By Temple Prime. Second edition. New York. 1897.

(14)

XI. THE GREEN BOOK. Contains Notes, Recollections, and Memoranda of the Seton Family. The earliest entry is 1797.

XII. THE BROWN BOOK. Contains Notes and Memoranda made by Archbishop Seton while visiting Scotland in 1855, 1861, 1889. and 1896.

XIII. AN OLD FAMILY, THE SETONS OF SCOTLAND AND AMERICA. By Monsignor Seton. New York, Brentano's. 1899.

XIV. WILLIAM WINSTON SEATON. of the *National Intelligencer,* Washington, D. C. A Biographical Sketch, with Passing Notices of His Associates and Friends. Boston, 1871. Written by his daughter, Josephine Seaton, and published by James R. Osgood & Company.

Robert Seton, D.D.

INTRODUCTION

BY

ARCHBISHOP ROBERT SETON,

OF

VIA DEI CAPPUCCINI, ROME, ITALY.

ALTHOUGH it has not been usual in Scotland to put an *a* in our name, yet there are several well-recognized cases in which it has been so written and printed in public documents, particularly in the seventeenth century.

As there can be no reasonable doubt that some who write their name Seaton are descendants of that noble race which was preeminently distinguished in Scotch history for over six hundred years, I welcome with pleasure the publication of a history of his branch of our illustrious family by my friend and kinsman Oren Andrew Seaton, Esquire.

The preparation of private records in that more endurable form which printing alone can assure, is a laudable object, and worthy of approval from all who value ancestral traditions, degrees of relationship, distinguished alliances, and examples of military and civic virtues. Intelligence, honesty, and courage--qualities which make for good in every country--have ever been characteristic of those who bear our ancient name. May it so continue.

Scotland is a small, but a very great country, and Americans of Scotch descent feel justly proud of the land of their forefathers. It is a land in which have been blended the best there was of Norman, Gael, and Saxon; and the Scot abroad has always been a gain to the people he settled among. The United States are in this respect the most favored nation in the world.

INTRODUCTION.

(By the Editor.)

It is natural for all persons of intelligence to desire to know who and what their ancestors were, and to speculate as to what their posterity will be in the future history of the most interesting world in the universe, to them.

The questions of the children in a family, as to their ancestors, will very soon bring out the lamentable fact that too little is known, in most families, of the men and women who bequeathed to them the varying cast of countenances they wear, and the tendencies of their minds to good or evil,—to acquiring useful knowledge, or frittering away their valuable time in useless, not to say harmful, amusements.

The person who feels no pride in his ancestry, nor love of posterity, like an army mule, is to be pitied. For him the past must be a barren waste and the future a dreary desert. God gave us parents to venerate and remember affectionately, and children to love, admire and plan and work for with the hope that they will grow up to be honorable men and women, who will do what they can for themselves, their country, and their posterity.

The poet said:

"Your son is your son till he gets him a wife;
But your daughter's your daughter all the days of her life."

A genealogist, however, like a fond parent, considers your children as yours for all of time and for eternity.

To belong to a family that has for generations continued to earn well-deserved respect, to be able to look back to forefathers who have lived well and done their life's work bravely, to know that before you were born your ancestors were honorable citizens who had done their best to uphold the right in domestic and national affairs, is a birthright of which anyone may well be proud.

Daniel Webster once wrote: "There may be, indeed, a respect for ancestry which nourishes only a weak pride, but there is also a moral and philosophical respect for ancestors which elevates the character and improves the heart, a respect which is laudably manifested by perpetuating their lineaments and describing their virtues."

An inheritance of wealth may be desirable, but an inheritance of character, an innate tendency toward that which is good and noble which has been intensified by generations of ancestors, who have themselves inherited a love of right and justice, is a dower beyond the ability of some persons to estimate or appreciate.

No one who sprang from a noble ancestry is justified in saying, as was once written:

"I am a nobody; who are you?"

A celebrated judge, long since deceased, used to contend that there was no such thing as bad port wine; while willingly admitting that one sample of his particular favorite wine might be better than another. We are inclined to believe the same of biographies. Any biography is better than none, for what one of God's creatures has done interests others, but we are none of us admirers of gravestone biographies in a family history.

Finally, tell us the history of the past and we may at least attempt to prophesy something of the future of a family. If our ancestors sprang from monkeys, as Darwin taught, why may we not expect our descendants to descend to donkeys? If our forbears were students, why may we not hope that we and our children may become scholars if we but direct our energies to that most desirable aim and end in life, especially if Addison was right when he wrote:

"Title and ancestry render a good man more illustrious, but an ill one more contemptible."

TABLE OF CONTENTS.

LIST OF ILLUSTRATIONS

SEATON COAT OF ARMS.

THE SEATON FAMILY.

CHAPTER I.

THE SEATON COAT OF ARMS.

THE armorial ensign, or coat of arms, in Scotland was a token of prominence of the possessor in his country. It was regulated by the ruler of the country, and many restrictions were placed upon those who aspired to support one.

The shield upon which arms were first displayed was three or four feet long, pointed below, and eighteen inches broad. The shield was carried in battle by its owner in the left hand (unless he was left-handed or ambidextrous), by a handle attached to its reverse side, as a means of defense from his enemies' weapons, while the spear, pike, axe, or whatever weapon suited his fancy or station, was used in his right hand.

The coat of arms signifies very little to peaceful Americans, where every one who behaves himself belongs to the nobility, but it is considered invaluable to the nobility of England and Scotland. In this country we know very little and care less about heraldry, as a rule.

Robert Seton says: "There is, perhaps, no family in Scotland—there is certainly not one in America—the heraldry of which is so ancient, so honorable, and so abundant as that of Seton."

George Seton wrote a work on "The Law and Practice of Heraldry" in which the number of colored shields of the family numbered over three hundred, and the Americans could add a dozen more; but W. Harvey McNairn, of Toronto, Canada, says there is only one coat of arms in the family, with marks of cadency, of course, and that the others are those of families allied to the Setons by marriage; that there are no *Seton* arms given, except the well-known coat with the crescents and tressure.

Each head of a family of proper lineage in Scotland could support a coat of arms with the consent of the sovereign, and each branch of our family seems to have one to itself.

Nesbit, the famous writer on Heraldry, says Dougal de Setoun possessed the earliest recorded arms of Seton in Scotland.

The coat of arms later came to be used as a decoration in castles, on carriages, and even on stationery and business cards.

For the benefit of those who have never looked up the subject of heraldry it may be said the shields were colored any one or more colors each having a special name different from its usual designation, as "Or" for golden yellow; "Argent" for silver white; "Gules" for red; "Azure" for blue; "Sable" for black; "Vert" for green; "Purpure" for purple, etc. And on shields in black and white each color was represented by certain marks to denote the color; thus, the part of the shield that should be golden yellow was represented by points or dots ⦂⦂⦂; silver white, by a plain white field; red, by perpendicular lines ⦀⦀⦀⦀; blue, by horizontal lines ☰; black, by perpendicular lines crossed by horizontal ones ▦; green, by diagonal lines from upper left to lower right ⧄; purple, by diagonal lines from upper right to lower left ⧅: and blood-red, by lines representing green crossed by those denoting purple ⧓. So by examining a printed coat of arms the colors in which it was originally painted may be determined.

A "Charge" in heraldry is any figure or picture contained in the field of an escutcheon. That on our Seaton arms, as represented herein, is a sheaf of wheat, signifying that we as a family are bound together by mutual interests and love, and that in union is strength, and if we scatter we lose our greatest element of strength. The birds hold a branch of holly, an emblem of the House of Avenel, from which we sprang.

"Supporters" are the pictures at the sides of the shield; ours are the same birds as in the charge, and they also hold a holly

COAT OF ARMS WITH SLOGAN AND MOTTO.

spray. Supporters were allowed only to chiefs of the principal families in Scotland.

The scroll-work at the sides of the shield is called "Mantling." A "Crest" is some figure above the top of the shield. Crests were marks of honor, worn only by heroes of great valor or those who had been advanced to high military command, though later every one with a coat of arms appears to have thought himself entitled to use a crest with it. The crest in the accompanying copy is a military arm with a drawn sword ready to strike. Different branches of the family sometimes had different crests, though the same crest has answered for many different arms in the family. A wyvern issuing out of a ducal coronet was, perhaps, the greatest favorite for a crest in our family at an early date.

The "Slogan," or war-cry, usually accompanied the crest, either surmounting it or being placed at the sides. The Seaton slogan is given by Scott as follows: "A Seyton! A Seyton! Set on! Set on! Bear the knaves down!" Others give only "Set on! Set on!" and I have seen it given "St. Bennet and set on!" Saint Bennet, or Benedict, it appears was the patron saint of the family. The slogan was the battle-cry, shouted aloud upon making a charge upon the enemy.

"Scrolls" were placed below the painted shields, for the family name or motto. Our motto was and is, "Hazerd zet Forward." This is presumed to signify, at whatever hazard yet go forward. This motto appears in some of the arms of the family, and it was carved over the castle gateway and over doors, and was also used in interior decorations.

The "Fitché" on the shield is the cross with the sharp point downward. It is said by G. T. Clark, in his work on Heraldry, to have been added by the eldest son, who used his father's arms with the fitché added, to distinguish between them, or as a mark of cadency, or difference.

The "Crescents" in the upper part of the shield are said by Monsignor Seton to have been used as emblematical of the three crescent-shaped bays into which the lands of Lord Seton divided the southern portion of the silvery Frith of Forth, but Mr. Clark, just quoted, says they were used to distinguish between the arms

of the father and those of the second son when he was allowed to
support that honor, as the fleur-de-luce, commonly called the
fleur-de-lis, denotes that a sixth son had used the same arms as
his father and first and second sons.

> "The fleur-de-lis, that lost her right,
>   Is queen again for a' that!"—*Scott.*

The markings on the coat of arms that precedes this article
denote that the upper part of the shield was gules, or red, and the
sides, between the mantling and the body of the shield, were mur-
rey, or blood-red, both of which colors were supposed to indicate
valor, magnanimity, and the like, and are regarded as the most
honorable colors, according to Chambers, Vol. V, p. 144.

Mr. John Seaton, of Greenup, Kentucky, has a print of a coat
of arms printed from a copper plate that was brought to this
country by John Seaton, the Irish emigrant, from which the writer
had photographs taken.   And there are other prints in possession
of some other members of the family in America.

James Seaton, of the Charlestown Navy Yard, had a copper
plate from which copies were printed in Boston, Massachusetts,
as late as A. D. 1830.

Some well-posted members of the family doubt this being a
genuine coat of arms of our family, but, after noting their reasons,
the writer is inclined to accept it as all right.

In his article on Heraldry in the Encyclopædia Britannica, C. F.
Clark mentions Seton as a writer on the subject; also, that in
Scotland an early Lord Seton had a concession from King Robert
Bruce of a sword supporting a crown, and that his descendant in
1601 received as an augmentation, "azure, a blazing star of eight
points within a double tressure."

> "The tressured fleur-de-lis he claims
>   To wreath his shield."—*Scott.*

The arms of Governor Gordon, of Pennsylvania, show the tressure and three crescents of the Setons in one of its quarters.   And
in the volume quoted above, Seton is mentioned as one of the
critical writers on the subject; and in another place there is a
quotation from Seton's "Law and Practice of Heraldry."

CHAPTER II.

THE SCOTCH TARTAN.

THE Scotch Tartan was a worsted, or linsey-woolsey, cloth woven with alternate stripes or bands of colored warp and weft, or woof, so as to form a checkered pattern in which the colors alternated in sets of definite sequence. The tartan was worn like a shawl, or an Indian's blanket, and great antiquity is claimed for it. It has been asserted that the numerous clans into which the Highland population of Scotland were divided had each a special pattern by which their clan could be distinguished from others.

After the rebellion of 1745 various Acts of Parliament were passed disarming the Scottish Highlanders, and prohibiting the use of Highland dress in Scotland under heavy penalties. But those Acts were repealed in 1782 and the tartans were again permitted to be worn. Macaulay says that the sight of a Scotch tartan in London would inflame the populace of that city with hatred.

The Seaton tartan in Scotland is said to have been principally of a red color with small lines, or stripes, of green, purple, and white. It is more than likely that a "top-coat" has now taken the place of the tartan with nearly every one, being much handier for working-people and of a considerably later style in polite society; though the same plaids, made of different materials, have frequently been used for lining ulsters and other overcoats.

CHAPTER III.

THE NAME SEATON GIVEN TO MANY PLACES.

In the north of England there are several places that have been given the name Seaton, being mostly, if not altogether, localities where persons of the name had settled and were extensive land-owners. Sir William Dugdale (1605–1668), an eminent English antiquary, mentions, in the northeastern part of England, an "Ivo de Seaton" and a "Capella de Seaton"; also a "villa et territorium de Seaton." And William Camden (1551–1623), a "celebrated and conscientious antiquarian and historian," gives a Seaton in Northumberland as part of the barony of De-la-Vall in the thirteenth century, and Seaton Delavell and Monk Seaton are plainly marked on a superb collection of maps spoken of by Robert Seton as being in the Theatrum Orbis Terrarum of William and John Blaeu, published at Amsterdam in 1648. He further remarks that these names of places are now mostly written Seaton, but that it was not so formerly, evidently meaning that the spelling was Seton at that time.

In Rand & McNally's Atlas there is given a harbor at Cockenzie, in Scotland, called Port Seaton; and in Cram's a Seaton village in the city of Toronto, Canada, in which village there is a Seaton street. The village is said to have been named for Baron Seaton, whose title was derived from the City of Seaton, a watering-resort on the sea, in Devonshire, England.

In the United States of America we find a town of Seatonville in Marshall county, West Virginia, the northwest corner county of the State, located on the Ohio river. This place is given on some maps as Wolf Run. The town was named for John B. Seaton.

There is a village of Seatonville in Jefferson county, Kentucky, on the Ohio river, where the river forms the boundary between that State and Indiana. This village was very appropriately named Seatonville by its founder, Charles Allen Seaton, who with Kenner, George, Richard, and Kenner Seaton Jr. all lived on adjoining farms in the vicinity. When a postoffice was granted the village, some one at the Postoffice Department saw fit to give it the name of Malott instead of Seatonville as petitioned for.

The village of Seaton, Blount county, Tennessee, was named for Mr. "Gran" Seaton, son of Alfred Seaton, whose father was Philip Seaton, of Sevier county. The postoffice has been discontinued or renamed. This village seems to have been located inland and not on any large stream, or other body of water, as has been the almost unvarying custom among persons of our name when establishing towns.

Coming on west, we find a village of Seaton on the Iowa Central Railroad, in Mercer county, Illinois, which was founded by George Seaton, president of the Bank of Seaton, for whom the town was named. This county is located on the Mississippi river. There is also quite a village called Seatonville in Bureau county, of the same State, and a Seatonville Junction,—both of the latter places being located on the Indiana, Illinois & Iowa Railroad.

In Hamilton county, Nebraska, a village and postoffice of Seaton were established by Robert Seaton, the first settler and first merchant in the place. Along the northwest corner of this county flows the Platte river.

Again, in far-away Oregon we find a postoffice of Seaton, in the western part of Lane county, on the Siuslau river, about fifteen miles from where it empties into the Pacific ocean. This office must have been named by some person in the Department for we are assured that no Seaton ever lived in the neighborhood. The name of the office has lately been changed to Mapleton.

Cram's list gives a Seaton postoffice in Fayette county, Iowa, but a letter to the postmaster was returned with the notation upon it that there is no such office in the State.

There is a postoffice of Seaton in Bell county, in about the central part of eastern Texas, but the postmaster informs us that
—3

no person of the name ever made his residence there, but that the office must have received its name from some one connected with the Postoffice Department of the Government.

There is a curious letter in the British Museum (addit. 19,185), dated Pianketank (Virginia), 21st July, 1730, from Dorothy Seaton, widow, to Sir Robert Kemp, Bart., of Ulston Hall, near Yoxford, in Suffolk, by the way of London. It bears the following indorsation: "Rec'd the 20th of October, 1730,—not answered." The writer's maiden name appears to have been Kemp, and after making out a relationship to Sir Robert, she narrates some of her misfortunes. In a postscript she gives her address as "Seaton's Ferry on the Pianketank, Virginia."

Last of all, so far as we know, there is a street in the city of Washington, D. C., that has been given the name of Seaton street.

CHAPTER IV.

THE FAMILY NAME.

"Have regard for thy name; for that shall continue with thee above a thousand great treasures of gold."—*Ecclesiasticus*, xii. 12.

THE manner in which we came to be called Seaton is a curiosity, indeed. At first, only individual names were given to anyone, Indian fashion, for some peculiarity of the one receiving it. It appears our earliest known ancestors used pikes or spears in the almost continual wars in which they were engaged. For that reason they were called Picot, which means Pikemen in the early Norman language. Later, these people seem to have settled down to the more quiet life of agriculturists, and, oats being their principal crop, they soon gained such a reputation for the wonderful crops of this valuable grain that their section came to be known by a name derived from the Latin name of oats, which are called *avena* in that language. So the vicinity came to be known as Avenelle, and our forefathers as Avenel.

This manner of calling a section of country after its principal crop has its counterpart in Alexander county, Illinois, where so much wheat was formerly produced as to give the name Wheatland to that section and a town therein.

We find a Baron Walter Avenel, descended of a very ancient border family, who once possessed immense estates in Eskdale, mentioned in "The Monastery," by Scott; also, a Mary Avenel. In the same story he describes the arms of Glendenning and Avenel, two ancient families.

As the family increased in numbers they began to spread out, as they did nearly a thousand years later in the eastern part of this country, and some of them lived at a place called Say; hence that branch became Picot Avenel de Say; the *de* meaning of. Say is said to have been located near Argentan, Normandy.

One Saher de Say went to Scotland and located in the Lothians. where he built a "toun" which was called Sea-toun, or Say toun. One of his descendants was made Lord of Sea-toun, and some of his posterity took the name Seatoun or some one of the twenty-five other ways in which the name has been spelled. So the family was Seatoun until when Sir Alexander Seton IV., Knight, died. That was the last of the Seatouns in direct descent, but his daughter, Margaret Seton, married Alan de Winton, a distant kinsman, who assumed the name Seton in order to secure the titles and estates. Had Alan de Winton been possessed of superior titles and estates to those belonging to Margaret Seton he would doubtless have retained his own name and all succeeding generations who are now called Seaton would have sported the euphonious name of Winton, as some of his descendants did.

Monsignor Seton, from whom we learn these and many other interesting facts, says Avenel was one of the great names of Normandy, and that the Avenels were kinsmen of Rollo, first Duke of Normandy.

In an article on Seton Chapel, in Provincial Antiquities of Scotland, by Sir Walter Scott, it is said: "They took their original name from their habitation, Seaton, 'the dwelling by the Sea,' in East Lothian."

In this way the name came to be Seaton, or any one of the other ways of spelling the name, for it should be remembered there was no established spelling of any name by legal enactment at that time, each writer spelling any word as seemed proper to him from the way he heard it pronounced, as often happens even at this late date. But, in spite of the numerous different ways in which the name has been spelled, all of the persons most vitally interested, with barely one exception, pronounce the name alike, so far as we have been able to learn.

We have the word of Archbishop Seton that he has known instances where those of the family who had the *a* in their names have dropped it; and Leonard Seaton of Henderson, New York, informed me that some members of our branch of the family spelled the name Seton until about 1817, when they added the *a*.

In the Dictionary of National Biography the name of Alexander

Seton, a Scotch friar and reformer, who took a prominent part in the Reformation, is given as in this sentence Bishop Burnett, writing almost contemporaneously, spells it Seaton, while in a Recantation, published by the friar himself in London in 1541, it is spelled Seyton.

Mr. Samuel W. Seton, for many years Superintendent of Education in New York city, an uncle to Archbishop Seton, told Samuel Seaton, of Greenup, Kentucky, many years ago, that there was originally only one family of the name. And many others have expressed the same opinion to the writer.

With one exception, all persons of the name with whom we have had any correspondence on the subject agree that their ancestors were descended from a Scotch family; so there can be no reason for a doubt, it seems to us, that we are all descended from one common ancestor, though Monsignor Seton claims the Setons were a Highland clan, while the Seatons were a great Lowland family. There is no reason to doubt the correctness of his claim, but our researches seem to prove that condition of affairs to have existed many generations after the foundation of the family. And even if it were originally so, we may console ourselves by reading "Tales of a Grandfather," by Scott, where it is said: "But the Highlands and the Borders were so much wilder and more barbarous than the others [Lowlands] that they might be said to be altogether without law."

It has been explained that the name was spelled differently according to the locality. Those of the family who went to Germany during the troubles of the Stuarts spelled the name Seytoun; the emigrants to Ireland, and many of those who went to England, used the *a*, as do most of the name in America who are known to the writer either personally or by correspondence; though there are many who write the name Seton, and not a few spell their patronymic Seeton.

In Buchanan's History of Scotland, which was originally written in Latin and afterward translated into English by John Watkins, the name appears in each of several spellings; see pages 199, 201, 203, 306, 353, 393, 439, 446, 455, 457, 629, and 638.

In the Encyclopædia Britannica the name is spelled Seton, as

SEYTON WITH MACBETH.
(See wyvern on shield.)

it is in Who's Who and Who's Who in America. In the former
work the name appears in Vol. XI, pages 362, 690 and 712; in
XIV, 670; XV, 597–598; and in XX at 593.

Sir Walter Scott uses one form of the name for several of his
characters in his Scotch story, "The Abbot," where it is Seyton,
and Shakespeare gives our name to one of his creations in Macbeth, where he gives it the same as Scott. In commenting on this
fact, Monsignor Robert Seton says the name was almost always
spelled in Shakespeare's time as he used it.

In a "Group of College Stories," one tale by Catharine Young
Glen makes use of an Arch Seton as attending college at Windham.
And Alice Louise Lee uses the name of President Seton of James
Seton's School for Boys.

Abbott, in his Life of Mary Queen of Scots, uses the name of
one of the Queen's maids of honor as Mary Seaton, but Monsignor
Seton spells her name as he does his own, Seton.

But, after all has been said, the Seaton coat of arms, a copy of
which was brought from Scotland to this country by way of Ireland when John Seaton came over in 1729, settles the question as
to some of the family having used the name as we do now before
they left Scotland.

However, the writer has no doubt that the original name was
Seatoun, and has no desire to have it changed, since it has been
handed down to us unstained by criminal performances.

A few more words about names, and we will close the subject
and leave it for each person who is interested in the matter to decide whether there was only one family of the name in the beginning of the family history, or whether there might have been as
many families as there are spellings. We will also let each one
concerned decide how the name should be spelled.

It was no very uncommon affair to change the family name in
the early history of the Scottish nation. In fact, it has been
stated that there were no family names, or surnames, except
among the nobility, until many generations had passed away
after the settlement of the country. But, in this connection, we
read in the Bible that Simon's surname was Peter,—and that was
at the beginning of the Christian era.

It is claimed that it was in the reign of Malcolm Canmore (1058–1093) that surnames were first given indiscriminately to the favorites of the king.

Quite often, in the marriages of the upper classes, it occurred, where the bride was an heiress, that the groom would assume the surname and titles of the bride's family, after surnames had become somewhat common. As an instance apropos we might mention that Alexander of Seton, son of Sir William Seton, married Elizabeth of Gordon, the heiress of Sir Adam Gordon, about 1408, and was created Lord of Gordon about 1431. Their son took the name Gordon and was made Earl of Huntley, and Lord of Badenoch a few years later.

In several cases, where some one married a Seton heiress, the groom took the name Seton after the same fashion. Even in the royal family, Mary, daughter of King James V., was the first to spell the name Stuart according to the present custom. Before that time the name was Steward and later Stewart. A Norman baron had a son, Walter, who was a steward in the household of David I., King of Scotland. Afterward the name Steward became attached to his family and it was written Steward, or Stewart, until Mary went to France, when the form *Stuart* was adopted by her, and was continued in use by succeeding generations.

More than that, the name of the country was not known as Scotland until in the ninth century, when Kenneth Macalpine was king, having been called Caledonia before that time, at least by the Romans.

It has been considered a sure sign of high rank in the country to have possessed a surname as early as the beginning of the eleventh century, as most persons had only individual names at that time, which names were given as descriptive of the person, or some of his doings, after the custom of the American Indians of this country, at our first acquaintance with them, as well as the savages of all other countries.

The family Christian names, as well as surnames, follow in direct descent, though very irregularly, through many generations, often given from father to son, or from mother to daughter, and perhaps quite as frequently from uncle to nephew and from aunt to niece and from grandparent to grandchildren. The names John, Andrew, James, and George, common enough even at the present, have descended from the earliest immigrants, as have those of Charles, William, Henry, Samuel, and Robert. The more common female Christian names in the family have been Margaret, Mary, Martha, Ann, and Elizabeth, of which the latter has been very much the most common of all names among the ladies who have married into the family circle.

CHAPTER V.

THE EARLY ANCESTRY IN NORMANDY.

THE earliest recorded ancestors of the Seaton family were Normans, who derived their remote origin from the Goths, the latter of whom took such an active part in the affairs in Europe from the third to the eighth century of the Christian era. "The Goths," says E. A. Freeman in his History of the Goths, "may on many grounds claim foremost place among Teutonic nations which had a share in breaking up the Roman power. . . . No Teutonic people has left behind it such early remains of a written literature. The Goths first appear in history in the ancient land of the Gatæ. . . . In the third century they were still settled outside the empire, and appear as invaders and ravagers of the Roman territory from the outside. In the middle of the fourth century they were a great power under the Gothic king, Ermanaric, whose domain stretched from the Danube to the Baltic."

Some writers claim the Goths had always been Catholics, but others say they embraced Arianism before the end of the fifth century. In the sixth century the Goths overran Spain and Italy, but many were finally overcome, and some joined their conquerors, the Romans.

Written laws were put forth among the Goths in the fifth century, but the great collection of their laws dates from about the year 654. In the seventh century the Goths and the Romans were again Catholics.

Alexander Gibson, M. A., says of Normandy, the country from which our remote ancestors went to Scotland:

"Normandy is the name which was given to part of northern Gaul in consequence of its occupation in the early part of the tenth century by Northmen, whose name was, on Gaulish soil, gradually changed into Normans."

The chief of the early Scandinavian settlers in Normandy was Rolfe, known in Latin as Rollo and in French history as Rou, a viking leader to whom many early exploits, real or imaginary, are attributed. He received a grant of a tract of land of which Rouen was the center, from Charles the Simple, King of Carolingia. The land was cut off from the duchy of France, yet the grant was from the king and not from the duke of France, and the king received Rolfe's homage. The two princes were presently engaged in war with each other, but Rolfe seems to have been faithful to King Charles.

The Normans were thus at war with the French from the moment of their settlement. In the next century the land was "parted out" among the successful contestants, and before the end of the tenth century there was an oppressed peasantry in the land, who were evidently the conquered descendants of the earlier inhabitants. These people were either slaves or serfs, the latter of whom were considered as belonging to the land on which they lived and with which they might be transferred. They were not regarded as personal property, as were the slaves. Serfdom existed in Normandy at an early date and in Scotland as late as the eighteenth century, while in Russia serfdom was not abolished until 1861.

A nobility gradually sprang up among the Normans, consisting of those who could claim kindred with the reigning house. The leaders among the soldiers had a share of the land to be divided among the conquerors, and the slaves and serfs made the noblemen wealthy in the course of time.

The country was frequently, if not continually, at war with some power, and generally after each decided defeat on either side some of the participants on the losing side sought refuge in some other country, disposing of what property they could and taking as much as possible of what remained with them.

It is stated by some writers that it was in Normandy that surnames, that might be handed down to their descendants, were first given to the nobility, from which country they were said to have been introduced into near-by countries; but evidently those writers forgot their Bible lessons. However, the fact that Saher de Say, who was later the founder of our family, possessed a surname, proves to some that he was of the Norman aristocracy, which fact is further confirmed by his possessing enough wealth to purchase and improve such extensive properties in each of the three Lothians in Scotland. For it is to be remembered that the aforesaid Saher de Say was a refugee from Normandy, who settled in the southern part of Scotland, taking part with his countrymen the Wallaces, Bruces, etc., in the almost continual wars between the different claimants for the crown of the latter country.

We learn that Picot Avenel de Say, one of our forbears, lived in Normandy under Robert, sixth duke of that country, about 1030. "He was a son of Robert de Say and Adelaid his wife, of the charter of Saint Martin of Seez, where he held no less than twenty-nine lordships. He was the ancestor of all the Says in England and Scotland, and probably of Jean Baptiste Leon Say in France, a noted statesman, Minister of Finance, etc., and was a baron of England under the Conqueror's reign. He also held the Castle of Marigny, with other possessions in Normandy, while he still continued, like many others, to be represented in both countries. He erected a church and a monastery in honor of Saint Giles within the boundaries of Camboritum, the relics of which are said to still exist."

CHAPTER VI.

DE SAY IN SCOTLAND.

"The first appearance of de Say in Scotland was in the reign of Alexander I. (1107–1124), and it antedated by some years the peaceful invasion of the Anglo-Normans under his brother, David I. Then they came to the number of at least a thousand.

"The immediate cause of de Say's going to Scotland for a home was a dispute between a baron and his suzerain, something quite common in that turbulent age. Robert Fitz-Picot was Baron of Brunne, in Cambridgeshire, in 1068, where 'the moat of his castle and a few other traces of the buildings yet remain.' His oldest son, Robert Fitz-Picot, the viscount, forfeited the barony for rebellion against King Henry I., who granted it to Pain Peverill, said to be the husband of Robert's sister."

Had the result of the quarrel been different, who can say that de Say might not have remained in Normandy? Then there would have been no Sea-toun and consequently no Seatons.

The first of the great house of Seatoun established in Scotland was Saher de Say, as has been told. He had a grant of land in the Lothians, which was called in different histories Saytun, Saytoun, Seatoun, etc., all evidently meaning the home of Say, or, as is claimed by others, the home by the sea.

"This settlement gave rise to a name and family which became preëminently distinguished in the annals of Scotland," as Sir Bernard Burke puts it. The account continues:

"The knight or baron, having secured his grant of land, proceeded forthwith to build a castle and a church—both of rude material and ruder in architecture—a mill, a brew-house, and huts for the serfs, and thereby formed about himself a hamlet which, in the practice of the age, was called a "toun" of the owner. . . . The place where Saher de Say settled is between Tranent and the sea, about ten miles below Edinburgh, and it continued to be the principal home of his descendants for over six hundred years."

The son of Saher de Say is known in our family history as Dougall de Say-toun. His Christian name is unknown, as he was usually described by a familiar appellation of the people around him. The Normans wore a strong coat of mail, which made them objects of dread and wonder to the Britons, Picts, and Celts, in whose ancient songs they were called Dugall, the "Black Strangers," from the appearance they made when incased in armor. Dougall de Saytoun, then, literally means "The Black Stranger [lord] of the toun of Say." He flourished in the reign of Alexander I., A. D. 1107–1124, and married Janet, daughter of Robert de Quincy.

"SEHER DE SETOUNE succeeded to Dougall, his father." Just how or why the name was changed from Saytoun to Setoune is impossible to say, unless it was through an error of some recorder. "Whom he married I find not certainly in any register of the house," quaintly remarks Maitland. Seher de Setoune lived in the time of David I. (1124–1153).

" PHILIP DE SAYTOUN succeeded to Seher, his father. He made a strong alliance by marrying Helen, only daughter of Waldeve, fifth Earl of Dunbar and March, by Aelina, his wife. Philip got a charter from King William, the Lion, in 1169, confirming to him certain lands, which remained in possession of his descendants for more than five hundred years.

"ALEXANDER (1) DE SETOUN succeeded his father Philip, who died in 1179. He married Jean, daughter of Walter Berkley or Barclay, chamberlain to the king—an office of great influence and dignity. He subscribed a charter given by Secher de Quincy, Earl of Winchester, in England, his kinsman, to the Church of Saint Mary of Newbattle in the thirteenth century, which is interesting because it contains the earliest mention of coal-mining in Scotland. . . . Sir Alexander died in 1211."

" BERTRAND or BERTRAM DE SETOUN succeeded Alexander, his father, and married Margaret, daughter of William Comyn, Earl of Buchan, Great Justicar of Scotland.

" He died about 1230, leaving two sons: Adam, of whom below, and Alexander, who witnessed the confirmation of a charter to the burgh of Glasgow by King Alexander II., dated November 22, 1225."

" ADAM DE SEATOUNE. He succeeded his father Bertram, and is described by Maitland as 'ane maister clerk'; *i. e.*, a well-read man. . . . Adam de Seatoune married Margaret Gifford, daughter to Hugh de Gifford, Lord Yester, a neighboring baron. . . . The original 'Goblin Hall,' described in *Marmion,* is still a part of this old, ivy-clad castle, now in ruins, and but a few miles from Seton. Adam died in the reign of King Alexander III. (1249–1292), but the year is not known. He left, besides a son and successor, a daughter, who married Sir William de Keith, ancestor of the great family of Keiths, Earls Marischal of Scotland. This lady, 'who was,' says Chalmers in his *Caledonian,* 'of a gallant race,' seems to have infused a new spirit into the Keiths. Her husband died before 1290. By him she had three sons, one of whom, Philip, was a priest and rector of Biggar, in Lanarkshire."

" SIR CHRYSTELL OR CHRISTOPHER DE SETON (1). He succeeded his father Adam, and married Maud, daughter of Ingelram Percy, Lord Topcliff in Yorkshire." Here we have another change in the spelling, without any reason being given. " The illustrious family of Percy derived its descent from one of the Norman chieftains (William de Percy) who accompanied the Conqueror to England in 1066. The line of Percy is traced back in Normandy to the time of Rollo, first duke, in 912. Sir Christopher was a very pious man, 'more given to devotion than to worldliness,' says Maitland; and another family chronicler tells us that he was a man that loved neither strife nor wrong, but rather to read and pray. He was a considerable benefactor of the Church, particularly out of the estates in England, which he administered during his father's lifetime. His brother settled also in that part of England in which many Scoto-Normans (originally Anglo-Normans) were large land-owners, and is described as 'Sir John Seton of Seton, in Yorkshire.' He died in old age, before 1270."

> "The knight's bones are dust,
> And his good sword rust;
> His soul is with the Saints, I trust."

"SIR CHRISTOPHER SETON (2) succeeded his pious father, and married Agnes, daughter of Patrick, Earl of March. He was a valiant knight, and did many brave deeds against England when the crown of Scotland was in dispute between Bruce and Baliol. He was a friend and companion of the national hero, Sir William Wallace, and when driven off his own lands by the enemy, took refuge with forty followers in Jedburgh Forest, 'ay awaiting his tyme contrare the English,' says Maitland. He was finally killed at the battle of Dillicarew, on the 12th of June, 1298, leaving two sons, Christopher and John."

"SIR CHRISTOPHER SETON (3), succeeded his unfortunate but gallant father in those troublous times of the War of Independence. He was knighted by King Robert Bruce, and for his courtesy and valor was called by the common people, with whom he was a favorite, Good Sir Chrystell. He is mentioned by Lord Hailes, the restorer of Scottish history, as one of the twenty chief associates of Bruce in his arduous attempts to restore the liberties of Scotland. He is there styled Christopher Seton of Seton." This is the first time I remember to have seen the English *of* take the place of the French *de* in the family name.

A. C. Swinburne, in his History of Scotland, as given in the Encyclopædia Britannica, gives the name of this Christopher Seton as early as 1301. In that year he married Lady Christian Bruce, sister of the heroic Robert Bruce, afterward King of Scotland. Sir Christopher was twenty-three years old at that time, having been born A. D. 1278. Christian Bruce was the daughter of Robert Bruce, Lord of Anandale, and Margaret, heiress of Niel, Earl of Carrick.

The account continues: "On March 25th, 1306, Robert Bruce was crowned at Scone, but though a king, he had as yet no kingdom. In his efforts to obtain it he was defeated at Methven by

Pembroke on June 19th, 1306, and on August 11th of same year he was surprised at Strathfillan, where he had taken refuge, by Lord Lorn, and was impelled to take refuge on the island of Rathlin, off Antrim, Ireland." Some of the ladies of the household were sent prisoners to England; some were confined in cages and shown as curiosities. Nigel Bruce, Robert and Christian's brother, was beheaded at Berwick by the victorious English, as was Christopher Seton, their brother-in-law, sometime before June 7th, 1307, for the crime of faithfully upholding the cause of the rightful heir to the Scottish crown, as they professed to believe.

At the battle of Methven, Bruce was thrice unhorsed, and once so nearly taken that the captor, Sir Philip Mowbray, called aloud that he had the new-made king, when Sir Christopher Seton felled Mowbray to the earth and rescued his master. The large two-handed sword, wielded by our common ancestor, is now in the possession of George Seton, Esq., of Edinburgh, representative of the Setons of Cariston, as we are informed in "An Old Family."

In G. A. Henty's story, "In Freedom's Cause," it is stated that Sir Archibald Forbes, whose mother was a Seaton, was with Sir Christopher Seaton at Methven, and assisted him in rescuing Bruce from Sir Philip Mowbray and his men.

After many notable acts against the English, Chrystell was taken prisoner at last, in the castle of Loch Doon, near Dalmelington, in Ayrshire, through the treachery of one of his retainers named MacNab. Sir Christopher was immediately conveyed to London, to be exhibited to the king, and then was brought back to Dumfries and executed there, because he was present and permitting Bruce to kill the Red Comyn in a sudden quarrel in the Greyfriars' Church in that town, on February 10, 1305.

In a quaint Life of Robert Bruce, published in the early part of the 18th century, Sir Christopher is enshrined in verse:

> "The noble Seton, ever dear to Fame,
> A Godlike Patriot, and a spotless name,
> By factious Treason in Lochdown betrayed,
> And to Augusta's hostile towers conveyed;
> For Scotia's sake resigned his gallant breath,
> Great in his life, and glorious in his death."

—4

The historian Tytler says: "So dear to King Robert was the memory of his faithful friend and fellow-warrior, that he afterward erected on the spot where he was executed a little chapel, where mass was said for his soul." But Robert Seton says that it was the widow of Sir Christopher who was really the one who built the chapel for her husband, in honor of the Holy Cross; but her royal brother so generously endowed it by a charter dated at Berwick-on-Tweed, the last day of November, 1323, that he is sometimes called the founder.

Sir Richard Maitland, whose mother was a daughter of George Lord Seton, left in manuscript a history of the family of Seyton, as we learn from the Encyclopædia Britannica, from which it appears he had seen the king's charter endowing the chapel, and that he had heard mass there, and that it was still standing in the year 1552.

In Jane Porter's "Scottish Chiefs" mention is made of this Sir Richard Maitland of Thirlstane, the Stalwarth Knight of Lauderdale, noted in Scottish traditions for his bravery. She says that his valiant defense of his castle against the English in his extreme old age is still the subject of enthusiasm among the people of Lauderdale. One of Sir Richard's daughters was married to Lord Mar, but in giving birth to a daughter, who was named Isabella and afterward became queen of Scotland by marrying Robert Bruce, she died.

Sir Christopher's widow was confined for a time in a nunnery in England, but was liberated in a few years, and died in peace, we are told by Robert Seton, D. D., in "An Old Family."

Sir Walter Scott thus touchingly refers to our friends, Nigel Bruce and Christopher Seton, in his "Lord of the Isles," Canto second, xxvi:

> "Where 's Nigel Bruce and De la Haye,
> And valiant Seton—where are they?
> Where Somerville, the kind and free?
> And Fraser, the flower of Chivalry?"

"The large family estates in England were confiscated at this time. The manor of Seton, at Whitby Strand, in Yorkshire, was conferred upon Edmund de Manly who was later killed at the battle of Bannockburn. The more extensive domain in Northumberland was granted to William, Lord Latimer, who was made a prisoner at the same battle, which occurred June 24, 1314, and which determined the independence of Scotland and confirmed the title of Robert Bruce as King of that country."

CHAPTER VII.

" Sir Alexander Seton of Seton (2) succeeded his good father, and was knighted by Robert Bruce. He was employed both in civil and military affairs, for in January, 1302, he had a safe-conduct into England, and three years later the Scottish king applied for another one for him to treat of a peace with the English. In 1306 there was a mutual indenture made between Sir Gilbert Hay of Erroll, Sir Niel Campbell of Lochaw, and Sir Alexander Seton of Seton, knights, at the Abbey of Lindores, to defend King Robert Bruce and his crown to the last of their blood and fortune.

"Upon sealing the said indenture they solemnly took the sacrament at Saint Mary's altar in the said abbey church." "Seton," says Alexander Laing, "came of a race that fought bravely and suffered much for the independence of Scotland." Sir Alexander Seton shared in the glorious victory of Bannockburn, June 24, 1314. Sir Thomas Gray, on the testimony of his father, who was then a prisoner in the Scotch camp, tells us that Alexander Seton rode to Bruce's tent in the woods the evening before the battle with important information, and advised him to take the offensive and attack the English next morning with vigor.

"Sir Alexander got from his royal uncle, Robert Bruce, important grants of land for services rendered by his father, and also certain honorable and uncommon additions to his paternal coat of arms. A little later he received another grant—this time of the Barony of Barnes, in East Lothian, for his own services, particularly in Ireland, whither he had accompanied the king's brother, Edward Bruce.

"The appeal of the Irish chieftains for deliverance from their English conquerors, the Scottish expedition to Ireland, the crowning of Edward Bruce as King of Ireland in 1316, his victorious march at the head of a small army of Scotchmen, with very little native assistance, from Carrickfergus to Limerick, his unsuccessful siege of Dublin, his retreat northward, and his final defeat and death with nearly all of his followers at the battle of Dundalk, on October 5, 1318, is one of the most chivalrous episodes, as it was one of the most ill-advised measures, in the history of Scotland.

"Sir Alexander Seton was one of the thirty-nine nobles and others who assembled in Parliament at the Abbey of Arbroath on April 6, 1320, and addressed that famous letter to Pope John XXII. at Avignon, which is one of the most spirited and patriotic documents in history. It induced the Holy See to recognize the independence of Scotland and the title of King Robert Bruce.

"Sir Alexander was a benefactor of the monasteries at Hadding-ton, and looked only to pass his remaining years in piety and repose; but the peace of the kingdom was violently broken by the attempt of Edward Baliol to seize the crown after the death of Bruce, and during the minority of his son David II."

Maitland tells us in his History of Scotland, page 201, that Edward Baliol, who wished to be made king, came to Kinghorn and there landed his forces on August 1, 1331. On the arrival of the fleet, Alexander Seton, a nobleman who happened to be there at the time, strove to oppose them, but he had so few followers at hand, in comparison with those of Baliol, that he and most of his followers were cut off.

Sir Alexander married Isabel, daughter of Duncan, tenth Earl of Fife. In this connection Robert Seton remarks that up to the eighteenth century, there is not another family in Scotland that made so many advantageous marriages and gave so many younger sons to heiresses.

Sir Alexander Seton (3) succeeded to Alexander II., his father, and was truly a noble knight and renowned in Scottish prose and verse.

He was made captain and keeper of Berwick in April, 1333, bringing as his contribution to the defense of that important town, one hundred men-at-arms and five gallant sons. Buchanan here comes to our aid, telling us that Edward Baliol was made king in August, 1332. About four months later the party of Bruce, thinking Baliol sought the kingdom for the English, made preparations for war, strongly fortifying Berwick because they believed the English would attack that place first. Alexander Seton, a worthy knight, was made governor of the town. The English king demanded Berwick of the Scots, but they replied among other things, that they were resolved to die a noble death rather than consent to a peace unjust to themselves and their kingdom. They appeared to appreciate the Latin motto, *Aut mors aut vita decora.* The English king then besieged Berwick by sea and land with vast forces, giving the besieged no rest either by night or day. The Scots boldly sallied out upon the English every day. They also threw fire into the English ships which lay in the river, and burned many of them.

In these skirmishes William Seton, the Governor's son, was lost, and was much lamented by all on account of his singular valor; for while he endeavored to leap into one of the English ships, his own being driven too far off by the waves, he fell into the sea and was drowned. Another son of the governor, Alexander, in too great eagerness, proceeded so far in a sally that he was taken by the English.

The siege began on the 13th of April, and it was now July. The garrison became straitened for want of provisions; so the town, no longer able to hold out against such great odds, made an agreement with the English to surrender if no help arrived by the 30th of the month. For a guarantee of the faithful carrying out of the arrangement, Thomas Seton, the governor's eldest son, was given to the English as a hostage. Archibald Douglas, captain general, hearing of the agreement made by Alexander Seton, changed his plan of marching into England, and went toward Berwick. When his force came in sight of the English king, he sent a herald into the town to tell Governor Seton that unless he surrendered at once, he would put his son Thomas to death, although the day had not arrived for the surrender according to the agreement. The English set up a gallows where it could be easily seen by the Scots, and caused the governor's two sons, Alexander and Thomas, the one a prisoner of war and the other a hostage, to be brought forth for execution. At this dreadful sight Governor Seton was in a most miserable state of perplexity, but encouraged by his heroic wife, the mother of the boys, and one of the most patriotic, courageous and far-seeing women of any age, it was decided to defend the town that had been committed to his care, at all hazards, rather than betray his trust. What a terrible position for parents to be placed in, all who have children of their own can perhaps realize! The English king, Edward III., carried out his threat, and executed the boys. In the battle that followed from ten thousand to fourteen thousand Scots were slain, the most of them of the better class, as Buchanan assures us. After the battle, when there was no further hope of relief, Alexander Seton surrendered the town of Berwick upon condition that the people should march out with all their goods.

The heroic wife of Alexander Seton was Christian Cheyne of Straloch, who belonged to a Norman-Scotch family, a family of well-connected notables of Scotland. He died at a good old age, and was buried at Seton Church, leaving two sons, Alexander, who succeeded him, and John, founder of the Parbroach branch of the family.

"SIR ALEXANDER SETON, KNIGHT (4), succeeded to his patrimonial estates, yet lived to enjoy them only a few years. He was the third, but eldest surviving son of the late Governor of Berwick. He married Margaret, sister to Sir William Murray, Captain of Edinburgh Castle, by whom he left an only child, a daughter, named Margaret for her mother; so that in him the direct male line of the family came, partially at least, to an end."

Taylor says that Sir Alexander sought refuge from his sorrows and troubles in a hospital of the order of Saint John of Jerusalem, and his daughter Margaret became the heiress of his extensive estates.

"MARGARET, HEIRESS OF SETON, Lady Margaret Seton, was forcibly abducted in 1347 by a neighboring baron, Alan de Winton, a distant kinsman of her own and a cadet of the Seton family. This outrage caused a bloody contest in Lothian; on which occasion, says Fordun, a hundred plows were laid aside from labor."

In a ballad entitled "Alan of Winton and the Heiress of Seton,"

we find some verses, in one stanza of which an allusion is made
to the family crest and slogan:

> "One hundred ploughs unharnessed lie,
>   The dusky collier leaves his mines.
> A Seton! is the gathering-cry,
>   And far the fiery Dragon shines."

When Margaret Seton was rescued and Alan de Winton con-
fronted by the Seton family, she was handed a ring and a dagger,
with permission to give him either love or death. She gave him
the ring, and they were happy ever afterward. It is supposed
that Henry de Wynton was a younger son of this marriage. He
was one of the heroes of Otterburn, August 19, 1388 Alan de
Winton assumed his wife's name, and died in the Holy Land, leaving a daughter, Christian, who became the Countess of Dunbar
and March, and two sons, Sir William Seton, his successor, and
Henry, who retained his father's surname and inherited Wrychts-
houses. He married Amy Brown, of Colston.

CHAPTER VIII.

"Sir William Seton of Seton. first Lord Seton. He was a famous knight in the middle of the fourteenth century, and visited Jerusalem. On his return he took part, in 1383, with the Borderers of Scotland, in that raid into England described so graphically by Froissart (who names him), 'for they said there had been such damage done to their lands as was disagreeable to themselves and friends, which they would revenge the very first opportunity.' They came back with a rich booty in prisoners and cattle. Froissart mentions in the same year a Sir John Seton, who took part with the English in the counter-raid into Scotland. He must have been one of the Yorkshire Setons. Those were days of murderous and almost constant fighting between the Scotch and English; and one of the battles is forever celebrated in poetry and romance. The battle of Otterburn. which furnished material for the ballad of *Chevy Chase*, was fought on the 19th of August, 1388, and Sir William Seton was there. . . . Maitland informs us that Sir William Seton 'was the first created and made lord in the parliament, and he and his posterity to have a vote therein, and be called Lords.' Several of his ancestors sat in Parliament. . . . In a manuscript of the British Museum. Sir William Seton is styled 'Wilhelmus primus Dns. Seton.' and several other documents confirm the title to him. His descendant refused an earldom in the sixteenth century. because he preferred the distinction of being the premier Baron of Scotland. The precise date of the creation is unknown. but it is reasonably presumed to have been sometime before 1393. Lord Seton married Catharine. daughter of Sir William St. Clair of Herdmanston. a great house at that time. By her he had two sons and six daughters. The eldest son, John, succeeded his father, while the second son, Alexander, married, in 1408, Elizabeth. daughter and heiress of Sir Adam Gordon by his wife Elizabeth. daughter of Sir William Keith, and founded a family of Seton blood which rose to fame and importance and the highest rank of the peerage. . . .

"Alexander Seton was created Lord of Parliament as Lord Gordon about 1437. His son, Alexander Seton, Lord Gordon, assumed his mother's surname, and was created Earl of Huntley. While some of the descendants of this marriage took the name of Gordon, others retained that of Seton. The Marquess of Huntley (Premier Marquess of Scotland) is descended from him in the male, and the Duke of Richmond and Gordon in the female line. The daughters of William and Catherine all married well. Margaret— John, Lord Kennedy; Marion—Sir John Ogilvy of Lintrathen; Jean—John, Lord Lyle; Catharine—Bernard Haldane of Gleneagles; Anna—Hamilton of Preston; Lucy—Lauder of Poppill. All these were men of old family and personal distinction. . . .

"Lord Seton belonged to the third Order of Saint Francis, and dying in February, 1409, was buried in the Church of the Franciscan Friars in Haddington, to whom he left by will six loads of coal weekly, out of his coal-pit of Tranent, and forty shillings annually, to be charged to his estate of Barnes. His widow is described as a virtuous and energetic woman, who got husbands for four of her daughters, and built a chantry on the south side of the parish church of Seton, prepared a tomb for herself there, and made provision for a priest to say mass perpetually for the repose of her soul."

Chambers's "The Family of Gordon" says: "The last of the Gordons in direct line came to an end in Sir Adam Gordon, who fell at Homildon in 1402, leaving an only child, a daughter, Elizabeth, to inherit his lands." This Elizabeth Gordon married Alexander Seton, son of Sir William of Seton, before 1408, who, before 1437, was created Lord of Gordon. Their son, Alexander, who took the name Gordon, was made Earl of Huntley in 1445, and Lord of Badenoch a few years later. In Sir Robert Gordon's Genealogical History of the Earl of Lutherland, written in 1639 by Sir Robert Gordon and published in 1813 in Edinburgh, it is stated that George Gordon, Lord Byron, the poet, was descended from a younger son of the second Earl of Huntley, grandson of Alexander Seton.

Another Gordon, Patrick, a soldier of fortune, being a younger brother, became the Lieutenant-General and finally the General of the Russian army. King James II, of England wished him to enter the English service, but he was unable to obtain permission to leave the Russian service. He died at Moscow, November 29, 1699. "The Czar Peter visited him five times during his illness, and had been twice by his bed during the night, stood weeping by his bed as Patrick drew his last breath; and the eyes of him who left Scotland a poor boy were closed by the hands of an emperor."

The first Lord Seton owned extensive tracts of land in each of the three Lothians, East, Mid and West Lothian, the Lothians being later created into the counties of Haddington, Edinburgh, and Linlithgow of Scotland. In this connection it may not be considered out of place to mention the fact that there is a village of Linlithgow in Columbia county, New York, which was probably named for the place of the same name in Scotland, as there were many persons of Scotch descent among its early settlers.

In the "Lost Heir of Linlithgow," by Mrs. E. D. E. N. Southworth, Eglantine Seton, Baroness of Linlithgow in her own right, orphan, niece, and ward of the Earl of Torsach, is given a very singular and interesting history. She was said to have been presumptive heir to four great estates, situated severally in Scotland, England, Wales, and Ireland. Before her twelfth year she had succeeded to each of these rich estates, and so came to be called "the combined heiress." Her father was the tenth and last Baron of Linlithgow, and upon his death Eglantine became Baroness Linlithgow in her own right. Her home was Seton Court, and her tutor was the Rev. Mr. Graham, a retired clergyman. She was possessed of a "colossal fortune," and Alexander, Earl of Ornoch, was attracted and delighted by her "glad eyes" and fell in love with her at first sight. Eglantine, however, loved William Douglas, a nephew of Dougald Douglas of Inch Trosach, and married him.

There was also mentioned a Dr. David Seton, of the village of Seton, who was a distant relative of the Setons of Linlithgow, and who was educated in Edinburgh.

Lord Seton owned a castle situated about midway between the

capital city, Edwin's Burgh (Edinburgh), and the village of Lin-lithgow, about fourteen miles west of the former place. This castle was known as Niddry Castle, or Seton's Niddry. It appears to have descended from generation to generation until George, fifth Lord Seton, finally owned it.

Sir Walter Scott, in "The Abbot," mentions Mary Queen of Scots having visited the castle, and every Life of the unfortunate Queen that I have seen confirms the statement of the story. The castle was finally confiscated with other immovable property belonging to the family, and at last account was nothing but a ruin belonging to Lord Hopetoun.

Lord Seton also owned a palace in Edinburgh, which has been mentioned by many writers. The best description of this magnificent structure known to the writer is that of Scott, who calls it the Palace of Seyton. From his description it appears to have been entered through an arched gate from Cannongate street, which arch was graced by a shield supported by two huge foxes of stone. There was a paved court before the house that was decorated with large formal vases of stone, in which yews, cypress and other evergreens vegetated in somber sullenness and gave a corresponding degree of solemnity to the high and heavy building in front of which they were placed as ornaments, aspiring toward a square portion of the blue hemisphere, corresponding exactly in extent to the blue quadrangle in which they were placed, and all around which rose huge black walls, exhibiting windows in five stories, with heavy architraves over each, bearing armorial and religious devices. In the center of the lower front of the court was a large door where hung a bobbin attached to a heavy and massive latch, which admitted to the large hall, or vestibule, lighted dimly by latticed casements of painted glass. The walls were surrounded with suits of ancient and rusted armor, intercharged with huge and massive stone scutcheons, bearing double tressures, fleured and counter-fleured, wheat sheaves, coronets, and so forth. Several folding doors led from this apartment to the other parts of the massive building where the family lived during a portion of each year.

FRONT VIEW OF SETON HOUSE IN RUINS, 1790.

CHAPTER IX.

"JOHN, SECOND LORD SETON, was intended for the Heiress of Gordon, but secretly wedded Janet Dunbar, daughter of the Earl of March, much to his father's displeasure. He had one son by her, who predeceased him, and three daughters. Lord Seton was appointed Master of the Household by King James I., and was sent on a mission to France. He is described as a good fighter and a great hater of the English, and was taken prisoner at the battle of Homildon Hill, in 1402. He had several safe-conducts to England between 1409 and 1421, and died about 1441, when he was buried in his mother's chantry at Seton Church.

"His daughters were disposed of as follows: Christian married Norman Leslie of Rothes, by papal dispensation from the fourth degree of consanguinity, obtained in December, 1415; Janet married Sir Robert Keith, son of the Earl Marischal; Marian married Sir William Baillie of Laminton, in Lanarkshire, now represented by Baillie of Dochfour, County Inverness, and in Ireland by Baillie of Ringdufferin, County Down."

William, Master of Seton (eldest son of a baron) "first appears in a charter which he witnessed in 1423, where he is described as 'William Seton, son and heir of John, Lord Seton.'"

In the wars of France there were Scotchmen on both sides. An Alexander Seton, who cannot now be identified, took forty lances and forty men-at-arms . . . to the assistance of King Henry V. in 1421. The Master of Seton accompanied the Scotch Auxiliaries to the assistance of the French, and after sharing in the victory of Bauge was slain at the bloody battle of Verneuil, August 17, 1424. By his wife, whose name is unrecorded, William, Master of Seton, left a son George, who succeeded his grandfather, and two daughters: Catharine, who married Alan Stuart of Darnley, and was mother of the first Earl of Lennox; and Janet, who married John, second Lord Haliburton.

From a work on "The Scots Guards in France," by Father
William Forbes-Leith, S. J., Robert Seton gives an account of
some matters of family interest not found elsewhere: "As early
as the first dispatch of Scotch Auxiliaries to France, two Setons,
Thomas and his brother, are found each at the head of a company
of men-at-arms and archers, and were 'conspicuous amongst the
most faithful followers of the Dauphin. Thomas was favored
with the estate of Lingeais and appointed to accompany Charles
wherever he went.' Sir Thomas Seton was killed a few years
later, before the fortress of Cravant. . . . To conclude a
short digression, Setons are found officers and gentlemen-privates
in this celebrated corps [the Scots Guards] from 1419 to 1679, the
last of our name on the list and muster-rolls being David Seton,
Brigadier."

" GEORGE, THIRD LORD SETON, succeeded to the title and estates
while still a minor, 'being bot nyne yeirs of age,' and was secured
as a rich prize by Sir William Crichton, the powerful but unscrupu-
lous Lord Chancellor, who then held possession of Edinburgh
Castle. . . . When George grew up he accompanied Crichton, who, after all, could not have meant him wrong, on an em-
bassy to France and Burgundy, and had a safe-conduct to pass
through England, April 23, 1448. He was very tall and handsome,
a good scholar, and an accomplished courtier. He made a great
match, marrying Lady Margaret Stewart, only daughter and heiress of the gallant John, Earl of Buchan, younger son of Robert,
Duke of Albany, Regent of Scotland, and grandson of King Robert
II., of which branch of the royal Stuarts the Setons are the only
representatives. For his victory at Bauge 22d March, 1421, the
earl was made Constable of France. His wife was Elizabeth,
daughter of Archibald, fourth Earl of Douglas in Scotland, and
Duke of Touraine in France. He was one of the foremost warriors of his time."

By this marriage Lord Seton had a son called John, of whom
hereafter, and a daughter Christian, who married Hugh Douglas of
Corehead. This lord kept a great house, and was given to entertaining. He restored and embellished the parish church of Seton.

"After he had lived a long and honorable life," says Maitland, "he died in the Convent of Black Friars (Dominicans) at Edinburgh, and was buried in the choir of their church. He left them, by will, twenty marks to be paid annually out of his estate of Hartsyde, in Berwickshire."

"JOHN, MASTER OF SETON, died during the lifetime of his father, and was buried in the parish church of Seton. He married Christian, daughter of the first Lord Lindsay of the Byres, by whom he had three sons and a daughter, who married the second Lord Lyle. The eldest son, George, succeeded his grandfather; the next son was John, who had a son killed by robbers in Annandale while returning, with too small an escort, from a military expedition into England; the youngest son was Alexander, who had, besides a son called John, Baillie of Tranent, who married and had issue, a daughter Christian, who was wedded to Preston of Whitehill."

GEORGE, FOURTH LORD SETON, succeeded his grandfather, and exemplified in his person the hereditary love of learning in his family. Maitland says: "He was much given to letters, and was cunning in divers sciences, as in astrology, music, and theology. He was so devoted to study that even after his marriage he went to the University of Saint Andrew's, and after a while to that of Paris, to prosecute his researches." Between 1485 and 1503 he was engaged in the public affairs of the kingdom, while at the same time devoting considerable attention to his patrimonial estates, with a fine eye to architecture and to the dignity of religion. In this line he built Winton House, and laid out the garden and park around it; but his most enduring memorial is the Collegiate Church of Seton. A Church of Seton, *Ecclesia de Seetbun*, is mentioned as early as 1242, and the Rev. Joseph Stevenson, S. J., discovered "a presentation of the Church of Seyton, in the year 1296." It must have been a considerable church even before it was made collegiate by papal authority, because a Brief of Pope Paul II., in 1456, which is preserved among the treasures of the society of Antiquaries at Edinburgh, mentions the "Provost of Seton—*Prepositus de Seton*." Schools of elementary instruction were almost always attached to these old Scottish churches.

There exists in the Advocates' Library at Edinburgh a Brief of Pope Alexander VI., written on vellum, and dated 1492, *dans protestatem . . . ad procedendum ecclesia collegiata de Seton.* In consequence, Lord Seton, on June 20, 1493, had the provisions of the Brief carried out by the ecclesiastical authorities to whom it had been committed, viz., the Bishops of Candida Casa (Whithorn) and Dunblane, and the Abbot of Newbattle. It is one of the only two remaining churches in Scotland that are roofed with stone."

The following is Robert Seton, D. D.'s, description of the collegiate church of Seton :

"This little church, whose original pile was very ancient, is situated near the sea-coast of Scotland, about twelve miles below Edinburgh, and rears itself close to the mansion-house of the Setons. It enclosed for many centuries their family tomb, and received from them whatever decorations, endowments, furniture of sacred vessels, and ornaments they imagined could add to its magnificence. The present structure was erected in the thirteenth century, and King Robert I. granted to the ' town of Seton the liberty of having a weekly market every holiday after mass,' when the traders would expose their goods in booths beside the church, where the presence of the clergy and the sanctity of the place, under the invocation of Our Lady and Saint Bennet (Benedict), patron of the family, tended to preserve order among the people and justice in their dealings. In the year 1493 it was made a collegiate establishment for a provost, six prebendaries, two singing-boys, and a clerk, to whose support George, Lord Seton, assigned the tithes of the church and various chaplainries which had been founded in it by his ancestors. At later dates other members of the family made additions to the edifice, multiplied its ornaments, increased its wealth, and raised within it some sumptuous monuments. In 1544 the English invaders, while destroying the neighboring castle, desecrated the church ; and after removing the bells, organ, and other portable objects to their ships, burnt the beautiful timberwork within. The church was soon restored, and during the commotions of the Reformation had the good fortune to escape almost uninjured. It remained perfect until the Stuart troubles of 1715, when the Hanoverian

—5

SETON CHURCH.

troops quartered in the castle and vicinity defaced the interior of the building, broke the tombs, and tore up the pavement in search of hidden treasures and for the lead that encased the bodies.

"Seton Church while undamaged was a handsome cruciform Gothic structure with a central tower. Now it stands desolate amid ancestral oaks entwined by ivy—the family badge- retaining little of its former self, and showing only an impressive and death-like beauty of an architectural ruin. The Earl of Wemyss and March, a descendant, but not the representative of the original owners, is the present proprietor, and has arrested the further progress of decay. It has long been a favorite subject with artists."

The illustration in this book was taken from the one in "An Old Family" which was made from Swon's engraving in the Maitland Club edition of the History of the House of Seyton which was published in 1829 for the Maitland Club. It was brought down to the year 1559 then, and Alexander, Viscount Kingston, wrote a continuation to 1687.

"A curious feature of Seton Church is the hagioscope, vulgarly called 'squint,' which is an opening frequently found on one side, and sometimes on both sides, of a chancel arch, arranged obliquely and converging toward the altar in order to enable the worshippers in the side aisles of a church to witness the Elevation of the Host during mass. It is the only one now existing in Scotland. It may be an interesting item that the last burial in this old church (until within these later years, when the Weymes family are beginning to be interred there) was that of Miss Matilda Seton, on December 8, 1750," says Robert Seton, adding: "I do not know who she was."

The following short excerpt from "The Ruins of Seton Chapel," by David Macbeth Moir, taken from "An Old Family," tells its own story:

> "And, O! sad emblem of entire neglect,
> In rank luxuriance, the nettles spread
> Behind the massive tablature of death,
> Hanging their pointed leaves and seedy stalks
> Above the graves, so lonesome and so low
> Of famous men, now utterly unknown,

Yet whose heroic deeds were, in their day,
The theme of loud acclaim,—when Seton's arm
In power with Stuart and with Douglas vied.
Clad in the robes of state, or graith of war,
A proud procession, o'er the stage of time,
As century on century wheeled away,
They passed; and, with the escutcheons mouldering o'er
The little spot, where voiceless they sleep,
Their memories have decayed; nay, even their bones
Are crumbled down to undistinguished dust,
Mocking the Herald, who, with pompous tones,
Would set their proud array of quarterings forth,
Down to the day of Christal and De Bruce."

"The most notable affair in the life of this lord was his capture
by Dunkirkers in the course of one of his voyages to France.
After losing all of his baggage he was obliged to ransom his life
from these Flemish pirates or privateers, but with the firm resolve
to bide his time and punish them severely.   This he did soon after,
although at great cost to himself in land and money.   On the 22d
of January, 1498, as appears in the Registry of the Privy Seal,
he bought a ship from the King of Scotland called the Eagle,
fitted her for war, and put to sea against his enemies, slew many
of them, took and destroyed several of their vessels.   The stream-
ers and flags, embroidered with the family arms, used on this occasion were preserved at Seton Castle, and were seen and described
by Alexander Nesbit, the writer on Heraldry, over two hundred
years later.   Lord Seton married Lady Margaret Campbell, eldest
daughter of Colon, first Earl of Argyll, and had three sons and two
daughters: George, his successor; John, who died without issue;
Robert, a man-at-arms in France, who died in the Castle of La
Rocca, at Milan, during the Italian wars of Louis XII., leaving
two sons: William, also a man-at-arms, in the Scotch Guards in
France, and Alexander, who married Janet Sinclair, Heiress of
Northrig, and founded the line of Setons of Northrig; Martha,
who married William Maitland of Lethington, of an ancient family,
and was ancestress of the Earl of Lauderdale.   Catharine, refusing many good offers of marriage, entered the Convent of Saint
Catharine of Siena at Edinburgh, and died there a professed sister
at the age of seventy-eight."

CHAPTER X.

"GEORGE, FIFTH LORD SETON. During his brief career he completed certain portions of the house at Seton, and repaired the great dungeon. He was also a generous benefactor to his Collegiate Church. By his wife, Lady Janet Hepburn, daughter of Patrick, first Earl of Bothwell, he had, besides a daughter Mariota (or Marion), who in 1530 married Hugh, second Earl of Eglinton, three sons, the first and third of whom died young, and the second succeeded to the title. This lord was very familiar with the chivalrous King James IV., and was among the valiant ones who died at Flodden on September 19, 1513. His body was brought home and buried with great lamentation in the choir of Seton Church beside his father:

> " 'Sleep in peace with kindred ashes
> Of the noble and the true,
> Hands that never failed their country,
> Hearts that never baseness knew.'

"Lady Seton continued a widow until her death, forty-five years after, and was a wise mother to her children and grandchildren, and a very pious woman. Sir Richard Maitland enumerates some of her many benefactions to Seton Church—a silver processional cross, sacred vessels, rich and complete sets of vestments, antependiums of fine woven arras, besides adding new furniture to the revestry, founding two more prebends, and enlarging the priest's chambers near the church, parts of which remain. When her son came of age she retired to the Convent of Saint Catharine of Siena, at Edinburgh, of which she was a large benefactress, as others of the family had been before. . . . Lady Seton died in this convent in 1558. Her body was honorably transported to Seton, and buried in the choir of the church beside her husband. Saint Catharine's Convent, commonly called 'The

Sciennes,' was destroyed at the Reformation, and the inmates dispersed.   Nothing now remains of it, and even the site is built over, the only memorial being the name, 'Saint Catharine's Place.' . . .

"GEORGE, SIXTH LORD SETON, succeeded his father in 1513, and was 'a good, wise, and virtuous man.' This lord repaired the older parts of Niddry Castle, in his Barony of Wynchburgh, and enlarged it. The top of the old square tower is distinctly seen among the trees as the train from Edinburgh speeds northward.

"'In former days the traveler to Stirling commonly went by the way of Linlithgow, which is the place where Mary Stuart was born, and he was all the more prompted to think of that enchanting woman because he usually caught a glimpse of the ruins of Niddry Castle—one of the houses of her faithful Lord Seton—at which she rested on the romantic and memorable occasion of her flight from Lochleven.'—William Winter: *Gray Days and Gold.*

"Maitland describes this Lord Seton as much given to manly games and outdoor sports, especially hawking, and says that he was reputed to be 'the best falconer in his day.' On November 17, 1533, he first appears in public life as an extraordinary Lord among the Senators of the College of Justice, an institution which had only been founded the preceding year. In 1542 he was associated with Lords Huntley and Home in command of a strong force organized to watch the operations of the English troops while King James V. himself assembled a large army at Edinburgh. In March, 1543, he was intrusted with the keeping of Cardinal Beton, who was accused of treasonable correspondence with France. In May, 1544, Seton Castle was burnt, and the church greatly injured by the English invaders, who carried away everything they could. This unfortunate nobleman died on July 17, 1549, at the Abbey of Culross, and was buried in the choir, because the English then garrisoned Haddington and harried the lands of the Barons round about. When they evacuated the country, his body was conveyed to Seton by his wife and a large company of kinsmen and friends to be entombed in his own church. He was twice married. His first wife—1527—was Elizabeth Hay, eldest daughter of John, third Lord Yester, by whom he had two boys and five girls. The eldest son, George, succeeded as seventh Lord Seton. John, the second son, founded the Setons *of Cariston* by marrying Isabel, Heiress of David Balfour of Cariston, in the County of Fife, 'of a very old standing family,' which is traced back to Sir Michael Balfour, who died in 1344. Of the five daughters, Beatrix married George, eldest son and heir of Sir Walter Ogilvy of Dunlugus. Their grandson was created a peer in 1642 as Baron Ogilvy of Banss, for his eminent services in the royal cause. The title is dormant since 1803.

"Helen [Maitland says Eleanor] married Hugh, who succeeded as seventh Lord Somerville, a peerage created in 1430 and dormant since 1872.

"Lord Seton married, secondly, a French woman of noble birth, Lady Mary Pyeris, who came to Scotland in the suite of Mary of Lorraine, daughter of the Duke of Guise and second wife of King James V., by whom she was the mother of the ill-fated Mary Queen of Scots. By this foreign marriage, something most unusual at that time, and in Scotland,

"'Land of the brown heath and shaggy wood,
Land of the mountain and the flood.'

Lord Seton had two sons, who left no descendants, and an only daughter, Mary, who was one of the Four Marys."

From Chambers we learn that George, sixth Lord Seton, was immovably faithful to Queen Mary during all the mutabilities of her fortune, and that he was master of the household of the king, in which capacity he had a portrait of himself painted with his official baton and the following motto:

"In adversitate, patiens;
In prosperitate, benevolous.
Hazard, yet forward."

But Robert Seton ascribes all this to the seventh lord.

Chambers also describes the joyous times at Seton, and the beautiful necklace won as a prize by Mary Seton at golf in a game against the queen.

Scott mentions a George Seyton, son of this Lord Seyton as

having been wounded in the Leslie-Seyton skirmish in the streets of Edinburgh. He also writes of a Dick Seyton of Wyndygoul, who was run through the arm by Ralph Leslie in the same encounter, but says two of the Leslies suffered phlebotomy at the same time. He likewise speaks of a Catharine Seyton and a Henry Seyton, twin brother and sister, children of Lord Seyton, both of whom assisted at the escape of Queen Mary from Lochleven Castle, where she was held a prisoner. From Scott's remarks it seems that Catharine and Mary Seyton were one and the same person. He describes her as "a modest young lady of sixteen, with soft and brilliant, deep-blue eyes, well-formed eyebrows, rich wavy tresses, of excellent shape, bordering perhaps on embonpoint, and therefore rather a Hebe than a Sylph, but beautifully formed, with round and taper fingers. She was an attendant of Queen Mary's at Lochleven Castle."

Henry Seyton was described as being a fiery youth, bold and fearless, with laughing full blue eyes, a nose with the slightest possible inclination to be aquiline, of a firm, bold step. He is represented as applying his riding-whip to the shoulders of a lout who stood before him and maintained his position with clownish obstinacy, or stupidity. He was dressed in purple velvet and embroidery. To a maid of the inn he promised a groat to-night and a kiss on Sunday, "when you have on a cleaner kirtle," for some slight service she was to perform for him.

To Adam Woodcock, the falconer of Sir Halbert Glendenning, who offered him a drink, by way of courtesy, and to sing him a song railing at the Pope, he replied: "He who speaks irreverently of the Holy Father of the Church in my presence is the cub of a wolf-bitch, and I will switch him as I would a mongrel cur." And when the singer started in again, Henry struck him a blinding blow across the eyes. He is said to have killed one Dryfesdale, who spoke slightingly of his religion and collared Henry and tried to have him arrested, and was himself killed in the battle of Langside, following the flight from Lochleven Castle, at which time George Douglas also met his death, as the story goes.

During the time of this Lord Seton, in the year 1539, King James V. came to Edinburgh and from thence removed to Seaton,

where he caused James Hamilton. Sheriff of Linlithgow, to be
brought to his trial and the king's court was duly convened there
when the prisoner was convicted of breaking open the royal bed-
chamber with a design to kill the king, and condemned. His
head was struck off, his body dismembered, after execution, and
the quarters hung up in the public places in Edinburgh. Such
was the inhuman practice in England and Scotland in that barbarous age, as we are assured by Buchanan in his History of
Scotland.

CHAPTER XI.

"George, seventh Lord Seton, was born in 1531, and succeeded his father in 1549.   It was to this 'noble and mighty lord'
that Maitland dedicated his history of the Seyton Family, begun
at the request of his father.   He was addicted to horse-racing and
to hawking in his youth, and on May 10, 1552, won a silver bell
which was run for at Haddington, the county town.

"Before he was twenty he married Isabel, daughter and heiress
of Sir William Hamilton of Sanquhar, at the time one of the Senators of the College of Justice in Edinburgh Castle, a singular
combination of peace and war.   She brought him the Manor of
Sorn and other lands in Kyle.   A number of gold medals were
struck to commemorate this union, on account, especially, of the
bride's relationship to the Earl of Arran, Regent of Scotland and
Duke of Chatellerault in France.   The medal is now very rare.
The Hamiltons have ranked for upward of four hundred years
among the most prominent and powerful of the Scottish nobility.

" Sir William Hamilton of Sanquhar was also Lord-Treasurer to
James V., and invited his Majesty to Sorn Castle, in Ayrshire, to
be present at the marriage of his daughter to Lord Seton.   On the
eve of the appointed day the king set out on the journey ; 'but he
had to traverse a long and dreary tract of moor, moss, and miry
clay, where there was neither road nor bridge ; and when about
half-way from Glasgow, he rode his horse into a quagmire, and
was with difficulty extricated from his perilous seat in the saddle.
Far from a house, exposed to the bleak wind of a cold day, and
environed on all sides by a cheerless moor, he was compelled to
take a cold refreshment in no better position than by the side of a
prosaic well.'   The well at which he sat and swore is still there,
and is called the King's Well ; and the quagmire in which his
horse floundered is ironically called the King's Stable.

"Soon after coming of age, Lord Seton was elected Provost of Edinburgh, and governed the capital for several tumultuous years with firmness and discretion. On one occasion there was an uproar in the city, whereupon two of the municipal officers hurried out to the Provost at Seton; but he, finding that they were to blame, promptly confined them in his castle dungeon, while he rode into Edinburgh, summoned the guard, and suppressed the riot."

When the marriage of Mary Queen of Scots and the Dauphin of France, afterward Francis II., was under consideration, in 1558, eight ambassadors were chosen in Scotland to go over to France to complete the arrangements. Among these was named George Seton, Governor of Edinburgh. Soon after they had embarked a violent gale of wind arose, in which two of the ships were sunk. The rest of the fleet was scattered, but sometime later arrived at different ports in France. The commissioners could not come to any satisfactory agreement with the French court, and were dismissed the court. Before they had time to embark for Scotland, four of their number died, from poisoning as some thought, but George Seton's name does not appear among those who died, and he returned to Scotland, as Buchanan tells the tale. On this occasion we are told that the king made George, Lord Seton, a present of magnificent silver plate, superior to anything seen in Scotland, which, after serving at banquets prepared for royalty at Winton House and Seton Castle, was finally stolen and beaten to pieces or melted down, at the time the castle was plundered in the troublous times of 1715. One of the noteworthy deeds of Lord Seton was the bringing of the first coach to Scotland when the Queen returned from France.

After the marriage of Mary Stuart and Francis II. was finally consummated, Lord Seton was sent to England to present Queen Mary's portrait to her cousin, Queen Elizabeth, and was entertained in a sumptuous manner at the English court. He also went to France to accompany Queen Mary back to Scotland after her husband had died, and she made him one of her Privy Council, and appointed him Master of the Household. He was also a knight of the most noble Order of the Thistle.

In June, 1567, Queen Mary and Bothwell, with several lords, who had answered their unhappy sovereign's appeal, and a considerable force assembled for battle, marching along gathering friends and distributing arms among her subjects as she went. Before night they reached Seton, but, there being so many of them, they could not all be quartered there, so they divided their numbers, some going to each of two neighboring villages.

On various parts of his castle he inscribed, as representing his religious and political creed, the following French legend:

> "Un Dieu, un Foy, un Loy."

Robert Seton gives a slightly different rendering of this inscription, as follows:

> "Un Dieu, Une Foy, Un Roy, Une Loy."

He is said to have declined to be promoted to an earldom which Queen Mary offered him at the same time she advanced her natural brother to be Earl of Mar. On refusing this honor, Mary wrote or caused to be written, according to Chambers, the following lines in Latin and French:

> "Sunt comites, ducesque alii, sunt denique regis,
> Setoni dominum sit sates esse mithi.
> Il a des comptes, des roys, des duces, ainsi
> C'est assez pour moy d'estre Seigneur Seton."

Which was rendered by Sir Walter Scott as follows:

> "Earl, duke or king, be thou that list to be;
> Seton, thy lordship is enough for me."

Robert Seton says this inscription was written by Mary, herself, with her diamond ring, upon a window of the great hall called Sampson's Hall, at Seton.

Lord "Seyton" was described by Sir Walter Scott in "The Abbot" as he appeared at his castle after the encounter with the Leslies in the streets of Edinburgh, as a tall man whose dark hair was already grizzled, though his eye and haughty features retained all the animation of youth. On that occasion the upper part of his person was undressed to his Holland shirt, whose ample folds were stained with blood. But he wore a mantle of crimson, lined with fur, cast around him, which supplied the deficiency of his dress. On his head he wore a crimson velvet bonnet, looped up on one side with a small golden chain of many links, which, going twice around the hat, was fastened by a medal, agreeable to the fashion among the grandees of the time.

In a poem by Aytoun of Bothwell at that time, Lord Seton is described, as we learn in "An Old Family," as follows:

> "He was of a noble stamp
>   Whereof this age hath witnessed few;
> Men who came duly to the camp,
>   Whene'er the Royal trumpet blew.
> Blunt tenure lords, who deemed the Crown
>   As sacred as the Holy Tree,
> And laid their lives and fortunes down
>   Not caring what the cause might be."

CHAPTER XII.

THE FLIGHT FROM LOCHLEVEN.

LOCHLEVEN CASTLE, where Mary Seyton and Mary Fleming were in attendance upon their beautiful and otherwise charming, but ever unfortunate queen, is described by Scott as "a sequestered, water-girted fortress consisting of one large donjon keep, surrounded with a court-yard with two round flanking towers at the angles, which contained within its circuit some other buildings of inferior importance. A few old trees, clustered together near the castle, gave some relief to the air of desolate seclusion. The gate of the court-yard was kept locked so no one could pass in or out without the consent of the owner of the castle."

While confined in Lochleven, Queen Mary had some of her maids of honor with her, as well as a page or two, who tried to entertain their beloved sovereign by reading, singing, and friendly converse, and 't is even said that they danced for her, perhaps at her request, to keep the time from passing too slowly for her followers.

The following is taken from Scott's description of the flight from Lochleven Castle, and is the most interesting of any of the accounts at hand and probably as reliable, if what Napoleon said of history is true. Here is his definition of history. Who can improve upon it? "What is history, but fiction agreed upon?"

"'We have but brief time', " said Queen Mary; 'one of the two signal lights in the cottage is extinguished—that shows the boat is put off.'

"'They will row very slow,' said the page, 'or keep where depth permits, to avoid noise. To our several tasks. I will communicate with the good father.'

"At the dead hour of midnight, when all was silent in the castle, the page put the key into the lock of the wicket which opened into the garden, and which was at the bottom of the stair-case

which descended from the Queen's apartment. 'Now turn smooth
and softly, thou good bolt,' said he, 'if ever oil softened rust!'
and his precautions had been so effectual that the bolt revolved
with little or no resistance. He ventured not to cross the thresh-
old, but exchanged a word with the distinguished Abbot, asked
if the boat were ready.

"'This half-hour,' said the sentinel. 'She lies beneath the wall,
too close under the islet to be seen by the warden, but I fear she
will hardly escape his notice in putting off again.'

"'The darkness,' said the page, 'and our profound silence may
take her off unobserved, as she came in. Hildebrand has the
watch-tower—a heavy-headed knave who holds a can of ale to be
the best head-piece upon a night-watch. He sleeps for a wager.'

"'Then bring the Queen,' said the Abbot, 'and I will call Henry
Seyton to assist them to the boat.'

"On tiptoe, with noiseless step and suppressed breath, trembling
at every rustle of their own apparel, one after another the fair
prisoners glided down the winding stair, under the guidance of
Willie Douglas, and were received at the wicket-gate by Henry
Seyton and the churchman. The former seemed to take instantly
upon himself the whole direction of the enterprise. 'My Lord
Abbot,' he said, 'give my sister your arm and I will conduct the
Queen—and that youth (Willie Douglas) will have the honor to
guide Lady Fleming.' . . . Catharine Seyton, who well
knew the garden path, tripped on before like a sylph, rather leading the Abbot than receiving assistance. The Queen, her native
spirit prevailing over female fear, and a thousand painful reflec-
tions, moved steadily forward, by the assistance of Henry Seyton;
while Lady Fleming encumbered with her fears and her helpless-
ness, Willie Douglas, who followed in the rear, and who bore under
the other arm a packet of necessaries belonging to the Queen.
The door of the garden, which communicated with the shore of
the islet, yielded to one of the keys of which Willie had possessed
himself, although not until he had tried several—a moment of
anxious terror and expectation. The ladies were then partly led,
partly carried, to the side of the lake where Lord Seyton, George
Douglas and several others awaited them. Henry Seyton placed

the Queen in the stern: the Abbot offered to assist Catharine, but she was seated by the Queen's side before he could utter his proffer of help.

"They rowed to the mainland, where they found horses awaiting them, and long before daylight they ended their hasty and perilous journey before the gates of Niddry, a castle in West Lothian nearly midway between Edinburgh and Linlithgow, belonging to Lord Seyton. When the Queen was about to alight, Henry Seyton, preventing Douglas, received her in his arms, and kneeling down, prayed her Majesty to enter the house of his father, her faithful servant. 'Your grace,' he added, 'may repose yourself here in perfect safety. . . . Do not dismay yourself should your sleep be broken by trampling of horses, but only think that here are some score more of saucy Seytons come to attend you.'

"'And by better friends than the saucy Seytons, a Scottish Queen cannot be guarded,' replied Mary. 'Rosabell went fleet as the summer breeze, and well-nigh as easy; but it is long since I have been a traveler, and I feel that repose will be welcome.— Catharine, *ma mignonne*, you must sleep in my apartment to-night and bid me welcome to your father's castle.'"

The next day the Queen with her attendants proceeded to Hamilton Palace, where six thousand men were soon assembled in her defense. While Mary's headquarters were at Hamilton the regent and his adherents had, in the king's name, assembled a host at Glasgow to oppose the Queen's followers. And when the latter came opposite Glasgow on the way to Dumbarton, they were attacked near Cathcart Castle, in which battle, called the battle of Langside, Henry Seyton met his death while defending the Queen.

The Queen's forces were defeated, and nearly suffered annihilation in this battle. Mary is said to have fled sixty miles from the field of battle before she halted at Sanquhar, and for three days of flight, according to her own account, she had to sleep on the ground and live on oat-meal and sour milk. On the third day she crossed the Solway and landed at Workington, in Cumberland, May 16, 1568.

After this disastrous encounter Lord Seyton was obliged "to retire abroad for safety," and was an exile for two years, during which time he was reduced to the necessity of working for his daily bread like common people. The work he succeeded in securing was driving a team in Flanders. He is said to have risen to favor in King James VI.'s reign, and returned to his home and resumed his accustomed life. As a reminder of his trip abroad he had a picture painted on one of the walls of the picture gallery at Seton Castle in his wagoner's costume as though driving four of those stocky Flemish horses.

Robert Seton says: "Lord Seton here displayed the hereditary valor of his race, repeatedly charging the rebel heights with the cry, 'God and the Queen! Set on! Set on!' He was wounded and taken prisoner and came near being put to death. When he was brought into the presence of Moray, he was bitterly rebuked by him as having been the prime author and the chief performer in this tragedy; whereas, according to Moray, it was his duty to have been one of the first to protect the infant king. Seton answered that he had given his fidelity to one prince, and that he should keep it as long as he lived, or until the Queen should have laid down her right of government of her own free will. Irritated by the reply, Moray asked him to say what he thought that his own punishment ought to be, and threatened that he should undergo the extreme severity of the law. 'Let others decide,' said Seton, 'what I deserve. On that point my conscience gives me no trouble, and I am well aware that I have been brought within your power, and am subject to your will. But I would have you know that even if you cut off my head, as soon as I die there will be another Lord Seton.'"

"As it was, he got imprisoned in Edinburgh Castle, but after a year's confinement went into exile," as above stated. "Lord Seton returned to Scotland in January, 1571, and is then constantly mentioned in letters and state papers, and always as an incorruptible and untiring agent of the imprisoned Queen and the Catholic cause.

"Lord Seton died on the 8th of January, 1585, and was buried in his family church, where on a slab of black marble embedded in the wall there is a lengthy epitaph from the pen of his son Alexander, who was an elegant Latin scholar."

--6

CHAPTER XIII.

MARY SEATON AND THE MAIDS OF HONOR.

MARY SEATON was the only daughter of the sixth lord by his second wife, and consequently she was half-sister to the seventh lord. She was one of the "Four Marys," celebrated in song and tradition, daughters of Scottish noblemen, all of the same age and Christian name as Mary Stuart. They were brought up as her playmates at the Priory of Inchmahome, on an islet in the lake of Monteith under the shadow of the highlands, and afterward accompanied her as little maids of honor when she was taken to France in childhood.

The New York *Tribune* is quoted by John Seaton of Greenup, Kentucky, as saying that Mary Seaton was the most beautiful and the favorite of the Four Marys that figured as maids of honor to the ill-fated Mary Queen of Scots, accompanying her from Scotland to France, and finally back to Scotland and into captivity. The same paper further says: "There is not a chapter in the annals of Scotland which does not contain mention of the Setons. They are represented to this day in the aristocracy of Sweden, and have occupied for three centuries a conspicuous place in the patritiate of Milan; while students of Shakespeare may remember that a Lord Seyton is described as being in attendance on Macbeth. The present head of that branch of the Seton family which has remained in the United Kingdom is Sir Bruce Maxwell Seton of Abercorn, while the head of the American branch known as the Setons of Parbroath descended from a Seton who came to America in the reign of George II. is William Seton, elder brother of the right reverend author of the family record, 'An Old Family.'

"The words of an old ballad founded on the dying lament of one of the four Marys have often been quoted to us:

> " 'Yestereen the Queen had four Maries,
> This night she'll have but three;
> There was Mary Seton, and Mary Beton,
> And Mary Carmichael, and me."

"They remained in France from 1548 to 1561, receiving there a finished education. Mary Seton was the only one who never married, although not for want of noble suitors, among whom the most ardent and persistent was Andrew Beton, nephew of the murdered Cardinal and brother of the then Archbishop of Glasgow. He was a faithful friend and servant of the Queen; but Mary Seton had cherished from her earliest years, amid the monastic cloisters of Inchmahome, a pious inclination to retire from the world, when she could do so without seeming to desert her unfortunate sovereign, whose captivity she had shared in Scotland, France and England. Once, on being pressed by her kind-hearted mistress to marry, she declared she was not free to do so, having made a vow of virginity. She would never admit an earthly bridegroom.

"Finally, in September, 1583, she obtained the Queen's permission to retire from her services and fulfill her desire of entering a convent. She became a nun at Saint Pierre-aux-dames in Rheims, of which the Queen's aged aunt, Renée de Lorraine, was abbess, and died there some time after 1615."

There is a letter in the Manuscript Department of the British Museum from Mary Seton to the Countess of Roxburgh, dated at Rheims, September, 1614. But the most curious of several memorials of Mary Seton is a Mori watch made in the shape of a human skull, that was given her by Queen Mary.

I have seen several different pictures of this watch, and while it must have been quite a curiosity, it was surely rather a ghastly affair. From the Philadelphia *Ledger* and other papers we learn that the watch was about two inches and a half in diameter. It is supposed to have been purchased by Queen Mary when on a visit to Blois with her husband, the Dauphin of France, as it has the name of a celebrated Blois manufacturer engraved on it.

The entire skull is curiously engraved. On the forehead there is a picture of Death, with the usual scythe and the hour-glass and sand-glass. He is depicted as standing between a palace and a hovel, to show that he is no respecter of persons, and underneath is the familiar quotation from Horace: "*Pallida mors æquo pulsat pede pauperum tabernas Regumque turres.*" At the back of the skull is another representation, this one being of Time devouring everything. Time also carries a scythe, and behind him is the emblem of eternity—the serpent with its tail in its mouth.

The upper section of the skull is divided into two pictures. On one side is the crucifixion, with the Marys kneeling at the foot of the cross, and on the other side are Adam and Eve surrounded by animals in the Garden of Eden.

Below these pictures, running around the skull, there is an open-work band, to allow the sound of the striking of the watch to be heard. This open-work is a series of designs cut to represent the various emblems of the crucifixion, such as scourges, the cross, swords, spears, the lantern used in the garden, and so forth. All the carvings have appropriate Latin quotations.

By reversing the skull and holding the upper part in the palm of the hand, and lifting the under jaw on its hinge, the watch may be opened, and on the plate inside is a representation of the stable at Bethlehem, with the shepherds and their flocks in the distance.

The works of the watch are in the brains of the skull, the dial-plate being where the roof of the mouth would be in a real skull. This is of silver and gold, with elaborate scrolls, while the hours are marked in large Roman letters. The works are remarkably complete, even to a large silver bell with a musical sound, which holds the works in the skull when the watch is closed.

This curious old watch is still in perfect order, and when wound every day keeps accurate time. It is too large to be worn, and was probably intended for a desk or private altar.

Perhaps it may interest some to learn more of the four Marys. In addition to what we have learned from Archbishop Seton and other sources, we read from Abbott's Life of Mary Queen of Scots that they were Mary Beaton, Mary Fleming, who is also mentioned by Scott, Mary Livingston, and Mary Seaton. We have no explanation as to whether Mary Livingston or Mary Carmichael was really the Maid of Honor, and it is possible that both may have occupied that honorable station at different times.

But, evidently, the lament herein given must have been that of either Mary Fleming or Mary Livingston. Abbott further says the four Marys were educated with Mary Stuart, Queen of Scotland, and that the French king claimed that he had expended five million pieces of gold in their maintenance and education.

Knollys, writing of Mary Queen of Scots, speaks of her daring grace and openness of manner, her frank display of a great desire to be avenged of her enemies, her readiness to expose herself to all peril in hope of victory, her delight to hear of hardiness and courage, commending by name all her enemies of approved valor, sparing no cowardice in her friends, but above all things athirst for victory by any means, at any price; so that for its sake pain and peril seemed pleasant to her, and all other things, if compared with it, contemptible and vile. From this description we may form some opinion of those who were her favorites, among whom were the Seatons of her reign, and especially Lord Seaton and Mary Seaton the Maid of Honor.

In the *Metropolitan Magazine*, 1904, page 119, in the story of "The Queen's Quair," a story of Mary Queen of Scots, by Maurice Hewlett, mention is made of Lord Huntley, his sons, John and Adam Gordon, Mary Seton, Lord Seton, and Niddry House.

While on the subject of Mary Queen of Scots and the Seatons, it may not be out of place to give a few instances where the Scottish sovereign visited at the Seaton home, or made some use of their services, that are to be found in Buchanan and Watkins's History of Scotland:

In June, 1488, Buchanan tells us, when James III. was slain, his eldest son, the Prince, ordered the Admiral of the fleet, Andrew Wood, to come ashore to him. This, Wood refused to do unless hostages were given for his safe return, upon which Seaton and Fleming, two noblemen, were sent for that purpose. They were safely landed after a stormy interview between the Prince and the Admiral, which might have terminated differently had it not been for the hostages on board the ships.

In the reign of James VI., who began his reign August 29, 1567, the king found his finances running low, and that he had no prospect of pecuniary assistance from England; so he began to devise measures for the improvement of his treasury. With this object in view he appointed eight commissioners, all of whom were of the legal profession, and who, because of their number, were called the Octavians. Among these men was Alexander Seaton, president of the board, and seven other noblemen. To these eight men, or any five of them, was given full and free management of the rents and duties of the controllers and collectors, with almost unlimited power of jurisdiction. "The national affairs were so well managed by these men," says Buchanan, "that the king was relieved from his embarrassment and the country benefitted at the same time."

At the time of the murder of David Rizzio, the Queen's Secretary. Mary went with George Seaton, attended by one hundred mounted soldiers, to his castle, and afterward to Dunbar, where she gathered a force together and turned her fury against the murderers of her favorite.

After the murder of Lord Darnley, and before twelve days were passed, Queen Mary went to Seton and while there never allowed Bothwell, who was supposed to have been the cause of the murder of her husband, "to be one moment from her side." The palace was full of the nobility, and she went abroad every day to the usual sports, although it was proper for a widow not to be seen for some time after the death of her husband. The coming of M. de Crocq, the French embassador to Scotland, to Seton somewhat disturbed her arrangements, for he told the guests how infamous the matter looked among foreigners. Mary then returned to Edinburgh, but Seaton had so many conveniences the queen was not contented till she returned there again.

However, Mary was finally married to Bothwell, and during their nuptials their party were at Seton House, where it appears she was a frequent visitor, especially when she sought shelter from her enemies, as were many others of the Catholic portion of the citizens of turbulent Scotland. It was while at Seton House on this occasion that Moray (or Murray), the Prime Minister, was summoned to appear before the Queen, which he did, and the party was there for some days until, finally, he was banished from the country, receiving permission to pass through England into France and thence to any place he might choose.

In 1604, when James VI.—he who caused the Bible to be translated into English--was King of England, Scotland, Ireland and France, a quarrel arose between Alexander Seaton, Lord Fivie, the Chancellor of Scotland, and the Earl of Glencairn, for which, being a Catholic, he was cited to appear before the Council, and, on his disobedience of the order, was pronounced contumacious; but from the rapid advancement he made in the good graces of the king it does not appear that the decision of the Council amounted to very much in that case, for in 1605 he was made First Earl of Dunfermline, and in 1611, Keeper of Holyrood House during his life.

At the beginning of 1617, King James made known his intention of visiting Scotland in person, and about the middle of March he left London with a large train of attendants. On crossing the boundary-line of the two kingdoms he alighted from his horse and welcomed the English nobles into Scotland, then remounting, he went to the seat of the Earl of Hume, from whence he proceeded the next day to Seaton, the house of the Earl of Winton, and on the next day entered Edinburgh.

About a hundred years later, when Anne occupied the throne, at the opening of Parliament in July, 1704, the succession of the crown being under discussion, and Queen Anne very much desiring to have the matter so arranged as to preserve the Protestant religion, the commissioner addressed the assembly, making known the queen's wishes. Several others continued in a similar strain, but without producing much effect, as Buchanan assures us. When the ministers had finished, Seaton of Pitmedden introduced a motion that "the house would support the Queen without naming a successor to the crown during the session of Parliament, and would agree to settle such question of government as should best conduce, in the event of Her Majesty's death, to free the kingdom from all English influence, preparatory to a federal union." In consequence they passed an act of security, wherein it was decreed

FIVIE CASTLE, ABERDEENSHIRE.

that in case the queen died without issue, the estates of Scotland should have the power to nominate a successor to the crown.

This parliament was the last under the reign of the Stuarts, as Queen Anne died on the first of August, 1714, closing the reign of the House of Stuart in Scotland, which was begun when Robert II. began to govern the country in 1371.

Under the reign of George I., King of Great Britain, France, and Ireland, in the year 1715, summonses were sent to many persons of distinction in Scotland, calling upon them to appear by a given time at Edinburgh to give security for their submission to the reigning sovereign, on pain of being declared outlaws and rebels. A few complied with the requirements, but the majority determined to begin hostilities before the royal armies should be concentrated in force. On the fifth of October the laird of Mackintosh joined the Earl of Mar, who ordered him to cross to the south side of the Frith of Forth in order to coöperate with the English and Scotch partisans on the border. "Mackintosh accordingly landed in East Lothian, and, having taken Seaton House, marched toward Edinburgh, but, finding the city and suburbs well defended, he changed his course and went to Leith." He gained possession of Leith without much difficulty, and at once fortified it. But when the Duke of Argyll appeared there with twelve hundred soldiers, the Highlanders, "like the Arabs, silently folded their tents" in the night and marched away, returning to Seaton House, which he placed in such a state of defense that the royal troops did not care to attack the place at that time.

All Scotland was now in commotion, and most persons were compelled to take up arms on one side or the other. Several noblemen and gentlemen with their tenantry took sides against the English government, among whom were George Seton, fifth and last Earl of Winton. But fierce divisions broke out among the Scots, which proved their ruin. A battle ensued in which the carnage was great and many prisoners were taken by each side. Earl Winton and several other earls were taken prisoners not long after, at Preston, on the thirteenth of November. A court-martial was held at Preston for the trial of the prisoners, on the twenty-

first. Some were sentenced to be shot and others were taken to
the Tower in London and treated with great indignity. Many
escaped to neighboring countries without so much as a Scotch
baubee. Like Bedlam beggars they were literally turned out in
the highways of the world to beg their bread until such time as
they could find work.

In "A Jacobite Family." by Brown, we find mention of this
event:

"Mr. Moir had occasion to go to London, taking John [Gunn]
with him, of course. He visited his friend, the Earl of Winton,
then under sentence of death in the Tower for his concern in the
rebellion of 1715. The Earl was arranging his affairs, and the
family books and papers had been allowed to be carried into his
cell in a large hamper, which went and came as occasion needed.
John, who was a man of immense size and strength, undertook, if
the Earl put himself, instead of his charters, into the hamper, to
take it under his arm as usual, and so he did, walking lightly out.
Lord Winton retired to Rome, where he died in 1749."

Some of the exiles made their way, under assumed names, to
England. Among these were the ancestors of Ernest Thompson
Seton, who went by the name Thompson for some generations,
and the ancestors of John and Mary Seaton mentioned elsewhere
in this volume. Some went to France, others to Germany and
Italy, and quite a number to the neighboring island of Ireland.
where some of their ancestors had been with the army of Edward
Bruce, and from which country a good number emigrated to this
land of the free and home of the brave.

Scott, speaking of that time, says: "The horses remained almost constantly saddled, and the sword seldom quitted the war-
rior's side: where war was the natural and constant state of the
inhabitants, and peace only existed 'n the shape of brief and
feverish truces."

CHAPTER XIV.

"ROBERT SETON FIRST EARL OF WINTON. On the death of George, seventh Lord Seton, in 1585, he was succeeded by his eldest surviving son, Robert, as eighth lord. Although his father left the estates heavily incumbered by reason of the great expense of several embassies and of his losses suffered by adhering to the queen's party, yet by prudence and ability Robert was soon able to put his affairs in good condition and provide both sons and daughters with respectable fortunes. He was very hospitable and kept a noble house, the king and queen being frequently there, and all French and other ambassadors and strangers of quality were nobly entertained. He was a favorite with the king, and was created Earl of Winton with solemnity and pomp of banners, standards, and pennons inscribed with loyal mottoes and quaint devices, at Holyrood House, on the 16th of November, 1600. He was a great builder and a wise improver of his property, especially by working on the harbor of Cockenzie, along the most rugged part of the Frith of Forth, a curious fishing village of great antiquity, whose history is little known. It originally sheltered only small boats, but when improved by art accommodated vessels of larger size.

"In 1582 Lord Seton, as he then was, married Lady Margaret Montgomerie, oldest daughter of Hugh, third Earl of Eglington, by whom he had five sons and a daughter: Robert, second Earl of Winton; George, third Earl of Winton; Sir Alexander Seton of Foulstruthers, who succeeded as sixth Earl of Eglington, and in descent from whom is the present Earl of Eglington and Winton, Lord Montgomerie, Androssan, Baron Seton and Tranent; Sir Thomas Seton of Olivestob; Sir John Seton of St. Germains; Lady Isabel Seton, who married James Drummond, first Earl of Perth. Their only daughter married the thirteenth Earl of Sutherland. Secondly. Lady Isabel married Francis Stewart, eldest son of the attainted Earl of Bothwell, by whom she had a daughter, Margaret, and a son, Charles Stewart.

"ROBERT, SECOND EARL OF WINTON, was born in 1583, and married Ann Maitland, only daughter of John, Lord Thirlstane, Chancellor of Scotland, but by whom he had no issue. In his disappointment he resigned his titles and estates to his younger brother, George, and died, in a private station in life, in January, 1634.

"GEORGE, THIRD EARL OF WINTON. In 1620 he built the house of Winton from the foundation, which had been burned by the English of old, and restored the park, orchard, and garden around it."

The description of Setoun Palace in East Lothian makes it appear to have been a splendid structure. It had been visited in royal progresses by Queen Mary; by her son, King James VI.; by the unfortunate Charles I.; and by the Merry Monarch, Charles II.; and an account of the masque ceremonies on those occasions, it is said, would fill a volume.

"In 1639, at the commencement of the Scottish Rebellion, Lord Winton left the country and waited upon the king to offer his loyal services, for which the rebels did him great injury; and thereafter all through the Civil War he was constantly harassed. In 1645, when Montrose was in command of the royal forces, the earl's oldest son, Lord Seton, joined him, and was taken prisoner at the disastrous battle of Philipaugh, and remained long in hazard of his life. When King Charles II. came to Scotland in 1650, the Earl of Winton was in constant attendance on him, and died on the 17th of December of that year, while preparing to be present at the coronation. Like his father, he suffered a long series of petty persecutions from the Presbytery of Haddington on account of his attachment to the Catholic faith. . . ."

Lord Winton was twice married. By his first wife, Lady Ann Hay, eldest daughter of the Earl of Erroll, he had five sons and three daughters, of whom only three will find place here, as the rest died young or unmarried.

The children of Lord Winton and Lady Ann Hay were: George Lord Seton, of whom hereafter; Alexander, Lord Fivie, who was made Earl of Dunfermline and Lord Chancellor of Scotland, being the last Catholic to hold that position. He is spoken of as a man of magnificent tastes. He was made keeper of Holyrood House during his life, which gave him the right to an apartment in the royal palace. He was distinguished for his architectural skill and his writings. He died at Pinkie House on June 16, 1622.

Elizabeth Seton, daughter of Lord Winton, was married in 1637 to William, seventh Earl Marischal, by whom she had four daughters, who were all well married. She brought a large fortune to her husband, and died in 1650.

"By his second wife, Elizabeth Maxwell, only daughter of the seventh Lord Herries, Lord Winton had six sons and six daughters, of whom only the following are mentioned, the others dying either young or unmarried, or without succession: 1. Christopher; 2. William. Christopher was a scholar. The brothers and a preceptor, while going 'on their travels abroad, were cast away at sea, upon the coast of Holland, in 1648.' 3. John, the Honorable John of Gairmiltoun, or Garleton; 4. Robert, of whom more among the cadets in 'An Old Family.' 5. Ann, married at Winton in April, 1654, to John Stuart, second Earl of Traquair, by whom she had three sons and one daughter, Elizabeth, who died, 'a brave, hopeful, young lady,' at the age of twenty. 6. Mary, married James Dalzell, fourth Earl of Carnwath, by whom she had a daughter, also named Mary, who married Lord John Hay, second son of the Marquess of Tweeddale."

The Honorable Sir John, a younger son of Lord George Seton, third Earl of Winton, was born September 29, 1639, and was created a baronet on December 9, 1664. He received in patrimony the lands of Garleton, or Gair-mil-toun, and Athelstanford in Haddingtonshire, where the picturesque ruins of the old tower and castle are to be seen on Garleton Hills, about two miles from Haddington, Scotland. He married Christian, daughter of Sir John Home of Renton, and had ten children by her, who was his second wife.

"The Family of Seton," by George Seton, says that John Seton

PINKIE HOUSE, MIDLOTHIAN, FAVORITE RESIDENCE OF THE LORD CHANCELLOR.

of Garleton was twice married, and the names of the ten children given by him were by his second wife, the Hon. Elizabeth Maxwell, daughter of Lord Herries. We do not know the names of the children by the first wife, but Mrs. F. Catharine Dahl, *née* Seaton, of Frogner. The Park, Hull, England, thinks he had no children, or only daughters by the first wife. If her supposition is correct, there remains no doubt that our branch of the family belongs to the Parbroath instead of to the Garleton branch. But Josephine Seaton makes the unqualified statement in the sketch of her father, William Winston Seaton, that Henry Seaton was the eldest son of Sir John Seaton of Garleton.

Sir David Seton of Parbroath married Mary, daughter of Lord Gray, by whom he had three sons, George, David, and John, the latter of whom went to Virginia from London, England, in 1635, and from whom some good genealogists believe Henry Seaton and William Winston Seaton were descendants. If it were not for Josephine's positive statement that Henry was the son of Sir John of Garleton, all would be plain enough. She gives no authority, but makes the statement that Henry was the son of Sir John of Garleton, and it is not for us to say she was mistaken, but both lines are given as we find them.

GEORGE SETON, FOURTH EARL OF WINTON, succeeded his grandfather, and the descent through that line may be found in "An Old Family," to which we are indebted for much the greater portion of what has preceded, and to which your favorable attention is directed.

"MOTHER" ELIZABETH ANN (BAYLEY) SETON.

Elizabeth Ann (Bayley) Seton, wife of William Seton, a member of the firm of Seton, Maitland & Co., of New York city, was born in New York city August 28, 1774. She married William Seton of the same city on January 25, 1794, Bishop Provost officiating. She opened a school in New York in 1805, and conducted it until 1808. In the following year she, with her sisters-in-law Harriet and Cecilia Seton, took the veil, and with eight thousand dollars, given by a recent convert to Catholicism, bought a farm at Emmitsburg, Maryland, and there founded the first community of the order of Sisters of Charity in the United States, together with a school for girls. Mrs. Seton becoming the Mother Superior.

Mother Seton wrote her Memoirs in 1817. Her father was Richard Bayley, M. D., and her mother, Catharine Carleton, whose father was Rector of St. Andrew's Church at Richmond on Staten Island. Mrs. Catharine (Carleton) Bayley died at Newton, Long Island, in May, 1777, leaving two daughters, of whom Elizabeth was the younger. By his second marriage, with Charlotte Barclay, June 16, 1778, a daughter of Andrew Barclay and Helen Roosevelt, he had a large family, of whom Guy Carleton Bayley married Grace Roosevelt. Their eldest son, James Roosevelt Bayley, who was Mother Seton's nephew by the half blood, was the first Bishop of Newark, New Jersey, in 1853. He founded Seton Hall College and was Bishop of Baltimore in 1872.

Helen and Grace Roosevelt were own cousins to President Roosevelt's fourth and fifth great-grandfather, as appears in the "Genealogy of the Roosevelt Family," published in 1902 by Charles B. Whittelsey, of Hartford, Connecticut.

The married life of William and Elizabeth Ann Seton was very happy. Their home was near the Battery, in New York, then the most desirable part of the city.

William Seton is said to have been the handsomest man in New York, and one of the few who were well connected in Great Britain. Their first child was born in 1795, and was named Ann Mariah.

Early in 1800 William Seton's affairs became embarrassed, and he found himself in difficulties which he was unable to surmount, and before two years were over he had lost his fortune, but he found his wife to be a woman of indomitable energy and a support in every trouble.

In November, 1797, Mrs. Seton, with a few other society ladies, formed the first organization in New York, and probably in the United States, for the relief of poor widows with small children. The one-hundredth anniversary of the society was celebrated with much *éclat!* in 1897.

Mrs. Seton had been strictly brought up in the tenets of the Protestant Episcopal Church, and became a particular favorite of Rev. Mr., afterward Bishop, Hobart. One of Doctor Hobart's daughters, Rebecca Seton Hobart, was a god-child of Mrs. Seton.

In September, 1803, William Seton, accompanied by his wife and eldest daughter, went on a voyage to Italy for his health, which he hoped would be restored by the mild climate at Pisa. Mrs. Seton kept an interesting journal during her absence, which has been published, and was edited by her grandson, now Archbishop Robert Seton.

William Seton died at Pisa, on December 27, 1803, of consumption. His body was buried in a Protestant cemetery at Leghorn, his modest tomb being next to Smollett's.

While in Italy, Mrs. Seton and Anna were much befriended by a noble and exemplary Catholic family named Filicchi. Chevalier Filicchi had traveled in the United States in 1785-86, and became a friend and correspondent of William Seton. After her return to New York, in June, 1804, Mrs. Seton and her children were received into the Catholic Church on March 14, 1805, after a severe struggle with herself, and after encountering the most intense opposition of her family and friends. She left New York and went to Baltimore, Maryland, in an almost destitute condition on account of the treatment received from her family. Her god-mother, a rich and childless widow, Mrs. Sartin, who had made her will in Mrs. Seton's favor, destroyed the will when Elizabeth became a Catholic, and left her large fortune to another.

Mrs. Elizabeth Ann Seton died on January 4, 1821, in Emmittsburg, Maryland. Her life has been admirably written by the late Rev. Dr. White, who made it one of the most interesting and edifying works in the Catholic literature of America. It has gone through several editions, and continues in constant demand. Her life has also been written in French by Mme. de Barbery, and translated into German and Italian.

The children of William and Elizabeth Ann Seton were: William, Richard, Ann Mariah, Rebecca, and Catharine, for an account of whose lives see "An Old Family."

From the Cincinnati *Commercial Tribune* we learn that:

"Search is being made here for the facts and deeds that will

—7

authorize the enrollment of the first native American to be included among the canonized saints. The Very Rev. P. S. McHale, C. M., President of Niagara University, has received authority to begin the work preliminary to the beatification of Mother Elizabeth Seton, who founded the order of the Sisters of Charity in the United States."

WILLIAM SETON.

"William Seton, brother to Archbishop Robert Seton of Rome, Italy, representative of the Setons of Parbroath, Scotland, died March 15, 1905, in St. Vincent's Hospital, New York. He was a most learned and distinguished gentleman, who always reflected luster on the ancient and honorable family from which he sprang. Born in New York January 28, 1835, he studied at Fordham College, and at Mount St. Mary's, of Emmitsburg. After traveling some years in Europe he returned to the United States to study, and passed his examination for the bar. The Civil War breaking out just then, he never practiced his chosen profession, but answered President Lincoln's earliest call for troops in 1861. He was a first lieutenant and later a captain of the Fourth New York Regiment of United States Volunteers, and was severely wounded twice in the battle of Antietam. After recovering he was appointed captain of the Sixteenth Artillery, and was under General Grant.

"After the war he began a life of study and literary occupation. He published several novels and stories, the best known of which is 'A Romance of Charter Oak.' 'The Pioneer,' a poem from his pen, won the admiration of William Cullen Bryant. In a few years he abandoned this line of literature and devoted himself to the study of Natural History, making yearly visits to Paris to meet there the most learned men in their special branches.

"Mr. Seton was a grandson of the venerable Mother Seton, foundress of the Sisters of Charity in the United States. His brother, Archbishop Robert Seton, of Rome, Italy, is a distinguished antiquarian and writer who knows more about the history and antiquities of Rome than any other living person. The Archbishop is now the last of his race. A sister, Miss Elizabeth Seton, a most graceful writer, lives at Huntington, Long Island.

"Mr. William Seton, before his lamented death, gave to the Bishop's Memorial Hall, Notre Dame, Indiana, all the Seton heirlooms which he inherited from his ancestors. Among the treasures is an original portrait of Mary Queen of Scots, given by that unfortunate princess to a member of the Seton family."

The foregoing interesting article was taken from the *Western Watchman*, a Catholic journal published at St. Louis, Missouri, April 20, 1905.

ARCHBISHOP ROBERT SETON.

Robert Seton was born in New York August 28, 1839. His father was William Seton and his mother Emily Prime.

Robert was educated by private tutors at his home, and at Rome University. He is an LL. D. and a D. D. He was the Private Chamberlain to Pope Pius IX.; Dean of all Monsignori in the United States; lecturer of Seton Hall College at South Orange, New Jersey, with its twenty-two instructors, one hundred and fifty students, and its library of forty thousand volumes; and of the Catholic University of Washington.

He has been a writer for Catholic magazines, is author of "An Old Family, or the Setons in Scotland and America," the best history of several that have been published, and "The Dignity of Labor," published in 1893. He was also editor of "The Letters and Journal of Elizabeth Ann Seton."

The New York *Tribune* is quoted by John Seaton of Greenup, Kentucky, as saying that Monsignor Seton is not only one of the most eminent genealogists in the United States, but likewise enjoys the distinction of being the only Roman Catholic prelate of American birth who ever had been admitted to and graduated from the Academia Ecclesiastic at Rome, Italy, which is restricted exclusively to theological students of noble birth, and from the graduates of which the nuncios and diplomatic officials of the Pope are exclusively recruited.

The New York *Daily Sun* in 1899 said that Monsignor Seton was made Prothonotary Apostolic by Pope Pius IX. in 1867, when only twenty-eight years old, and that he was the first American to be so honored.

The Chicago *Tribune* of January 3, 1905, contains a letter by Marquise De Fontenoy, mentioning the college where Robert Seton, the only American-born person who ever entered, was educated. Also Sir Bruce Maxwell Seton, head of the Seton family in Great Britain, and William Seton of New York, head of the Setons of Parbroath, whose ancestors came to America in the reign of King George II., and who married a Miss Curzon, of Baltimore, Maryland.

Fontenoy further says: "I know of few families whose record is more interesting or more closely interwoven with national history on both sides of the Atlantic than the Setons."

At present Robert Seton is an Archbishop in the church that is "Roman in its center and Catholic in its circumference." His story is very modestly told in "An Old Family."

William Seton, Robert's father is reported to have been the first person to introduce Percheron horses into this country for breeding purposes, having sent two brood mares and a stallion from near Chartres, in Eure et Loire, France, in August, 1856, to his son, also William Seton, who then owned property at Dixon, Lee county, Illinois.

ERNEST THOMPSON SETON.

Ernest Thompson Seton, artist, author, and noted lecturer, was born in 1860, and educated at Toronto Collegiate Institute and the Royal Academy of London, England. He lived in the backwoods of Canada during the time from 1876 to 1880, when he was Official Naturalist to the Government of Manitoba, and on the Western Plains of the United States from 1882 to 1887. He studied art in Paris, France, during the years from 1890 to 1896 inclusive, and married Grace, daughter of Albert Gallatin, of San Francisco, California, on the first of June in the latter year, having before that time published the "Birds of Manitoba," in 1890.

He is now well known as an animal painter and illustrator, having been one of the chief illustrators of the Century Dictionary. He has written several popular books, among which "Wild Animals I Have Known" is probably the best known.

Mr. Seton is one of those who have changed their names for cause, having at different times written it Ernest Seton-Thompson, Ernest Thompson-Seton, and Ernest Thompson Seton without the hyphen. He is also reported to have spelled the name Seaton at an early period of his career.

Grace (Gallatin) Seton is a writer and book-maker of assured reputation. She did praiseworthy newspaper work in Paris, France, in 1894, and she plans the makeup of some of her husband's books, especially as to the arrangement of the text and illustrations.

Mr. and Mrs. Seton now make their home at Cos Cob, Fairfield county, Connecticut, except during the time he is out upon his lecturing tours.

In the Kansas City *Star* of February 14, 1904, a long article is copied from the New York *World*, telling that Mr. and Mrs. Seton had been blessed with their first child after eight years of wedded life, and that their intention was to raise little Miss Ann Seton out of doors, "An Indian child."

CHAPTER XV.

THE FAMILY IN AMERICA.

"The family is the first institution and lies at the basis of everything that is good in society," says C. H. Parkhurst, D. D. Then let us study the history of our family and try to improve wherein our ancestors may have done amiss in the past, or at least maintain the record of sobriety, patriotism, and honor handed down to us.

It ought to be an inspiration to every one to know he has descended from a long line of upright, intelligent men and women, and vicious indeed is the one who would intentionally bring reproach upon a name that has been maintained in honor for many generations.

"Seek not the idle fame derived from dead ancestors," as Scott says, but put forth your best efforts to so live that the world may be made better in some degree by your having lived in it, is fit advice for children in this and all coming generations of the family.

The same fate that made you Scotch by descent gave you head and heart and hands to uphold the good name so nobly handed down to you by a long line of honorable ancestors, no one of whom, so far as we have learned, was ever the inmate of a penitentiary. Those of our name and blood who have suffered confinement or death at the hands of the law have done so through the efforts of the enemies of their king or country for fighting in defense of the one or the other.

"It were a great pleasure," says Maitland, "to a man to know the origin and beginning of his house and surname, and how long it has stood, with good actions and virtue of his predecessors."

Should anyone claim the Seatons have not always been loyal, brave, and honorable citizens of their respective countries, you may, with a clear conscience, tell him as Marmion told Douglas of old:

> "And if thou saidst I am not peer
> To any lord in Scotland here,
> Lowland, or Highland, far or near,
> Lord Angus, thou hast lied."

And to the best of our knowledge and belief, no man has ever found a mistress of the Seaton name or blood.

Both tradition and history declare that the Seaton family originated in Scotland, as has already been explained, and George Buchanan and John Watkins's History of that country is especially explicit on that point; and to prove their competency as witnesses we will quote from Reverend Allan Menzie's History of the Church of Scotland, as follows:

"One of the best Latin scholars that modern Europe has produced was George Buchanan. His last and most important labor was his History of Scotland, originally printed in 1582, of which there have appeared seventeen editions."

So much for the man who lived with and wrote of the ancestors of our family and the people of whom they formed no unworthy part.

George Buchanan had the direction of the later education of James I. of England, who was also James VI. of Scotland, he who authorized the translation of the Bible.

THE FIRST SEATON IN AMERICA.

In the "Virginia Historical Magazine," volume 6, page 406, under the head of "Virginia Land Patents," is to be found the earliest record of a Seaton in this country, so far as we know; mention being made of 1200 acres of land on the north side of the James river, the patent issued July 12, 1637, in consideration of the transportation of twenty-four persons by Harvey. Among the names is to be found that of "Jon." Seaton, who is doubtless the John Seton mentioned on page 196 of "An Old Family" as the sixth child of Sir David Seton of Parbroath, who went from London to Virginia on August 7, 1635.

Hotter's "Our Early Emigrant Ancestors" says that "Jo."

Seaton sailed August 7. 1635. on the ship "Globe," and that he was nineteen years old at that time.

In "The Genesis of the United States," by Alexander Brown, is an extract from the record of the Stationers' Company of the City of London, dated "1609, 7th mo.," which shows that a Mr. Seton was a member of the "Stationers," and was one of those among whom £125, to be used in the Company's adventure in the voyage to Virginia, was levied and disbursed. Mr. Seton's share was three pounds.

In the Virginia Historical Magazine, volume 2, page 280, it is recited in a long deed in Stafford county, dated March 8, 1759, from William Fitzhugh, of Calvert county, Maryland, to Bailey Washington, of Stafford county, Virginia, that Richard Carey and George Seaton obtained a patent in 1662 for six thousand acres of land on the Potomac, in Westmoreland county, which had been granted in 1659 to Mr. Hugh Gwinne, who sold it to said Seaton and Thomas Morris; that Morris and his wife Mary sold their share to said Carey, etc. Carey's will, dated November 29, 1682, is referred to, and discloses the fact that George Seaton was then dead and that he left heirs.

This George Seaton may probably be safely considered as a son of Jon. Seaton mentioned heretofore, as least until we learn more of them.

HENRY SEATON, son of the Honorable John Seaton of Garleton, or Gairmiltoun, in East Lothian, Scotland, or of John Seton, son of Sir David Seton of Parbroath, with others of the family, were devoted adherents of the Stuarts of Scotland "for whose throne they had unflinchingly fought in opposition to the Prince of Orange," making themselves somewhat noticeable to the government of England by their Jacobite schemes for its overthrow in Scotland. Finally, convinced of the futility of any further resistance to the authority of William III., Henry Seaton and a number of his co-workers sought refuge in the wilds of America, locating in the Colony of Virginia in 1690.

In volume 1, page 479, of the Virginia Historical Magazine, a George Seaton is mentioned as a Justice of the Peace of Gloucester county and as having taken part with the insurgents in Bacon's

Rebellion; and it is further stated that some of his descendants probably lived in King William county, and that W. W. Seaton of the *National Intelligencer* was of the latter family. This may or may not have been the George Seaton mentioned as of Westmoreland county; but the inference that he may have been George Seaton, son of Henry, the ancestor of W. W. Seaton of the *National Intelligencer*, appears to be very doubtful.

Henry Seaton settled first in Gloucester county, where others of the name had been located since 1637, and who may have been, and probably were, relatives, who had influenced the decision of Henry as to a proper starting-place for a home, the Pyanketank seeming to be the most eligible site for that purpose. For some years Henry Seaton continued to reside upon the banks of the Pyanketank, in Gloucester county, during which period, in 1709, he was married to Elizabeth Todd, daughter of a gentleman of standing in that county, and had issue.

Mr. George Fitzhugh, of Rappahannock, a gentleman remarkable for his wit and abstruse learning, in his papers on the "Valleys of Virginia," quotes Bishop Mead's list of the early justices and Vestrymen,—at that time offices of mark,—among whom, in Pentworth Parish, Gloucester county, were mentioned Henry, Richard and Bailey Seaton, and says: "None but men of substance and consideration were made vestrymen," and the reader will find that the descendants of these gentlemen have retained their high social position.

Henry Seaton subsequently removed to an estate in King William County, on the Mattapony, which for several generations continued to be the home of his descendants.

By a deed a century and a half old, in possession of the family "An Indenture Tripartite, made in the first year of the reign of 'our most gracious Sovereign, Lord and King, George the Second,' between Colonel Taylor, George Seaton, only son and heir of Henry Seaton, and Elizabeth his wife, now the wife of Augustine Moore, Gentleman," we learn that Henry Seaton's widow had remarried.

Henry and Elizabeth Seaton had been blessed with only one child before the death of the former, and to him had been given the name of George Seaton.

CHAPTER XVI.

THE ONLY CHILD OF HENRY AND ELIZABETH SEATON.

GEORGE SEATON, the only child of Henry Seaton, was born on the family estate on the Mattapony, in Virginia, on December 11, 1711, and of course was given all the advantages of the then new country in the way of an education. We have no extended account of his boyhood, but on December 27, 1734, when he was twenty-three years old, he married Elizabeth, daughter of Leonard Hill, of King William county, Virginia, gentleman. He seems to have succeeded in a financial way, holding large properties in Spottsylvania county, besides the paternal estates, which at his death in 1750 were left to his eldest son, after the legal fashion of the country as a royal colony of England. The daughters and the younger son must have been compelled to be satisfied without any of the real estate belonging to the family.

The names of the children, according to the old family Bible, were, in the order of their birth: Elizabeth, Augustine, George 2d, and *Betty*, of the record, but *Elizabeth* in the Biographical Sketch of her nephew, William Winston Seaton.

THE CHILDREN OF GEORGE AND ELIZABETH SEATON.

Elizabeth Seaton, the first child in the family, was born December 19, 1735. Further than this we know nothing more of her, except that she died December 9, 1738, but we surmise that she was born at the estate on the Mattapony, where her grandfather, Henry Seaton, had established his home in 1709.

AUGUSTINE SEATON, son of George, was evidently born at the same Virginian home as his sister. His birthday was October 17, 1737. The facts in our possession regarding the early life of Augustine Seaton are very meager, indeed, but from the nature

of the case we feel sure his education was carefully looked after
by private tutors and his morals guarded with loving kindness.
And in confirmation of this thought we learn that he was "a
gentleman noted for his high-toned bearing, winning manners,
and strong good sense."

In the year 1776—a year never to be forgotten by any loyal
American—Augustine Seaton was married to Mary Winston,
daughter of Samuel Winston, Esquire, of Louise county, Virginia, who was of the same family as the mother of the immortal
Patrick Henry.

Colonel John Henry, Patrick's father, a native of Aberdeen,
Scotland, and a nephew of the historian Robertson, came to this
country in quest of fun, fighting and fortune, enjoying the patronage and friendship of Governor Dinwiddie, of Virginia, by
whom he was introduced to Colonel Syme, of Hanover, whose wife
was Miss Sarah Winston, in whose family he became domiciled,
and whose widow he subsequently married, continuing to reside
on the family estate of Studleigh, where their son, Patrick Henry,
was born. It is said that it was from his mother's side of the
house that Patrick derived his genius of eloquence.

The home of Augustine and Mary Seaton, "Chelsea," since
passed into the sixth generation on the mother's side, is described
as "one of the most ancient houses in Virginia, its brick having
been imported from England, and it is still, despite the dilapidations of two revolutions, an imposing and stately residence."
This account is found in "A Biographical Sketch" of William
Winston Seaton, the third son of these aristocratic people, and
continues: "Here were the graves of young Seaton's forefathers,
and within the venerable mansion were gathered cherished Old
World family relics, with worm-eaten wills and musty parchments,
while on the walls were portraits of his progenitors of a century
and a half."

The name of Augustine Seaton, Regimental Quartermaster in
Grayson's Additional Continental Regiment of Virginia, May 24,
1777, is given in Heitman's Register. He resigned December
20th of that year.

Augustine Seaton died suddenly at West Point, the residence

of his daughter, Mrs. John West, of York River, York county, Virginia, on October 10, 1794, being nearly fifty-seven years old.

The children of Augustine and Mary Seaton were: 1. Lucy; 2. Augustine Hill; 3. Leonard Hill; 4. William Winston; 5. Elizabeth; and 6. John. For an account of what is known of the lives of these people, see further along in this book.

GEORGE SEATON 2D, the only other son in the family, was born February 8, 1739, according to the record in the old family Bible, that was printed in the year 1638, and which is now in the possession of Seaton Schroeder, of Washington, D. C., a son of Caroline Seaton, daughter of William Winston Seaton.

Of the children of George Seaton 2d and his wife we have as yet found no record, except that they had one son, Asa Seaton, of whom all that is known to us will be given later.

George Seaton 2d died in the year 1791, as recorded in the Bible referred to before.

Elizabeth Seaton, called Betty, was born March 28, 1741, doubtless on the family estate on the Mattapony, in Virginia, and carefully nurtured until in good time she merged her identity with the one man of her heart by marrying John West, of York River, gentleman, a scion of a noble British house.

The Wests are a family of great historical distinction, John being a direct descendant from father to son of Lord De la Warre, the famous and gorgeous Governor of Virginia of long ago.

We have no account of the children of John and Elizabeth (Seaton) West, except that Thomas West, their son, married a Miss Bolling, who is claimed to have been a direct descendant of the Princess Pocahontas, daughter of the Indian chief, Powhattan; but they left no issue.

John Randolph, the Virginian statesman and United States Senator, is also said to have been a descendant of the Princess Pocahontas.

CHAPTER XVII.

THE CHILDREN OF AUGUSTINE AND MARY (WINSTON) SEATON.

Lucy Seaton, the eldest child, was born on December 10, 1778. When she was grown to womanhood and had been educated, she was married to Thomas Rose, of Richmond, Virginia.

AUGUSTINE HILL SEATON was born on November 15, 1780. He died in February, 1810, without issue.

LEONARD HILL SEATON was born October 13, 1782. He died in April, 1826, without heirs.

WILLIAM WINSTON SEATON has been given another write-up, much more in detail than can be attempted here; but for those who have no opportunity to read the "Biographical Sketch" of him, we give the following, gleaned from several sources:

He was born January 11, 1785, at Chelsea, in Virginia, the ancestral home of this line of Seatons. From the sketch mentioned we learn that "Under the paternal roof passed young William's childhood in happy companionship of brothers and sisters, his tastes refined by gentle maternal influences, his intelligence quickened by the noted society frequenting his father's hospitable home, which numbered among its cherished guests the illustrious Patrick Henry."

A domestic tutor directed the education of the youth, and of course his brothers and sisters, in the earlier paths of learning, until he reached, in Richmond, Virginia, what was then the culminating academic polishing of Ogilvie, the Scotchman, "whose earldom of Finlater slept while he was playing pedagogue in America."

Young William belonged to a military company in Richmond from his boyhood, and he was a sportsman skilled in the use of firearms. We are told that at the early age of eighteen his mind was quite matured, his ambition aroused, and he passed into the arena of public life, entering with manly earnestness upon the career of political journalism, of which he was one of his country's pioneers, and which his well-earned fame and social distinction crowned with honor.

WILLIAM WINSTON SEATON.

He made his first essay into the stormy field of politics as assistant editor of a Richmond journal, having acquired a practical knowledge of "the art preservative of all arts" in the same office with that master of journalism, Thomas Richie.

William Seaton soon received an invitation to take charge of a more prominent journal, in Petersburg, Virginia, then edited by Colonel Yancey. This was in the spring of 1806, and in the next year he accepted an advantageous offer and the persuasions of the retiring editor to assume proprietary editorship of the *North Carolina Journal*, of Halifax.

On March 30th, 1809, he was married to Sarah Weston Gales, daughter of Joseph Gales and Winifred Gales, of Raleigh, North Carolina, formerly of Sheffield, England; and it appears to have been a most happy union of hearts as well as hands and a bright feather in his cap in the way of social advancement, for Mrs. Seaton proved to be one of the brightest and most fascinating ladies of the nation's capital city.

In October, 1812, he joined his fortunes with those of his brother-in-law, Joseph Gales, which association transferred the names of Gales and Seaton from the head of the *Register* to that of the *National Intelligencer*, of Washington, D. C., of which journal the subject of this sketch was editor at the accession of James Madison to the presidency; and still he was in the same position during the administration of our first martyred President, the lamented Abraham Lincoln, and was yet hale and hearty and in full possession of his magnificent powers though eighty years of age.

"Had it not been for the industry of Gales and his partner, William W. Seaton, an important part of the proceedings of the Senate and House of Representatives .which they reported, would not have been preserved. Especially is this true of the great debate between Hayne and Webster." (Continental Encyclopædia.)

William Winston Seaton enrolled himself as a private in a volunteer company commanded by Captain John Davidson, at Fort Warburton, and was in the various expeditions on which his command was detailed during the War of 1812. He was with the company on August 24, 1814, at East Branch, and also at Bladensburg, when they were engaged with the enemy.

The *Intelligencer* office was sacked by orders of Admiral Cockburn, a British officer, as a petty spite against the publishers for the help they gave the cause of their country.

A letter to Mr. Seaton from General G. H. Stuart, of the British army, is addressed to "Colonel" W. W. Seaton, though we have no other evidence of his having been promoted at such a surprising stride. But he was at least Captain of the Washington Guards in October, 1824, and his son, Augustine F. Seaton, was also the Captain of the "Young Guards," who eclipsed even the veterans commanded by his father, and it was declared to be the best drilled volunteer corps at the reception of General Lafayette in Alexandria on that memorable occasion.

Mr. Seaton is reported to have offered this toast at the reception given to the distinguished guest of the nation:

"The United States and France, their early friendship—may it ever be maintained by mutual acts of kindness and justice."

He also entertained the noble Frenchman at his home on December 15, 1824, when all of the President's cabinet, except Mr. William Harris Crawford, were present, as was every member of the diplomatic corps, except Baron Marenit, the French minister, who was precluded from society for three months at that time by some rule of court etiquette.

Lafayette attended the Unitarian church with the Seatons during his stay in Washington, being desirous of hearing the Reverend Mr. Little, of whose fervid eloquence he had heard. And Mr. Seaton accompanied Lafayette as far as Baltimore on his departure from the capital, and visited the cattle show with him in that city. He was also chosen, with the Mayor of Washington, at another time, to escort Lafayette from the President's to a private *en famille* evening at the home of Mr. Barlow, a personal friend of the titled foreigner, from which place Mr. and Mrs. Seaton accompanied him to a concert.

William Winston Seaton was for ten years elected to the Mayoralty of the city of Washington, D. C., and in that capacity entertained the city's guests in the persons of General Bertrand, Charles Dickens and wife, and many others, at his home.

He was an active member of the Washington Monument Society, of which organization he was chosen vice-president. And the corner-stone of the monument was laid during one of his terms as Mayor, which event, by the way, was the last appearance in public of President Taylor, July 4, 1848.

Winfield Scott and William Winston Seaton were intimate companions in their youth, both living in Richmond, Virginia at the time, there being only one year difference in their ages, and both attended the same school, that of Ogilvie, the Scotchman, mentioned before.

Daniel Webster and our Mr. Seaton were quite intimate, often visiting back and forth in each other's homes in Washington, and quite as frequently writing to each other, as is shown by letters given in the Biographical Sketch of our subject.

Far ahead of the time in which he lived, he emancipated his slaves of his own volition, and assisted as many as desired in colonizing themselves in Africa, being an active and practical member of the Colonization Society at the time. It has been said of him that he freed more of his own slaves, at his own suggestion, than all of the Abolitionists in the North had ever done up to the time of the Emancipation Proclamation of the President.

There are many letters in existence that were written to him by noted men of several countries, among the number one from Lord Durham, Governor-General of Canada, who is reported to have pronounced Mr. Seaton "the most charming American he ever met."

In Nicolay and Hay's Life of Abraham Lincoln in the *Century* magazine, is a portrait of W. W. Seaton, of Washington, D. C., and in the Continental Encyclopædia it is stated that he and his brother-in-law were the only reporters in Congress for eight years, from 1812 to 1820, one working in each house. And W. W. Seaton is mentioned in the Encyclopædia Britannica in connection with Joseph Gales, where it is said they formed a partnership in 1812, and that the *Intelligencer* was changed from a tri-weekly to a daily in 1813; and further, that the files of the *Intelligencer* form an important part of the authentic documents relating to United States history.

The children born to William and Sarah Seaton were as follows, in the order of their birth: 1. Augustine Fitzwhylson; 2. Julia; 3. Altona; 4. Gales; 5. William Henry; 6. Ann Eliza; 7. Josephine; 8. Caroline; 9. Virginia; 10. Malcolm; and 11. Arthur.

Mr. Seaton retired from the management of the *National Intelligencer* on December 31, 1864, and if we are not much mistaken, considerably reduced in fortune on account of the war, for when the South seceded from the Union, in 1861, his subscription list must have suffered to the number of subscriptions carried in the Confederacy.

— 8

Mrs. Sarah (Gales) Seaton died on December 23d. 1863. and was buried on Christmas day. Mr. Seaton survived his wife only about three years. dying at Washington, D. C.. June 18, 1866. aged about eighty-one years.

The reader is referred to the Biographical Sketch of William Winston Seaton for fuller particulars regarding the life of this most excellent gentleman. The said sketch is said to have been written by his daughter, Josephine Seaton.

Elizabeth Seaton. born October 9, 1786. married Samuel Scott. of Richmond. Virginia. and had issue. one daughter. Mary Seaton Scott. Elizabeth died September 5, 1818.

John Seaton was born August 18, 1788, and died July 18, 1808, without issue.

CHAPTER XVIII.

Asa Seaton, the only child of George Seaton 2d, of whom we have any mention, was born in Virginia, about the year 1758, as nearly as we can ascertain. When he was a young man he struck out on his own behalf, as many another son has done when it would probably have been better for them to have remained with their loving parents.

When the War of the Revolution broke out he was to have been found enlisted in the United States Navy, and later he served his country in the army. It is more than likely that he took to the water like a young duck when he first left his Virginia home, and thus naturally gravitated into the navy when there was need of sailors and marines to defend the best interests of his country, for it has run in the blood of the Seaton family to go to the rescue of their government at the first possible moment when their services were needed.

Asa Seaton is said to have been a magnificent specimen of manhood, being of dark complexion, with black hair and eyes, and of a large, powerful build, weighing over two hundred and fifty pounds and measuring two inches over six feet in height. He possessed broad shoulders and great physical energy and resolution. He married Rebecca Barnes on January 8, 1778, in Connecticut. Rebecca was born at Bradford, Connecticut, in 1759, and was well educated for her time, being a botanist of some repute and a diligent biblical student. It has been said of her that she could give the verse and chapter of almost any Bible passage quoted in her hearing. She died in Henderson, New York, in 1845, aged eighty-six years.

From the best information at hand it seems reasonable to suppose that Asa Seaton lived at Bradford, Connecticut, from the date of his marriage to about 1790. My uncle, Leonard Seaton, Jr., wrote me that he remembered hearing his grandmother,

Rebecca (Barnes) Seaton, relate incidents concerning her older sons that happened after they were men grown and while they still lived at Bradford. One of the stories follows: It seems that according to the Blue Laws of Connecticut there was a prohibition against traveling on the Sabbath day, but at one time Truman and Willard were away from home and were naturally anxious to return as soon as possible; but a Sunday intervened. So one of the young men muffled the other up, and they continued their journey homeward, telling every one who asked them about their traveling on the Lord's day that they were going to a safe and isolated place, as they did not desire to give the much-dreaded smallpox to anyone,—all of which may have been true in a sense. They thus reached home without molestation for violating the law, and without doing harm to anyone except themselves, and afterward enjoyed telling of the unceremonious way in which people they met scrambled out of the way of the loathsome disease, as they supposed.

It was from the same source we learned that Asa Seaton served as a volunteer in the Revolutionary War, as well as in the United States Navy. My uncle said he had the word of his grandmother for the facts, she having lived in Henderson, where Uncle Leonard resided, for some years before her death.

Asa Seaton and his family moved to Ellisville, Jefferson county, New York, from Columbia county, in the same State, about 1814 or 1815, buying and paying for six hundred acres of land in that township, as is shown by the records at Watertown, the county seat. There is a tradition that he moved to Columbia county, from Connecticut, about 1790, though we have no documentary evidence of the date of the removal. He deeded a small farm to each of his four married sons about the time of the removal to Ellisville, and sold a large part of his remaining realty in 1818 and the rest in 1820. He emigrated to Ontario, Canada, soon after the close of the War of 1812, settling near Coburg, where he spent the remainder of his days. He died at the home of his son Willard, at the age of seventy-two years.

Asa Seaton accumulated quite a good amount of this world's goods. He was a brainy man, successful in his business, and one who gave his children as good educational advantages as were possible at that time in a new country.

There were born to Asa and Rebecca Seaton eleven children, as follows: 1. Willard; 2. Tina; 3. Keziah; 4. Truman; 5. Roswell; 6. Welthy; 7. Ann; 8. Asa, Jr.; 9. Leonard; 10. Samuel; 11. Pamelia.

THE CHILDREN OF WM. WINSTON AND SARAH (GALES) SEATON.

AUGUSTINE FITZWHYLSON SEATON, the eldest son of these most estimable people, was early interested in military affairs, having commanded a company of "Young Guards" at the reception of the great friend of our government, General Lafayette, in the city of Baltimore, on the occasion of his visit to this country in 1824. And we are pleased to record the fact that his company was pronounced to be the best drilled command that took part in the parade, his father's company of the "Old Guards" not excepted.

Augustine was a cadet at the West Point Military Academy, and graduated from that institution July 1, 1828. He was Brevet Second Lieutenant in the Seventh Infantry in July, 1833; Second Lieutenant September 28, 1834. After his graduation from that great training-school, from which have been sent out so many of the best commanders of the nation's army, Augustine was ordered to Fort Gibson, on the then far frontier.

During an expedition against the Indians in 1835 he shared all the hardships of a soldier's life, advancing into the wilderness of the plains and the Ozark mountains. The health of the young soldier failing, he suffered intensely, and in a few weeks was discharged at the summons of the Angel of Death, and passed over and was enrolled with the army of warriors in the "happy hunting-grounds" of the red savages whom he was opposing, where he will forever hear the glad songs of reveille, but the bugle-calls to fatigue duty and taps never.

He was born at Raleigh, North Carolina, on August 10, 1810, and died a Lieutenant of the Seventh Regiment of United States regulars in the "Ozark Territory," on November 18, 1835, without issue.

Julia Seaton, the first daughter to bless the happy pair, was born on June 9, 1812, at Raleigh, in the "Old North State." In the course of time she was married to Mr. Columbus Munroe, at Washington, the capital of the country. Two sons were born to this couple, Seaton Munroe, and Frances Munroe, the latter of whom died at Washington, D. C., August 7, 1889.

Altona Seaton was born after the removal of the family to Washington, or on March 10, 1814, to be exact. She died on October 3d of the same year.

Gales Seaton was born at Washington, July 27, 1817. He attended school at Georgetown College, and he was at one time located in Richmond, Virginia, for a short time at least, for he wrote quite an interesting letter to the guest of his father's home, Charles Dickens, the great novelist, soon after the latter's visit there, and the letter was dated at Richmond. Gales died February 9, 1857, unmarried.

William Henry Seaton, the son who is mentioned in the Biographical Sketch of his father as having come to his death in the spring of 1827 by being thrown and dragged by his pony while taking his morning canter, was born at Washington, June 20, 1819. His death is recorded by Mr. Seaton Schroeder as having occurred on September 21st, 1826.

Ann Eliza Seaton was born in June, 1821, and died the same year.

Josephine Seaton was born at Washington, D. C., on September 7, 1822. From that time until the day of her death we find no mention of her name, except that she was the author of the Biographical Sketch of William Winston Seaton, her father.

Caroline Seaton was born at the Washington home of the family, on March 25, 1824. She was married to Francis Schroeder, of Baltimore, Maryland. Both Francis and his father, Henry Schroeder, were born in Baltimore. When their son, Seaton Schroeder, was two months old, the family went to Sweden, Francis having been appointed United States Minister at Stock-

holm, where they remained eight years, during which time Caroline
(Seaton) Schroeder died on February 24, 1853.

Their son, Seaton Schroeder, now one of the best known officers
of the United States Navy, was born August 17, 1849. After
the return from Sweden, Seaton remained a year in this country,
then passed two years in Paris, France.

In September, 1864, he was appointed a midshipman at the
United States Naval Academy by President Lincoln, entering the
Academy that month with Richard Wainright, who was also one
of Lincoln's appointees, and who was also born in the District
only four months later than Schroeder. They grew up together
in Washington, were graduated from Annapolis at the same time,
in June, 1868, Schroeder having the higher standing; and to further cement their lifetime friendship, the subject of this sketch
married Wainright's sister, Maria Campbell Bache Wainright,
the daughter of Captain Richard Wainright of the navy, who had
commanded Farragut's flagship, Hartford, at New Orleans, during the Civil War. Through her mother she was the great-grand-
daughter of Benjamin Franklin. They were married in January,
1879.

Seaton and Maria Schroeder have had six children, of whom
the last five are living, and whose names follow: Winston Seaton
Schroeder, died in infancy. Sarah Franklin, Caroline Seaton,
Joanna Anchmuty, Seaton, and Wainright, complete the number.

Among the interesting episodes of Mr. Schroeder's service at
sea, which began on the Pacific station, where he was promoted
to Ensign in 1869, may be mentioned the following:

In June, 1871, while on the sloop-of-war Benicia, he took part
in the attack on the Korean forts, and was mentioned by name in
dispatches of the commander-in-chief, Rear Admiral John Rodgers.

In 1879-80 he was associated with his friend Lieutenant Harry
H. Gorrings in the removal of the Egyptian obelisk in Alexandria,
and its erection in the city of New York.

In 1890 he was put in command of the dynamite gun-vessel,
Vesuvius, and for three years carried on experimental work with
that vessel and her guns.

While a lieutenant, also, in 1888, in coöperation with Lieutenant

SEATON SCHROEDER.

FAMILY OF SEATON SCHROEDER.

W. H. Driggs, he invented and perfected the Driggs-Schroeder rapid-fire guns, which have since shared with the Hotchkiss in the composition of the secondary batteries of United States war-ships.

During the war with Spain he was Executive Officer of the battleship Massachusetts, and was advanced three numbers in his grade for services during that war.

In May, 1900, Mr. Schroeder went to the Island of Guam as Governor, remaining there until February, 1903. Upon his return to Washington in March of this year, he was appointed Chief Intelligence Officer of the Navy and a member of the General Board, which position he occupies at this writing.

Since entering the service he has passed considerably more time at sea duty than on shore. He has lately finished the work of revising the Naval Regulations.

VIRGINIA SEATON, daughter of William Winston and Sarah (Gales) Seaton, born at Washington, D. C., on September 20, 1825, died at about two years of age. Thus was added another sorrow to the many sustained by this estimable family.

MALCOLM SEATON was born at Washington, on May 12, 1829. He married Jane E. Spriggs, daughter of Major Benjamin Spriggs, of Washington, November 19, 1857, but had the great bereavement of losing his loving companion after twenty years of married life, she dying on September 27, 1878. After fourteen years of mourning for his departed helpmeet, he again married, his choice this time falling upon Mary, daughter of Captain Henry Graybill, of Savannah, Georgia, and the impressive ceremony being performed on September 22, 1892.

Malcolm Seaton we find listed as principal examiner of Division Fireman's Navigation and Wood Work. His death has lately been reported to us as having occurred at Washington, D. C., on September 6, 1904.

Arthur Seaton, the last child given to the family was born at Washington, on January 24, 1831, and died on the succeeding 19th of August.

MALCOLM SEATON.

MRS. MALCOLM SEATON.

CHAPTER XIX.

THE CHILDREN OF ASA AND REBECCA (BARNES) SEATON.

WILLARD SEATON was born March 23, 1779, in the State of Connecticut. He married Mary Adams, a descendant of John Adams, the second President of the United States.

Their children, in the order of their ages were: 1. Laura; 2. Asa; 3. Daniel; 4. Josiah Wellington; 5. Hiram; 6. Mary; 7. Riley; 8. Leonard Barna; 9. Willard 2d; 10. Harriet; 11. George; 12. Benjamin Franklin; 13. Louise; and 14. Ira Hamilton.

With his brother Roswell, Willard moved his family from New York to Canada soon after the close of the War of 1812, and settled near Coburg, Ontario. Here his son Benjamin F. was born, and at least two of the other children. Willard left Canada in 1830, returning to the States. He stopped at Henderson, New York, to visit his brother Leonard for a short time, then they pulled out for the West.

When they left Canada, Willard's mother went with them to Henderson, her husband having died in Canada at a good old age.

After leaving Henderson this time, the family of Willard went to Forestville, New York, then to Chardon, Ohio, and later to Massillon, in the same State, where both Willard and his wife Mary died and were buried.

TINA SEATON, the first daughter in the family, was born January 25, 1781, at Branford, New Haven county, Connecticut. She was never married, preferring to live the life of a celibate, with a society of Shakers, a religious community whose official title is "United Society of Believers in Christ's Second Appearing." They came from England to New York in 1774, and settled near Albany, New York.

We have the word of Mr. Chauncey Miller, a leader of one of the

"families," that Tina Seaton was a member of the society from
early childhood. She died at the Village of "Shakers" in Albany
county, New York, January 13, 1860, aged seventy-eight years,
eleven months and nineteen days.

KLZIAH SEATON seems to have left no obtainable record of her
life. We only know that she was born on December 17, 1782, in
the State of Connecticut.

TRUMAN SEATON was born on December 12, 1784, in Connecticut.
He was married, but to whom we have yet to learn. He owned
the farm given to him by his father in Jefferson county, New
York, but how much more we are unable to say. He sold his real
estate in New York before 1830, and moved to the new and grow-
ing West, after which time we have no account of his own or his
family's doings.

ROSWELL SEATON, one of the Connecticut boys, was born on September 8, 1786. He married a Miss Olmstead, who died when her
daughter Aurilla was quite young. He was one of the married
sons to each of whom his father gave a farm, which land with all
other owned by him was sold before 1830, and Roswell moved his
family and personal effects to Canada and became a loyal subject
of the King of England, no doubt. In Canada he located near
Coburg and Port Hope, Ontario, where his brother Leonard visited the family in 1851, returning a visit Roswell made him in
1848-9.

Roswell's mother, Rebecca (Barnes) Seaton, lived with him
after the death of her husband in 1827, until in 1833, when she
made her home with her son Leonard at Henderson, New York,
for a year or two, when she returned to Roswell, and stayed until
in the fall of 1837, when she once more took up her residence in
Henderson, where she continued to reside until the day of her
death, in September, 1845.

Roswell Seaton lost his first wife, and their daughter, Aurilla,
lived with her grandparents, Olmstead, at Ogdensburg, New
York, until she was a young lady. In the meantime, Roswell had
married again, and had children by his second wife, Elizabeth

Hollenbeck. Aurilla and one of her half-sisters, Arletta, went West to visit their uncle Willard's family; and Arletta's brother Albert went later, and worked for Daniel Seaton for two years. Then Arletta and Albert returned to Canada, where their home had been, near Hamilton.

Although Aurilla only went West for a visit, she remained, and was married to her cousin, Daniel Seaton, and did not go back to see her grandparents for three years, and then took her two little boys, George P. and John Hill Seaton, with her to make a visit.

Aurilla Seaton reared a family of eight children, and died at Sandwich, Illinois, September 2, 1887, aged seventy-nine years and ten days, having been born in the State of New York, August 22, 1808.

WELTHY SEATON was born June 30, 1788. She married a De Sany, or Desany, and lived with him in Canada. They had children who visited the Henderson Seatons with their mother in 1835, since which time we have no account of them, and we have not been advised as to their Christian names.

ANN SEATON, daughter of Asa, was born September 18, 1790. She was married to a Mr. Hart, with whom she lived at Flint, Michigan, as late as 1855; or possibly it may have been some of their children who lived at Flint at that time.

ASA SEATON, JR., was born September 12, 1792. He was once married, but parted from his wife on some terms and joined the Shakers near Albany, New York. He owned a farm in New York State, which he sold to his brother Leonard after having lived on it for some time with his wife. Probably there were no children.

Mr. Chauncey Miller, for many years the leader of one of the families of Shakers, having succeeded Asa Seaton, Jr., in that honorable and responsible position after the death of the latter in 1867, says that Asa joined the Society about 1822, and died steadfast in the faith on April 18, 1867, at the age of seventy-four years, seven months and six days. It is understood that whatever property Asa possessed at the time of joining the Shakers was contributed to the common fund.

LEONARD SEATON, senior, the writer's paternal grandfather, was born at Granville, Washington county, New York, on August 1, 1794. He was evidently named for Leonard Hill, father-in-law of George Seaton, or Leonard Hill Seaton, son of Augustine, a man very highly respected in the family, his name appearing in other instances. At the age of thirteen years, in 1807, Leonard Seaton went to Fort Stanwix, now Rome, Oneida county, New York, to learn the trades of tanner and currier, and boot- and shoemaker, with his uncle, Rufus Barnes, with whom he continued to make his home, and for whom he worked as an apprentice. He stayed there six years, except while serving his country as a soldier during the War of 1812. He first enlisted in Captain Rudd's Company, Detachments 131 and 157, Regiments of New York Volunteers, War of 1812. His first term of enlistment began March 10, 1813, and expired on March 25 of the same year. He afterward volunteered in Captain Brooks Harrington's company of Colonel Allen's Fifty-fifth Regiment of the New York Militia, for which service he received a land warrant for one hundred and sixty acres of land.

After Leonard's apprenticeship was out, he worked as a journeyman for his uncle and others in Utica and other villages in Oneida county, New York, until about 1816, when he went to Henderson, in Jefferson county, of the same State. The records show that he owned a tract of land in 1816, and his son, Leonard, Jr., has in his possession a deed which shows that he bought eighty-eight and three-fourths acres from his father, Asa Seaton, paying $1,200 for it. The deed bears date of June 18, 1818.

He worked at his trade in Henderson in 1817 for Allen Kilby, after which he was agent and foreman for Giles Hall, at Belleville, in the same county, as well as for Samuel Borden, of that village.

In 1822, when twenty-eight years old, he married Polly Pennell, daughter of Andrew and Sabrina Pennell, of Belleville, New York, by whom he had five children, as follows: 1. Andrew Pennell; 2. Boyington Chapman; 3. Leonard, Jr.; 4. Frances Phidelia; and 5. Samuel G.

The family moved to his farm that was bought of his father in

LEONARD SEATON, SR.

1824, which he carried on until 1830, when he moved to Mather's Mills.

On July 6, 1834, Polly Seaton died at the farm, four days after the birth of her son Samuel G. Seaton. In the fall of the same year that he lost his wife, he married Sarah Chapman, of St. Lawrence county, New York. Of this union there were born eight children, viz.: 1. Mary Miranda; 2. Cornelia; 3. Arminda Dorleska; 4. Chauncey Eugene; 5. Ambrose Barnes; 6. Louise; 7. George Luman; and 8. Herbert Julian.

In 1836 Leonard moved to the farm known as the Oliver Smith farm, three-fourths of a mile northeast of Belleville. And from 1830 to 1837 he owned and managed two other farms, known as the Sturtevant farm, at Roberts Corners, and the Jotham Little-field farm, just south of the Roberts Corners burying-grounds, in Ellisburg township.

Having sold all of the before-mentioned property before April 1, 1837, he bought the Amasa Whitney farm, in Henderson town-ship, to which he moved at that date. He bought the tanning and currying business of S. D. and A. D. Kilby, at Henderson village, at some time in 1839, but, though taking possession and running the business, he did not move the family to the village until in April, 1840. He continued to run this business and a boot-and-shoe business, as well as a small farm, until his death on August 15, 1872, though he did very little work except around the house and garden for some years before his death.

In company with his eldest son, Andrew Pennell Seaton, the writer's father, he bought the tanning, currying and boot-and-shoe business of Foster Lewis, at Burrville, Jefferson county, New York, which business was personally managed by the son and partner.

The writer remembers quite distinctly hearing his grandfather tell of putting out an orchard on one of his farms near Henderson after he was a middle-aged man. His neighbors tried to convince him, for what reason I cannot guess, that it was useless at his age to plant an orchard expecting to receive any remuneration for his labor. However, he planted the trees, and, as it proved, outlived the longest lived of them, and received good pay for his labors. Besides that, he received much credit for his success, and his example encouraged others to thus beautify and enhance the value of their farms, and helped to prove that part of the State to be adapted to the production of fruit, which was doubted by many at that time.

Grandfather Seaton received a newspaper gratuitously for many years from his cousin William Winston Seaton, editor of the *National Intelligencer*, of Washington, D. C., whom he admired very much as a man and an editor.

The subject of this sketch was a strictly honest and honorable man in all of his dealings, almost painfully prompt at all of his appointments, exacting immediate obedience to all his requests and commands from his children, all of whom, excepting Herbert, perhaps, stood in considerable awe of him. I remember hearing Uncle Boyington tell of his and Uncle Leonard's jumping up from the table and running to the window to see something that was going on out in the street. When they returned to finish their meal Grandfather pointed with his thumb over his shoulder toward some chairs, saying: "You boys have finished your supper." The boys took the hint, and after that were sure to eat all they wanted before leaving the table.

That he possessed a keen sense of humor is certain. On one occasion when he was going away to be gone for some time, he gave instructions to Herbert about the chores. Among other things to be done there were some pigs to be fed. He cautioned Herbert against forgetting to feed them regularly. "for," said he. "if you do there will be a streak of lean meat for every feed you forget to give them, and we will find it out when we come to kill the pigs." Uncle Herbert is said to have attended to the pigs with great faithfulness on that occasion.

My recollection of Grandfather Seaton is that he was full six feet tall, and straight as an Indian. He appeared to me a very austere man, one who made use of as few words as possible and one who seldom smiled, at least not on noisy children. He dearly loved a game of draughts or checkers, and would play for half a day at a time, after he gave up active work, without passing a word with his opponent, who was probably as little inclined to talk as himself at the time. I have often seen him and a Mr. Brown playing, or rather studying how to play, for so long a time that I became tired of waiting and ran off to play with some other boys without having seen either of them make a move, though always feeling a deep interest in a good game of checkers myself.

Leonard Seaton, Sr., died of bronchitis, at his home in Henderson, New York, on August 15, 1872, being seventy-eight years and fourteen days old at the time of his death.

Mrs. Sarah (Chapman) Seaton was a large, fine-looking lady as I remember her, and her photograph shows her to have been. She was a fine housekeeper and needlewoman, and was as kind to the grandchildren as any grandmother could have been; and the fact that grandparents always spoil their grandchildren with kindness has become proverbial. I can remember going to her home often, when I was a small boy, hoping and expecting she would give me some cookies or apples, of which it was soon learned there was always an abundance. And I do not remember ever to have gone in vain; nor was the giving skimped. She, being usually busy, would send me to the cellar and tell me to fill my pockets, a permission I was not slow nor backward about improving. She died at her home in Henderson on the fifth day of October, 1887.

Samuel Seaton, the youngest son in the family circle, was born June 10, 1797, probably at Granville, Washington county, New York. He died in Ellisville, Jefferson county, New York, when a young man, and was buried in the Evergreen Cemetery at Mixer's Corners.

Pamelia Seaton, the last child as well as youngest daughter, was without any possible doubt the pet of the household, or the regular order of nature must have been reversed in this particular case. On the 17th of July she was born, in the year 1799, probably at Granville, New York. She was married to William P. Jones, of Ellisburg, about 1819. They moved to Bishop Street, in Henderson township, about 1839. There were born to them nine or ten children whose names were: 1. Arletta; 2. Leonard S., for his grandfather; 3. Philetus; 4. Riley; 5. Lorenzo; 6. Alsom;

—9

7. Cordelia; and 8. Evalin. And there were one or two more whose names do not appear on our list.

The sons, Leonard, Riley and Philetus, moved to Battle Creek, Michigan, in 1845. Lorenzo left New York about 1847, since which time we have heard nothing from him. The rest of the family, except William, the father, who died in 1841, in Henderson, continued to make their home in Henderson township until in 1851, when Grandfather Seaton went with them to Battle Creek, Michigan, where he saw them comfortably settled in a good home.

Pamelia (Seaton) Jones died more than twenty-five years ago, but some of the children were still living at the Michigan home the last we heard of them, in the first year of the twentieth century.

CHAPTER XX.

THE CHILDREN OF WILLARD AND MARY (ADAMS) SEATON.

LAURA SEATON. when grown, married a gentleman named Becock, and lived in Stark county. Ohio. They had a son, Leonard Becock. who was a member of the Thirty-fourth U. S. Zouaves with his cousin Warren Seaton; and a daughter. Aurilla Becock, who married a Brow, and lived with him at Massillon, Stark county. Ohio.

After the death of Mr. Becock. Laura married a gentleman named Waldo. since which time we know nothing of them.

ASA AND DOROTHY SEATON.

ASA SEATON was born on Independence Day of 1803. and died at Chetopa. Kansas. January 16, 1891.

Dorothy Wilcox, daughter of Clement and Kate (McDougal)

Wilcox was also a second child of the marriage which took place in 1806. These two were married in Canada, in 1831, and both died at the home of their son, Robert Seaton. Asa was a farmer all of his life, and lived to be eighty-seven years of age.

The children of Clement and Kate Wilcox were as follows: Hiram, Dorothy, Charles, Warren, Miranda, George, Millie, Mary, and Susan; and here may be found some of the names that Asa and Dorothy gave to their children, viz.: Loraine, Polly, Warren, Clarinda, Valentine, Miranda, George, Robert, and Chauncey.

Dorothy (Wilcox) Seaton died November 24, 1884, at the age of seventy-four years.

EARLY HOME OF ASA AND DOROTHY SEATON.

DANIEL SEATON, son of Willard, was born in New York State, and moved to Canada with his parents when he was quite young. He married his cousin, Aurilla Seaton, daughter of Roswell. He bought land in Canada that was situated near that owned by Willard and Roswell, and all three did their trading at Coburg. The family moved to Illinois, and Daniel set men to work with ox teams and continued until he had about three hundred acres ready for crops. The next year he raised a great crop of wheat and corn. He had to haul his grain to Chicago, which took three days to go and return, but wheat was worth a dollar per bushel. He lived in a log house until his land was fenced, and he had a fine stock of horses and cattle; then he built a large new house and barn. He was one of the leading men in the neighborhood, one whose word was as good as his bond. He was hospitable and charitable, never turning those away who were in distress, and many a load of wood and sack of flour or wheat he was known to take to the sick and needy. He had a houseful of young folks, and was able to indulge the Seaton love for large families and fine horses to the full, with carriages to go with them.

There were born to Daniel and Aurilla Seaton ten children, all but one of whom lived to become men and women. The family lived near Newcastle, Hamilton township, Ontario, Canada, and Daniel's brother Josiah lived near them. When Daniel moved to Illinois, Josiah went and lived with him until he had bought land and built a house. Another brother, Leonard Barna Seaton, lived near enough so they could visit back and forth, both in Ontario and in Illinois.

The children of Daniel and Aurilla Seaton were: 1. Aurilla; 2. Harriet Louise; 3. Mary; 4. Samantha; 5. George Perry; 6. George Hill; 7. Leonard; 8. Albert; and 9. Ira Daniel. They were one-half of them light-complexioned and one-half dark, but all had black eyes. Who was the other child?

Daniel Seaton settled at Campton, Illinois, at an early date, buying and "taking up" four hundred acres of prairie land and buying another hundred acres of timber land. At a later date he moved to Sandwich, Illinois, where he died September 8, 1884, at the age of seventy-nine years, five months and eight days.

JOSIAH WELLINGTON SEATON was born in Castleton, Vermont, in 1806, moved to New York, and later to Canada, where he was married in Coburg to Sarah Gifford of that place. He died March 17, 1895, in Illinois.

The children who blessed this union were: 1. Humphrey Gifford, who was twice married, first to Helen Gilman, who died several years ago, leaving two children,—Willard, who now resides in Chicago, Illinois, and Jennie, who married Lee Moore, and claims Chicago as her home. Humphrey next married Mary Carver, of Plano, Illinois, by whom he was presented with two children: Georgie, now Mrs. Fuller, of Plano, Illinois, and Frank Seaton, of Chicago.

2. William Albert Seaton went to California many years ago. He married Emma Cross, of Oakland, California, whose mother was a second cousin to Daniel and Noah Webster. Mrs. Emma (Cross) Seaton is now living in Reno, Nevada, having once made her home in San Francisco. She has a son in Reno, Nevada.

3. Nelson James Seaton, of Elburn, Illinois, has two sons, Lyle and Wert, residing at Elburn.

4. Henry Wellington Seaton, of Chicago, has three sons, James and Harry, of Jackson, Michigan, and Clinton, of Chicago, Illinois, and one daughter, Mrs. Corrinthe Angeline (Seaton) Crosby, who lives in Chicago.

All of Josiah Seaton's children, except Henry W., were born in the Dominion of Canada. (Henry's birthplace was Campton, Illinois.) and all were raised in the Methodist faith, were Republicans, and all were blondes.

Mrs. Sarah Seaton was a daughter of Humphrey and Elizabeth (Smith) Gifford, of Coburg, Ontario, Canada.

Josiah W. Seaton was a County Commissioner and a member of the School Board, though he had no ambition to be a public official, preferring to attend to his own affairs on his farm.

HIRAM SEATON, son of Willard, was married, and had at least two children, a son who returned to New York State with his parents, after they had been West, and lived in Ellisburg, Jefferson county, a year or so about 1836, and a daughter, Abby Seaton. After leaving New York the second time, Hiram took his family to Indiana or Michigan, from one of which States he went to Canada on a visit to relatives, and was taken sick there. When it was certain he could not recover, Daniel, at whose home he was at the time, sent for Hiram's wife, and she and her little daughter went to Canada. After the death of her husband, Mrs.

Seaton, Hiram's widow, married Samuel Sanderson, and moved away. Hiram died at his brother Daniel's home, of quick consumption.

MARY SEATON, daughter of Willard, died in infancy.

RILEY SEATON was living at his brother Daniel's home when Hiram died there, and on the day of Hiram's funeral Riley contracted a bad cold, which was accompanied with the usual chill and fever. Some cattle broke out of the pasture, and Riley ran out without coat or hat to assist in driving them back, caught more cold, became decidedly worse, and in six weeks from the day of Hiram's funeral Riley died of the same complaint at the same hospitable home.

WILLARD SEATON 2D was married, and had one son, Dallas Seaton, who died of smallpox in the army during the Rebellion, and a daughter, Frances Dallas Seaton, who, as well as her mother, is deceased. Willard, Jr., went to California in 1848, evidently in search of gold, and has not since been heard from by his friends and relatives. He was living in Kendall county, Illinois, when his brother Daniel moved to that State.

HARRIET SEATON, daughter of Willard, married a man whose name was Parmelee. They lived at Massillon, Ohio.

GEORGE SEATON lived in Kendall county, Illinois, was married and had one child, when his brother Daniel moved to that State.

LOUISE SEATON married a Mr. Moblie. They lived at Fulton, Ohio.

IRA HAMILTON SEATON, son of Willard and Mary, lived at Springfield, Ohio. He was born April 9, 1824, in Hamilton, Duken county, C. W., and died January 25, 1884, at Springfield. He was married to Hester Ann McBride on February 12, 1846, at Canton, Stark county, Ohio, by Rev. Mr. Mower. Hester Ann died February 24, 1852, aged 26 years and 21 days, at Massillon, Ohio, having been born February 3, 1826, at Shippenburg, Franklin county, Pennsylvania.

The children of this family reported to us were:

1. Benjamin Franklin Seaton, born at Canal Fulton, Stark county, Ohio, December 1, 1848. He was married to Miss Lucilla Everett, of Decatur, Illinois, at Quincy, in that State, August 7, 1871. He lives at 773 West Jefferson street, Springfield, Illinois, at which address he has domiciled for fourteen years, having lived at Quincy, Illinois, from 1871 to 1876. He was a letter-carrier for twenty-seven years, is a Republican and a Methodist. The children of Benjamin F. and Lucilla Seaton are: John Benjamin, born at Burlington, Iowa, October 11, 1871, and married January 31, 1899, at Belleville, Illinois, to Miss Lulu Bertha Caviness, in the court-house. His sister, Edith Everett Seaton, was born at Springfield, Ohio, January 27, 1885. She was married by Rev. J. L. Duckwall, at Springfield, Ohio, April 18, 1904, to George H. Keller, of Baltimore, Maryland.

2. George Arthur Seaton, who died December 28, 1853, aged one year and fourteen days.

3. John Ira Seaton was born in Massillon, Ohio. He married Sarah Ann Nagley at Springfield, Ohio, her birthplace, in April, 1876. He died December 11, 1883, at Springfield, aged thirty-three years and twenty-eight days. The children of John Ira Seaton as reported to us are Harry McBride Seaton, of Delray, Michigan, and William Rea Seaton. The latter son was born August 20, 1879, at Springfield, Ohio, and is a telegraph operator at Holly, Michigan, where he has resided for about two years, before which time he had always made his home at the place of his birth. Harry is a Republican in politics, and his religious belief is Episcopalian.

4. Charles Willard Seaton, son of Ira H., died February 1, 1886, aged thirty-nine years and two months.

Ira Hamilton Seaton was at one time extensively engaged in fancy poultry, owning 1500 fine birds. He made a visit to his nephew, Robert Seaton, at Muncie, Indiana, about 1875. It is said he had a son, Leonard Seaton, who was a railway mail clerk. Ira was twice married, but had no offspring by his second wife.

BENJAMIN FRANKLIN SEATON, son of Willard, was born near

Coburg, in the province of Canada, on November 11, 1820. He left the Dominion with his parents in 1830, returning to the United States and stopping for a short visit with relatives at Henderson, New York. After a brief rest and visit at Henderson, they continued on their way west to Forestville, in that State, and later to Chardon, Ohio, and finally to Massillon, Ohio, where they resided until Willard and his wife died and were buried there.

The subject of our sketch married Ruth Maria Hurlbert at Ashtabula, Ohio, on December 14, 1852. There were born to them seven children, whose names follow: 1. Carrie Elizabeth; 2. May Goodwin; 3. Anna Ruth; 4. Grace; 5. Fannie Louise; 6. Frank Hurlbert; and 7. Grace Lillian.

Mrs. Ruth (Hurlbert) Seaton died at Marion, Iowa, on March 2, 1901, where the family had resided since 1860. Mr. Seaton was engaged in the agricultural implement business at Marion for a long period of years, and was serving as Mayor of the city when he was elected Sheriff of Linn county, "in which position he served five years, having been twice reëlected." From several different newspapers we learn that Mr. Seaton had some very thrilling experiences in the line of his duties as Sheriff. The August number of the *Detective* for 1885 gives a full page to his experiences while in office, as well as a portrait of him.

It appears the election in 1880, when Mr. Seaton was first elected Sheriff, was very close, Colonel Ed. Swem, who then held the office, being a very popular candidate for reëlection; but when Mr. Seaton was reëlected, four years later, after having served the county faithfully, his majority was 1,008 votes. During the last four years of his service he had under his charge eight hundred prisoners, twelve of whom were charged with murder, conviction following in nearly every case. These eight hundred prisoners included housebreakers, "gophers," fanners, and in fact almost every class of criminals from murderers to common vagrants.

Among the notorious characters arrested by Mr. Seaton were Albert Mitchell, O'Connor, "Doc" Mohler, and "Doc" Diets, murderers. The account says that although Mr. Seaton is of slight build, he is one of the hardiest and most successful in the pursuit and capture of criminals.

The St. Joseph *Gazette* gives a description of the capture of the notorious Bill Carl, a most desperate man, by Mr. Seaton at Greenleaf, Kansas, that shows the latter to have been a very courageous man. It appears that Carl knew officers were out for him, and had often made the statement that he would never be taken alive, and went armed and kept in company with a companion, each keeping guard over the other.

Mr. Seaton and his deputy, W. W. Graham, of Atchison, Kansas, went to Greenleaf, and after a few preliminaries the former walked into a barber shop and arrested Carl, who commenced backing toward a door and turned and ran. The deputy arrived in time to fire three shots at the fleeing man, but neither of them took effect. Carl ran into the cellar under a grocery, closely followed by Sheriff Seaton, by whom he was again arrested, and was brought to the street at the point of the Sheriff's revolver. By this time Carl regained his nerve, and as soon as he was in the street he began to show fight. Had Carl not lost his self-possession while in the cellar he might easily have killed the Sheriff, being hidden and protected behind a barrel of vinegar. A desperate struggle ensued while the officers were putting the handcuffs on the prisoner, who succeeded in drawing his revolver, and would have killed the Sheriff had that gentleman not knocked the weapon out of range. He bit the lobe of Graham's ear nearly off, and by some means got Mr. Seaton's middle finger of the right hand in his mouth and lacerated it fearfully. All this time the City Marshal and peace officers, together with a large crowd of curious people, stood by looking on, but not one of them lent a hand to the struggling captors; in fact, their sympathies seemed to be with the outlaw. It was said to have been the most desperate hand-to-hand struggle ever witnessed in that part of the country. The prisoner was immediately taken to the depot and shipped to Marion, Linn county, Iowa.

From the Omaha *Bee:* "On the 20th of last March a man by the name of Thum, an ex-convict from the Iowa penitentiary, was brutally murdered upon the railroad bridge of the C. M. & St. P. road at Cedar Rapids, Iowa, and his mangled remains thrown into Cedar river. The murderer escaped. Albert Mitchell, alias Harry Wood, was suspected, and officers were put upon his track; but he seemed to vanish into thin air. Later, Sheriff Seaton, of Linn county, got word that Mitchell was in Omaha, and immediately went there; but again the culprit had flown. At a still later date Mr. Seaton was notified that Mitchell was again in Omaha. Accompanied by George Pollins, a constable of Cedar Rapids, he again went to that city, and saw Mitchell walking on a street. Pollins remained where he was while Sheriff Seaton crossed the street and spoke to Mitchell, at the same time grasping him by the wrist to prevent his using a weapon. Mitchell broke loose and made a move toward his hip pocket, but the sheriff was too quick for him, and almost in the twinkling of an eye his revolver was in his hand and the muzzle was full upon Mitchell's face. At this stage of the game Pollins appeared upon the scene and clapped the bracelets upon Mitchell's wrists. He was marched up to the city jail and placed behind the bars, and later in the day was taken to Iowa."

The Cedar Rapids *Republican* is responsible for the following: "Marion, the county seat, was shaken from center to circumference by the wildest excitement yesterday afternoon. At about one o'clock four prisoners confined in the county jail made a desperate attempt to regain their lost liberty, and in doing so one of them almost lost his life. The men were: Albert Mitchell, the supposed murderer of Thum; Will Carl, who was recently captured by the Sheriff in Kansas after a desperate resistance; Albert Taylor, the insurance agent, in for forgery; and J. H. Smith, bound over for burglary.

"At one o'clock yesterday, Frank Seaton, the Sheriff's son, entered the jail proper for the purpose of putting water for bathing in the cell in which the four men were confined. As customary at the entrance of an official into the cage, the men retired to the inner cell and shut the door. The bolts were shot, and Frank entered. No sooner was he inside than the door was burst open and the four desperate men rushed at him. Mitchell led the gang, and with a powerful push overthrew the young man, and in an instant the party were out and hurrying along the passage. Miss Fannie Seaton, the Sheriff's daughter, heard the shout of her brother, and running from the kitchen, where she was at work, caught Taylor as he attempted to pass her. The desperate man caught the frail girl and with one effort hurled her from him. Before she could recover the men were out of the front door, and like frightened sheep were running down the street toward the outskirts of the city. Frank Seaton had not been idle, however, and was on their heels. A party of forty or fifty men, who had gathered at the postoffice corner on their way to the ball grounds, joined in the pursuit, led by the Sheriff himself, he being among the party.

"Frightened by the repeated shots of Seaton, Taylor and Smith surrendered before going a block from the jail, and were turned over to men and taken back to their cells. Mitchell and Carl, however, ran south on Market street for a block, and then struck off along an alley running east. As they crossed the sidewalk there was a declivity of several feet, and there Mitchell tripped and fell. He recovered his feet in a few seconds, but Carl was some distance ahead. The crowd had in the meantime stopped when Taylor and Smith were caught, and Mitchell was pursued by only two men, S. L. Waters, a contractor, and George Holland, one of his employees. The Sheriff, meantime, had gone past where the prisoners turned into the alley, and made a detour for the purpose of heading them off. Mitchell, when he had reached the center of Parmenter & Son's lumber yard, turned on his pursuers, flourishing a heavy club, and even started toward them. Backing off a few feet. Waters and Holland armed themselves with clubs, and seeing this, Mitchell attempted to escape, but they were on him before he could do so, and a desperate encounter ensued. In the first few blows Holland was struck on the left temple, and a serious gash, some two and a half inches in length, inflicted. Waters still kept up the fight, which was of the fencing order and resulted in no wounds, but catching sight of the Sheriff advancing on Mitchell from the other direction, Waters said :

"'Well, here comes Seaton, and he will finish you.'

"'No, he won't,' said the desperate prisoner, at the same time facing about. At this moment Waters could easily have knocked him senseless, but, weak from his long encounter, he was satisfied to wait till the Sheriff came, feeling that that official now had command. Seaton and Mitchell advanced toward each other, the former with a drawn revolver, the latter swinging above his head his heavy club. The Sheriff was the first to speak and said: 'Surrender, or I will shoot you.' 'I will never surrender,' replied Mitchell; 'shoot and be damned!' Twice the officer commanded him to surrender, but no attention was paid to the order, and when Mitchell was within a few feet of him the Sheriff fired. The man wavered, but before he could do anything, Holland, who had by this time recovered, rushed upon him and threw him to the ground. A fierce struggle ensued, during which Mitchell succeeded in getting hold of the Sheriff's revolver and tried to wrest it from him. The officer's hand was badly cut, but he managed to hold on to the weapon. Mitchell fought hard, but at last gave up and was sent back to jail.

"Carl meanwhile had taken refuge in a corn-field a little way beyond, and had crouched down, hoping to escape observation. However, it was known that he was there, and Seaton going into the field soon found him and compelled him to surrender."

Since the spring of 1903 Mr. Seaton has made his home with his daughter, Mrs. Fannie Louise Ives, at Galesburg, Illinois, having permanently retired from business.

CHAPTER XXI.

LEONARD BARNA SEATON, son of Willard and Mary (Adams) Seaton, was born March 14, 1814, either in Jefferson county, New York, or in Ohio, according to different correspondents. He went to Canada with his father's family "soon after the close of the War of 1812," lived there until about 1830, having married Almira W., daughter of Thomas and Sarah (Sperry) Wing, the latter of whom was a descendant of that Deborah Wing, a widow, who settled at Sandwich, Massachusetts, in 1629. Upon the death of Almira's father, her mother married a second time, her second husband being a Mr. Brisbin. Almira was born at Champlain, Clinton county, New York, April 22, 1817. The family moved to Hope township, Durham county, Ontario, where Almira met her future husband. She died at Aldercoign, Toronto, the residence of her son-in-law, J. H. McNairn, on February 26, 1895, and was buried at Mt. Pleasant Cemetery, Toronto.

Leonard Barna Seaton learned the trade of wagon- and carriage-maker at Port Hope, Canada. He worked seven years as an apprentice to learn the business, then some years as a foreman for the man with whom he learned his trade. He moved to Bletcher's Corners in 1838, and finally to Newcastle, in Clark township, where he bought a farm covered with timber. This tract he traded for eight acres in Newcastle, where he built several good houses for that time. He also built quite a large shop and started the manufacture of wagons and buggies on his own account. The business grew steadily for years, until he was possessed of a competency and retired from active business, leasing his shops to two young men who had learned the trade with him.

About the time he quit the business to enjoy the fruits of his labors, his health began to fail. His doctors said he would die of consumption in a short time, but, Seaton-like, he declared he would not die, but would outlive every doctor who said he would die of consumption. And he did outlive every one of them. After a few years he regained his old-time health, and, with the return of health, his ambition for business returned, and thinking he ought to be doing something, he launched out in the mercantile business and kept what is now denominated a department store, then called general store.

The Grand Trunk Railroad was in course of construction at that time, and business was booming. Like many others, he made plenty of money for a time, but business depression set in, as it is sure to do occasionally, and "down came baby, cradle and all." Mr. Seaton was undismayed, but with indomitable will determined to take Horace Greeley's advice and "go West and grow up with the country." So in 1859 he ticketed to Leavenworth, Kansas; but he remained there only a short time, then went to Plano, Illinois. This was about 1862. In Plano he made some property, not very much, but enough to be getting along nicely. Finally the time came for him to lay his burdens down, and he was summoned home to receive his reward, dying as he had lived, with no murmurings, at Plano, on the 20th of March, 1890. He was a Methodist in religion. In Canada he was a Reformer and in the United States a Republican.

The children of Leonard Barna and Almira (Wing) Seaton were: Sarah Elizabeth, born in Clark township, 3d of February, 1837, died, and was buried in Newcastle in 1847; Mary Elizabeth; Emeline Irene; and Leonard Turner Seaton.

THE CHILDREN OF DANIEL AND AURILLA SEATON.

George Perry Seaton, the eldest child of the family, was named for Mr. George Perry, a merchant who was an intimate friend of the family. George Perry Seaton was a great traveler in his younger years. He contracted the gold fever when only seventeen years of age and went to California, coming back after three years with gold enough to buy and stock a good farm, build a comfortable house and supply himself with many conveniences. His friends then thought he was about to settle down and take unto himself a wife, but a number of his young friends, including his brother John, wanted to visit the land of gold, and desired him to accompany them; so, after being at home for about a year, he again crossed the desert and the mountains. He put in two years there, and then returned around Cape Horn, having made the first trip across the Rockies and returned by way of the Isthmus of Darien. Going to California so young cut off his studies; so, after his second return, George attended Mount Morris Seminary for another year. He then married and settled down. He had two daughters and a son. The eldest daughter was named Mary and the son Frank, but we have not been advised as to the name of the other daughter nor of the wife.

George was a successful farmer until the end of his life, both he and his wife dying at Flora, Illinois, where it is supposed some of the children may be living.

JOHN HILL SEATON, son of Daniel and Aurilla, went to California in search of gold, remaining about a year. After his return he remained on the home farm until he was married, when he bought a place in Sandwich, Illinois, but he soon traded his town property for a farm, where he was living at the time of his death. He was named John Hill Seaton, for John Hill, who married Esther Olmstead.

John Hill Seaton had one son, John Channer Seaton, a pharmacist, who resides at Somonauk, Illinois, and who has furnished us quite an amount of copy, but neglected to give his own biography, though asked especially for it:—another example of the extreme modesty of the Seatons when speaking of themselves.

John Channer Seaton was married to Josephine, daughter of Mr. T. J. Phillips, of Newark, Illinois, (where Josephine was born, September 14, 1862,) on her nineteenth birthday. They made their home in Newark and Plano for about six years, then removed to Somonauk in the fall of 1887, where Mr. Seaton has since been in business continuously.

A daughter, Nina Seaton, was vouchsafed to these loving parents, and it is a safe prophecy that she has seldom known an unsupplied want.

Mrs. Seaton had three brothers: Carson E., of Springfield, Missouri; Thomas Leland and Charles B. Phillips, of Aurora,

Illinois; and two sisters, Mrs. Ida R. Flower, of Paw Paw, Michigan, and Mrs. Louise Harding, of Aurora.

Mrs. Seaton was a prominent church worker, and was a member of the Congregational choir for seventeen years. She was also the contralto in the Somonauk Ladies' Quartette, and an active member of the Eastern Star. She died from the effect of a tumor, on November 26, 1904, and the funeral was held at the Congregational Church in Somonauk, Monday, November 28, the Rev. W. L. Lewis officiating. The members of Pearl Chapter, O. E. S., attended the funeral in a body. The remains were interred at Millington Cemetery.

Aurilla Seaton, the eldest daughter, married D. Gardner Cook. They had a son, Willard Cook, who lives in Chicago, Illinois. He married Edith Kisnor, and has two children, Lorie and Harold Cook.

Aurilla Seaton taught school a few summers, the school-house being located on her father's land, only a short distance from the home. She went to spend a summer with her uncles Willard and George Perry, and there met Mr. Cook, who was a maker of wooden pumps and was doing well. They were married, and he built a house and shop in Sandwich, Illinois. Their children were: Willard, born five years after the marriage, and Mary, who was born when her brother was six years old.

After Mrs. Cook died, November 25, 1881, Mr. Cook rented his place in Sandwich, and went back to Red Bank, New Jersey, his old home, where all of his relatives were, stayed ten years, and then returned to Sandwich.

Willard went to Chicago to work when he was old enough, and is a pattern-maker in the McCormick reaper works. He is said to have made all of the models shown by the McCormicks at the Paris Exposition, and is considered a genius at his business.

Mr. D. Gardner Cook died in 1898.

Harriet Louise Seaton married E. K. Freeland, at Sycamore, Illinois, September 18, 1865. Mr. Freeland was born at Newark, New Jersey, in 1840. He is of German descent, and had six sisters and two brothers. Captain A. W. Freeland and John

—10

M. both served in the Federal Army during the Civil War, and in the Regular Army afterward. The Freelands reside at Sandwich, Illinois, and have lived there for nearly forty years, and they expect to continue to reside there, having a nice home that satisfies their moderate desires. At one time they had a home at Campton, Kane county, Illinois, where Daniel Seaton settled at an early date. Mr. Freeland was a soldier in the Union Army, having enlisted in the One Hundred and Fifth Illinois Volunteers, Company H, and served through the war. Mrs. Freeland's three youngest brothers were in the army as drummer-boys, and her uncle, Leonard Barna Seaton, was a Drum Major. Mr. Freeland has been Marshal, Constable and Deputy Sheriff in his home county, and is now Constable and Fish Warden. He is a Republican, and a member of the Congregational Church.

The children of Harriet (Seaton) Freeland are as follows:

1. Hattie L. Freeland; died in 1860, in infancy.

2. Elizabeth B. Freeland was born in 1864. She was a bright, active girl, and in time graduated from the Sandwich High School. Then she went to Aurora, Illinois, and learned shorthand and typewriting, and secured a position there; but after about a year she went to Chicago and worked in an office, making her home with her aunt, Mary (Seaton) Miller. In 1897 she went home to spend the holiday-time, was taken sick, and, after three weeks of suffering, died. She was a beautiful young lady, and was to have been married in two months.

3. Daniel Freeland was born in July, 1867. He was a young giant in strength when he was grown. He married Jessie Everest in 1890. Their daughter, Grace Freeland, is eight years old, and her brother Robert is five at this writing. "Dannie" had never been sick except with childish ailments, until he was overcome by pneumonia, that carried him away after a day and a night's sickness, March 4, 1904. He worked in a manufactory in Sandwich, never having been away from home for any length of time.

4. Dwight A. Freeland, when through school, learned the printer's trade and the barber business, but he works at neither. He is a member of the International Brotherhood of Electric Workers, and his home is in Chicago. He married Belle Whit-

more in 1884, losing her by death in 1900. Their two little boys,
Donald Edward, eight years old, and Henry Eugene, six years of
age, live with their paternal grandparents. Donald is said to be
a very bright scholar for an eight-year-old boy. He can repeat
whole chapters from the Bible, and literally searches the Scrip-
tures.

SAMANTHA SEATON, daughter of Daniel, was married on her
eighteenth birthday to Edwin Miller, who was an engineer on the
Northwestern Railroad, but he owned a farm near Campton,
Illinois. They have three children: 1. Mary, now Mrs. Alfred
Steffen, of Chicago, a bookkeeper in the Phœnix Insurance Company's office, who translates all their German correspondence.
2. Frederick Miller, who married Maud Stewart and has two
children, Ida and George Frederick Miller. At the time of his
death, in 1896, he was cashier for a gas company in Chicago. 3.
Carrie Miller, now Mrs. Herbert Elliott of Chicago, completes the
list of Samantha (Seaton) Miller's children. Four years after the
death of Samantha, Mr. Miller married Mary Seaton, sister to his
first wife. They had two children, Grace, who died in infancy,
and Harvey, who is a bookkeeper for the Swift Packing Company.
He married Jessie Parks, and has one little girl, the idol of her
grandmother Freeland's heart.

LEONARD SEATON, son of Daniel, went through the Civil War as
a Drum Major, then married Belle Drake, of Chicago, and lived
there the most of the time till his death, in 1894. His two sons
are in the People's Gas Company, and in Chicago you could find
very few, if any, better or steadier boys than Willard R. Cook,
Henry Miller and Earl and Grant Seaton, not one of whom has a
vicious habit.

ALBERT SEATON, son of Daniel, is said to be a confirmed bache-
lor, a good, steady man, always to be relied upon. He lives at
Aurora, Illinois.

IRA D. SEATON, the youngest son of Daniel and Aurilla, was born
at Campton, Kane county, Illinois, February 15, 1850, and died
at Sandwich, in the same State, at the home of his sister, Mrs

IRA D. SEATON.

Harriet Louise Freeland, January 31, 1895. Up to the time of the Civil War he lived on the farm where he was born. During the progress of the war he enlisted as a drummer-boy in Company G, One Hundred and Forty-first Illinois Infantry. After serving about a year he was honorably discharged, and returned home broken in health. Ira was a musical genius, and was an invalid for some years before he died. His funeral was held at his late residence, and the body was interred at Lawn Ridge Cemetery. He had no family, but was a man whom every one liked and respected.

CHAPTER XXII.

THE CHILDREN OF LEONARD AND POLLY (PENNELL) SEATON.

ANDREW PENNELL SEATON, the writer's father, and the eldest son of Leonard and Polly Seaton, was born at Belleville, Jefferson county, New York, on November 19, 1823. He was named for his maternal grandfather, Andrew Pennell, through whom he traces his descent to a certain John Pennell, who came to America in 1728. He was a Captain in the Cumberland Militia, and served his country from August 18, 1778, to July 24, 1782, in the War of the Revolution.

When the subject of our grateful remarks was old enough, he helped on his father's farm until he understood the business as then carried on in New York State. Like most young men who lived in the vicinity of the "Great Lakes," he followed sailing in one capacity and another. He also worked in a tannery with his father until he became a master mechanic in the business of tanning leather.

In 1846 he was married to Laura Ann Ferguson, daughter of John and Clara (Wilson) Ferguson, who lived near Burrville, or Burr's Mills, in Watertown township, Jefferson county, New York. Her father was a soldier in the War of 1812, and later a farmer. Her maternal grandfather served his country in the Revolutionary War.

The Fergusons trace their descent to a son of King Fergus of Scotland, who was, according to the custom of the time, called Fergus' son, and later, Ferguson. The name is frequently mentioned in the history and literature of Scotland.

Robert Burns, the most beloved Scottish poet, wrote of Ramsay and Ferguson as his models in poetry. Sir Samuel Ferguson was, perhaps, the most widely known poet in the family, though not the only one by any means. There were historians, soldiers

ANDREW PENNELL SEATON.

poets, teachers, and scholars, to say nothing of lords and other dignitaries in the family, that were spoken of as praiseworthy in the histories of their country. A plan of the Cathedral of Norva is given in Chambers's Cyclopædia that is credited to Ferguson's Handbook of Architecture.

MRS. LAURA A. SEATON.

In company with his father, the tanning and currying and boot-and-shoe business of Foster Lewis at Burrville, New York, was purchased by Andrew P. Seaton, who was the resident partner and manager of the business.

It was while living at this picturesque little village that the first child was born to Andrew P. and Laura A. Seaton, and the writer of this book was that child.

Soon after this time the Burrville business was disposed of to advantage, and Father moved his little family to Henderson village, where he worked in his father's other tannery.

In after-years the writer frequently helped his father in the tanning process, taking boyish delight in plunging the hides into the clear water-vat to soften them, then fishing them up with a long hook and sousing them into the lime-vat to loosen the hair.

When that object had been accomplished the hides were again
ished for, the hair removed and the surplus flesh skived off, and
mce more baptized, this time in the bate or hen-manure solution,
o extract the remaining lime; then the clear water was once more
mployed to remove the ingredients of the bate, when the sides,
is they were now called, having been split along the back, were
eady for the tanning process proper. The sides were carefully
aid away in other vats, flesh side up, alternating them with a
iberal sprinkling of ground tan-bark; then the water was turned
m to make the tanning liquor. The object of this whole process
vas to impregnate the sides with tannin or tannic acid, which
makes leather of the skins and renders them firm and durable,
md, in some measure, impervious to water.

When the tanning was complete I helped spread the sides
mt on the piles of unground tan-bark in the sun to dry before
urrying, or finishing. It soon became evident that wet leather
ould be burned by the hot sun as readily as by a hot stove. The
rocess of drying had to be watched very closely and the sides
aken in at just the right moment or there would be burned spots
hat were worthless. The currying, including slicking, stuffing,
oarding, blacking, smoothing and polishing, followed; but that
art of the work was beyond my ability.

When we boys were old enough to begin to work at some ad-
antage and to pick up considerable knowledge on the streets
hat was better for us not to know, Father moved from Henderson
illage to the "Overton farm," a short distance east of town, and
ngaged in dairy-farming. During the time we lived in Hender-
on we occupied, at different times, the Wooley house, across the
reek; the Chapman house, adjoining the school-grounds on the
vest; and a house known as the Kilby house. Then Father
ought the Bullard place, north of the Universalist Church. It
vas from the last-named place we moved to the Overton farm,
about the beginning of the War of the Rebellion. And it was from
his farm I went to the army in the summer of 1864. On May 31,
1864, Father bought the "Court farm," down on Sixtown Point.
On this latter farm Father continued to keep a dairy, and hauled
he milk a part of the time to Tyler's cheese factory, in Henderson

village. Later, there was a factory built on the farm of Albert Wilkinson, less than a fourth of the distance from our place to the village, and the milk was delivered there for a time. But Father prided himself more on the butter we made than on the cheese that was made for us; so he returned to making butter for special customers, from whom he received quite a premium over the regular market price.

Father was a very particular man about the way his work was done. We were all required to milk the cows at exactly the same hour, morning and evening, every day, and there was to be no changing of milkers or trading cows among the boys. Each milker must milk the same cows from the time they were fresh until they went dry. And he was as exacting in the dairy-house as in the milking-yard. Nothing was allowed to be taken into the milk-room except the new milk and the utensils for making it into the very best butter it was possible for us to make. Even the swill-pails were not allowed to be taken in to be filled with skim-milk, but the milk must be taken out-of-doors before being emptied. I said *us* advisedly, for Brother James and I had the churning to do, and Mother did the dairy-work while the hired help attended to the other housework. If the temperature of the cream was such that a whole hour was required to do the churning, Father was so much the better pleased, whatever we boys thought about the subject.

The diary kept by Father in his farming days lies before me as I write, and in several places mention is made of selling butter to so-and-so at thirty cents, and from that price to forty cents per pound, which shows his efforts to make first-class butter were appreciated. He had several regular customers for whom he filled a firkin with butter each year, that held enough to last the family for whom it was made a whole year. I once heard Captain Eggleston, one of the regular customers, say to Father: "We have just used the last pound of butter from the firkin you put up for us a year ago, and we thought it was as good as the first pound we used from it." While the honor has been given to Father, it will readily be understood that at least a share belongs to Mother, who did the part of the work that brought success to our door.

In the sugar-bush, as everywhere else, the same painstaking
care was observed. Nothing was neglected that would insure an
extra quality of the product. All the straining and skimming
was done that could be of any benefit, and when the syrup was
thick enough it was allowed to cool; then sweet milk and fresh-
laid eggs were beaten up together and added to it. It was then
re-heated, and again skimmed, to clarify it. When the syrup was
so clear that a newspaper could be read through a two-quart
Mason's fruit jar filled with it, all hands were satisfied.

While we lived on the Court farm. Father raised some wheat to
sell, and engaged in fishing on Lake Ontario and in Henderson
bay, with gill-nets, when the ciscoes came down the lake to spawn
in the bay. In 1865 and 1866 we pushed the fishing, sometimes
catching as many as six or eight barrels of ciscoes in a night, that
were sold for the Catholics during Lent, when they were not allowed to eat any kind of meat, bringing from six to eight dollars
per barrel. But on account of a law having been passed by the
New York law-makers in 1867 that no fishing was to be done in
the waters of the State with nets, Father sold his boats, nets and
other fishing outfit on August 28, 1867; but later it was decided
that the law did not apply to the international waters of the Great
Lakes, so we helped others for wages during that season.

After the farm-work was done in the fall of 1867, Father sailed
on a lake propeller and left us boys to run the farm until it was time
to begin fishing; when he returned I helped run a pound-net and
a string of gill-nets for a firm from up the lake, while he took care
of the farm and helped neighbor Peter Demelt what he could with
his fishing.

During the summer of 1867 a swamp fire raged on the Point,
and the road overseer, or path-master as he was called there,
ordered out all of the able-bodied men and boys in his district
with their teams to haul water and fight fire. It was a terrible
experience. The fire swept everything before it, roaring and rag-
ing like a very unquenchable burning lake of fire so often pictured
to us by the preachers of that day. Large trees were burned
down, falling with a thunderous crash and a great scattering of
sparks and burning branches. Even the ground, composed as

it was of branches and leaves that had fallen from their parent limbs, burned to the depth of two feet or more in places and often the fire would run beneath the surface of the ground for some distance and break out where it had not been looked for before, often setting fire to some building or fence. Sometimes in walking along a person would suddenly fall into a seething pit of fire which had not shown aboveground. When these underground fires were found, the teams were directed to unload their water there, and quite frequently it required many loads of water to quench these fires and prevent their spreading in the direction of buildings or other valuable property. Thousands of dollars' worth of stately monarchs of the woods were destroyed, the homes of the farmers threatened, and weeks of valuable time consumed in fighting these destructive fires; and once in a while some fire-fighter would lose his life by being struck by falling trees or falling into the underground fires and being asphyxiated before help could reach him.

In the spring of 1868 Father traded his dairy cows for sheep, thinking there would be more profit in raising sheep than there was in dairying, but he sold the sheep in the fall of the same year, and returned to butter-making as better suited to his tastes and training.

The Point was a great place for sociability. Neighborhood visiting, card-playing and dancing were of frequent occurrence during the winters when the sailor-boys were at home. And apples, cider, cards, and checkers were the regular order at home on those evenings, when we were not invited out or entertaining others. Mother never played, being busy with her work. I usually read or wrote while the others played one game or another as the notion came to them; and that seemed to be the regular order at the other homes in the neighborhood.

During the winter of 1867-8 we had a severe siege of typhoid fever, each member of the family, except Father, taking a turn at it. Brother James had a relapse, the second spell being worse than the first. If it had not been for the kindness of Julia White and Sarah Manning, who came to Mother's aid, I do not see how she could have endured the strain of both work and worry, for she was completely prostrated as it was. Doctor Eugene Chapman, a brother to my particular chum, I. W. Chapman, was our physician, and he was faithful even to coming the distance on foot on at least one occasion when the snow-drifts were so great that no horse could make the trip. With neighborly assistance we pulled through the sickness without the loss of any member of the family, but without their aid it is doubtful what the issue might have been.

My parents and brother George and sister Clara moved from Henderson, New York, in 1870, and located at Floyd, Floyd county, Iowa, where Father bought a farm not far from town, but soon moved to town and rented the farm. He was engaged in merchandising for some time in Floyd, and was a Justice of the Peace there for several years.

Father was a stockily built man, and was able, when in his prime, to do a full day's work with any company, having cut five acres of heavy grass in a day, using an "Armstrong" reaper—a hand-scythe and snath. The nearest the writer ever came to doing an equal task was when he mowed five acres of rather light barley in one day. After that day's work the boy had a pretty good opinion of his father's ability as a hay-maker.

He was extremely punctual and exact to all of his appointments and engagements, even in attending to his meals,—so much so that one of his good neighbor ladies said she could safely set her clock by Mr. Seaton when he went to his dinner. And what is perhaps more strange, his favorite cat would almost invariably meet him at about a certain place on the sidewalk and accompany him the rest of the way home at meal-times.

Father was an Ensign in the New York State Militia, but he never was required to leave the State to take an active part in the war, though he had one son and four brothers engaged on the side of the Union in the War of the Rebellion of 1861–5.

In the diary that has been mentioned I notice that Father belonged to a temperance society, probably the Good Templars, and mention is frequently made of his attending lodge during the winter. The fact is also mentioned that he was loaning money quite often about 1866-7-8.

MRS. LAURA A. SEATON.

Laura Ann (Ferguson) Seaton, my mother, was born near Watertown, New York, on the Ferguson homestead, July 11, 1822, died at Floyd, Iowa, March 29, 1887, and was buried in the cemetery there, where a fine marble monument marks her last resting-place. I have in my possession a document from the War Department at Washington, D. C., saying that William Ferguson, Mother's grandfather, served in the Twenty-fifth Massachusetts Regiment in the Revolutionary War.

Also, that John Ferguson, her father, was a sergeant in the

Seventy-sixth Regiment of the New York Militia, War of 1812, and received a land warrant for one hundred and sixty acres of land for the service.

I have often been told that my mother was a beautiful lady, which exactly agrees with my estimate of female loveliness. I can add that she was a consistent Christian and a regular attendant at the Methodist Episcopal Church when I lived at home. I have often written of Mother in both prose and verse, and always to speak in her praise. She was my ideal of a lovely woman, possessing all of the virtues and none of the vices of womankind.

On the 27th of July, 1887, Father was married to Minerva J. Carpenter, at Waterloo Iowa, by the Reverend J. O. Stephenson. Mrs. Carpenter was a fine-looking and wealthy widow and an old acquaintance of the family, and, if she could add any happiness to Father's old age, I would be the last to object to such a marriage.

Andrew Pennell Seaton died at the residence of Brother George F. Seaton, at Floyd, Iowa, February 22, 1897, and was buried beside my Mother.

MRS. MINERVA J. (CARPENTER) SEATON.

MONUMENT OF A. P. AND LAURA A. SEATON.

CHAPTER XXIII.

THE CHILDREN OF LEONARD AND POLLY SEATON (CONTINUED).

BOYNTON CHAPMAN SEATON, the second son, who has always been a "boy" to all of his friends, was born on August 25, 1825, in Ellisburg, Jefferson county, New York. In 1847 he was married to Cornelia Wallace. They lived a long time in the county of his birth, where as a farmer I first remember him, and it was one of my greatest delights at that time to go out from town to visit at Uncle Boy's. He was probably the most friendly and sociable Seaton of them all, and had more closely intimate friends. It was aptly said of him by an admiring personal friend: "He is the Seaton with the least money and the most friends."

There were born to these good people four children, one dying in infancy. The other children are P. N. Cushman, Wallace, and and Maud; of whom more will be told later.

Cornelia (Wallace) Seaton died in March, 1884. Boynton was a sailor on the Great Lakes for some years. The last vessel that he commanded was the "Jennie White," which he sailed during the season of 1885.

He served his country in the War of the Rebellion as a gentleman private in the Tenth New York Heavy Artillery, enlisting on August 21, 1862, and being mustered out in July, 1865; and he used to talk very entertainingly of his experiences while in the army. I have heard that he repeatedly refused an office in the regiment when one was offered to him.

After the capture of Petersburg, Virginia, by the Federal army in April, 1865, while our brigade was marching through the captured city he hunted me up, secured my exemption from the regiment for a short time, and showed me many of the interesting sights of the defeated and badly wrecked city, he being on some kind of detached duty in the city at the time. He also filled me

—11

up with some of the toothsome food of civil life, which tasted remarkably palatable in comparison with the hard-tack, wormy beans and "sow bosom" of the army rations.

It is my impression that Uncle Boy kept a first-class hotel in Henderson after the war, from which time I do not remember to have met him until the date of my visit to Rochester, New York, in the summer of 1901, when he was living with his daughter, Mrs. Maud Smith, wife of Charles N. Smith, a barber, at No. 852 St. Paul street, in that beautiful city. Uncle Boy appeared to be perfectly contented with the treatment the world had given him so far along the journey of life.

It was a pleasure to the writer to walk along the streets of Rochester with the subject of this sketch and notice how familiar he was with every one we met, even to the little toddlers on the sidewalk; for every one of whom he had a pleasant word, often accompanied with a chuck under the little one's chin. It was also a pleasure to see the courtly grace with which he saluted the older portion of the citizens with his lifted hat and cheery good-morning. He seemed to know, and be known by, everyone.

Boynton C. Seaton died at No. 16 Straub street, Rochester, New York, on September 5, 1903, of apoplexy, aged seventy-eight years and eleven days. The remains were taken to Henderson, in the same State, for burial, and interred at the Roberts Corners Cemetery.

It is with great regret we find it necessary to close this poor sketch of a prince of good men without some of his help in the way of some of the interesting stories that he delighted in telling, and told with such infinite gusto, of his many experiences, both in and out of the army.

LEONARD SEATON, JR., the third son of the family, was born in Ellisburg, Jefferson county, New York, July 18, 1827. He was brought up on a farm and learned the tanning, currying and shoemaking trades with his father, his first experience in the business being at grinding bark in 1839 with one horse on a sweep, —the same the writer operated a good many years later. He attended the district schools in Ellisburg and Henderson, also

Richard Ellis's select school and Union Academy at Belleville, in the same county.

In 1845 he worked for Gen. A. N. Corse in his boot-and-shoe manufactory, assisting in the store, where now stands Washington Hall, Watertown.

From 1847 to 1848 he worked in Burrville, at tanning and shoe-making, for his father and brother Andrew P. Seaton, and in the

LEONARD SEATON, JR.

next year he bought his father's currying and boot-and-shoe business in Henderson, which he carried on until August 21, 1862, when he enlisted in the Tenth New York Heavy Artillery.

In the course of time he married Mary Brown, of Henderson. This Mrs. Seaton lived only about one year after their marriage, and left no offspring, so far as I know.

The second lady he chose for an helpmeet was Harriet Ann Bates, to whom he was married in Henderson, March 17, 1850. I remember Aunt Hattie as a very pleasant lady—one of my favorite aunts, in fact. She was of a remarkably lively temperament, and took particular interest in making the visits of children agreeable when they visited her, which I for one did quite frequently. Of this marriage there were born a daughter, Florence, in 1857, and a son in 1859. The son died in infancy, and Florence married Dr. W. G. Terry, of Henderson.

Harriet Ann Seaton died at Henderson, in 1859.

In 1850 Mr. Seaton bought the Spaulding & Ivory Furnace Company property in Henderson, and converted it into a tannery. In 1860 he was appointed as Assistant Census Marshal of the towns of Henderson and Hounsfield, and in September of that year he was appointed Postmaster at Henderson; but in 1861, by reason of political affiliations, he was succeeded by L. B. Simmons.

In 1861 Mr. Seaton bought the C. H. Overton farm, near the village of Henderson, and let it for a term of years. He also sold his boot-and-shoe stock, and having closed his tannery and sold the stock in the vats to Sylvanus Pool, at something of a sacrifice, he joined his regiment on September 18, 1862, at Watertown, immediately before it left for New York city, where it was quartered at Park Barracks, where the New York postoffice now stands. He was appointed battalion quartermaster, and later ordnance officer.

On March 27, 1864, the regiment was ordered to the front, and in May of that year was embarked on transports at Alexandria, arriving at Front Royal, Virginia, May 31, and on the march to Cold Harbor Lieutenant Seaton was in command of the rear guard. The regiment arrived at Cold Harbor at midnight, June 4, 1864, and commenced active work in building defenses, digging ditches, etc.

The regiment was under fire, and, though in no actual battle, war was to be seen on every side. From drinking filthy water at that time Mr. Seaton was severely poisoned, and had a serious time with some eruptive disease, which caused a scab to form over his whole person. This scab finally peeled off in great flakes, and from the effects of which he never fully recovered, and he was afterward pensioned.

In July, 1864, he was assigned to the command of a provisional battalion of six hundred men, and receipted for their outfit of arms, ammunition, clothing, etc. The battalion was made up of convalescents from sixteen different regiments. The provisional battalion was reorganized into companies, and Mr. Seaton assigned to command the second company and take charge of Fort Simons, D. C. In September the regiment was ordered to report to General Sheridan, in the Valley; but from having ridden on top of a box-car in the rain all night, Mr. Seaton was taken sick and sent to the hospital.

On December 17 he was assigned to general court-martial duty, and so continued until February 18, 1865, when he was discharged for physical disability incurred in line of duty. He had been trying to settle up with the department for liabilities incurred by receipting for the property of the provisional battalion in July, 1864, the department having him charged with about $36,000; but after several weeks' work in procuring affidavits, the debt was canceled.

On April 4, 1886, Mr. Seaton married Mrs. Marian J. Chapman, of Belleville, New York, a very estimable lady, who kindly entertained me at their home on the occasion of my visit to New York in June, 1901. They lived on the farm one year, when he sold the farm and engaged in the general mercantile business at Henderson, in which he continued until 1878, except in 1874-5-6. There are no children from this union, but each has one child by a former marriage. Mrs. Seaton's son, Arthur L. Chapman, is a successful physician in the city of Watertown, the county seat. He married a Miss Tyler, of Henderson Harbor, daughter of the gentleman who owns the Tyler cottages along the bay shore, where a large company of people congregate every summer to enjoy the beautiful scenery and the healthful lake breezes that have the scent of evergreens and enjoyable health in every breath. Arthur and his wife own a beautiful cottage contiguous to the Tyler group.

In 1872 Mr. Seaton and his brother George bought the Daniel Smith farm, in Henderson, and in the same year he was elected

RESIDENCE OF LEONARD SEATON, JR.

Supervisor of the township and was reëlected in 1873-4-5, although a Democrat, while the town was strongly Republican.

During the years 1871 and 1872 he built at Henderson Harbor the vessel "Leonard Seaton," and sold her for $22,000. He built and sold the "James Wade" in 1873 for $28,000. She proved too large for the Welland Canal, and her stern had to be cold-chiseled down, her wales taken off and her load taken out before she could get through, when she sailed to Chicago. Heavy damages for demurrage and delay were demanded by other vessel-owners, but their claims were eventually compromised.

Mr. Seaton afterward built the vessel "Jennie White," named for a schoolmate of the writer's, which was sailed by her father, Captain J. M. White, and others for fifteen years, when she was sold in 1890; she was finally lost in the Gulf of St. Lawrence, in 1894. The "James Wade" foundered in Lake Michigan in 1878, and all on board were lost. The "Leonard Seaton" was wrecked in Lake Erie in 1888, but no lives were lost. This vessel business proved to be a great financial loss, and although no one else shared the losses, many profited by the enterprise.

In 1873 Mr. Seaton bought the Reeves farm, in Henderson. He was nominated for Sheriff in 1875, but was defeated by Hon. A. W. Peck by only 186 majority. In 1876 he attended the Democratic State and National Conventions; besides, he was for a short time at Democratic headquarters in New York city.

He was elected Sheriff of Jefferson county in the fall of 1878. At the expiration of his term of office he was appointed chief deputy and jailer by G. Harrison Smith, Sheriff-elect, and took substantially the sole charge and responsibility of the office throughout Mr. Smith's term, which ended December 31, 1884, thus having been a Democratic Sheriff for two terms in a county strongly Republican.

In 1884 he was again nominated for Sheriff, but was defeated by J. M. Felt, though with a reduced majority. On January 1, 1885, he returned to Henderson with his family. He attended the National Democratic Convention in Chicago in 1884, and in 1887 and 1888 he made several trips to Kansas on important business for others, which he transacted to their entire satisfaction. He attended the Republican National Convention, witnessing the nomination of Benjamin Harrison for President. He also attended the National Democratic Convention in 1892, when Cleveland was renominated for President.

In 1860 he visited Wisconsin, Iowa, and other Western States. On that trip he also visited Toronto and London, Canada, where he saw the Prince of Wales, who was then making a tour of Canada. At that time he traveled by mule teams in Iowa, as there were then no railroads in the northern part of the State. In 1867 he again visited the West, accompanied by his father. At Winona, Minnesota, they met Bishop Whipple, who was born and raised in Jefferson county, New York. He, having known Mr. Seaton, Sr., came forward and introduced himself, and an agreeable visit resulted.

In the fall of 1885 Mr. Seaton commenced to practice law in justices' courts in Henderson, Ellisburg and Hounsfield, and occasionally in Worthville and Rodman, and even in the city of Watertown. He almost invariably appeared on the side of the defendant, and, as he himself said, never advised the commencement of suits unless as a last resort; and in obtaining settlements he was usually quite successful.

Mr. Seaton was a Democrat, voting first in 1848 for Cass, then for Pierce, Buchanan, Breckinridge, McClellan, Seymour, Greeley, Tilden, Hancock, Cleveland, and Bryan. Greeley was the hardest medicine for him of any in the list.

He was a member of no church, but contributed liberally for the support of churches. He was a Mason and a member of Joe Spratt Post G. A. R. His knowledge of affairs and business was most excellent. His judgment was good and his foresight and initiative perceptions of the means necessary to be used to accomplish his purposes were of a high order.

But it was rather as a kind and lovable friend and acquaintance than as a business man, soldier, politician or legal adviser that he made his most favorable impression upon all who knew him.

Leonard Seaton, Jr., died at his home in Henderson, New York, on December 5, 1903. The funeral was held on the 7th, conducted by Rev. L. Black, and the interment was made at Roberts Corners Cemetery.

CHAPTER XXIV.

FRANCES PHIDELIA SEATON, the first daughter in the family, was born at Henderson, Jefferson county, New York, on April 25, 1830. She was married to Elliott Monroe Clark, of New Haven, Madison county, Vermont, December 24, 1846, by Elder Slater, of Henderson. Mr. Clark was born May 15, 1826, as above.

Mrs. Frances Phidelia (Seaton) Clark died many years ago, and Mr. Clark married again and lived somewhere in Missouri at the last account we had of his whereabouts.

The children of E. M. and Frances Clark were:

1. Leonard Anson Clark, born February 11, 1847, in St. Lawrence county, New York. He was married to Clara V. Smith at Charles City, Iowa, November 22, 1878, by D. U. C. Duncan. Their children are named as follows: 1. Frank Ray Clark, born August 27, 1879, at Charles City, Iowa; 2. Arthur Earl Clark, born at Charles City, Iowa, July 15, 1881; 3. Maud Belle Clark, born August 28, 1883, at Faulkton, South Dakota; 4. Rollin Vern Clark, born at Faulkton, South Dakota, October 3, 1886; 5. Roy Leonard Clark, born April 7, 1889, at the same place as above; 6. Hugh Harold Clark, born as above, on September 8, 1892; and 7. Daisy Maree Clark, born April 7, 1896, at Elmore, Minnesota.

2. Mary Angelia Clark, who was born at Henderson, New York, October 18, 1848. She was married to Horace Jerome Dawley at Austin, Mower county, Minnesota, October 20, 1866, by C. J. Shortt, a Justice of the Peace. Their children were: 1. Hubert Jerome Dawley, born March 27, 1869, at Charles City, Iowa; 2. Hurel Guy Dawley, born March 6, 1872, at Charles City, Iowa; 3. Herbert Macy Dawley, born February 16, 1878, at Sibley, Osceola county, Iowa; and 4. Edith Aurilla Dawley, born September 4, 1881, at Sibley, Iowa.

3. Ella Genevieve Clark was born at Henderson, New York, August 29, 1851, and was married to her cousin, P. N. C. Seaton, December 16, 1871, at Charles City, Iowa, by C. B. Hamlin. They have four children, as follows: 1. Zua Olga Seaton, born at Charles City, Iowa, July 8, 1873; 2. Jennie Cornelia; and 3. Jessie and Angelia, the twins, born at Algona, Iowa, on Independence Day, 1879; and 4. Fay Cushman Seaton, born at Algona, Iowa, July 28, 1883.

4. Ernest Danford Clark, born November 13, 1863, at Waukon, Hardin county, Iowa. He was married to Beezie Henrietta Morgan, in Charles City, Iowa, on February 26, 1884. Mrs. Clark was born November 4, 1865, in Waukegan, Illinois. They have four children: 1. Jessie Mae Clark, born December 7, 1884; 2. Eddie Clark, born December 22, 1885; 3. Florence Henrietta Clark, born February 24, 1889; and 4. Hazel Frances Clark, born April 10, 1891.

5. Clara Eva Clark was born August 12, 1865, at Charles City, Iowa, and married to William J. Smith on January 20, 1882, in Charles City, Iowa, by John S. Bradley. Their children are named as follows: 1. Effie Smith, born November 12, 1882; 2. Bertha Smith, born June 12, 1885, 3. Frank Smith, born June 12, 1885, evidently twins; 4. Oren Smith, born June 17, 1887; 5. Millard Smith, born November 25, 1889; 6. Ruby Smith, born November 13, 1891; and 7. Willie Smith, born December 15, 1898.

SAMUEL GREENLEAF SEATON, the youngest child of Polly (Pennell) Seaton, was born at Mather's Mills, Jefferson county, New York, on July 2, 1834. He lived at Elyria, Ohio, for twelve years, and went to Kingston, Wisconsin, in 1848, where he continued to reside until in 1856. In the next year he was married to Ellen Graham, eldest daughter of John and Elizabeth Graham, on the 10th of January, 1857, since which time his home has been in and around Chicago, Illinois; though five of his children were born in Wisconsin, as follows: 1. Fred Albert; 2. Mary; 3. Fannie; 4. Jane; 5. Ellen Graham. The youngest child, 6. Louise, was born at Chicago.

Samuel Seaton has been an expressman nearly all of his life,

since he was old enough to take a position with the American
Express Company, having worked his way up from the bottom
round of the ladder by mere force of executive ability until he
was Superintendent of the Western Division, with an office in
Chicago. He has since been with the Adams Express Company
in the same capacity, and now is in the employ of the United
States Express Company and is still in Chicago, though his home
is now at Lagrange, Cook county, Illinois.

While he lived at Kingston, Wisconsin, he was the President
of the place in the year 1860. He was a Reform Alderman in the
twelfth ward in the city of Chicago during 1877 and 1878.

CHAPTER XXV.

THE CHILDREN OF LEONARD AND SARAH (CHAPMAN) SEATON.

Mary Miranda Seaton, the first-born of the second marriage, was born at Henderson, New York, on October 19, 1835, where she lived and attended the village school, except while finishing her education at the Belleville Academy, perhaps, until she was married to Danford Butts, who was a tinner and hardware dealer in the latter place when I attended the academy there.

The children born to Danford and Mary (Seaton) Butts were:

1. Lenora Holly Butts, born May 23, 1858, who was married to Benjamin Stretton on April 6, 1881. Mr. Stretton was in the employ of the American Express Company at Atchison, Kansas, when the writer visited them many years ago. "Nora," as we called her, died at Kansas City, of typhoid fever, on August 2, 1891, leaving two little girls, Nina Claire Stretton, born July 31, 1884, and Nellie Louise Stretton, born January 6, 1887.

2. Nellie Louise Butts was born October 1, 1860. She was married July 10, 1894, to William Herrick Putnam, of Red Wing, Minnesota. Their children were: Danford Seaton Putnam, born May 25, 1895, and died January 3, 1896; and Richard Herrick Putnam, born July 15, 1901.

3. William C. Butts was born February 15, 1863. He is a steamboat captain on the Great Lakes; has had command of several different boats, but was in command of the "Nimich" in 1891.

4. Sarah E. Butts was born November 3, 1865. She was married to Dewitt Hungerford on November 15, 1883. A daughter was born to them March 15, 1888, who was given the name Beulah N. Hungerford.

5. Mary E. Butts, the youngest of the children, was born October 30, 1868, and married to Orvis K. Estes, on the 8th of May,

1889. One daughter was born to them, on August 15, 1895, and given the name Marian Estes. Danford Butts, the father, died December 22, 1890. His relict lives at Henderson, New York, where I spent a few pleasant hours on my visit to New York in 1901.

If I am not mistaken, she and her only son, who is her only unmarried child, live together, when he is not engaged at his business on the lakes, and they own a summer cottage at the bay-side, where Aunt Mary passes the heated term with the company of campers during the absence of her son.

CORNELIA SEATON was born at Henderson, New York, in 1837, and died at the same place about a year later.

ARMINDA DORLESCA SEATON was born in the town of Henderson, New York, May 10, 1838. Her girlhood was passed, like that of other girls, in attending school and helping about the housework. She was married in Henderson on Thanksgiving evening in 1857, to Daniel J. Sprague, by the Reverend M. M. Rice. Their only child was Elwin Delay Sprague, born August 15, 1858. He lives in Arizona. Mr. and Mrs. Sprague lived together for about ten years, when, for reasons of their own, a divorce was obtained. Aunt Arminda resided in Henderson up to February 14, 1883, when she was married to Arthur J. Armstrong, of Rochester, New York, by Reverend L. B. Fisher, and went to the city of Rochester to make their home. Their residence is at No. 31 Harris avenue, where I visited them in 1901, and found them nicely located and apparently as happy as we mortals often are. With Mr. and Mrs. Armstrong at that time were living Hattie (Armstrong) McBirney and her husband, Wesley McBirney, and their sweet little baby-girl, Helen McBirney. Uncle Armstrong was a night-watchman somewhere in the city when I was there, and Mr. McBirney was working at his trade, a gilder.

CHAUNCEY EUGENE SEATON, fourth child, but first son of Leonard and Sarah Seaton, was born at Henderson, New York, on January 19, 1840. He was married to Sarah Eugenia Grannis on the 15th day of October, 1866, in Grace Church, at Madison, Wisconsin,

by the Reverend James Maxwell. Mrs. Seaton's death occurred
at Owatonna, Minnesota, on the 20th of August, 1869. They had
one child, Julia Seaton, who was born May 11, 1868, at Owatonna.

Chauncey E. Seaton was married a second time, and his choice
his time fell upon Florence Ida Potter. The ceremony was
pronounced at Meadville, Pennsylvania, in Christ Church, by the
Reverend William G. W. Lewis, on February 11, 1874. Chauncey
was a lieutenant in the Tenth New York Heavy Artillery during
the Rebellion. He has been engaged in the express business most
of the time since the close of the war. His present address is
360 Calumet avenue, Chicago, Illinois. He has an office in Chicago, where he has charge of all of the property of the western
division of the American Express Company, and is their purchas-
ing agent.

AMBROSE BARNES SEATON was born at Henderson, New York,
September 21, 1841. He attended the village school, and probably Union Academy, at Belleville, in the same county, and when
he was old enough, helped at the farm work, but probably never
enjoyed it as much then as later in life. I remember hearing
Uncle Danford Butts tell of Ambrose helping him harvest some
wheat. As long as Ambrose could rake and bind as fast as Danford cradled he worked away cheerfully enough, but when the
cradler let out a few links in his speed Ambrose lost confidence in
his ability as a binder, and quit in disgust. We have not heard the
other side of the story, and do not know how it looks from that
point of view. Ambrose went into the army in August, 1862,
enlisting in the Tenth New York Heavy Artillery as Quartermaster Sergeant, in which capacity he served until made First
Sergeant, in January, 1863. He was promoted to Second Lieutenant of Company B, about July, 1863, and to First Lieutenant
of Company F, in May, 1865. I believe he took part in all the
engagements of the regiment during his term of service. He was
mustered out of the service in August, 1865. After wintering in
Henderson, he went to Montana with ox teams in the spring of
1866, and remained there until 1872, being engaged in farming for
two years, and the rest of the time in mining. From 1872 to 1876

he worked for an express company. He was married to Amelia Frances Selfridge, at Champaign, Illinois, by the Reverend Theodore Morrison, of Bloomington, Illinois, on January 10, 1875. Their only child, Charles Chauncey Seaton, was born on October 16, 1880, but lived only about nine months, dying at Marshalltown, Iowa, July 3, 1881. Ambrose owns nearly one thousand acres of land, part of it at least being near Running Water, South Dakota. He lives in the city of Mitchell, South Dakota, and is engaged in farming and small-fruit raising. He has lived in South Dakota since the year 1876.

LOUISE SEATON, the next daughter, was born at Henderson, New York, February 22, 1843, and was married to James Pettengill, of the same place, on her twenty-third birthday, February 22, 1866. Their first child, Jennie Louise Pettengill, was born December 29, 1866, and died on August 20, 1873. Florence Pettengill was born May 5, 1878, and died May 19, 1878. Reuben C. Pettengill was born October 23, 1879, and Herbert A. Pettengill on November 14, 1883. Both boys are bright and well educated and great readers. Reuben has taught school, but seems to prefer some other line of work. He worked at market gardening for about two years near Rochester, New York, where he was married to Hattie Cole. They moved to Kansas in the fall of 1905, where Reuben planned to engage in raising garden truck and small fruits for market, locating at Jewell City.

Herbert A. Pettengill is a sailor on the Great Lakes. Aunt Louise is one of my best correspondents, and is much more given to expressing her thoughts and feelings than most of the Seatons, who, as a rule, are not demonstrative even to a slight degree, and especially not addicted to talking of themselves, much to my regret when I speak as a writer of the family genealogy.

Uncle James Pettengill died September 20, 1885, aged fifty years. I remember him as a first-rate horseman, and often have I, as a boy, thought that to have such horses as he drove, or rode, with such unusual skill, would be all that could be wished for in this world.

CHAPTER XXVI.

THE CHILDREN OF LEONARD AND SARAH SEATON (CONTINUED).

GEORGE LUMAN SEATON, the next son, was born at Henderson, New York, on December 24, 1844. He attended the village school in his native town for several years, showing especial proficiency in penmanship more than in any other branch of learning. He was grand company for we younger boys, and could tell such wonderful tales as fairly fascinated us. At this date it appears that he was repeating the tales he read in some book or story-paper, of which he was especially fond.

After a while George and Talford Jeffers, a playmate, who was also an interested reader of the New York *Ledger* and Mrs. Southworth's stories, as well as all tales of adventure, took the notion into their heads that they, as well as the heroes of the stories they read, could go out into the world in their youth and return after many days of wandering up and down the land and sea, laden with honors and rolling in wealth. So they started out, after telling their plans to some of us smaller boys, and cautioning us not to mention where they were. As good luck would have it, the parents of the two adventurers never thought of asking us if we knew where their boys were, and we were saved the ordeal of trying to deny knowing anything of their whereabouts.

Mr. Jeffers, Talford's father, was greatly worried, and fairly flew around trying to find the boys, or to learn where they had gone. When he appealed to Grandfather Seaton to secure his coöperation in the task of following the boys, he received but little satisfaction. Grandfather, in his dignified and almost stoical way replied: "I think they will return by the time they need a clean shirt." But Mr. Jeffers, not liking to trust to such procedure, started out, and finally overtook the boys at Albany and brought them back with him, thus proving Grandfather's prediction true, but not in the sense intended.

Like most boys raised near the lakes, George finally began life as a sailor. He once told me of making out a report to the auditor of the company for which he worked. When he handed the report in, the man who received it said it was not right. "I will wager you the cigars that it is correct," replied Uncle George. The auditor took his pencil and pointed out wherein the report was defective. "You are right," said George, and he set up the choicest smokes he could secure, thinking that a cheap way to learn how to make out the report without letting anyone know that he did not before quite understand the *modus operandi*.

George Seaton was married to Sarah Viola Hutchins, at Lamotte, Jackson county, Iowa, February 25, 1869, by James Hays. Viola was born in the town of Orleans, New York, on the 17th of April, 1845. Their children were: 1. Anna Lee; 2. Lena Louise; 3. Benjamin Levi; and 4. George Louis.

Uncle George spent many years as a purser on one of the large lake steamers, and finally lost his life when the Manistee went down in Lake Superior on November 15, 1883. It seems he had a premonition that he would lose his life on the lakes, and expressed the feeling that it was not safe for him to return to his boat the last time he was at home, but he said the company for whom he worked had been so kind to him that he disliked to disappoint them, or cause them any inconvenience in finding another man to take his place, so he left his home and loved ones after a lingering and reluctant fare-you-well, and never returned to them again. But he had thoughtfully insured his life in the interest of his family and left them quite well provided for in this world's goods.

THE MANISTEE.

To Mrs. G. L. Seaton.

"Proudly sailed the Manistee,
  O'er the waters so glad and free,
    Bearing on board in captain and crew,
    A group of men both loved and true,
    And in every port where they chanced to be,
    They welcomed the crew and Manistee.

—1

"And as gaily they swept away from land,
 'Twas with many 'God keep you' and waving of hands,
  For the boat was a favorite and all were kind;
  And in searching the lakes you could scarcely find
 A crew more civil and good to see,
 Than that which belonged to the Manistee.

"As around the lovely lake she flew,
 And the pictured rocks came into view,
  More beauties of nature, it would seem,
  Than ere was known in wildest dream,
 Much of the pleasure, all could see,
 Was due to the men of the Manistee.

"But where is she now? O, who can tell
 What happened to her, what really befel
  That beautiful boat, and that gallant crew
  Of husbands, fathers, and heroes true?
 Tell me, O, tell me, merciless sea,
 Did you take our all with the Manistee?

"O, you cruel, cruel, treacherous sea,
 Can you ever know what you did for me?
  While counting the days until he come,
  You robbed me of him, you spoiled my home,
 For it never, never more can be,
 As it would had you spared the Manistee.

"Can it be that the dear ones we knew went down,
 He with the black eyes, he with the brown,
  Are their bodies lying 'neath the blue wave,
  Their spirits with one that's 'mighty to save'?
 We trust that united the friends may all be,
 With the ones that were lost with the wrecked Manistee.

"O! dear Lord in Heaven I pray that before
 They knew they must cross to the other shore,
  They saw helping hands reaching out through the wave,
  From the Father who's ready to rescue and save,
 And safe in thy home may all of them be,
 The crew of the ill-fated, lost Manistee."

After about ten years of widowhood, Mrs. Seaton was married to Mr. Hyland Millen, on October 27, 1893, by the Reverend C. G. Sterling.

Mr. Millen was killed by the cars at Buena Vista. Colorado, on September 20, 1895, after which time Auntie Millen kept the family together until they were ready to begin work on their own account. She gave them a good education and a lovely home at 3857 Charles street, Omaha, Nebraska, up to the time of the Trans-Mississippi Exposition, when my wife and I visited them.

In the summer of 1904, during the Louisiana Purchase Exposition, George L., his wife, Benjamin L. and their mother were living in St. Louis, the boys working for the express company, in whose office I had a few moments' visit with the boys.

HERBERT JULIAN SEATON, the youngest child in the family, was born at the Seaton home in Henderson, New York, on January 2, 1852. He attended the village school, and helped some with the farm work after he was old enough. He was different from most boys in having decided, before he was fifteen years old, what girl he was to marry, and in making no secret of his choice. He had also determined at that time that he was to be a merchant, and tried to shape his education with that object in view. He seems to have changed his mind on the first proposition; as it has been stated that "Wise men change their minds, fools never." But he did enter the store of his brother Leonard when he left school in 1866, and remained there until 1875, when he went sailing as clerk of the steamer Olean, running between Buffalo, New York, and Toledo, Ohio.

He had a spell of typhoid fever that fall, but after his recovery, finished the season on the steamer Tioga as her clerk. During the winter of 1875-6 he was bookkeeper at the New York Central dining-hall, at East Buffalo, New York. In the spring of 1876 he sailed as clerk of the Jay Gould, running between Buffalo and Detroit, and again in the winter of 1876-7 he clerked at the same dining-hall as the winter before.

He was married to Helen Ida Barber, at Munnsville, Madison county, New York, on June 26, 1877. Of this union two children were born, viz.: Leonard Barber and Donald Adelphas.

This marriage was not entirely congenial, and the parties most concerned decided to separate, Mrs. Seaton to have the home and everything they had, as well as the custody of the children. She is said to have married another man within three months of the separation.

Herbert married again on May 10, 1898. His second wife was Mae Anna Dodson, eldest daughter of Mr. N. H. Dodson, of Chicago, Illinois, where the wedding took place. Miss Dodson was born at Wakefield, Clay county, Kansas, on September 6, 1871. This time the little winged god seems to have pierced two hearts with one arrow, and all is well.

Herbert was clerk of the Canisteo, running from Buffalo to Green Bay, in the summer of 1877, and again spent the winter at the usual dining-hall. In the spring of 1878 he shipped as clerk of the steamer Atlantic for the run from Buffalo to Lake Superior.

He was then for two years Under-Sheriff of Jefferson county, New York, with his brother Leonard, at Watertown, the county seat.

In the spring of 1881 he engaged with the Lake Michigan and Lake Superior Transportation Company, and while in their employ has been clerk of the Heard, Peerless, Fremont, City of Duluth, Traverse, and Manitou, and ticket agent in Chicago, Illinois. Since 1898 he has been agent for the company at Hancock, Michigan, where he lives at the present writing, January 8, 1901.

Herbert thinks his grandmother lived to be nearly one hundred years old, and was totally blind for some years before she died. He further says Asa Seaton, Jr., his uncle, was at the head of one of the four Shaker settlements, or families, at Lebanon, Mount Lebanon, New Lebanon and Shakers, near Albany, New York, holding that position from sometime in 1850 to 1865, when he was succeeded by Chauncey Miller, from whom the writer has lately received a very pleasant letter in reference to the lives of Asa, Jr., and Tina Seaton.

CHAPTER XXVII.

THE CHILDREN OF ASA AND DOROTHY (WILCOX) SEATON.

LORAINE SEATON was born near Coburg, Ontario, Canada, January 5, 1833. She married a Mr. Dombaugh, December 11, 1858. They lived near Muncie, Indiana, and were the parents of four children as follows: Anna Belle Clara, born March 3, 1859; married Lewis Cowing, September 28, 1881. Mr. Cowing was at one time Commissioner of Delaware county, Indiana, and was living at Muncie, in that county, in 1903. Edward Dombaugh, born October 3, 1860; died August 23, 1862. Fannie G. Dombaugh, born December 24, 1865; died October 30, 1867. Harry I. Dombaugh, born November 18, 1867; was in Mexico when last heard from.

Loraine (Seaton) Dombaugh married a second time, George W. Leith, August 23, 1871. One child, Ernest Irven Leith, was born February 6, 1873, to bless this marriage. He lived in Bakersfield, California, at the last word from him.

POLLY SEATON was born December 11, 1834, and died in less than a year, October 8, 1835.

WARREN SEATON was born in 1835. He married Margaret Blades, in 1865, at Mount Pleasant, West Virginia. He is the only living brother to Robert, of Kansas City. Their children were Dimmie and Catharine. Warren Seaton is said by more than one to resemble the writer so closely that the picture of either might be mistaken for that of the other.

CLARINDA, or CLARA SEATON, born April 5, 1838, married Sylvester Gray, in 1860. They live in Wooster, Ohio, and their children are: Edward Gray, born in 1863; Alice Gray, born in 1865, and married to William Kilgore. They reside in Duluth, Minnesota. Lillie Gray was born in 1867, and Howard Gray in 1871, and died in 1902. The family address is Wooster, Ohio.

VALENTINE SEATON was born in Stark county, Ohio, February 4, 1840, and died in Pulaski county, Indiana, September 7, 1901. Margaret L. Jurey, born in Wyandot county, Ohio, July 29, 1843, died in Pulaski county, Indiana, February 15, 1898. They were married at Wyandot, Ohio, by Rev. Mr. Jackson, November 13, 1867. They lived with his father for a time, then made a home for themselves in Dunkirk, Jay county, Indiana, afterward moving to Muncie, Indiana, and finally to Pulaski county, Indiana, where both died as stated above.

The children of Valentine and Margaret L. Seaton are: Albert Jurey, born in Crawford county, Ohio, October 4, 1868, died in Pulaski county, Ind., April 3, 1890; Charles H., born in Dunkirk, Ind., May 27, 1873, married Della Martin at Jansen, Neb., December 22, 1902. They are now living near Minot, North Dakota, on a farm. Frank W., born in Muncie, Ind., November 7, 1875, is at present a merchant in Glenburn, North Dakota, and unmarried; Edward A., born in Pulaski county, Ind., January 19, 1887, is now a junior in the Muncie, Ind., High School, living with Mrs. Lewis G. Cowing, his cousin.

After the death of his wife, Margaret, Valentine Seaton married Martha J. Stout, December 1, 1898. She is still living, in Winamac, Indiana.

MIRANDA SEATON was born December 29, 1841, and married Jesse McClelland in 1868. They live at Wooster, Ohio. Their children are George McClelland, born in 1870, and Blanch McClelland, who was born in 1872.

GEORGE SEATON was born July 7, 1843, and died on April 29, 1844.

ROBERT SEATON, born July 1, 1845, at Crestline, Ohio, married Mary Stewart, of Nevada, Wyandot county, Ohio, in 1872. Robert was born and raised on a farm, where he continued to live until he went to learn the printer's trade, at the age of fourteen years. He worked on the Cincinnati *Commercial* when Murat Halstead was editor and publisher, from which position he enlisted three times in the Federal Army during the Civil War. The first and second times he was rejected on account of age and a truss that he was compelled to wear, but on the third attempt to become a soldier the inspection was less rigid and he was accepted. . He served in the One Hundred and Thirty-sixth Ohio National Guard, and went to Washington, D. C., where his regiment did garrison duty, serving from May 2, 1864, to September 4th of the same year. He was in no regular battles, but that was no fault of the soldiers; for who ever knew a soldier who did not prefer an active campaign to being shut up in a town with nothing but drilling and guard duty to do?

Since his return from the army he has been engaged in the mercantile business. He lived at Muncie, Indiana, about 1875, where two of his children were born. Later he founded the village of Seatonville, in Nebraska, was the first postmaster, built the first store building, and was the first merchant.

From Seatonville, Nebraska, the family went to Chetopa, Kansas, continuing the same business, and from the latter place to Kansas City, Kansas, where he was having a rushing trade when the Kaw river flood occurred, in May, 1903. The flood put an end to his operations, wiping out all of his accumulations for years, but he soon started again in a modest way in Kansas City, Missouri, in a grocery and bakery, in which his son Chauncey Alfred is associated with him. Each member of the two families lends a helping hand as needed, and the business is having a good run of trade.

The present address of the Seaton Grocery Company is 2610 East Eighteenth street, Kansas City, Missouri.

The children of Robert and Mary (Stewart) Seaton are: Chauncey Alfred; Lulu Stewart; Wallace Robert; Mabel Helen; Carrie Loraine; Ruth Marie; and Dorothy Margaret.

Robert Seaton is First Day Adventist in belief, but worships with the Methodists in his present location. He is a six-footer without obesity, a mild-mannered, quiet gentleman, in whom all have implicit confidence as soon as they become acquainted with him. He is a Republican in politics.

Mrs. Seaton is a model housekeeper, an ideal hostess, and a lady of education. She is a Seventh Day Adventist in belief, but at present affiliates with the Methodists.

CHAUNCEY SEATON, the youngest son of Asa and Dorothy, was born March 17, 1848, and died December 12, 1896. He was married to Ella Stewart in 1884, at Upper Sandusky, Ohio, Ella being a sister to Robert's wife, Mary. Chauncey died at Spokane Falls, Washington.

THE CHILDREN OF BENJAMIN F. AND RUTH (HURLBERT) SEATON.

CARRIE ELIZABETH SEATON was born at Massillon, Ohio, on October 8, 1854, and died at Marion, Iowa, February 6, 1885.

MAY GOODWIN SEATON was born at Massillon, Ohio, on the 17th of May, 1856. She was married to L. M. Lillis, a druggist, on March 7, 1887, and died at Marion, Iowa, on April 27, 1895.

ANNA RUTH SEATON was born at Massillon, Ohio, July 30, 1859. She died single, at Marion, Iowa, September 1, 1899.

GRACE SEATON was born after the family moved to Marion, Iowa, the date of her birth being July 30, 1861, the year the Civil War began. She died in October of the same year.

FANNIE LOUISE SEATON was born in Marion, Iowa, December 21, 1863. She was married to Norman E. Ives, United States Pension Examiner, September 9, 1885. One incident of her life is mentioned in the sketch of her father. They have two children, Haroldine C. and Norman Seaton Ives, born at Marion, Iowa, September 19, 1890, and Chicago, Illinois, March 5, 1897, respectively.

FRANK HURLBERT SEATON was born at Marion, Iowa, April 3, 1865, and died at the same place on July 30, 1895, unmarried.

GRACE LILLIAN SEATON was born at Marion, Iowa, December 2, 1874. She was married to Leslie C. Bolton, a lawyer of Oskaloosa, Iowa, on September 5, 1894. They have two children, both born at Oskaloosa: James Seaton Bolton, born June 14, 1895, and Frank Lesley Bolton, born July 30, 1896.

SARAH ELIZA, the first-born of the family, was born in Clark township. Ontario, on the 3d of February, 1837. and died and was buried in Newcastle, Canada, May 3d, 1847

MARY ELIZABETH SEATON was born at Bletcher's Corners, Ontario, on the 26th of February, 1839. She was married August 4, 1857, by the Rev. Canon Henry Brent, in Newcastle, to Robert Jones, son of Elias Jones, of Coburg, one of the oldest and most respected Ontarian families. He was a Conservative, a member of the Church of England, Clerk of the Court in Millbrook, and subsequently a traveler. They lived at Millbrook, Ontario, during 1857–62, Newcastle 1862–77, Toronto 1877. He died, and was buried in Toronto August 15, 1892. The present address of his widow is 255 North Lisgar street, Toronto, Canada. They had the following family: Frank Elias Jones, died 1879; Emma Mary Jones was born in Newcastle, Ontario. She married William Sinclair Duncan. He is an expert marksman, the winner of the Governor-General's prize (championship of Canada), and a member of the team sent by the Canadian Army to Bisley, England, to compete with marksmen from all parts of the Empire. He was a Lieutenant in the Second Regiment, "Queen's Own Rifles of Canada," and Adjutant in the Twelfth Regiment "York Rangers." They had the following children: Helen Emma, married John Campbell Hunter; Gertrude Florence.

Jessie Seaton Jones married Arthur Augustus Martin, of Toronto, and died in that city February 16, 1902. They had five children: Jessie Edith, Frank, ob. inf., Mary Helen, Arthur Burnham, and Henry Edwards.

Margaret Louise Jones, Frederick and Edith Helen complete the names of the children of Robert and Mary Elizabeth (Seaton) Jones. Frederick died about 1897.

EMELINE IRENE SEATON, daughter of Leonard Barna, was born at Newcastle, Ontario, on the 19th of January, 1842. She was married in Newcastle, by the Rev. Canon Henry Brent, December 11, 1861, to James Harvey, son of John Norman and Deborah

(Pierce) McNairn, of Dickinson's Landing. Ontario. He was born there August 15, 1837. They lived at Whitby, Ontario, 1861-62, Port Hope 1862-66, Toronto 1866-. He was a captain in the Grand Trunk Rifle Brigade during the Fenian Raid of 1866, and has the General Service Medal and a military land grant in New Ontario for his service on that occasion. He edited the "Sower" in 1891, and published "The Apocalypse" in 1899. He is a member of the Law Society of Upper Canada, and is a Commissioner. He is a manufacturer of waxed paper in Toronto and proprietor of the Dansville Paper Mill at Dansville, New York. His residence is Aldercoign, 4 Harvard avenue, Toronto, Canada. They have had six children: Mary, ob. inf.; Alice Maud, ob. inf.; Frederick Harvey, ob. inf.; Edgar Norman, born 15th July, 1869, died 27th June, 1884; Harvey Turner, ob. inf.; William Harvey McNairn, born 3d of September, 1874. The latter is a scholarly gentleman, very much interested in the subject of genealogy, and consequently well versed in the mysteries of heraldry. He has rendered us considerable assistance with this branch of the family history. He is a member of the University of Toronto, matriculated in 1895, and graduated B. A. in 1899 and M. A. in 1900. For two years he was an assistant in the mineralogical laboratory, and while an undergraduate he won some scholarships and prizes, and held one or two offices. He is a charter member of the Toronto Chapter of the Delta Upsilon college fraternity, and at present is his father's assistant in the office in Toronto. He is a member of the choir and of the board of managers of the Parkdale Presbyterian Church.

LEONARD TURNER SEATON, son of Leonard Barna and Almira (Wing) Seaton, the youngest child and only son of his parents, was born July 26, 1848, in Newcastle, Ontario, and moved to Plano, Illinois, with his parents. He married Nancy Alice Robbins in Plano on the 2d of April, 1873, Elder F. Curtis performing the ceremony. Their children are: Frank Grant; Earl Garfield; Sidney Blaine; Emeline Mary; Stanley Wing; Harrison Ingalls; and Jessie Caroline,—all Republicans, like their father, as their names plainly indicate.

Leonard Turner Seaton learned the trade of cabinetmaking while quite young, and in 1870 opened a furniture and undertaker's store in Plano. He continued in active business there until in 1877, when he sold out and went to Pecatonica, Winnebago county, Illinois, and bought a furniture business. In 1882 he sold that establishment and returned to Plano, where he took up the same line of work and continued it until finally he retired from that business, and now devotes his time to the sale of a patent milk-can washer of his own invention, of which he is selling machines and territory. He seems to be of a lively temperament, positive in his opinions and likes. He sums up the Seaton characteristics by saying that as a class they are very radical, and are slow to change their minds when once convinced they are in the right.

CHAPTER XXVIII.

THE CHILDREN OF ANDREW P. AND LAURA A. SEATON.

OREN ANDREW SEATON, the first child born to the worthy people whose names head this chapter, was born at Burr's Mills, or Burrville, Watertown township, Jefferson county, New York, on August 11, 1847, but the family moved to Henderson village, in the same county, soon after that important event occurred, and all the recollections of his boyhood days are associated with Henderson and its surroundings. He attended the village school in the latter place until far enough advanced in his studies to make it advisable to continue the good work at Union Academy, at Belleville, in the same county. He helped with the work in the tannery, grinding bark and doing other light jobs, during the vacations of the school, after he was old enough, until the day arrived when his father moved from town to the Overton farm, probably for the children's good. After that time he assisted with the farm work, milking cows, feeding calves, plowing, or whatever was the order of the day, until August 22, 1864, when he enlisted in what was later Company B, One Hundred and Eighty-sixth New York Volunteers, Infantry, and went to the war. The regiment rendezvoused at Madison Barracks, Sacket's Harbor, on the bank of Lake Ontario, where the soldiers took their first lessons in guard duty, drilling, and especially in eating the army rations. This latter experience was a revelation to our soldier-boy. In comparison with his mother's cooking the meals dished up at the barracks tables appeared to him as though the potatoes had been boiled with their jackets on, in the same water in which they had been washed, although Lake Ontario kissed the shore a few steps back of the dining-hall. The potatoes were piled, a peck in a place, on the bare, rough pine board tables, alternating with great hunks of boiled beef; and baker's yeast bread, which the

FAMILY OF O. A. SEATON.

boy never had been able to eat, was scattered along the tables at frequent intervals. Our tin cups were filled with black, drastic coffee, "strong enough to bear up an iron wedge," as some one said, and we were told to pitch in and help ourselves. No butter, no cream, no sugar, no anything inviting, and, worst of all, no appetite for such food. But later in the war there were times when such a spread would have been considered a feast.

At about this stage in the game the youngster began to wonder if he had ever complained of the food or cooking at home, and heartily repented having done so, if he had. Some of the boys ate with an appetite worth having, some made uncomplimentary remarks, and others looked down their noses as though they saw eternal misery at the end thereof. Three or four skedaddled for Canada, unable to face the music, and were marked on the rolls as deserters. It was explained that the Commissary Department was not quite ready for so many boarders, and that matters would mend in a day or two.

When the company was dismissed more than one boy went to the sutler and bought something he could eat. And for about four days this order of exercises was repeated three times a day, without tasting a bite at the regular meals. "How do you live?" asked an acquaintance. "Oh, I am boarding with my pocket-book," was the answer; and many another could have truthfully made the same reply. On the fourth day some one asked the boy if he intended to board and clothe himself and serve his country for nothing during his term of enlistment. This set the boy to thinking, and he said to himself: "See here, my young man, can you not muster up spunk enough to take things as you find them, when they cannot be improved, or must the Government of these United States maintain a wet-nurse for its baby-boy?" After that view of the case was taken, yeast bread, bean soup and baked beans, salt fat pork and several other items on the bill of fare were introduced to the soldier-boy's stomach, but in this case, to know them was not to love them. It was a tough proposition, but in his veins were a few drops of blood imbued with the "sand" that had stood a long line of sailor and soldier ancestry in good stead in similar circumstances, and he lived through the ordeal,

The first experience on guard duty is well remembered. The position chanced to be at the entrance to that part of the barracks used for a temporary hospital. The orders were not to permit anyone, except officers, or the hospital corps, to pass in or out, and a club about three feet long and an inch or less in diameter was handed over by the preceding guard with which to enforce the order. But the young and inexperienced guard, on duty for the first time, was not told how to distinguish officers and hospital em- ployés from the common soldiers and civilians, nor did he think to ask. As all wore citizen's dress, he was at a loss to know whom to admit or to allow to pass out. Even had some one appeared with the proper insignia of his rank, it would have been impossible for our soldier-boy to interpret his position without instruction. As he marched up and down the porch before the door, he won- dered there had been no password, or countersign, given him by which he could determine whom to allow to pass, as he had read was the custom in the army. Presently a man (not a gentleman) came along and tried to pass into the hospital. " Halt!" de- manded the guard in his best military tone. The approaching man paid no attention to the command, but kept advancing as though to crowd his way through. Again " Halt!" was called, and this time the club that did duty for a sword or gun, was raised. Still he came on. Then, preparing to strike, the boy called " Halt, you jackass, or you will get hurt!" The man stopped, drew back a step and said, " I'll teach you to call a superior officer a jackass! What is your name and company?" The question was ignored, with the remark that it was hard to see where he was superior to a jackass. Off he went in a towering rage to have the boy arrested, but the fighting blood of the young soldier was up, and he felt no fear of arrest under the circumstances. And that proved to be the last that was heard of the affair.

It would perhaps be interesting to follow the fortunes of the young man through the war in the Second Brigade of the Second Division of the Ninth Army Corps, but that experience has been saved for a sketch of itself, when opportunity offers, so we will only say he followed the line of duty in his regiment until the close of the war, taking part in all the marches, fortifying and fighting, without ever having failed to answer at roll-call, or being excused from any duty for disability, though twice slightly wounded.

After the war was over, returning to the farm he made a hand at anything there was to be done summers and attended school during the winter, taking a post-graduate course, until in the spring of 1868, when he shipped as landsman on the lake schooner, C. G. Mixer, Captain Eggleston, for a sailor on the Great Lakes. In a month's time he was promoted to ordinary seaman, though such promotion usually requires a whole season's service in the former capacity. But the experience as a fisherman and with the pleasure sail-boat at home made him familiar with the vessel, and the former acquaintance with sail-boats was counted in his favor. In another month he was advanced to seaman, with all the duties and pay of that position. But, not enjoying the night work on board ship, he went to St. Joseph, Champaign county, Illinois, to visit his aunt's family, and while there accepted a position as salesman, bookkeeper and assistant Postmaster in the store of his uncle, Albert R. Ralph, living in the family with Aunt Lydia and Cousins Jennie and Alta, who came to gain a place in his affection next to his mother and sister.

After the new town of St. Joseph was started on the railroad, the store was moved there, and while boarding at a hotel the clerk somehow exchanged his usually good health for quite a disagreeable case of dyspepsia, and he decided to go to Kansas and rough it a while for health's sake, and to secure a homestead while they were to be had for the taking, almost.

In Kansas he taught school during several winters, farming summers, until in March, 1878, on the twenty-sixth day of that eventful month, he was married to Sadie Elizabeth Bartley, whose acquaintance he made while living at St. Joseph, the home of her father, James Bartley, a farmer of English and German descent.

Mr. Bartley's father, Jacob Bartley, went from Ohio to Illinois at the early settling of the latter State, having previously emigrated from Virginia, where he married Sarah West, a descendant of the original owner of West Point, Virginia, later made historic by General George B. McClellan in his campaign during the War of the Rebellion.

MRS. SADIE E. SEATON.

Here occurs another of those curious coincidences so often found in the study of genealogy: In 1741 Elizabeth Seaton married John West. of York River. Virginia, gentleman. and here in 1878 we find Oren Andrew Seaton, a blood relation to the said Elizabeth, marrying Sadie Elizabeth Bartley. a direct descendant of the aforesaid John West.

The children born to Oren A. and Sadie E. Seaton. all of whom are alive and well at this writing. are: Goldie Myrtle: Noble Fay: Roy Andrew; Guy Oren: and Sadie Gladys.

The next year after Goldie Myrtle was born a trip was made to Illinois. to see and be seen by relatives. and from there the journey was continued to Iowa for the same purpose.

A term of school was taught while the family visited at St. Joseph. and Noble Fay was born at the home of his grandfather Bartley.

Arriving at the Kansas home in the fall of 1882. an engagement was entered into with the officers of the home school district to teach their winter's term of school. after which the farming went on as before. until in July of 1883. when a position was accepted as weighman and bookkeeper with Messrs. W. R. West & Company. grain merchants. of Glasco. Cloud county. Kansas.

While the family resided at Glasco. Roy Andrew. the third child. was born, on April 17. 1884. And while there Mr. W. A. Walker. one of the partners in the grain business. who also owned the Bank of Glasco. offered the grain business bookkeeper the position of cashier of the bank. at better wages than he was receiving. but the other partners would not consent to release him from the grain office.

When the year was up for which he had hired. the bookkeeper accepted a better position with the remaining partner. A. T. Rogers. in his grain office in Beloit. in Mitchell county. there being a change in the Glasco firm by which Leo Noel became a partner and wished to do the office work.

After one year's experience in Beloit he bought, in partnership with Mr. Rogers. the grain business of John D. Robertson. in Jewell City. Jewell county. Kansas. and in another six months secured the whole business. and has since run the business in his own name.
—13

except for a few months when his father owned a quarter interest, and has added coal, thoroughbred Poland-China hogs, Shorthorn cattle and Percheron horses to his other business, besides owning three hundred and twenty acres of land, which is rented out.

Guy Oren, the third son, was born at the Seaton home in Jewell City, on August 8, 1886, and Sadie Gladys, the baby of the family, on February 13, 1890.

Besides attending to the regular business of his grain office, the subject of this sketch has written considerably for the agricultural press and the local newspaper, besides a volume of poems for his mother; a book of stories for children, many of which have been published in different periodicals; a History of Prairie Township, Jewell county, Kansas, published in the *Jewell County Republican;* and this Genealogy of the Seaton family. There is also in course of construction, as opportunity offers, a series of stories of army life as seen by a private in the rear rank and a corporal, and a book of quotations composed of interesting statements found in the writer's reading.

As a matter of gossip, which the greater part of this book is, and which does very well within the family but is decidedly poor business outside of that holy tribunal, it might be mentioned that the soldier-boy was more than once offered a commission while in the army, but very foolishly refused it because he thought one so young and inexperienced ought not to be put in command over older men with whom he had been associated all of his life, and who were much better fitted to command than a seventeen-year-old boy.

It might also be allowable to mention the fact that he was the Master of three different Granges of Patrons of Husbandry while granges were the fashion among farmers; that he is a Republican in politics, and a brother-in-law to the Methodists in religious matters; that is, he married a Methodist lady, and considers it the best day's work he ever did.

While in the army he took part in the battles of the Weldon Railroad, the Jerusalem Plank Road, Hatch's Run, and was in at the taking of Petersburg, and was on the way to Richmond when the assassination of President Lincoln occurred and the war came to an end.

CHAPTER XXIX.

THE CHILDREN OF ANDREW P. AND LAURA A. SEATON (CONTINUED).

JAMES HENRY SEATON, the second son in the family, was born July 2, 1849, at Henderson, New York, where he passed his youth attending the village school and enjoying all of the pleasures that came in his way. He was naturally sociable, fun-loving, and purse-free. He could find more to laugh at in a day than some others could in a week. He made friends wherever he happened to be, and apparently without effort. When he was sent to the field to hoe corn he was sure to need rest every time he came out to the fence where another boy was doing like work in an adjoining field, and he would become so interested in the conversation of his company that it was nothing uncommon for him to sit on the fence visiting while his brother would hoe another round.

His father once summed up his predominant traits of character by saying that he was always laughing, whistling or crying, when he was a small boy.

When James was grown to man's estate, he took to the water as naturally as a catfish to mud. He was a sailor on the Great Lakes for several seasons, spending his winters around Henderson, Watertown, Rutland, and vicinity, often spending all of the wages of the previous season before the winter was over. He seemed to care nothing for money, except as it could add to his and his friends' pleasure.

One winter, while enjoying himself around Rutland sleigh-riding, dancing, skating, etc., he made the acquaintance of Francelia Alma Cotton, with whom he was afterward spliced, as the sailors say. Miss Cotton was born December 26, 1848, at or near Rutland, New York, and was married to the sailor-boy at Black River, New York, on August 22, 1872.

When he had a family James quit the lakes and tried his hand at farming near Floyd, Floyd county, Iowa, where the family had located.

After an indifferent experience as an Iowa agriculturist, he set sail in a prairie schooner for sunny Kansas, to embark in the sod-house line of wheat- and stock-raisers. After waiting eighteen months for his first wheat crop to heave in sight, after it was sown, and when they had eaten everything they brought with them, without raising even a mouthful, they again hoisted anchor and set sail

FAMILY OF JAMES H. SEATON.

in their mover-wagons, steering their course back to Iowa as a sure haven; but there they again met adverse winds, and in course of time hove about and started a voyage of discovery over the billowy prairies of Nebraska. They finally landed at Wallace, in Lincoln county, where they had their port of refuge for a number of years. They had a comfortable home in town, and a half-section of land not far away.

James has always been a lover of fine horses and has owned a good many, some of which were well bred and excellent roadsters. One of his admirable conceits has always been that he did not intend to starve himself nor his team to death while going from one town to the next, and he never did the like if his team was able to make the distance on time with what encouragement he was able to give it, though it should be understood that he soon disposed of horses that needed to be urged to do their best, and that he was a good feeder and care-taker of his horses as well as of himself and his family.

During his eventful life, James has tried several different lines of business with the intention of making his fortune, having at different times been a sailor and a farmer, as has been stated; then he was remarkably successful at collecting bad debts for others for some years; has operated a livery stable, a natural outgrowth of his love for fine driving-horses; has doctored horses for those in need of such help; been the undertaker for all the country round, at no expense to anyone except himself; sold and set up agricultural implements and machinery. At the present writing he is superintendent of a line of creamery stations extending over four hundred miles of railroad lines in western and southern Nebraska. He owns a two-hundred-acre farm, where he lives, and enough other land to bring his holdings up to a thousand acres of Nebraska prairie farm-land.

James and "Frank," as he calls his wife, have raised quite a family of fine, bright children, among whom are now living, Hattie Maybelle; Charles Andrew; Laura Pearl; James Henry 2d; and Merton Robert. The children who have died are: Gertrude Alma; Kittie Isabelle; Perry Albert; and Cassie May, We may have more to say of these children further along in this book.

FRANKLIN PIERCE SEATON was born at Henderson, New York, on March 8, 1852, and died April 6, 1853.

GEORGE FERGUSON SEATON, named for his uncle, George Ferguson, was born January 21, 1854, at Henderson, New York. He is the heavy-weight of all our branch of the family since his great-grandfather, Asa Seaton, whom he resembles in having dark hair and being large in person.

George is a great stay-at-home practitioner. It is doubtful if he was away from home over-night of his own volition, except on

FAMILY OF GEORGE F. SEATON.

business, and once when he came to Kansas to spy out a better location for a home, and to visit the family of the writer. And then he would have turned back before bedtime the first night of his visit if he had only his own feelings to consult, or at east that is the opinion of his host on that occasion. He is always the same pleasant, quiet, honorable gentleman every day of his life, a friend to every one he knows, enjoying the confidence and respect of all his acquaintances.

On the thirteenth day of January, 1878, he was married to Clara Fannie Bulkley, of Floyd, Iowa, where they have made their home since that most momentous event of their lives, their marriage, unless we have to except the birth of their first child.

Mrs. Seaton, *née* Bulkley, was born May 9, 1857, receiving a fine education, and, if I mistake not, was a successful school teacher before her marriage. She is a bright, stirring, wideawake lady, a tidy housekeeper and a model entertainer, as the writer can testify from his own experience when he paid them a visit about as far back as the year 1880.

George has made steady progress in his business affairs, until the last we heard he owned a fine farm near the city of Floyd, which he rented out, and a lovely home within the confines of the city, where he lives and enjoys the fruits of his labors and serves the city in the capacity of Street Commissioner.

The children born to George F. and Clara F. Seaton were: 1. Maud Ethel; 2. Frederick Bulkley; 3. Andrew Pennell; and 4. Clara Bulkley Seaton,—of whom more as we proceed.

JENNIE CLARA SEATON, the baby and pet of the family, was born on November 16, 1856, at Henderson, New York. She was a handsome girl, having fair complexion and long, black, curling hair, which she usually wore in ringlets. So much favored was she in the matter of hair that she could comb it out straight before going to school and when she returned at eventide it would have coiled itself into ringlets, and wet weather that would ruin most girl's curls would only make hers curl the closer.

Clara was a very studious girl, and was usually at or near the head of her classes. She was especially a wonderful speller, having attended a whole term of school when quite small without missing a word in spelling. She and her cousin, Florence C. Seaton, won the prize as the best spellers in their school, if not in the county.

She went with the family to Iowa in 1870, and when old enough married William H. Morgan, at Floyd, Iowa, on October 29, 1876, the Reverend Samuel Sherin, pastor of the Methodist Church of that place, officiating.

JENNIE CLARA SEATON.

Their children, all of whom were born in Iowa, were: 1. Hattie Ethelyn Morgan, born in Floyd, on July 21, 1878; 2. Clara May and 3. Katie Mabel, the twins, born in Charles City township on December 19, 1880. Katie died December 25, 1890. 4. Oliver Clinton, born December 27, 1885, died January 20, 1891; and Lynn Ferguson Seaton Morgan, who was born at Riverton, Floyd county, October 12, 1894.

The family started from Iowa on November 15, 1895, to seek a new home in the fruit belt of Missouri, where they hoped to find a climate less severe. After a journey of a month and a day in snow, sleet, rain, and of course mud to hinder them, they arrived

at Bartlett, Shannon county. Missouri, on December 16, 1895.
They bought a small fruit farm, where they had every promise of
raising abundance of apples, peaches, cherries, and pears, not to
mention the small fruits of all kinds, which grow almost sponta-
neously as though native to the locality, or, as some one has stated
it, "as though the soil were own mother to them, as it is to the
weeds, instead of only stepmother."

From August 20, 1900, to February 11, 1902, they lived in the
city of Winona, Missouri, running a hotel during that time.

MR. AND MRS. W. H. MORGAN AND LYNN FERGUSON SEATON MORGAN.

They have given their children a good education, and at least
one of the girls has taught school. From the last-named date up
to the fall of 1905 they were back on the farm raising fruit and livestock, since which time they have made their home at Jewell City,
Kansas, where Mr. Morgan has worked at carpentry and Miss
Clara has been the proprietor of a "racket" store, called the Curiosity Shop.

Hattie Ethelyn Morgan married William T. Guider, a New-

Yorker, who has been a member of the fire department of Omaha, Nebraska, for twelve years, and has had several very narrow escapes from death in the line of his duty. The Guiders own two farms, one in Dakota and the other in Missouri.

Lynn Morgan is attending school in Jewell City, Kansas.

CLARA MAY MORGAN.

W. T. AND HATTIE (MORGAN) GUIDER.

CHAPTER XXX.

THE CHILDREN OF BOYINGTON C. AND CORNELIA SEATON.

PETER NEWCOMB CUSHMAN SEATON, the first-born son of "Uncle Boy" and "Aunt Cornelia," was born at Henderson, New York on October 10, 1850. He lived in the neighborhood of his birthplace until he was seventeen years of age, when he moved to Charles City, Floyd county, Iowa, and engaged in farming. "Cush" was as full of fun as a bee-sting is of poison, and that is about as full as it is possible to be, and it is a wonder that he, as well as most other boys, ever lived through the thoughtless scrapes of his younger days, after he began to run on the streets and mingle with other boys of his own age.

In the year 1871 he married Ella Genevieve Clark, his cousin, and daughter of Frances Phidelia (Seaton) Clark, who married E. M. Clark.

Cushman and Ella were married at Charles City, Iowa, on December 16, 1871, by C. B. Hamlin. Their children were: 1. Zua Olga; 2. Jennie Cornelia, 3. Jessie Angelia, the latter two being twins; and 4. Fay Cushman.

It was in 1877, I believe, that Cousin Cushman moved from Charles City to Algona, in the same State, and there followed farming for some time, then operated a tow mill and hay press. In 1887 the family made another move, this time to Orange City, where Cushman again managed a tow mill and hay press for several years. Then he took up electric-light work, directing the electric-light plant of that city for about two years, when, on account of poor health, he gave up that work and moved to Springfield, South Dakota, and began farming again. After raising one crop in Dakota he moved to Birch Tree, Shannon county, Missouri, starting on October 10, 1894. At the latter place he followed farming until in May, 1899, when he took the back track for Springfield, South Dakota, where he lived at the writing of this poor sketch of a superior gentleman, in January, 1902.

WALLACE SEATON, another son of this family, has kept his doings to himself, so far as the writer is concerned, except that he is a sailor on the Great Lakes.

MAUD SEATON, the daughter of the family, is the wife of Charles N. Smith, in Rochester, New York, where her father lived until the time of his death. They have no children, but lavish their affections on some choice cats of an aristocratic breed, Angoras. Their home is as tasty and tidy as anyone could wish,—a model, in fact. Their location was at St. Paul street when the writer was there in the summer of 1901.

THE ONLY CHILD OF LEONARD AND HATTIE SEATON.

FLORENCE C. SEATON, the only child of Leonard, Jr., and Hattie (Bates) Seaton, was born in Henderson, New York, in 1856. She was a bright, vivacious, happy girl, the particular chum of my sister, Clara Jennie Seaton. They were in the same classes at school, and jointly won a prize as the best spellers in the school, or county, neither having missed a word in spelling during the term.

In the course of time she married Doctor W. G. Terry, a practicing physician of Henderson, where we visited them for a short time in 1901, making the acquaintance of the rest of the family at that time.

Mrs. Terry was an active member of the Woman's Christian Temperance Union, having been the secretary of the society until her health failed. She was also a member of the Eastern Star Lodge and the Grange, as well as of the Daughters of the American Revolution, and of the Universalist Church of Henderson.

Doctor and Mrs. Terry have raised two bright, interesting children, now grown to manhood and womanhood. Richard Seaton Terry, the elder, is a full-fledged lawyer, having graduated from the Albany (New York) Law School, and Hattie, "the married baby," as her mother fondly spoke of her, has joined her fortunes with Professor J. Aiken Montague to found a home of their own, and is the happy mother of a son and heir, Terry Seaton Montague, born August 7, 1905, at Henderson, New York. Professor Montague is probably a cousin of the writer's room-mate at Union Academy, David A. Montague, and of Harrison Montague, who swung the birch over us in the Henderson school in the days of our callow youth, and still once more, of Joel Montague, who was the last teacher in the Old North School House while we attended that venerable institution.

Professor Montague was principal of the village school at Henderson in 1901, while we were there.

Mrs. Terry was a great sufferer from something like neuralgia during the closing years of her life. She died at the family home in Henderson, New York, on June 21, 1902, mourned by all who knew her. Mrs. C. L. Boyce was a constant attendant upon Mrs. Terry in her last illness. No daughter could have done more for a mother.

We are reminded that "Death loves a shining mark," and Mrs. Terry will be sadly missed in her home village, where she was always prominent in social, literary, and religious work. She was a fine elocutionist and was always ready to give her services in helping and training others to help in church and other entertainments.

Her funeral was held in the Universalist Church, of which she was an active working member, Rev. George Adams officiating. The interment was at the Evergreen Cemetery.

THE CHILDREN OF SAMUEL G. AND ELLEN (GRAHAM) SEATON.

Fred Albert Seaton was born at Kingston, Wisconsin, November 22, 1857. He was married to Mary E. Kellog, and they have three children: Florence, Blanch, and Hazel. Their home is in or near Chicago, Illinois.

Mary Seaton, daughter of Samuel G., was born at Milwaukee, Wisconsin, December 11, 1862, and married to Myron S. Kellog, by whom she has two children, Leorard Seaton Kellog and Florence Kellog, both of whom are unmarried, I believe.

FANNIE SEATON was first made acquainted with the other members of the family at Kingston, Wisconsin, on March 1, 1866. She was later married to Frank A. Mower, and has presented her husband with one child, Annie Louise Mower.

JANE SEATON was born September 12, 1868, at Kingston, Wisconsin. She married William F. Brabrook, Jr. They have one child, a son, whose name is Ralph Seaton Pope Brabrook.

ELLEN GRAHAM SEATON, born August 13, 1870, at Kingston, Wisconsin, married Cyril Larkin Coussens. They have no children, so far as we know.

LOUISE SEATON was born at Chicago, Illinois, on May 11, 1873, and married Fred Osborne Munn when she had finished her education in school and in the home. They have one heir, whose name is Robert Osborne Munn.

CHAPTER XXXI.

JULIA SEATON, only daughter of Chauncey E. and Sarah E. Seaton, was born on May 11, 1868, at Owatonna, Minnesota. On account of the well-known modesty of her father we have no account of her early life, though the proud parents of a first-born child are not usually chary of their praises of their treasure. But, from the nature of the case, we feel sure she had everything that could add to her happiness, including a liberal education. No home, however, can be made so attractive to young people that they do not, after a while, want one of their own, and this case was no exception to the general rule. So Julia Seaton gave her heart and hand into the keeping of Mr. Albert Walter Frost. The ceremony that made them husband and wife was performed by the Reverend George C. Tanner, of Faribault, Minnesota, at No. 3360 Calumet avenue, Chicago, Illinois, at the home of the happy bride's parents, on the last day of the year 1890.

THE ONLY CHILD OF AMBROSE B. AND AMELIA F. (SELFRIDGE) SEATON.

CHAUNCEY CHARLES, or CHARLES CHAUNCEY, SEATON, the only child of Ambrose B. and Amelia F. Seaton, was born October 16, 1881, at Marshalltown, Iowa, but was spared to his loving parents less than one short year, dying on the third of July of the year following that in which he was born, and in the same city.

Inscrutable are the ways of Providence, and past finding out, that this little rosebud should have been taken from his doting parents just as he began to twine the tendrils of his love about their hearts. They could have supplied his every want and educated him to fill an honored and useful place in the world, dispensing love and comfort to the needy of his abundance; while

in many other homes, where there is only a crust and a slip for the
little ones, they are to be found in numbers, though sometimes not
in good behavior and in the ways of wisdom.

THE CHILDREN OF GEORGE L. AND SARAH VIOLA SEATON.

ANNA LEE SEATON, the eldest child of Uncle George and Aunt
"Ola," was born at Lamott, Jackson county, Iowa, on the 27th
of March, 1870. After the careful training in the home of her
youth, under the direction of her competent mother, and in the
schools of Iowa and Nebraska, she was well fitted to fill any position that might attract her liking. As it proved, she decided to
take charge of a home of her own, and as a means to that end ac-
ceded to the earnest solicitation of Franklin Moore Borolin to
become his wife, and was married to him at Omaha, Nebraska,
on October 14th, 1896, the Reverend Frederick Tonge performing
the ever-interesting ceremony.

The only child in the Borolin home at the time of this writing
is a son, who was born on the last day of the year 1901. After
canvassing all of the names within their knowledge without finding one musical enough to suit so sweet a babe, they finally decided to call him Seaton Ayres Borolin; and who is there who has
the hardihood to say that their choice might have been improved
upon?

The Borolin home was located not far from Omaha, Nebraska,
but over the line in Iowa, at the thriving little city of Harlan, in
Shelby county.

LENA LOUISE SEATON, the second daughter, is a namesake of her
Aunt Louise (Seaton) Pettengill—of whom she reminds the writer
every time he sees her—and was born on March 24th, 1872, at
Henderson, New York. She is a lovely girl, and it is a wonder the
young men of Omaha would take no for an answer to their suit;
but, so far, she has resisted all of their pleading, and she stays with
her widowed mother at their modern home at 3857 Charles street,
Omaha, Nebraska.

Lena has had the benefit of the best teachers Omaha could
furnish, and is a scholar of no mean ability. If I am not mistaken,
—14

she was studying in the office of one of Omaha's leading physicians, at the date of our visit at their home on the occasion of the Trans-Mississippi Exposition.

BENJAMIN LEVI SEATON, the first son in the family, was born at Wyoming, Jones county, Iowa, on the Ides of March, 1879. After graduating from the best schools in Omaha, Nebraska, he accepted a position with the American Express Company, and has continued with that company since that time. There is no reason for doubt that he will serve the company well, and I take the liberty of predicting, although not a prophet nor the son of a prophet, that he wil reach a high and responsible position in the head office of the company. He was promoted to the St. Louis office, where we met him during the Louisiana Purchase Exposition in the year 1904.

GEORGE LOUIS SEATON, the youngest of the children, was born on the 24th day of October, in the year 1880, at Wyoming, Iowa, and received the finishing touches to his education in Omaha, Nebraska, where the family must have moved soon after his birth. As soon as he had reached the age when the American Express Company would accept his services, he began working his way up from the bottom round of the ladder in the city of Omaha, and he still continues with them. But after proving his fitness for the position given him, and his sterling honesty, untiring industry, and reliability, the company promoted him to a better position, and sent him to the St. Louis office, where he is yet working for them, and where he will, more than likely, be found as long as the company desires good reliable men and he wants a situation. We noticed, in our short visit at his office, that every one depended upon George to know where any desired information could be found, and he was competent to give the required information.

George Louis Seaton was married to Sara Bent Wall, of Washington, D. C., at the home of the bride's father, on the 22d day of May, in the year of our Lord 1902. An invitation to the wedding, received by the writer, says the happy couple, now made one flesh, will be at home, 2700 Russell avenue, St. Louis, Missouri, after June 15, 1902.

THE CHILDREN OF HERBERT J. AND HELEN IDA SEATON.

Leonard Barber Seaton, the first child and son, was born a Munnsville, New York, on December 11, 1878. He is supposed to be still among the living, but where, we are not advised. Doubtless he is making history that would be interesting to each of his relatives, could they learn the facts in the case.

Donald Adelphas Seaton was born, at the same place as his brother, on January 17th, 1882. If we knew more of his story it would be our delight to make the information known to the other members of the family at large.

THE CHILDREN OF ROBERT AND MARY (STEWART) SEATON.

Chauncey Alfred Seaton was born at Muncie, Indiana, on June 8th, 1874. He is a stirring business man, one who takes off his coat and goes into business as though he enjoyed it.

He married Anna May Mobray on November 18, 1902, at Plymouth, Missouri. Their address was 2610 East Eighteenth street, Kansas City, Missouri, when the writer visited them.

Mrs. Seaton is a lady who shows her good breeding and training in every act and word. She assists in waiting upon the customers in the store when her household and society duties will permit. Chauncey Alfred is a Methodist, and in all probability a Republican.

Lulu Stewart Seaton married F. E. Dent, of Oswego, Kansas, in her twentieth year, having been born on June 21, 1876, and married at Parsons, Kansas, September 29, 1895. They have one child, Marie Dent, born in the spring of 1897. Mrs. Dent is a Presbyterian in religious affiliation.

Wallace Robert Seaton, born October 4, 1878, is now a railway mail clerk on the Frisco line.

Mabel Helen Seaton was born March 28, 1881. She graduated from the Chetopa (Kansas) High School on May 17, 1898. She is described to us by a disinterested judge as a "fine-looking lady, with brains to take care of herself anywhere and at any time."

CARRIE LORAINE SEATON was born June 18, 1884. She died in Armourdale, Kansas, February 5, 1901.

RUTH MARIE SEATON was born July 21, 1891, and died on February 22, 1895.

DOROTHY MARGARET SEATON, a daughter by adoption, was born February 20, 1894, and of course lives at home with her parents.

THE CHILDREN OF LEONARD T. AND NANCY ALICE SEATON.

Frank Grant Seaton, the eldest child, was born at Pecatonica, Illinois, on December 1, 1878. He married Cornelia Cleveland ("no kin to Grover," we are told), at Plano, Illinois, on June 24 1903, the interesting ceremony being administered by the Rev. Doctor Henry, pastor of the First Baptist Church. Frank is a farmer in calling.

EARL GARFIELD SEATON was born January 26, 1881, at Pecatonica, Illinois, and is now his own man, or was before he was married to Georgia Potts, of Viroqua, Wisconsin, on the 6th day of August, 1905. The home of the happy couple is at the last-named place.

SIDNEY BLAINE SEATON was born at Plano, Illinois, September 28, 1883. He is a mechanic, and lives at 1874 Seeley avenue, Chicago, Illinois, since his marriage to Clara G. Vogelberg, in Plano, on the 21st of August, 1905.

EMELINE MARY SEATON, the first daughter to take up her residence with the family, was born August 15, 1886, at Plano, Illinois, where she still resides, a young lady with the best of life before her.

STANLEY WING SEATON was born at Plano, Illinois, on May 23, 1890, and is evidently striving for an education.

HARRISON INGALLS SEATON was born November 3, 1892, at Plano, Illinois.

JESSIE CAROLINE SEATON, the youngest of the children, was born February 18, 1896, at Plano, Illinois.

CHAPTER XXXII.

THE CHILDREN OF OREN A. AND SARAH E. SEATON.

GOLDIE MYRTLE SEATON.

GOLDIE MYRTLE SEATON, the first-born of the writer's family, was born on the Seaton homestead, in section thirty-three, in Prairie township, Jewell county, Kansas, on the 26th day of November, of the year 1879. She was a "wee bit morsel," with fingers like bird-claws, almost, weighing only six pounds with her clothes on, at the first weighing. She was quite a bright, observing babe, seeming to see and notice things about her at an early age. When only a few weeks old she startled her mother considerably by laughing aloud. Her father held her in his arms and was showing the canary to her. Every time her father would whistle the bird would chirrup and often sing a stave or two, and Goldie laughed at the bird's singing, a clear distinct laugh.

Goldie never learned to creep like other children, but would roll over and over on the floor when she wished to go from one part of the room to another. When she was about nine months old she began to climb up beside a chair, and stand, holding on with her hands, but before she was able to walk alone she had quite a bad spell of whooping-cough, which reduced her strength so much that she was over a year old when she first walked by herself.

She seemed to be entirely fearless as a little girl when in her father's company, and would stand perfectly erect and quiet on his hand when extended at the length of his arm, something none of her brothers or her sister could do.

Before she was two years old she made a trip to St. Joseph, Champaign county, Illinois, with her parents, in a covered wagon or "prairie schooner," to visit her Grandpapa Bartley and other relatives, and the next year made another journey to Floyd, Floyd county, Iowa, to see and be seen by the Seaton relations.

Goldie was not allowed to attend school until she was about seven years old, but she made good progress after she was once started. She usually ranked number one in her classes, except when she was obliged to stay at home on account of sickness. She graduated from the common school in the summer of 1895, before she was sixteen years old, her Common School Diploma being dated June 22, 1895.

At the examination of teachers after her graduation, she won a prize jointly with Miss Grace Price, a High School graduate, offered to the common-school graduate who should pass the best examination at the county Teachers' Institute. The prize was to be fifteen dollars, or the expenses of the teacher at the County Institute, and was offered by Honorable R. W. Turner, a Mankato lawyer, a former County Superintendent of Public Instruction, and ex-Minister to Spain from the United States Government. The following letter from Mr. Turner expla'ns itself:

MANKATO, KANSAS, September 11, 1895.
Miss Goldie Seaton, Jewell City, Kansas:

MY DEAR MISS SEATON—It affords me pleasure to herewith enclose draft for $7.50 as a promised prize to the Common School Graduate of Jewell county who should distinguish himself, or herself, above all others at the first examination for teachers' certificates taking place after the graduation of the class of 1895.

I have but one regret, and that is that my circumstances in life are such that I cannot make the prize more substantial. I can, however, enclose with it my best wishes for your success in life, and at the same time feel assured that the search after knowledge, so well begun, will not be abandoned even if it be true that,

> "Ever after mortal effort, ever after mortal pains,
> Something to which light is shadow, something unexpressed remains;
> Ever after human question, ever after human quest,
> Something farther than the farthest, something better than the best."

Faithfully, your friend,

R. W. TURNER.

Some time before this, Goldie won a gold pen and plush-lined case, offered by the editor of *The Jewell County Republican*, for the best essay, to contain fifty words of the editor's choosing. (Words chosen by editor given in italics.) The judges in the contest were Professor Cook, of the city schools, Mrs. Etta Harrington, and Mrs. Theodore Bartholow. The essay written by Goldie was as follows:

ALCOHOL.

Alcohol is an intoxicating drink and a *poison*. It is sold by *wholesale*, and some men make a *fortune* selling it. It is in *demand* in nearly every *city*. Some people who keep *boarders* think it is *generous* to use *wine* and *cider* on the table. *Once on a time* I heard a young *woman tell* one of her friends about a *father* that drank, who *died* and *left* a family. Their father wasted his *money* buying alcoholic drinks, and now they are *poor*. The mother tried to *coax* him not to *drink*, but it did no good. They were not *happy* or *jolly*. Sometimes the boys and *girls* had no good *clothes*. The girls seldom got a new *apron*, and they often went in *debt* for things. They were *young*, and wanted to *work* hard and *earn* a living. They were *dear* to their mother, and they *loved* her. These people often used *pounded* corn instead of flour, and considered it a treat to have *coffee* and *potatoes*. The boys did many *jobs* to earn a living, and were among the *best* in the city where they lived. Oftentimes the *ground* was covered with snow and they had no *shoes*. One of the boys used *tobacco*. All of the *housework* was done by the *mother*. She was strict and *taught* her *sons* not to drink, as she *herself* was a temperance woman, and they grew to be *good* and *true* men and they were liked and *respected* by all. She was *blessed* by them in after-years for making them temperance men. Their *practicing* to keep from drinking *will* help others not to use it. They worked like *beavers* to get *money* enough to get a good *education.* They were patient and *waited* for good times, and now it has come. Their mother is living happily with them, and expects to spend the rest of her life in peace with her children.

Jewell City, Kansas. Age 11. Words 318. GOLDIE SEATON.

On July 26, 1895, Goldie took part in a Demorest Contest at the Methodist Church in Jewell City. The title of her declamation was, "Prohibition Warriors." The essay she read at the graduating exercises of the common school on June 22, 1895, was "How Success is Won." And the subject of her essay at the Class Day exercises was "Chronicles." Her graduating oration was called "Probabilities of the Twentieth Century."

Goldie wrote the School Notes for *The Republican* during her last year in the High School, and was invited to attend a concert, with all of the other correspondents of the paper, and before the concert an oyster supper was served the writers who make a local paper interesting,—the correspondents,—all at the expense of the editor, Mr. William C. Palmer; the entertainment taking place on New Year's Day, 1896.

Goldie graduated from the Jewell City High School in the summer of 1896. Her High School Diploma is dated May 6th of that year, and she received a Teachers' County Certificate dated August 23, 1896, in which her grades were none of them less than 90, with two 99s and two 100s. She received another certificate, dated August 21, 1897, and in the fall contracted to teach the winter term of school in the Vance district, No. 34, which she carried through successfully, as young as she was at the time. She boarded at home and drove back and forth all through the winter.

On March 21, 1899, she entered Baker University, at Baldwin, Kansas, taking the Normal course, with a determination to secure a State certificate that would entitle her to teach any school in the State without further examinations. During her studies in the University she was employed to teach geography during one term, and to assist one of the professors in some other work. She graduated with honors in due time, and received recommendations from the professors under whom she studied that were calculated to satisfy anyone interested in the matter that she did faithful work and that she was fully qualified to manage any school in a creditable manner.

In the fall of 1899 she engaged to teach the winter term in the Wyland district, and again that winter she drove to and from her home all of the time, except a few nights when she visited with some of the patrons of the school.

After her graduation from Baker she was employed in the city graded school at Ionia, Kansas, and is at the present time one of the corps of teachers at Jewell City.

CHAPTER XXXIII.

THE CHILDREN OF OREN A. AND SARAH E. SEATON (CONTINUED).

NOBLE FAY SEATON.

NOBLE FAY SEATON, the second child and first son, making the "King's wish" complete, a son and a daughter, was born at St. Joseph, Champaign county, Illinois, at the home of his Grandfather Bartley, on March 16, 1882.

Being the first son in the family, and of course thought to be a wonderful boy, his mother chose the name Noble for him, as expressing at once her idea of what he was and what she desired and believed he would be. His father decided on the name Fay for him, because it was short, easy to pronounce, and besides, it could not be shortened into a nickname.

In the fall, when he was about six months old, he took a ride in a prairie schooner to the Seaton homestead in Prairie township.

Jewell county, Kansas, where he lived until in the summer of 1884, when the family moved to Glasco, Cloud county, of the same State, where his father worked at the grain business while Fay toddled around keeping his mother busy looking after him. After a year spent in Glasco, the family moved to Beloit, in Mitchell county, where they stayed another year, then made another move,- making the three removes that Franklin said were as bad as a fire. This time took the family to Jewell City, in Jewell county, where he has since been when at home.

He attended the city schools almost every day they were in session until he was graduated from the High School.

When Fay was eight years old he wrote an essay on "The Late War" for *The Jewell County Republican*, as explained in the sketch of his sister's life. Writing against boys four years older, he did not win the prize, but his essay was so well thought of by the committee of judges and the editor of *The Republican* that it was printed, and was as follows:

THE LATE WAR.

Once on a time there was a war between the Northern and Southern men. Many fathers and their *sons* went from the *city* and country, and were wounded and *died*. My *father* was a soldier. He says the officers were very strict. The soldiers had *coffee* to drink and sometimes *potatoes* to eat They slept on the *ground* and had a knapsack for a table. Some of them drank whisky and chewed *tobacco* by *wholesale*, and when off duty were *jolly* and *happy*. Some of the men who had a *fortune* before the war began wasted their money, buying every thing they liked, and thought it *generous* to treat the soldiers to things that did them harm. Others *waited* and worked with a *will* and did not go into *debt*, and by constant *practicing* saving their *money* they made themselves comfortable. *Clothes* were *dear* and the *girls* had to *work* like *beavers* to earn money. Even the *blessed* little boys and girls did a great many small *jobs*. Many a *young woman left* school and neglected her *education* to help her *mother*, who kept *boarders*, do the *housework*, or to work out to *earn* money to buy *herself* an *apron* Many parched rye and drank it for *coffee* when it was in demand, and *pounded* corn and used it for meal. I like to hear my papa *tell* how they *taught* the rebels to obey the law they could not *coax* them to do. Every loyal person *respected* the soldiers, who *loved* their country and wanted them to do their *best* and be *good* and *true* to it.

Jewell City. Age 8. Words used 264. FAY SEATON

When Fay was a little fellow about five years old a lady and gentleman called on his parents unannounced, and being a little short on pastry at the time, their mother told Goldie and Fay they must not ask for pie, as there were only two pieces, which would be served to the guests. All went along as merry as a wedding ball until the guests began eating their pie, when Fay said, as innocent as could be: "I must not ask for pie, for mamma has only two pieces." It is doubtful if Fay, or even Chauncey Depew, ever made a post-prandial speech that more completely brought down the house than that timely remark. The guests, who happened to be near and very intimate neighbors and friends, and the parents, laughed immoderately, while Fay gazed at them in big-eyed wonder, not understanding why they were so much amused.

When Fay was a small boy he had a habit of sticking his tongue in his cheek, when he was interested in his play, and making the most curious humming, buzzing, grunting noise I ever heard a child make. He seemed unconscious of making any noise, and would keep it up for a long time when busily engaged playing by himself. I do not know that he usually made the noise when playing with other children.

Fay was a good hand doing chores among the stock, but he never liked to work around machinery.

He was quick to learn, and might easily have been at the head of his classes, for his scholarship was the best, but his deportment usually brought his averages down so that he was most of the time rank two, which might have been much worse.

In the summer of 1900 he went to Salina, Kansas, to take a business course at the Wesleyan Business College, to fit himself with a good business training and be able to take charge of office work as stenographer, typewriter and bookkeeper. He graduated with the highest honors, being promoted ahead of his classes two or three times and after he had graduated, received a position with Mr. T. D. Fitzpatrick in his real estate and insurance business, which included the business of Grand Secretary of the Occidental Insurance Company, through the recommendation of Professor Roach of the college, as being the best in the school at that time.

The following clipping from the Salina *Herald* is perhaps worth preserving in this connection:

"Fay Seaton, of Jewell City, a late graduate of Kansas Wesleyan Business College, made one of the most brilliant records ever made by a student of that school. He finished the course several weeks ahead of the class in which he first started, and has the honor of being one of the fastest operators on the typewriter as well as the most swift in taking dictation. Prof. Roach has reason to be proud of Mr. Seaton, and his clean school record and upright, Christian character would be worthy of recommendation to anyone wishing to employ a stenographer. He went home last Saturday to spend Christmas."

Since beginning work Fay has saved his wages and even worked over-hours, investing his savings in Salina real estate, and selling again when he could do so to advantage, until he owns and rents some houses of his own, beside owning some unimproved city lots.

He is a member of the Epworth League and the Methodist Episcopal Church of Salina, Kansas, where he lived. He cast his first vote in the spring of this year of grace 1903, and is an active worker in the Republican party.

In addition to his other duties, Fay, has edited the *Occidental Monthly,* an insurance periodical, for the society of which it is the official organ, at the earnest solicitation of the management, doing the work mostly at night after a busy day in the insurance office.

Fay has since entered the Northwestern University of Evanston, Ills., with the view of taking a classical course.

CHAPTER XXXIV.

THE CHILDREN OF OREN A. AND SARAH E. SEATON (CONTINUED.)

ROY ANDREW SEATON.

ROY ANDREW SEATON, the second son and third child in the family, was born on April 17th, 1884, at Glasco, Cloud county, Kansas. Before he was two weeks old Roy had begun to cut his teeth, and by the time he was a month old he had two teeth fully cut through. He grew to be a full-faced, red-cheeked toddler, with black, curly hair that his mother usually curled in ringlets,— altogether a remarkably comely child.

One evening when he accompanied his father down-town, Mr. John D. Robertson, one of the most wealthy men in the county, said he would give the half of all he was worth for such a son. Very naturally the father placed a much greater estimate on the possession of such a son.

When Roy began to run around by himself in the yard he went out near the stable, where a young colt was lariatted, and, being too familiar on a short acquaintance, made an attempt to approach his coltship at the wrong end and received a kick from both the colt's hind feet on a soft spot just below his belt that knocked him down and scared him considerably, but did no other perceptible harm. From that day Roy's bad luck with horses has continued. He has had his full share of horses running away from him, though he never received any bodily injury in any of his runaways. Even after he began to like to visit a certain young lady, the saddle-horse that he rode out on that occasion broke loose just as Roy was about to mount for his return trip, and he was obliged to make the eight miles to his home just far enough behind the horse to be out of reach of it. So they walked home together, Roy and "Mack," in a sort of Indian file.

While Roy was yet wearing dresses he used to come up to the elevator and drive the horse that operated the cleaning machinery before the gasoline plant was installed. He would sit on a seat attached to the sweep and ride around and around for hours at a time. He had nothing to do, except to see that the horse did not stop, and could do that as well as a man. Sometimes he would fall asleep while the horse plodded on, but he seldom tired of his position of superintendent of the motive power.

One cold day, as he was driving away wrapped up in his shawl and mittens, his father noticed a tear on his cheek, and asked what was the trouble He replied that he was cold. It had never occurred to him that he could quit his place until the job was finished, and that has been his rule of conduct ever since. His one predominant trait of character has been to stick to his task until it was completed.

At one time while Roy was a little fellow there came to the house a negro woman with her brood of little pickaninnies, wishing to rent one of our houses. Roy had never before seen a negro, and watched the group in big-eyed wonder. When his mother told the woman she would send to the office for me, Roy was all eagerness to go. "I'll go, mamma! Let me go, mamma!" he exclaimed. So up to the office he came in a great hurry, arriving considerably out of breath. and called out: "Papa! there's a lady at the house who wishes to see you. And papa. she's *awful dirty!*" "Why. Roy." I replied, "you ought not say such a thing; you might hurt the lady's feelings if she knew what you said." "Well. but papa. she *is awful dirty.*" He did not know at that time that there is a black that will not wash off.

Roy has always been a studious boy. preferring books to street gossip. and has always shown a determination to fully comprehend any subject under consideration. not so much to be able to recite well as to understand the why and wherefore, the cause and effect of the subject. He was almost invariably reported by his teachers as ranking number one in all of his classes.

In the garret of his home are yet some of the many forms of apparatus that he and his classmate. Robert Sandborn, constructed while they were studying natural philosophy at school. Some of the models were very crude and rough. for their tools and materials were such as they could pick up about the place. but in every instance. so far as known to the writer. the contrivance illustrated the principle involved. They made induction coils, an electric friction-generator. electric bells. an electrophorus. an electric telegraph. and a miniature acetylene gas plant. that I now recall. besides a large number of little things hardly worth mentioning.

The telegraph line was located in the grain office, and extended from the southwest corner of the room. "Kansas City." to the northeast corner. "Chicago." the line running up and down the walls and along the ceiling. There the boys practiced for many an evening after school and supper were over. until, finally, Robert secured a position in a railroad telegraph office, assisted. no doubt. by the practice received in the grain office telegraph line.

The electric friction-generator was something of a curiosity. It consisted of a platform about fifteen inches square. with two uprights at the sides which supported an axle or shaft, on one end of which was a small pulley. A large driving-pulley was secured to another upright on the same side of the platform as the small pulley. These uprights were securely braced. and a belt connected the two pulleys. A large drenching-bottle, from which both ends were removed. was slipped over the middle of the axle between the uprights, and securely fastened. A handle or crank was fastened to the larger pulley with which to operate the machine. A cat had been killed, and its skin prepared for the purpose it was required to serve. This cat-skin was secured to a lever that was fastened to the platform by a hinge at one end of the lever, while the other end was loose, so that pressure could be applied to that end and thus hold the cat-skin against the circumference of the bottle when the crank was turned.

For the boys who may wish to try to make a machine like the one being described, it may as well be explained that the ends of the bottle were removed by winding a string soaked in kerosene around that end that it was desired to remove just at the place where it was desired to be severed, then the string was set on fire. This heated the glass just above the string so that when it was plunged into water to a proper depth the sudden cooling caused the glass to crack and fall off; after which the other end was given a like treatment. It may require a few trials to get the knack of doing this, but what man has done man can do.

In appearance the contrivance reminded the writer of the work of a New York carpenter, who said he could make anything if he could only have a cap-auger and a string to work with, but it did the work required of it in a surprisingly satisfactory manner.

Roy was president of his class in the senior year in the Jewell City High School, and was valedictorian in his class at the commencement exercises.

Up to this time he had shown a decided liking for, and an adaptability for, taking care of machinery about the elevator; so, on account of this natural predilection, he entered the class in mechanical engineering at the Kansas State Agricultural College, entering the sophomore class on September 19, 1901, being allowed nearly a year's credits on his preparation at the home school.

In the cadet corps at college he was promoted from private, after one year's drill, over all the corporalships, to first duty sergeant, and at the close of his second year upon taking a competitive examination, was advanced over ten first sergeants and

—15

lieutenants to Captain, and assigned to duty in Company D where he had served during his attendance at the college.

He was financially interested in the Students' Coöperative Association, which was running a book-store, in which Roy has held a position as salesman, and a dining-hall, where he takes his meals. He was also a stockholder in The Students' Herald Publishing Company and was Associate Business Manager on the *Herald* staff, to which periodical he was a frequent contributor.

While attending the college Roy filled the offices of president, corresponding secretary and critic in the college society to which he belonged, and was treasurer of the lecture course committee for the season of 1903 04. He was also president of the junior class during the spring term in 1903.

He has helped with the work at home during his vacations, and he graduated from the college in June, 1904. After graduation Roy was employed as assistant teacher in mathematics in his alma mater, something very seldom attained to by those who have never had experience as teachers, but his standing was such that the faculty decided to retain him in the college. He has classes in mathematics, including surveying and trigonometry.

Roy is a consistent member of the Methodist Episcopal Church and the Epworth League, and now that he is his own man, will doubtless vote with the Republicans in exercising the important privilege and duty of citizenship.

FAY, GOLDIE AND ROY SEATON.

CHAPTER XXXV.

THE CHILDREN OF OREN A. AND SADIE E. SEATON (CONTINUED).

GUY OREN SEATON.

GUY OREN SEATON, the youngest son and the most wideawake member of the family, justly claims Jewell City, Kansas, as the place of his birth, and celebrates each anniversary of the eighth day of August, 1886, as his birthday.

From his infancy Guy has been a lover of movement, seldom being quiet except when asleep, and not always so even then. As soon as he could walk about he would wander off and cause his busy mother so much worry as to where he was and trouble to follow him, that she finally resorted to lariatting him to a porch column.

When he was a little fellow in dresses he ran away from the home and went to the elevator to see who was there and what was going on. In trying to climb upon a heavily loaded wagon while there he put his foot before the wheel just as the team started and it was run over. Every one who saw the accident supposed of course his foot was crushed and ruined. A gentleman standing near caught him up and carried him to the house, where an examination showed the foot only slightly injured. There must have been a depression where his foot rested, as the wagon passed over it, and for once good luck counted for more than bad management.

Guy has always felt perfectly acquainted with every person he has come in contact with, or at least appeared to possess that happy faculty, and has always made friends readily. He has a great liking for bright colors, and if possible would wear a band-master's flowing plume, gold lace and braid, and other insignia of office, at all times, and be perfectly happy.

He is a most distressing rustler, doing whatever he undertakes with a rush and hurrah that sets more deliberate people's teeth on edge. He can do as much work as most boys, but is decidedly interested in knowing who is to receive the pay for his work. It can hardly be claimed that he likes work for work's sake, though he has planned more different ways to earn spending-money than any other boy known to the writer. And he never seems to have had a doubt of his ability to make his way in the world under any and all circumstances.

Guy learns readily enough, and might easily have been at the head of his classes, if his ambition had taken that direction; but he has experienced considerable difficulty in keeping his features composed enough to escape an occasional reprimand from his teachers, and he would much rather learn from Nature's great book than by steady application to school-books. If he was ever, before the last term in the High School, entitled to rank one in his classes, or if his activity permitted his deportment to be graded one hundred per cent., that fact escaped the notice of his parents; but he is quick to comprehend and has confidence enough in him-self to do almost anything that comes his way, and if he does not develop into a hustling business man, when once he settles down to some line of life-work, it will prove a great disappointment to his friends.

Guy has so far shown a decided liking for fine, high-headed, swift-moving horses, and when he holds the reins a current of magnetism seems to pass from driver to the team and they are up and going. He is much like his uncle, James H. Seaton, in not wishing to be on the road between two places long enough for team or driver to suffer from hunger.

Guy has just graduated from the Jewell City High School, at the head of his classes, having been declared valedictorian for the class, and it is to be hoped he will ever be an honorable gentleman, whatever his calling in life may be, for as Pope said:

> "Honor and shame from no conditions rise;
> Act well your part, there all the honor lies."

Guy is a member of the Epworth League, which he attends quite regularly, and of the Methodist Episcopal Church of Jewell City.

SADIE GLADYS, the second daughter and fifth and last child in the writer's family, was born at the Jewell City home on February 13, 1890. She is a bright, active, light-haired girl in her teens. She has never missed a day at school, except on account of sickness, and stands well in all of her classes, having received more times than any other pupil in her classes the honor of being rank one. She entertains a great liking for her teacher, Miss Mary McCoy, and will do all that is within her power to please the object of her admiration.

Her affection for Miss McCoy has prompted Gladys to write a number of "poems" in praise of her beloved teacher and friend. These "pieces," with several on other topics, Gladys has written in a little book for Miss McCoy. Gladys has the poetic temperament, and delights in expressing her thoughts and feelings in rhyme. She comes naturally by her talent for rhyming, and it is yet rather a natural than cultivated one, for among the Fergusons, from whom her descent is traced, there have been many poets, among whom Sir Robert Ferguson, the Scotch poet, a friend of Robert Burns, and Sir Samuel Ferguson, were perhaps the most widely known.

Gladys is easily the best musician in the family, readily playing any ordinary musical composition, and she sings quite well for so young a girl who has had the benefit of no more instruction, evidently inheriting her musical talents from her mother, or farther back in the Seaton family than her father. She accepted an invitation to preside at the instrument during the commencement exercises at the Ionia schools in the summer of 1903, and Professor Durett and several others expressed their approval of

SADIE GLADYS SEATON.

the manner in which she filled the position. And she has more lately officiated as organist at the Epworth League and at the services of the church and at prayer-meetings.

Gladys is also an elocutionist of some merit, considering her age and limited training, her services being in demand when there are any entertainments on the tapis, either at the public school or League.

CHAPTER XXXVI.

THE CHILDREN OF JAMES H. AND FRANCELIA SEATON.

HATTIE MAYBELLE SEATON, the first-born in the family, was born on Independence Day, in 1873, at Floyd, Floyd county, Iowa. She was given as good an education as the circumstances allowed, but was not so well instructed in the blessings of single life as to persuade her not to give herself in marriage to the man of her choice. She was married to John Conger, a broom-maker by profession, who at the last account was running a creamery station for the Beatrice Creamery Company of Lincoln, Nebraska, of which his father-in-law, James H. Seaton, is the Superintendent.

The children of these fine young people are Guy, Fay, Harold, and Joseph.

CHARLES ANDREW SEATON was born January 13, 1875. He was educated for a teacher, and was quite successful in that calling, but later he was managing a station for the Beatrice Creamery Company in Nebraska. He was married to Nettie Simmons at North Platte, Nebraska, November 8, 1905. They live at Wallace, Nebraska, near which place they own three hundred acres of land, which is devoted to raising horses.

GERTRUDE ALMA SEATON was born March 11, 1877. She was a very sweet child, too lovely for this world, and was called home to the other and it is to be hoped better world, on October 27, 1880, her death occurring at Floyd, Iowa.

LAURA PEARL SEATON, evidently named for her grandmother, Laura A. Seaton, was born December 14, 1879, at Floyd, Mitchell county, Kansas. After her school days were over she taught for some time near Wallace, Nebraska, where the family had located, with admirable success; then she established herself in the millinery business at Wallace, in the State of Nebraska. She was

JOHN AND HATTIE SEATON CONGER

married to George Myers at Wallace, November 20, 1902. They have one girl, Frances Myers. The family resides in Lincoln county, Nebraska, where they are farmers and stock-raisers, devoting especial attention to raising hogs.

KITTIE ISABELLE SEATON was born at Floyd, Iowa, on October 9, 1881, and died at Griswold, in the same State, July 29, 1882.

PERRY ALBERT SEATON was born September 20, 1883. He died at Wallace, Nebraska, on June 28, 1886.

JAMES HENRY SEATON 2d, named for his father, was born June 20, 1885. He attended the Wallace, Nebraska, schools while the family made that village their home, and moved with the others to Wauneta, in that State. He married Clara Fairbanks at Wauneta in October, 1904. They have one son, Clifford Clair Seaton, born 26th September, 1905. They live near Wallace on their farm, devoting their time to stock-raising.

MERTON ROBERT SEATON was born at Wallace, Nebraska, Lincoln county, March 28, 1887. He has been getting an education, and is in charge of the home farm of two hundred and ten acres on the Frenchman river.

CASSIE MAY SEATON was born at Wallace, Nebraska, April 21, 1889, and died at the same village in July of that year.

THE CHILDREN OF GEORGE F. AND CLARA F. SEATON.

MAUD ETHEL SEATON, the child that first made glad the hearts of her parents, was born December 6, 1878, at Floyd, Iowa. She spent her youth in getting an education and in learning housekeeping and home-making by assisting her mother. She was married to Charles Bird Kennard July 4, 1894, and has one girl, Blanch Ethel Kennard, born September 12, 1895. The Kennards make their home near Floyd, Iowa, and devote their energies to farming and stock-raising.

FRED BULKLEY SEATON, the son that made the wish of all parents complete, a daughter and a son, was born at Floyd, Iowa, on the tenth of April, 1881. He has grown to be a stockily built man, and has devoted some time to learning the carpenter trade, but is now engaged in farming.

ANDREW PENNELL SEATON 2d was given his grandfather's name complete. He was born at Floyd, Iowa, on February 15, 1885. He seems inclined to follow the honorable and independent business of farming for a livelihood. He was married February 22, 1905, at Floyd, to Laura Belle Reeser, and they are living on the farm where "Andy" was born.

CLARA BULKLEY SEATON, the baby-girl of the family, was born September 18, 1892, and is of course the pet of the household, and is helping her mamma and gaining knowledge.

THE CHILDREN OF PETER N. C. AND ELLA GENEVIEVE SEATON.

ZUA OLGA SEATON, the first child, was born at Charles City, Iowa, on July 8, 1873. She married Fred. J. Olerich at Orange City, Iowa, on March 16, 1893, the Reverend J. A. De Spelder performing the most interesting ceremony. Here ends the information we are allowed to know concerning these people, whose life history would doubtless rival the most thrilling romances were we permitted to know and tell the particulars of their lives.

JENNIE CORNELIA and JESSIE ANGELIA were twins. They were born at Algona, Iowa, on Independence Day, in the year 1879. The former died at Winona, Missouri, on the 22d of March, 1897. Jessie Angelia was married to Ode B. Odens on August 11, 1901, by the Reverend David J. Parrin, at Springfield, South Dakota.

FAY CUSHMAN SEATON was born at Algona, Iowa, on the 28th day of July, 1883. He must be his own man by this time, unless he has been married, and have an interesting life story if it could be told as it should be told.

CHAPTER XXXVII.

JAMES, JOHN AND ANDREW SEATON.

JAMES SEATON, of Scotland and Ireland. From Hayward's "Hancock, New Hampshire," Seccomb's "History of Amherst, New Hampshire," the "History of Washington, New Hampshire," and several other sources, we have gleaned the following: Three brothers emigrated from Scotland to Ireland, and thence braved the dangers of an ocean voyage to make a home in the wilderness of America. James Seaton came in 1727. His name with those of his two brothers and some younger members of the family are found on the tax lists of the new town of Amherst in 1760.

In "New Hampshire State Papers," volume XXVII, pages 67–70, is a quitclaim to certain lots in Amherst, dated December, 1759. Among others are mentioned John Seatown, Samuel Seatown, Andrew Seatown, and James Seatown, all of Souhegan. We have no mention of James having moved away from Souhegan or Amherst, so we suppose he died there at a later date, which has not appeared in our correspondence.

John Seaton, of Scotland and Ireland, a brother to the subject of the above sketch, was the next member of the family, so far as we know, to cross the stormy Atlantic to make a home in the New World. He came from Ireland, where he had taken refuge after some disastrous conflict of the supporters of the Stuarts with their enemies, in the year 1729.

After leaving Scotland in something of a hurry, probably, as he seems to have taken very little property with him, he was compelled to begin again to build a fortune for his old age and for his children, so he went to Newry, County Down, Ireland, and learned the tailor's trade.

John Seaton married Jane Edwards in Scotland, and more than likely some of his children may have been born there, for as nearly as we can learn, he lived in Ireland for only about fifteen years.

After their seven children were born, John Seaton, with his family, emigrated to what has come to be the United States of America, settling at Boxford, adjoining Andover, in Essex county, Massachusetts, bordering on the Atlantic ocean. His name appears on the records at Andover in the years 1737 and 1738, 1759 and 1760. He subsequently removed his belongings to Souhegan or Amherst, Hampshire county, New Hampshire, which county was also the home of another family of immigrants from Scotland, which is very closely related by marriage with some of the Seatons, —the Ferguson family, who first settled at Pelham, Hampshire county, of that State.

A "History of the Clan Ferguson," a book of considerable size and pretensions, was written many years ago in Scotland, and a continuation of the American branch of the family history, it being compiled by the writer's cousin, Miss Alta M. Ralph, of Watertown, New York. The names of the Fergusons first coming to America appear in C. O. Parmenter's "History of Pelham, Massachusetts," where they took an active part in the early settlement of that town.

John Seaton frequently wrote to his relatives in Ireland of the advantages of the new country over the old, until finally his brother Andrew came over in 1740. An account of his coming will follow. John Seaton sold his Amherst home to his son, John 2d. He it was who brought from Scotland the copy of the coat of arms.

The children of John and Jane Edwards) Seaton were: 1. Mary; 2. James; 3. Martha; 4. John 2d; 5. Samuel; 6. Elizabeth; and 7. Jane,—all of whom will appear further along in this book.

ANDREW SEATON.

At the frequent solicitation of his brother John, who preceded him, Andrew Seaton came to America with his family in the year 1740. He was born in Scotland, where he finally married Jane Blake, a daughter of one of the first families of that country. They lived at Tellehoague, Ireland, after his active and aggressive support of the house of Stuart had made him so interesting to the English that they declared his property confiscated and had decided to take his life upon the first opportunity.

Andrew kept a public-house at Tellehoague, County Tyrone, and was very wealthy before he left there,—so much so that he said when he left Ireland he could have given each of his children their weight in gold as their portion So we conclude that he must have saved a considerable sum from the wreck of his fortune in Scotland. It is probable that he left Scotland about 1715 as an exile, but in 1740 he set sail with his family from Ireland for this country, in one of the richest loaded ships that had ever crossed the ocean at that time.

We cannot help wondering whether Jane (Blake) Seaton ever asked her husband in the words of Arnold: "Wilt thou go forth into the friendless waste, that hast this Paradise of pleasure here?" Not she. Wherever Andrew thought it best to go, Jane was ready to accompany him. What a strange enchantment is love, to cause a woman to give up home and friends and comforts and native land to go with the one man of her heart across a tumultuous ocean, into a strange land, a wilderness, among savages, where none of the comforts and conveniences to which she had been accustomed from her birth, were to be had for love or money! Great is love, and too often greatly unappreciated!

Andrew Seaton shipped a valuable stock of merchandise from Ireland, intending to begin business in Boston, but the vessel in which they came was cast away one morning at about the break of day, on the Isle of Sable, then an uninhabited island, and he again lost his property. His family was providentially saved, but many of the other passengers on the ship at the time of the disaster lost their lives. The youngest daughter of the Seaton family was thought for some time to have been drowned, but was finally found washed ashore and partially buried in the sand, about two miles from where the wreck occurred, and resuscitated.

Andrew had the further misfortune of having his lower jaw broken at the time they were cast away, and his wife died a few days later, from fatigue and suffering.

The survivors from the wreck stayed nine days on the Isle of Sable without food, except a gill of dough and a thimbleful of butter to each individual per day, that being everything in the way of food saved from the sharks and fishes. At the end of the time named they managed to fit up the long-boat, and in it went to the Island of Cancer. All of the family, except Jane Seaton, the almost indispensable mother, who was probably buried at Cancer, went from Cancer to Cape Ann and thence to Boxford, near Andover, where afterward Andrew Seaton married Peggy Wood.

The name of Andrew Seaton appears on petitions at Andover dated May 13, 1747, and as late as 1753. At a later date the family moved to Amherst New Hampshire, where finally Andrew died.

The children of Andrew and Jane (Blake) Seaton were: 1. Andrew 2d; 2. Richard; 3. Sarah; 4. Ismenia; 5. Elizabeth; and 6. Anna, the last of whom was the one who was supposed for a while to have been drowned when the ship was cast away at the Isle of Sable.

Peggy (Wood) Seaton owned a farm near Amherst, New Hampshire, beside three other tracts in Souhegan, in the same county. She and her husband adopted two children to rear, Peggy never having had any of her own. To these two children she left a farm jointly, as they were at the time husband and wife. One of these children was Samuel Stanley and the other Jennie Seaton, a daughter of Andrew's Ismenia.

Peggy Seaton is reported to have once said to her husband's daughter: "You have so many children while I have none, you may give me one." The reply was, "You may take your choice." For this reason we conclude that Peggy Seaton must have been a remarkable woman, that a mother should be willing to give one of her daughters into her care to raise. According to the account, Peggy said to Jennie, the second girl, "Put on your bonnet and go home with me," which she did, and never returned except as a visitor. These two children that Peggy adopted lived on the farm given them by their mother by adoption, until their decease, Samuel being sixty-one and Jennie sixty-six when they died.

After the death of Andrew Seaton one of his daughters went to England and secured the services of an attorney, whose name, as nearly as we can make it out, was Nathan Haislup, to act for her in settling up the estate. But where much of an estate could have

come from after all of this indomitable gentleman's misfortunes is
a wonder. It further appears from the records that Mr. Haislup,
if that was really his name, was appointed as guardian for the other
children of Andrew Seaton, his widow having later married Joseph
Sewler, and very likely, Miss Abbott of Andover says, the younger
children may have lived with Mr. Sewler.

THE CHILDREN OF JOHN AND JANE (EDWARDS) SEATON.

MARY SEATON was born in Scotland or Ireland, and came to
America with her father's family in 1729, as has been stated.
The next information concerning her is that she was married to
John Mann. They had three children, as follows: Mary, John
2d, and Samuel Mann.

The family lived at Pembroke, Plymouth county, Massachusetts. The records in the case show that John Mann was published to Mary Seaton in 1737, in Andover, Massachusetts. It has
been claimed that this Mary Seaton had been married to a Mr.
Colton, who died before her marriage to John Mann, but if the
report is true, why was she published as Mary Seaton instead of
Mary Colton?

JAMES SEATON was doubtless born in County Tyrone, Ireland,
about the year 1718, and came to this country with the rest of the
family in 1729, locating near Andover, Massachusetts. The
records of the city say: "Married, May 5, 1748, James Seatown
to Elizabeth Robinson, by Rev. Barnard."

Elizabeth Robinson was the daughter of Joseph and Elizabeth
(Stevens) Robinson, honorable people of the vicinity. She was
the youngest of a large family whose births were recorded in
Andover up to 1723, and she was baptized in the North Church,
in 1727. Her father, Joseph Robinson, died April 9, 1756.

James Seaton is named by Seccomb and others as being on the
Association Tax List in 1760, and he was a Selectman in 1766 and
still in 1779; was on church committee in 1777, and subscription
papers at about the same time.

The city records show that there was "Born, July 13, 1750,
Elizabeth, daughter of James and Elizabeth Seatown." This

Elizabeth Seaton is said to have been married to Ebenezer Ellen-wood, and to have raised two children, John and Phœbe Ellen-wood.

The family is said to have moved to Amherst, New Hampshire, where they bought a farm, which was later given to the Ellen-woods, who finally gave it to their children, John and Phœbe, and bought another for themselves not far away. From John Farmer's History of Amherst we learn that James Seaton was a resident of Amherst before his brothers made their appearance there.

What has been written of the early life of Mary Seaton might be said of her sister Martha. The Andover records show this fact: "Married, May 22, 1744, John Wasson and Martha Sea-town, by Mr. Barnard." It has been stated that John Wasson and his family resided in Penobscot, Hancock county, Maine, and that they had eight children: 1. William, the first child was bap-tized on August 20, 1769, according to the records of South Church in Amherst; 2. John 2d; 3. Samuel; 4. Thomas; 5. Mary; 6. Martha; 7. Ann; and 8. Elizabeth.

CHAPTER XXXVIII.

John Seaton 2d was born in Ireland, about 1724, his father having emigrated to that country about 1715. He was five years old when the family crossed the Atlantic, locating at Boxford, near Andover, Massachusetts. The intention of John Seatówn of Boxford to marry Ismenia Seaton, his cousin, and daughter of Andrew Seaton of Andover, was published in the latter place in October, 1744, according to the records of the town. He moved to Souhegan West in the same year of the marriage, his father-in-law, Andrew, locating there at about the same time, and his brothers, Samuel and James, a short time afterward. Their names are all found on the tax lists of Amherst in 1760. He was a Deacon in the church at the time of his marriage, and continued to serve in that capacity there until 1783, when he resigned and moved to Washington, New Hampshire, where he died in 1793. He owned the old Seaton homestead at Amherst, having purchased it from his father, and, in course of time, sold it to his son, John 3d, just prior to moving to Washington in the same State. His name appears on petitions dated May 13, 1767, and others in 1778 and 1783, and on the Committee of Safety in 1778, and from other records it is certain that he was prominent in church affairs in 1779.

John Seaton 2d was a lover of music, like all of the family, and he taught vocal music and sang in the choir of which he was the leader in Andover, Amherst and Washington, as we have been informed.

After his removal to Washington, New Hampshire, he is said to have made his home with his son James Seaton.

The children born to John 2d and Isemenia Seaton, as given by Seccomb and others, were: 1. Elizabeth; 2. Jane; 3. Andrew; 4. Mary; 5. Margaret; 6. Martha; 7. John 3d, or John James, as some give it; 8. Ann; 9. Another Andrew on some lists and another Jane on others; 10. Is James on one list and Ambrose on another,—so it is not impossible that these loving people had twelve children instead of ten as some claim. The birth of Ambrose is not recorded in Andover, but it may have been at some other place. James is not mentioned in the Amherst History, but was added by John Seaton of Greenup, Kentucky, a member of this branch of the family.

John Seaton 2d made his home in Washington with his son James from 1787 until the angel of death made him a call with a summons to "come up higher," in the year 1793, as has been stated.

Ismenia Seaton, daughter of Andrew and wife of John 2d, was the mother of ten or twelve children. She suffered a stroke of palsy in 1764 which deprived her of the use of all of her limbs. When they moved to Washington in 1787 she was carried on a horse litter, and though helpless, her mind remained as vigorous as ever before. She was a great reader, and like many ladies of her time, indulged in smoking a pipe, though it was necessary to have every page of her book turned for her while she read, and her pipe held while smoking. Her daughter, Anna, with remarkable patience and cheerfulness did this without complaining, for the remaining seventeen years of her mother's life.

Samuel Seaton was one of the children of John and Jane Seaton, of whose descendants we will have no more say as we proceed, for they had only one child, a daughter, who married Henry Kimball, a hatter. Her name was Sarah Seaton, and she was born September 23, 1761, but further than that we are unable to say anything concerning her.

Samuel was one of the family on record at Andover, Massachusetts, but the *record* in the case is well described by a line in Gray's Elegy in a Country Church Yard:

"The *short* and simple annals of the poor."

But we do not know that the quotation describes the subject of this sketch in any way, even though it does the record in the case.

Samuel Seaton and Ruth Smith were published in Andover, Massachusetts, in November 1756, as both being of Andover.

The record was this: "Married, December 2, 1756, Samuel Seatown and Ruth Smith, both of Andover, by Mr. John Barnard." Miss Abbott, of Andover, is inclined to think that Ruth Smith was a Boxford girl, in spite of the record.

Samuel moved to Amherst a short time after 1744, where his name appears on the tax list in 1760. He was one of the Selectmen of Amherst, and he owned a farm near that city, which farm adjoined the one given to Samuel Stanley and his wife by Peggy Seaton.

Seccomb says Samuel Seaton's name was on a petition in Amherst in 1783; also that he was prominent in church affairs in that city in 1779, and was in trade early in some place in New Hampshire that looks like Hemiplus in our copy, and owned estates in Nashua, Hillsborough county, and in Salisbury, in Merrimack county, New Hampshire, though he lived in Andover at one time.

Samuel Seaton died in Wenham, Essex county, Massachusetts, about the year 1796.

ELIZABETH SEATON, daughter of John and Jane Seaton, was born in Bonny Scotland or the Emerald Isle, was never married, and died when about twenty-one years of age.

JANE SEATON, a sister to the above, was born in the old country, happily lived to be a woman, and was married to John Henderson. They had one child, John Henderson 2d.

CHAPTER XXXIX.

THE CHILDREN OF ANDREW AND JANE (BLAKE) SEATON.

ANDREW SEATON 2D, son of Andrew and Jane Seaton, must have been born in Scotland or Ireland, and made the voyage to America with his father's family. In "New Hampshire State Papers," Vol. XXVII, page 65, is a petition from the inhabitants of Amherst, dated at "Souhegan West No. 3, January ye 27, 1748," signed among others, by Andrew Seaton, Jr.; and in Wyman's "Charlestown Record of Families," he is mentioned as keeping a tavern called Indian Chief Tavern, on what is now the site of Harvard Church, near Charlestown Square. It is also recorded there that he sold some town lots to one Jonathan Bailey, a distiller, in August, 1766, and in 1809 he sold out his holdings and bought other land of Thomas Crown, on Washington street. His wife's maiden name is given as Betsy Gordon.

RICHARD SEATON appears to have been one of the minor children of Andrew and Jane Seaton, who were said to have been partly raised by their stepfather, Joseph Sewler.

SARAH SEATON was probably born in Ireland. She was married to Joseph Chaplin, and raised a family of four children: 1. Joseph 2d; 2. Mary or Mercy; 3. Anna; and 4. Sally. They lived in Londonderry at one time.

ISMENIA SEATON, we have already learned, married her cousin, John Seaton 2d, under whose name may be found the names of her children, who are the best and often the only history of a woman who merges her identity into that of her husband and family.

ELIZABETH SEATON, daughter of Andrew and Jane Seaton, was born in the old country. She married Richard Kimball. They lived at Boxford, Mass., for some time, then moved to Rindge. They had seven children: 1. Richard 2d; 2. Andrew; 3. Aaron; 4. Abel; 5. Lemuel; 6. Mercy; and 7. Ismenia.

ANNA SEATON, the youngest child of Andrew and Jane Seaton, was born in 1736. It was this Anna who came so near being drowned when the vessel was wrecked on the Isle of Sable during the twenty-one days' voyage over the Atlantic. When she was found it was supposed that she was dead, and she was laid aside for burial, but the other children took on bitterly to have Anna waked up. Her mother took her into bed with her, breathed into her mouth and did all she could to revive her, and after a while they perceived that her body began to be warm, and at last they succeeded in restoring her to life; but the mother, Jane Blake Seaton, died on the Island of Cancer, as has been told.

Anna was a person remarkable for her religious character, ever manifesting, from her earliest youth, a great regard for serious things and an aversion to everything light and trivial. She lived to become a lovely woman, and married Andrew Nichols. They lived at Newburyport, where he died, after which sad event, Anna went back to Londonderry and taught school. In the course of time she was married to James Donaldson, but it is believed that she died childless.

THE CHILDREN OF JAMES AND ELIZABETH (ROBINSON) SEATON.

ELIZABETH SEATON, daughter of James and Elizabeth, was born July 13, 1750, as mentioned in the life sketch of her father. She is said to have married Ebenezer Ellinwood, and to have had two children, John and Phœbe Ellinwood, to whom they gave a farm near Amherst, New Hampshire.

KENNER SEATON, son of James and Elizabeth, was born in Virginia, March 13, 1753. He was a soldier in the war for American Independence, called the Revolution. He was married at Andover, Massachusetts, to Elizabeth Sliger, who bore him seven children: 1. Elizabeth; 2. Margaret; 3. Rebecca; 4. George; 5. James Kenner; 6. Sarah; and 7. Richard.

With his family, Kenner Seaton moved to Jefferson county, Kentucky, where he and his sons settled at a place called Seatonville, in which village the postoffice was named Malott, and where Kenner lived the remainder of his days.

RODHAM SEATON, brother to Kenner, was a very religious man, belonging to the old Baptist Church. He was very strict in keeping the Sabbath day, and it is rather remarkable that he lost his life about 1788 by rupturing a blood-vessel in trying to remove a tree from the road one Sunday morning, the tree having fallen across the road during the previous night.

Rodham Seaton's children were four: two boys, Thomas and Kenner, and as many girls, whose names were Sarah and Elizabeth. Rodham is supposed to have been born about 1757, and consequently to have been about thirty-one years old when he died.

Thomas Washington Seaton, a brother to the above people, was born about 1755, probably in Virginia. From the records in the War Department at Washington, D. C., it appears that he served as a private in Captain Syme's company, Tenth Virginia Regiment, commanded by Colonel Edward Stevens, in the Revolutionary War. He is reported to have enlisted January 6, 1777, for a period of three years, but on the muster-roll of the company for the month of August, 1777, he is reported as "Invilade."

In due course of time, Thomas Washington Seaton married Barby Zinks, either in 1810 or 1811. They lived in Indiana at one time, and had an only son, Peter Seaton. Thomas died in the Hoosier State about 1813, and, some time afterward, Barby (Zinks) Seaton married Joseph Perisho. They resided in Indiana for a few years, then removed to Edgar county, Illinois.

Another ELIZABETH SEATON, a sister to Kenner, Rodham and Thomas, is said to have married Joseph Donaldson who lived and died at Eminence, Indiana. They had two sons and three daughters; Joseph and Jacob were the boys, both of whom are deceased. One of the daughters married John McGinnis, and they live near Eminence, Indiana. Another daughter married a Mr. Shoemaker, and lives near Eminence, a widow.

HOUSEN SEATON was born in Virginia. He married Sarah Kenner Pritchard, who was born in 1768 and died August 15, 1856. Housen built a flatboat in Virginia, probably at Huntington, and took his family down the Ohio river to Louisville, Kentucky. There he engaged in the hat business, but he is reported to have lived near Seatonville for a time. Soon after his trip down the river he died, leaving a widow and six children,—four boys and two girls.

The children of Housen and Sarah Seaton were:

1. JAMES SEATON, born March 27, 1796, at Winchester, Frederick county, Virginia. He married Nancy Wilhite, in Jefferson county, Kentucky, on December 16, 1819. They moved to Bureau county, Illinois, in 1835, and raised ten children. Nancy Wilhite was born July 25, 1801, in Old Virginia, and died in Illinois. James Seaton bought land in the above-named county, and lived there until the day of his death, in 1789. The village of Seatonville is on land formerly owned by James Seaton. The children of James and Nancy Seaton will appear later.

2. WILLIAM C. SEATON, son of Housen, was born in Virginia, January 8, 1804. He was twice married, first to Rebecca Stewart, by whom he was presented with four children, as follows: Eleanor Scott Seaton, born November 11, 1825; was married to Jefferson Durley, who is the Circuit Clerk of Putnam county, Illinois. They have one son, Leslie Durley, of Chicago; Sarah K. P. Seaton, born December 24, 1827, married a Burnham, now living in Hennepin, Illinois. Damarius Seaton, born June 9, 1830, married a Kay. She died in Nebraska City, Nebraska, where they made their home. James Hervey Seaton, born August 24, 1832, died at three years of age.

For his second wife William C. married Ellen Booth, who gave him two children, the first of whom was named James Hervey Seaton, the same as the child before him, who had died. His biography will follow.

The other child of the second wife of William C. Seaton was William Thompson Seaton, who was born February 1, 1839. He is now living at Bonanza, Alaska, unmarried.

William C. Seaton lived eighteen miles from Louisville, Kentucky. From there he moved to Clay county, Indiana, about seventy years ago. He died July 22, 1838. He was married to Ellen Booth, in August, 1835. Ellen was born in Hoosierdom, where she also died, in 1847. William is said to have come to his death by drinking too much cold water while overheated.

3. HERVEY SEATON, son of Housen, lived and died in Kentucky. He was Chief of Police in Louisville at the time of his death, having served on the police force thirty-eight years. He was twice married, having four children by his first wife, Anna Campbell.

4. SARAH SEATON, daughter of Housen, married William Zenor. They had ten children: 1. Housen K. Zenor had nine children, as follows: Mary; Amanda; John; Pritchard; Henry; Ardelia, who married James H. Seaton and presented him with the following children: Nellie B. Seaton, now Mrs. W. M. Studyoin, of Hennepin, Illinois; Alice Ardelia Seaton, born in Hennepin, December 14, 1868; is assistant postmistress and saleslady in a store in her native city, where she has passed thus much of her life, except while traveling in different States. She has always been an attendant at the Methodist Episcopal Church; is a member of the Rebecca branch of Odd Fellowship. We are under many obligations to Miss Alice for facts concerning the descendants of Housen Seaton, which she secured from an old Bible more than a hundred years old, and from relatives. Anna Geneva Seaton and Anna Eleanor Seaton are both deceased. Ida Frances Seaton; married W. J. Read, of Peoria, Illinois. 2. Jacob Zenor, William Zenor, Betsy Zenor, all three deceased; 5. Squire Zenor lives in the State of Washington; 6. Levi Zenor; 7. Amanda Zenor (Cecil); 8. Ann Zenor (Patterson); 9. Harvey Zenor; the last four are all deceased; 10. James Zenor; is living in Hennepin, Illinois. Each of these Zenors has children and grandchildren. Some were pioneers in Illinois and some of the sons participated in the Black Hawk War.

5. BETSY SEATON, daughter of Housen, married a Rose, but they were not permitted to raise any young Roses, how-

ever. They owned a plantation in Virginia, where they owned slaves.

6. PRITCHARD SEATON, son of Housen, died young.

THE CHILDREN OF JAMES AND NANCY (WILHITE) SEATON.

The children of James and Nancy Seaton, whose names I have learned, were James Hervey Seaton, of Seatonville, Illinois, who was born February 21, 1828, in Oldham county, Kentucky. He

JAMES HERVEY SEATON.

married Elizabeth Ann Harris, April 8, 1857, in Bureau county, Illinois, where they made their home until she died there, on December 12, 1893.

Mr. Seaton is now a retired farmer, living at Ladd, where his home has been for sixty-eight years, having previously resided in Oldham county, Kentucky, for seven years, and from which place he emigrated in 1835. He has held several local offices in his time, but his business has been farming, to which the greater portion of his time has been devoted.

The children of James Hervey and Elizabeth Ann Seaton are Emma Isabel, born February 17, 1858; Franklin Willard, born May 31, 1859; Oliver H., born June 27, 1862; Nora Edith, born January 8, 1868; William Arthur, born July 4, 1870, is a farmer and stockman, and lives in Bureau county, Illinois, probably; George Pritchard, born February 22, 1874, is a stockman and farmer. From one of the heifers owned by him were born four calves at a birth, all of which were perfectly formed and were registered.

Isam Seaton, son of James and Nancy, is deceased; Sarah Seaton is now Mrs. Porter, of Princeton, Illinois. Eliza Seaton lives at Spring Valley, Illinois, as Mrs. Munson. Lucretia Seaton married a Mr. Lee. They live at Seatonville. America Seaton is deceased, and Betsy Seaton is Mrs. Ott, of Chicago, Illinois.

James Hervey Seaton, son of William C. and Ellen (Booth) Seaton, the second son in the family of the same name, was born December 12, 1836, and died of pneumonia, at Hennepin, Illinois, on February 17, 1899. He was President of the Village Board, a member of Hennepin Lodge No. 118, I. O. O. F., and of Hennepin Post No. 231, G. A. R. Having lost his parents early in life, he went to live with an aunt. He attended school several years, then taught school in Missouri.

At the breaking-out of hostilities between the North and South, he enlisted from Clay county, Indiana, July 15, 1862, as a private in Company D, Sixth Indiana Volunteers, Cavalry, to serve three years or until the close of the war.

The regiment was assigned to the Second Division, Cavalry Corps, Army of the West, under Brigadier-General Stoneman, and he participated in the following engagements: Richmond, Kentucky, August 30, 1862, where the regiment lost 215 men killed and wounded, and 347 prisoners, 225 escaping capture. After some severe fighting, which resulted in very much reducing the regiment, what was left of it returned to Indianapolis for a time, probably to recruit their numbers. They then took part in the siege of Knoxville, Tennessee, November 17 to December 4, 1863; also in the Atlantic campaign, including Resaca, Cassville, Kenesaw, Altoona Pass, Lost Mountain, the Macon raid of July 27; Pulaski. Tennessee, September 27; Nashville, December 15-16. 1864; and a number of other engagements.

He was promoted to hospital steward, but took part in all the battles of his regiment, and was honorably discharged July 17, 1865. at Pulaski, Tennessee, on account of the close of the war.

He was united in marriage with Ardelia Zenor, daughter of Housen K. Zenor, who was born in Kentucky, in 1811, and died February 1, 1870, and Flora (Patterson) Zenor, a native-born Kentuckian, born October 29. 1815, and died November 2. 1902. The marriage of James Hervey and Ardelia Seaton took place May 29. 1866. at Hennepin, Illinois.

For about twenty years he was a teacher in the Methodist Sunday school, taking a deep interest in the work and being always present. He was a charter member of the Grand Army Post to which he belonged, and was initiated into the brotherhood of Odd Fellowship on October 15. 1870, serving as treasurer of the lodge from April in 1887 to the day of his death.

For the greater part of his residence in Hennepin he conducted a drug store and news depot, having graduated from the Bennett Medical College of Chicago, on May 23, 1871, and practiced medicine from that time until stricken down. In fact, it was in the discharge of his professional duty that he was exposed and contracted the fatal disease.

He was elected and served with credit to himself, several terms as Superintendent of Putnam county schools, and was also President of the Village Board of Trustees a number of terms.

The funeral services were held at the Methodist Episcopal Church in Hennepin, February 18. 1899, Rev. L. F. Zinser, pastor, assisted by Rev. J. C. Zeller, of Magnolia, conducting the religious services. The interment was in Riverside Cemetery, under the auspices of Hennepin Lodge No. 118. I. O. O. F., assisted by Hennepin Post No. 231, G. A. R.; and both lodges, as well as the Board of Trustees, passed resolutions of respect for the deceased and sympathy for the family.

CHAPTER XL.

THE CHILDREN OF DEACON JOHN AND ISMENIA SEATON.

ELIZABETH SEATON was born November 8, 1744, probably at Amherst, New Hampshire. She married Richard Godman, or Goodman, who later gave his life for his country at Valley Forge. Sometime later, on June 2, 1780, she married Henry Hendley, as some say, or Henry Hawley according to others, by whom she had one child, that was stillborn. Both of her husbands were Englishmen. She died on November 8, 1819.

Jane Seaton, second child of John and Ismenia Seaton, was born on the 6th of October, 1746, at Amherst, New Hampshire. She was adopted and raised by Peggy Seaton, as related elsewhere, with the consent of her parents. She married Samuel Stanley, who was also adopted and raised by Peggy Seaton, on May 3, 1774, and had seven children:

1. Andrew Stanley, born February 3, 1775; married Fanny Price. They had one child, Samuel Price Stanley, who died May 7, 1857. Andrew Stanley died January 10, 1849.

2. Peggy Stanley, born September 19, 1776. She married Joshua Wyman, December 25, 1796. They had two children, Stanley Wyman and Mary Wyman. Joshua Wyman died before his wife, and she married William Fox for her second husband.

3. Ismenia Stanley died of scarlet fever, at the age of fifteen years and six months.

4. David Stanley is unaccounted for in our record.

5. Sally Stanley was born July 25, 1789, and married Nathaniel Shattuck, Esq., being his second wife. They had seven children: 1. Annie Shattuck, born in Milford, on May 12, 1809. She married B. F. Wallace, of Antrim, August 13, 1829, and died in Bedford, August 16, 1847. 2. Mary Wallace Shattuck, born March 28, 1817, and died March 6, 1819. 3. Algernon Parker

Shattuck, born February 15, 1819; married Catharine Sweet, of Newark, on July 17, 1851. 4. Catharine Kendall Shattuck, born December 15, 1823; married Rev. Aaron W. Chaffus, on April 20, 1848. 5. George Freeman Shattuck, born October 9, 1825; lived only a little over a year. 6. Henry Campbell Shattuck, born August 9, 1827; died within eight months. George Henry Shattuck, born December 9, 1830. He wrote to John Seaton, of Greenup, Kentucky, two letters, one from Philadelphia and the other from Niagara Falls, in 1857, asking for the genealogy of the Seatons, which was sent him, and which he corrected as to the Jane Seaton Stanley and Shattuck families by adding a few names and dates which are included in this book.

George Henry Shattuck taught penmanship and bookkeeping in Philadelphia, New York, and Niagara Falls at that time. Sally Stanley Shattuck died in Manchester, February 7, 1865. Nathaniel Shattuck was born in Temple, February 27, 1774, and died in Concord, September 1, 1864.

Samuel Stanley, the husband of Jane Seaton, died of spotted fever, April 19, 1814, aged sixty-one years; and Jane preceded him, dying December 5, 1812 at the age of sixty-six.

MARY SEATON, fourth child of Deacon John and Ismenia Seaton, was born January 14, 1750, at Amherst, New Hampshire. She consented to take Peter Robinson's name, and to multiply his comforts and divide his troubles with him.

Peter was a soldier in the war of the Revolution, and lost his right arm at the battle of Bunker Hill. He was a baker by profession, and kept a public house in Concord, New Hampshire. They are reported to have had six children, but we have an account of only the following: 1. Peter 2d, like his father, was a baker, and kept a public house in Concord; 2. John Robinson; 3. Polly Robinson; 4. Ismenia Robinson, married William Butters, or Butten, of Concord. They had two boys, one of whom was named William Butters; the other's name was not given us. After the death of Butters, Mary Seaton married a man named Shaw, but they had no children.

MARGARET SEATON, fifth child of John and Ismenia Seaton, was

born April 22, 1752, and married Timothy Hartshorn. They had
one child, a daughter, who was left an orphan. Her name was
Peggy Hartshorn. She married Daniel Densmore, and moved
with him to Genesee. It is stated in other places that Margaret
Seaton's husband was Timothy Hawley, and again that his name
was Timothy Sleartson; so we conclude that she was married
more than once, or that a mistake was made by some one or the
other of our informants.

MARTHA SEATON, sixth child of John and Ismenia Seaton, can
be given only a short biography, for we only know of her that she
was born February 27, 1754, was married to Jesse Stevens on the
13th of April, 1786, moved to Genesee, and had four children:
1. Andrew; 2. John; 3. Patty; and 4. Nancy.

JOHN SEATON 3D, or Deacon John James Seaton, as one writes
of him, was the seventh child of John and Ismenia Seaton. He
was born in Amherst, New Hampshire, on the eighth of April,
1756, and married Rebecca Kendall daughter of Nathan Kendall
and Rebecca Converse, April 28, 1787. They lived on the old Seaton
homestead, one and a half miles from Amherst plain, on the east,
the same farm on which his father and grandfather had lived before him. He succeeded his father as Deacon in the Congregational or Presbyterian Church in Amherst, having been chosen for
that responsible position on September 3, 1795, and continued to
officiate until the time of his death, which occurred at his residence
on October 3, 1836, when he was over eighty years old.

It appears that John James Seaton was so well versed in the
pleasing art of music that he taught vocal music, sang in the
choir in the church where he worshipped, and was the leader of
the choir for a number of years.

The children of John 3d and Rebecca Seaton were four in number: 1. John 4th; 2. Nathan Kendall; 3. Samuel; and 4. Ambrose.

"She was never idle," the motto on her tombstone, was literally
true of Rebecca (Kendall) Seaton. Besides doing her own housework, she did carding, spinning, weaving, knitting socks, and other
work of that kind for market. She drove a "one-horse shay"

on her trips to market, going to neighboring villages, and at times as far as Salem. She was born in September, 1763, and died at Greenup, Kentucky, in August, 1839.

ANN, or ANNA SEATON, daughter of John and Ismenia Seaton, was born July 5, 1760. She devoted seventeen years of her life to the loving care of her palsied mother, proving herself a most patient and affectionate daughter. She afterward married the Hon. John Duncan, of Antrim, New Hampshire, who had been a Selectman, Town Clerk, Justice of the Peace, Representative for sixteen years, State Senator, and, best of all in the estimation of many of the Seatons, a Deacon in the church.

It was this Anna (Seaton) Duncan who, in 1827, at the home of her brother John, related the history of the early Seatons to her nephew Samuel Seaton, of Greenup, Kentucky. She died at Antrim, on October 4, 1834.

AMBROSE SEATON. From Miss Charlotte H. Abbott, of Andover, Massachusetts, we have received the information that there was a son Ambrose in the family of Deacon John and Ismenia Seaton, but we are inclined to believe that he was a son of Deacon John 3d and Rebecca (Kendall) Seaton, and will figure elsewhere.

ANDREW SEATON, son of John and Ismenia, was born on November 4, 1762. He married Polly Bowers. It is claimed there was another son in this family who was given the name of Andrew, and that he was born August 22, 1748, and died January 10, 1749.

Andrew and Polly (Bowers) Seaton are said to have "lived all about." They lived in Merrimack, Nottingham West, Hancock, and in Charlestown, Massachusetts, about 1803, in which latter city they kept a public house; thence they moved to Boston in 1818, and later to Medina, Ohio, where Andrew died September 12, 1826. In Boston he continued to maintain a public house and in Hancock he engaged in trade, being a member of the firm Seaton & Gordon.

Andrew Seaton was a "thoroughgoing business man," owning several stage lines: one to Providence, another to Andover, besides some others.

There were ten children born to Andrew and Polly (Bowers) Seaton: 1. Mary, born at Merrimack. August 14, 1790; died on September 24th of the same year. 2. James, born at Nottingham West, March 31, 1792; died January 2, 1834. He was a clerk in the Navy Yard in Charlestown, Massachusetts. 3. Ismenia, born at Nottingham West, September 10, 1793; died in 1870. 4. John. 5. Andrew, died at three years and nine months. 6. Mary. 7. Andrew. 8. Tyler. 9. Reed Page; and 10. Isaac Bowers Seaton.

JAMES SEATON, son of John and Ismenia, married Abigail Stevens, in Washington, New Hampshire, according to the records of that city, where his father lived with him in his later years, and where he (John) died. James moved to New York State, near Canada, at a more recent date. This family is reported to have been blessed with no issue.

—17

CHAPTER XLI.

THE CHILDREN OF KENNER AND ELIZABETH (SLIGER) SEATON.

1. ELIZABETH SEATON, born February 14, 1773, in Virginia; died in 1848. She married John Rose August 24, 1787, and had six children: Allen; Mary, who married a Buckner; James; George; and William.

2. MARY SEATON was born April 4, 1775, and died February 15, 1776.

3. MARGARET SEATON was born May 25, 1777, in Virginia, and died in June, 1835. She married Levi Whittaker, November 8, 1796. To them were given six children: Blaney; Grafton; Kenner; Levi; John; and Mary.

4. REBECCA SEATON was born in Virginia, June 31, 1779; married John Patterson August 8, 1799, and died September, 1836. To them in due time came three children: Rachel, who married a Kinsalo; Seaton Patterson; and Sarah Patterson, who married Joseph Frederick and had five children: Kitty; Margaret; Richard; George; and Alexander Frederick.

5. GEORGE SEATON, son of Kenner, was born in Virginia, on April 23, 1781, and died July 6, 1835. He married Sarah Drake, whose grandfather was Charles Drake, a brother to Sir Francis Drake, the famous English circumnavigator of the globe, February 3, 1803. Sarah was born February 20, 1783, and died December 14, 1863. To them were born eight children: Charles D.; Allen Rose; John Simpson; Jesse D.; Mary (Polly); Elizabeth; Apphia Ward; and Sarah.

George Seaton was for many years a magistrate at Seatonville, Kentucky, and after his death, his son, Charles D., was appointed under the old Constitution to be his successor.

6. JAMES KENNER SEATON, son of Kenner, was born in Virginia, March 6, 1783, and died September 2, 1826, in Jefferson county, Kentucky, where he had moved. He was married November 24, 1807, to Margaret Scott, who was born in Scotland, August 10, 1780, and died in Jefferson county, Kentucky, October 27, 1863. The fruit of this marriage was two sons and five daughters: Cynthia Ann; Levi W.; Richard Aliph; Mary; Sarah; Margaret; and Rachel.

7. SARAH SEATON, born October 23, 1787; died in 1836. She married Joseph Frederick, in April, 1806. She was left a widow, and later married Hezekiah Woodsmall.

8. RICHARD SEATON was born January 10, 1790, and died April 21, 1873. He was married to Eleanor (Nellie) Mundell, May 11, 1817, and moved to Illinois in 1835, settling at Camp Point, where he continued to reside to the day of his death.

Miss Mundell was born July 26, 1795, in the same county as her husband, where they were doubtless married "at the home of the bride's parents," with all the pomp and circumstance of such occasions. Richard and Eleanor Seaton were blessed with seven children: Margaret, Rebecca, Kenner, James, John, Richard 2d, and Sarah (Sallie).

THE children of RODHAM SEATON, as stated, were Thomas and Kenner; the latter of whom was born and died in Jefferson county, Kentucky. He married Mary Sliger. Their children were: Charles Allen and William Chesley. Mrs. Seaton was born in Bullitt county, Kentucky, where they were married about 1832, he having probably been born about 1796, and died in 1872 at the age of seventy-six, and she in 1871, aged sixty-five.

SARAH SEATON, daughter of Rodham and Elizabeth, married George Risinger. They had two children, a son, Kenner Risinger, and a daughter, Mariah Risinger. The former married a Miss Sliger, sister to his uncle Kenner Seaton's wife. Mariah Risinger was married to Ephraim Risinger, perhaps her cousin, and raised a large family, whose names have not been made known to us.

THE ONLY CHILD OF THOMAS WASHINGTON AND BARBY (ZINKS) SEATON.

PETER SEATON, the only child of the above persons who has been reported to us, was born about eighteen miles north of Louisville, Kentucky, on May 12, 1812. He married Lucinda Seain, on September 24, 1835. They had children to the number of sixteen, as follows: 1. Jonas W. Seaton was born December 10, 1836, and died October 18, 1855. 2. Nancy Jane Seaton was born March 15, 1839, and 's probably among the living, as no record of her demise appears among our papers. 3. Elizabeth A. Seaton was born August 5, 1841, and died November 1, 1901. 4. John W. Seaton was born October 22, 1843, and lost his life in the War of the Rebellion, on November 20, 1862. 5. Lucinda F. Seaton was born April 1, 1846, and died on the 7th of July, 1883. 6. Jacob N. Seaton was born on March 19, 1848, and died September 30, 1848. 7. Barby A. Seaton was born November 28, 1850. She was evidently named for her grandmother, Barby (Zinks) Seaton. The rest of her life story remains to be told. 8. James H. Seaton was born April 18, 1854. 9. Christopher C. Seaton was born November 30, 1855. 10. Peter Harry Seaton was born April 11 1858. He lives at Rose Hill, Jasper county, Illinois. He is married, but to whom we cannot say, and has four children, as follows: Frederick, born October 8, 1881; John W., born May 25, 1884; Charles L., born October 12, 1885; and Sylvia C., who was born on the 22d day of August, 1892. 11. William T. Seaton, son of Peter and Lucinda, was born March 15, 1860. 12. Jonathan S. Seaton was born June 6, 1862. 13. Phœbe Seaton was born April 23, 1864. 14. Emanuel W. Seaton was born August 10, 1866. 15. Daniel E. Seaton was born January 19, 1869, and died January 1, 1872. 16. Rose E. Seaton was born June 8, 1874, and died June 6, 1880.

THE CHILDREN OF JAMES KENNER AND MARGARET (SCOTT) SEATON.

CYNTHIA ANN SEATON was born in Jefferson county, Kentucky, August 25, 1808, and was married June 18, 1826, to William Rose, her cousin, by whom she had three children: Margaret Rose, who married James Vaughn, and died in Neosho, Missouri, without issue; James Rose, died without children; and Alice Rose, married in Albright, and lives at Glen Cove, Texas. Cynthia Ara Seaton Rose died in Texas, May 3, 1896.

LEVI W. SEATON, born near Fisherville, Jefferson county, Kentucky, December 18, 1810; died unmarried, July 8, 1833, of small-pox.

RICHARD ALIPH SEATON, born at the Fisherville home, March 12, 1812, died in Dade county, Missouri, October 21, 1895. He was married to Eleanor Mitchell Bayne, who was born November 16, 1817. The children born to this marriage were: Hester A. Seaton, born January 26, 1834 and died February 4, 1840; Margaret Ann Seaton, born November 16, 1835, married Taylor Boswell January 26, 1855, and died July 1, 1860, leaving three sons: Clinton Boswell, now living in Louisville, Kentucky; Edward Boswell also lives in Louisville; and Everett Boswell, who died young.

MARY ELIZABETH SEATON, daughter of Richard Aliph, was born July 14, 1840, and died June 24, 1841. Her sister, Sarah L. Seaton, born July 30, 1842, married James W. French, October 27, 1859. They live at Veachdale, Kentucky, and have two children: William S. French, of Monte Vista, Colorado, who married Georgia Kellar and has two children, Nora and Louise French. Nellie French, a sister to William S., married Foster Conner, and lives at Veachdale, Kentucky, and has several children.

CYNTHIA ISABEL SEATON, daughter of Richard Aliph, was born November 6, 1844, and died November 22, 1877, unmarried.

JAMES RICHARD SEATON, son of Richard Aliph, born April 18, 1847, at the family home at Fisherville about fifteen miles from Louisville, married Mary Frances Bidwell, born March 3, 1847, in Kentucky, October 29, 1872, near Mansfield, Missouri. They lived in Jefferson county, Kentucky, until 1870, when they moved with his father to Dade county, Missouri, where they lived for twenty-five years, then moved to Springfield in the same State, where they now reside, James R. being engaged in the coal and wood business. He is a Democrat in politics, and belongs to the

Baptist Church. The family consists of Elmer Bidwell Seaton, born July 23, 1847; Anna Eleanor Seaton, born September 21, 1876; James Richard Seaton, Jr., born April 13, 1879; married Mary Grand June 17, 1903; Ida Pearl Seaton, born May 15, 1881; died August 3, 1901.

ELODIA ARTEMESIA SEATON, daughter of Richard Aliph, born October 14, 1849; died August 22, 1880. She married Virgil I. Long, April 1, 1869. Besides two children who died young, they have two daughters: Olive, who married a Malone, and lives in Louisville, Kentucky, and Virgie, who married a Duval, and lives in Louisville.

SAMUEL EUGENE SEATON, son of Richard Aliph, born near Fisherville, Jefferson county, Kentucky, July 8, 1852, married Jennie Watson in Greene county, Missouri, February 11, 1874. He moved from Kentucky to Greene county, Missouri, in 1871, where he lived until 1891, when he removed to Center, Saguache county, Colorado, where he now resides. Samuel E. is a Democrat in politics and a Baptist in religion. Of this family there were five children: Cortey Eugene, born October 18, 1875, and died February 21, 1877, at Springfield, Missouri; Dalton Estelle, born April 6, 1877, at Willard, Greene county, Missouri. He married Pearl Carlin, in Del Norte, Colorado, January 14, 1903, and now resides at Alamosa, Colorado. Maud Inez, born October 9, 1878, at Willard Missouri, now lives at Center, Colorado; Eleanor Pauline, born April 13, 1880, at Cedarville, Missouri, married Struble Miles at Del Norte, Colorado, September 25, 1900, and lives at McPherson, Kansas; Grace Irene, born June 26, 1883.

WILLIAM FRANK SEATON, son of Richard Aliph, born September 4, 1860, in Jefferson county, Kentucky, moved to Missouri in 1870 with his brothers, and settled in Dade county, where he married Tempa Slinker, on October 3, 1883. They subsequently moved to Hooper, Colorado, where he died June 3, 1899. In the family there were three children: Leslie Everett, of Greeley, Colorado; Eula, who died in 1898 without issue; and Frank, of Mosca, Costilla county, Colorado.

CHAPTER XLII.

MARY SEATON, daughter of James Kenner, was born at the family home near Fisherville, Jefferson county, Kentucky, on October 14, 1814, and died March 7, 1892, at Dunksburg, Pettis county, Missouri. She married Milton William Tyler, March 14, 1833, and lived happily with him for fifty-nine years. They celebrated their golden wedding March 14, 1883, the family being all present for the first time in twenty-seven years.

Mr. Tyler was born near Fisherville February 28, 1812, and died at Dunksburg, Missouri, September 6, 1892. A full biography of each of the children in this family, including all of their descendants, would make a good-sized book of itself, but we will give a brief outline of such as appear on our files: The children born to Milton William and Mary (Seaton) Tyler were: James Kenner Tyler; Louisa Jane Tyler; Samuel Levi Tyler; Charles Thomas Tyler; Martha Josephine Tyler; Milton William Tyler 2d; and Richard Seaton Tyler.

Milton W. Tyler, Sr., removed from Jefferson county, Kentucky, to Johnson county, Indiana, in October, 1852. From that place he moved to Johnson county, Missouri, in 1869, and to Dunksburg, Missouri, in 1890, where he lived until his death, in 1892.

James Kenner Tyler was born in Jefferson county, Kentucky, on the 30th day of September, 1834. His father was Milton W. and his mother Mary (Seaton) Tyler, both natives of the same State. His paternal grandfather was Moses Tyler, of Irish-English extraction. James Kenner Tyler obtained his early education at the private schools of his neighborhood. When about twenty years of age he attended Franklin College, in Indiana, a Baptist institution. After attending this college one term he taught school, and then went home and spent a short time on the farm. In 1856 he emigrated to Missouri, first stopping at Knob Noster, where he secured a position as clerk in John A. Pigg &

Company's establishment. After that he engaged in numerous enterprises until in 1859. when he embarked in the mercantile business on his own account and continued the enterprise till the war broke out, in 1861.

He was a member of the State Guards at the time, and was ordered out in June of that year, in defense of his noble State, and served his country faithfully, participating in several hotly contested battles. among which were Wilson Creek and Lexington. In the latter, his side captured three thousand prisoners. He was finally captured in the spring of 1862. in Grover township, and taken to Sedalia and held there a short time. after which he was released and returned home, where he engaged in farming and stock-raising.

During the war he engaged in teaching school a few terms in the State of Indiana. In 1865, when matters had become settled, Mr. Tyler resumed his farming. and engaged in raising and buying stock and shipping the same, which business he followed successfully until the fall of 1880. when he was elected by the Democrats to fill the responsible position of Treasurer of Johnson county, a position for which his mild and genial ways. and especially his strict honesty, particularly fitted him.

In 1860. April 17. he was married to Amanda Jane, daughter of Larkin Hocker, Sr., a prominent farmer and stock-raiser of their county. The children by this marriage were: Mallie May Tyler; Sterling Price Tyler; Larkin Milton Tyler; James Seaton Tyler; and Elmer Hocker Tyler.

The last we heard of Mr. Tyler he was in the real-estate business at Warrensburg, Missouri.

Amanda Jane (Hocker) Tyler died January 4, 1880, at Knob Noster, Missouri, and was buried at Hocker Cemetery. She had long been a faithful member of the Mt. Zion Christian Church, and was so at her death.

In 1860 Mr. Tyler became a member of the Christian Church, and one of its most liberal supporters. He served as Township Clerk and School District Clerk for several years, being a friend to the public schools.

On March 29, 1882, James Kenner Tyler married Annie Cruce

at Warrensburg, Missouri, by whom he had one daughter, Edith Cruce Tyler, who was born August 20, 1887.

He owns a handsome residence in Grove township, called "Summit Home." As a man he is liberal and charitable, and is held in high estimation by all who know him.

Louise Jane Tyler, born September 24, 1838, near Fisherville, Kentucky, died September 24, 1896, at Franklin, Indiana, and was buried at Hopewell Cemetery, near there.

She was married to James Kerlin, August 24, 1870, at Knob Noster, Missouri, and raised three children: Seaton Tyler Kerlin, born November 23, 1872, at Franklin, Indiana, was a train-dispatcher at Charter Oak, Iowa, in 1894, and is now a telegrapher at St. Louis, Missouri, his address being 1803 Belienolt avenue.

Lulu Lenora Kerlin, born August 24, 1875, at Franklin, married Henry B. Harbaugh, April 6, 1903. Their present address is 602 East Second street, Indianapolis, Indiana. Mr. Harbaugh is cashier of the Claypool Hotel. Mrs. Lulu L. Harbaugh was a teacher, a Baptist, and a Democrat.

Mary Wyota Kerlin, born May 7, 1877, married Doctor H. R. Byfield, June 5, 1896. Their present residence is at Franklin, Indiana. They have one daughter, Halene Edell Byfield, born October 16, 1899.

Charles Thomas Tyler, born October 1, 1841, in Jefferson county, Kentucky, married Mary Elizabeth ———, March 24, 1868, near Franklin, Indiana. She died July 23, 1891, near Knob Noster, Missouri, and was buried in Hocker Cemetery. She was the mother of five children, as follows: Samuel Ira Tyler, born November 9, 1870, died January 11, 1872; Ida Maud Tyler, born November 15, 1872, married Arthur Layanley, March 4, 1897; Cecil Guy Tyler, born December 17, 1873; Charles Thomas Tyler, Jr., born August 6, 1880, married Nannie May Smith, November 5, 1902, and lost his wife by death, March 6, 1904; Neva Blanch Tyler, born December 14, 1881, is the last of the five.

Charles Tyler, Sr., traveled overland from Franklin, Indiana, to the Pacific coast in 1862, and, after many hardships, reached San Francisco after being on the road six months. He returned home by steamer to New York by the way of Panama. In religion he is a Christian and in politics a Democrat. His business is farming, stock-raising and fruit-growing, at Knob Noster, Missouri, on the rural free delivery route No. 2, where he has made his home for thirty-two years. He lived at Franklin, Indiana, until 1869, when he removed to his present place of residence.

Martha Josephine Tyler, born January 28, 1846, in Jefferson county, Kentucky, married Hume Edward Forsyth February 25, 1868, near Franklin, Indiana. Their home is "Edgewood" on the "Woodlawn Farm," Knob Noster, Missouri, where they are evidently happy, being Baptists and Democrats.

The children of the family are: Ora C. Forsyth, born March 14, 1874; Emory Tyler Forsyth, born December 14, 1877, and died February 10, 1878; Earl Thomas Forsyth, born January 13, 1884, died September 25, 1886.

Ora C. Forsyth and Stella T. Winston were married December 27, 1897. To them one daughter has been born: Velma Gladys Forsyth was born June 9, 1900. She was fatally burned, and died March 29, 1904.

Mr. H. E. Forsyth has made his home at Knob Noster, Missouri, for thirty-two years, having emigrated to Missouri from Johnson county, Indiana, in 1869.

Milton William Tyler, Jr., was born March 2, 1850, in Jefferson county, Kentucky. His present address is Sweet Springs, Missouri.

Richard Seaton Tyler, born December 3, 1855, at Franklin, Indiana, married Florence Shanks, November 3, 1880, at Sweet Springs, Missouri. He is a practicing physician and surgeon at Dunksburg, postoffice No. 2, Sweet Springs, Missouri. He has lived at his present home for twenty-five years, having made his home at Franklin, Indiana, fourteen years, and at Knob Noster, Missouri, nine years. He is a graduate of St. Louis Medical College, class of 1879; is Medical Examiner for the New York Life Insurance Company, the Mutual Life Insurance Company of New York, and the Master Woodmen of America. He is also a member of Pettis County Medical Society and the Missouri State Medical Society, etc., etc.

Samuel Levi Tyler, born July 28, 1839, near Fisherville, Kentucky, was married to Emma Eugenia Holland, March 6, 1866, in Centerville, Texas. The children in this family were: Charles Holland Tyler, born December 30, 1868, and died January 1, 1870, at Bryan, Texas; Lulu May Tyler, born December 27, 1870, and was married to Robert L. Hancock, November 28, 1899; Pearl Estelle, born January 26, 1875, married Romeo Wood April 18, 1897; Daisy Eugenia Tyler, born May 13, 1880, married Jesse Wiggin June 20, 1897; Samuel Lee Tyler was born May 16, 1882.

Emma Eugenia (Holland) Tyler died November 17, 1899, at Ellenton, Florida.

The following grandchildren have been born to Samuel Levi Tyler: Myrtle May Wiggins was born April 11, 1898; James Clyde Wood, July 29, 1898; Thelma Pearl Wood, June 24, 1901; and Samuel Leonard Wood, March 4, 1904.

Samuel Levi Tyler and his family are Baptists in religion and in politics they are always Democrats. They are orange-growers at Ellenton, Florida.

During the Civil War Samuel Levi Tyler was in the service of the Confederacy, having enlisted in the army under General Ben McCulloch, in Texas, May 1, 1861, and remained until the last general surrendered. The command in which he served, General Wharton's Cavalry Corps, never surrendered. They disbanded at Columbus, Texas. Mr. Tyler was a prisoner of war at Fort Leavenworth, Kansas, from November 19, 1861, to February 1, 1862, when he broke away from the guard and made his escape by running across the Missouri river on the ice. He was only about six feet from the guard, who had a gun with six loads in it, when he scaled the wall and ran for the river. Mr. Tyler with five others were to have been shot the next morning, as they supposed, for being Confederate soldiers. Mr. Tyler traveled five hundred miles to General Price's army, which was then at Boston Mountain, Arkansas, arriving in time to participate in the battle of Pea Ridge, or Elkhorn Tavern, and to receive two slight wounds. He remained in the army to the close of the war, taking part in all the Red River campaign and all battles in lower Louisiana. He was in the "Forlorn Hope" of two hundred who captured Brazier City, taking 1400 prisoners and $20,000 worth of supplies. He was also in the Battle of Wilson Creek and Lexington. Missouri, and was one of the guards placed over General Lyon where he fell.

The children of James Kenner Tyler and Amanda Jane Hocker, his wife, were: Mallie May Tyler, born October 4, 1862, at Knob Noster, Missouri. Married William Layan Hickman, January 29, 1882, at Warrensburg, Missouri. He is a merchant at Warrensburg, selling clothing and boots and shoes. They are members of the Christian Church, and "Democratic to a finish." This family has had nine children: Jennie Tyler Hickman, born April 16, 1883, at Warrensburg, Missouri; married Charles C. Clay April 25, 1901, at the place of her birth, where they reside at the present time. Mr. Clay was a Captain in the Third Infantry, National Guard of Missouri. They have one son, Charles Hickman Clay, who was born March 8, 1902, and whose great-great-grandmother was Mary (Seaton) Tyler. Elsie Lee Hickman, born April 26, 1886; Mary Allan Hickman, born March 28, 1891; James Larkin Hickman, born October 24, 1893, died December 11, 1893; Lydia A. and Mallie L. Hickman, the twins, were born April 26, 1895. Mallie L. died December 1, 1896, and Lydia A. July 15, 1897. Louise Hickman was born May 2, 1897.

Sterling Price Tyler, born October 25, 1864, at Franklin, Indiana, married Pearl H. Williams July 2, 1890, at Warrensburg, Missouri. Their children have numbered four, as follows: Encell Ellis Tyler, born October 1, 1891; James Kenneth Tyler, born June 8, 1894, died April 20, 1896; Sterling Price Tyler, Jr., born March 30, 1897; and Lhekla Tyler, born October 17, 1902.

Sterling Price Tyler is City Clerk, and he is a Democrat.

Larkin Milton Tyler, born September 7, 1866, at Knob Noster, Missouri, married Rachel Wofford, December 5, 1893, at Kansas City, Missouri. They have one daughter, Aniel Louise Tyler, born January 19, 1901. Larkin is a United States mail clerk, and resides at 3319 East Eighteenth street, Kansas City.

James Seaton Tyler, born June 7, 1868, near Knob Noster, Missouri, married Olive M. Campbell, December 20, 1891, at St. Louis, Missouri. They have two children, and reside at Dublin, Idaho where James is engaged in general merchandising.

Elmer Hocker Tyler was born December 27, 1870, at Knob Noster, Missouri.

Edith Cruce Tyler was born August 20, 1887.

SARAH SEATON, daughter of James Kenner, was born July 31, 1817, and married James Stout, June 9, 1836. Their children were two: 1. James Stout, Jr., who is practicing medicine at Omaha, Nebraska; and 2. Amy Stout.

MARGARET SEATON, daughter of James Kenner, was born February 2, 1820, in Jefferson county, Kentucky, and died January 2, 1893, in her native State. She married Nelson Tucker, March 22, 1837. Into this family were born four children: 1. Margaret Tucker, married Frank Davis, and lives at Morganfield, Kentucky; 2. James Tucker, married, and resides at the place last named; 3. William Tucker, died without issue; and 4. Alice Tucker, d. y. s. p.

RACHEL SEATON, daughter of James Kenner, born January 27, 1823, died at Billings, Missouri, August 9, 1891. She married Washington Smith, December 2, 1841, in the State of Kentucky. Their children were: Marcellus, Canning, and Chalmers Smith.

CHAPTER XLIII.

THE CHILDREN OF JOHN 3D AND REBECCA (KENDALL) SEATON.

JOHN SEATON 4TH, son of John and Rebecca, was born November 2, 1791. After a course at school he studied law with Aaron F. Sawyer. But, while it was his intention to be a first-class lawyer, it appears that both he and the family considered it a greater honor that he should be a Deacon in their church, succeeding his father and grandfather in that position, and he took especial pains to prepare himself to worthily fill that place, which was in their estimation no less worthy nor responsible than to be the pastor of the church. In this admirable ambition they were, however, disappointed, for he died on August 5, 1813, when he was about twenty-one years old, having up to that time taught school and vocal music in Amherst, where he also sang in the choir and, a part of the time, played on the bass viol therein.

NATHAN KENDALL SEATON was born October 24, 1794. It is said of him that he did not enjoy attending school in his youth, preferring to assist his parents on the farm and allow his brothers to obtain good educations, which they did,—Samuel as a teacher and lawyer, and Ambrose as a teacher and physician. However, he could not have neglected his own education to any great extent, for he was an officer in the Boston Custom House for about twelve years during Jackson and Van Buren's administrations, his term of office expiring in 1840.

He married Nancy D. Richardson, of Mount Vernon, New Hampshire, on December 25, Christmas Day, 1817. They are reported not to have been blessed with any children to make life doubly worth the living, once for themselves and more especially for the children. While Nathan was engaged at the Custom House, one of his cousins, Timothy Converse Kendall, was also serving his country at the same place, and another cousin, James Seaton, was a clerk in the Charlestown Navy Yards.

Nathan had copies of the coat of arms printed from his cousin James's plate while they were in the employ of the Government, and while he was in the Custom House at Boston, Nathan would occasionally go up to the old home place to visit his parents and to see how they were getting along, and, especially after his father's death, he would go up and hire a girl to do the housework and try to persuade his mother not to work so hard, but shortly after his departure his mother would discharge the help and do the work herself.

As she was a great knitter, and that being the easiest work she could do, often knitting while asleep in her chair, and awakening when she dropped a stitch, and, after picking up the stitch, dropping off to sleep again while the knitting went on, Nathan thought he would make use of her skill at that art to lighten her labors. So he told her there was a demand for socks in Boston, and that he would hire a girl to do the housework and give fifty cents a pair for all the socks she would knit. He did not take the trouble to inform her that socks were worth only twenty-five cents per pair in Boston. These arrangements completed, he returned to his business. In a short time socks began to come to Boston in such quantities that the son's salary was likely to prove insufficient for the demands upon it. Upon inquiry into the matter, it appeared that his mother had told all of the neighbor ladies of the great demand for socks in Boston and the good prices Nathan was willing to pay for them; so all hands went to work knitting for that market. That scheme had to be abandoned, so he persuaded his mother to go to Kentucky to make her son Samuel a visit, which she did, and she continued to live there to the day of her death, which occurred on August 30, 1839, when she was buried in the Seaton burial-grounds at Greenupsburg.

The subject of our sketch moved from Boston, Massachusetts, to Greenup, Kentucky, where his brother Samuel lived, in 1843, and engaged in merchandising, which business he continued to operate until the day of his death. He died March 11, 1859, and was buried at Greenup, after which his widow, Nancy Seaton, moved to Champlin, Illinois, where she finally died, but she was buried beside her husband at Greenup, Kentucky.

Samuel Seaton, son of the aforesaid Christian people, was born July 3, 1796. He was a student, devoting considerable time to fitting himself for a teacher and for the practice of the honorable profession of the law, teaching school as a stepping-stone to the vocation of his choice.

He married Hannah, the youngest of the four children of Nathaniel Eddy and Hannah Shepardson of Washington county, Northwest Territory, August 22, 1822. Her parents moved from Rutland county, Vermont, in 1798, to the above-named place, arriving at Marietta, Ohio, October 14. Hannah was born in Adams township, as above, on January 9 of the next year. Her grandfather, Nathan Eddy, was born in Plymouth county, Massachusetts, September 8, 1773. He married Eunice Sampson, of Middleboro, Massachusetts, on November 17, 1757. They moved to Sherburne, Vermont. The above Eddys were descended from Rev. William Eddy, vicar of St. Dunstan Church, in Cranbrook, England, from 1589 to 1616. His two sons, John and Samuel, left London for America August 10, 1630, in the ship Handmaid, John Grant, master. They arrived at Plymouth, Massachusetts, October 29 of that year. Samuel was the ancestor of Hannah Eddy, she being the eighth generation from William of Cranbrook, thus: William, Samuel, Obediah, Samuel, Samuel, Nathan, Nathaniel, and Hannah.

The Seaton brothers, James, John, and Andrew, from whom John of Greenup was descended, arrived at Plymouth in 1727, 1729, and 1740, respectively; therefore the children of Hannah Eddy and Samuel Seaton, being the descendants of both families, are the fifth generation in America of the Seatons and the ninth of the Eddys.

Samuel and Hannah (Eddy) Seaton had six children: 1. John of Greenup; 2. Rebecca; 3. Emily; 4. Emma; 5. Samuel; and 6. Mary Peck. Samuel learned the printer's trade in Amherst, and also learned to make hand-cards for carding wool and cotton. At the age of nineteen he went to Harrisburg, Pennsylvania, where he taught school, and from there to Ohio, where he again engaged in teaching, in Meigs and Athens counties. From Ohio he went to Greenupsburg. Kentucky, where he continued in the work of teach the young idea to shoot. Among his pupils in Kentucky were some of the grandchildren of Daniel Boone, and it was in the home formerly owned by one of the Boones that his children, or part of them, were born. When they went to Greenup they commenced housekeeping in the house where Daniel Boone had lived with his son Jesse. It was near there that Daniel Boone cut the poplar tree from which he made the pirogue in which he went to Missouri. Samuel commenced reading law with John M. McConnell, in Greenupsburg. But about 1818 he went to Portsmouth, Ohio, and continued to read there with a Mr. Clough, and was admitted to the bar. He practiced his profession in Piketon, Ohio, in 1819-20, then went to Meigs county, in the same State, but finally returned to Greenupsburg, where he practiced for a time, then engaged in merchandising. In the fall of 1826 he took his family, consisting of his wife and two children, John and Rebecca, on a trip to New Orleans, on a flatboat loaded with produce for sale along the route. His cargo consisted of leather, bacon, apples, castings made in the iron foundry in Greenup county, and various other articles, all together making a large boat-load. He traded along the Ohio and Mississippi rivers as he found opportunity, till the arrival at their destination. The boat was frozen in the ice at Shippensport, near Louisville, during the winter, but in the spring of 1827 the trip was continued, and the trading resumed until they arrived in New Orleans, where the remainder of the cargo and the boat were sold.

In trading along the river he had received a considerable sum of money, which he carried in a belt around his waist for safekeeping. One very dark night on the lower Mississippi river, while managing the steering-oar, his boat came into collision with a vessel at anchor in the stream. The shock threw him into the river, loaded as he was with his clothes and the money-belt, and he also had his overcoat on. As he went down he heard his boat crash against the other, and, as he could see nothing, he supposed his boat had sunken. He started to swim to shore, but could see nothing for some time, but after a while he saw a light some dis-

—18

tance down the river and swam in that direction. He soon heard his wife's voice calling. "Man overboard!" so he continued to swim down the river in the direction of the voice. He became greatly exhausted and could make but slow progress toward overtaking his boat and family that were floating with the current, his clothing hampering his movements and making his efforts almost of no avail, but by great efforts and persistence he finally overtook the boat and was carefully helped on board. He said afterward that if the pole that was reached to him had been carelessly pulled from him, he would not have been able to swim any longer and must have drowned.

From New Orleans he took his family by sailing-vessel to Boston, Massachusetts, and from there they went to Amherst, New Hampshire, to visit his parents and relatives, after an absence of about thirteen years. His parents, and brothers Nathan Kendall and Ambrose, were then living at Amherst.

On their return to their home they went by way of the lakes and stopped at Niagara Falls, where they saw a vessel containing live animals and geese sent over the falls for a show, gotten up to attract visitors to the falls.

It was upon his return from this trip, in 1827, that Samuel Seaton began his career as a merchant, which business he continued to manage successfully until his death. He was a Whig in politics, and was twice a member of the Kentucky Legislature, in 1833 and in 1846. He was the author of the law passed in 1847, called the "Seaton act," which secures to married women certain property inherited or given to them separate from their husbands.

Samuel Seaton was engaged in many enterprises: In 1847, at an expense of about five thousand dollars, he built a large stone dam twelve feet high across Little Sandy river at the falls one mile from the Ohio river, and a large mill. In the same year he commenced building a large charcoal iron furnace twelve miles westerly from Greenup, in the same county, on a tract of twenty thousand six hundred and twenty-six acres of land—the Thomas Keith patent—which he had bought of the heirs of Thomas Keith, who was before his death a paymaster in the Revolutionary War, and was an uncle of Chief Justice John Marshall, of the United States Supreme Court. The furnace was completed and in blast in November, 1849, at a cost of fifty thousand dollars, and was named the "New Hampshire," after his native State. He died of lung fever, at the furnace, on the 29th of March, 1850, and was first buried there, but afterwards his remains were removed to the Seaton family burial-ground on the hill back of Greenup. All gave him the name of being a "friend to the poor," an honest man.

His will is a pattern of brevity, and shows the great respect and confidence he reposed in his wife. It is as follows:

"I bequeath to my wife Hannah Eddy Seaton all my estate, real, personal and mixed, rights, credits, moneys and effects; and I appoint my said wife my sole executrix without security, and desire that no bond be taken nor oath administered.   SAM. SEATON."

Samuel Seaton began to trace the genealogy of his family at the time of his visit to Massachusetts in 1827, receiving some assistance at that time from his father, mother and others, but his father's sister, Mrs. Anna Duncan, who was the daughter of John and Ismenia Seaton, gave him the most help. He continued to collect material, as opportunity offered, for the remainder of his life, all of which was given to his son, John of Greenup, through the kindness of whom we are allowed to reproduce it here. Samuel was satisfied from his researches that there was originally only one family of the name, though some spell the name differently.

His son John, who continued to investigate the family history, and has added considerably to what his father had accumulated, has found no reason to believe otherwise than his father did on this point, and the writer of this book is more and more convinced that all Seatons are descended from the same common ancestor.

Samuel Seaton was personally acquainted with Samuel W. Seton, of New York, an uncle to Archbishop Robert Seton, who was Superintendent of Schools in New York city between 1838 and 1842, and was told by him much concerning the Seatons, ancient and modern, and especially that they were originally all of one family.

He was also personally acquainted with William Winston

Seaton, of Washington, D. C., and his partner, Joseph Gales, publishers of the *National Intelligencer* newspaper under the firm-name of Gales & Seaton, Seaton having married a sister of Gales. He took their newspaper up to the time of his death, and his son, John of Greenup, continued to take it until publication was discontinued by that firm. As Samuel had been well acquainted with them, he corresponded with William Winston Seaton concerning the family, and sent him a copy of the Seaton coat of arms in 1858.

CHAPTER XLIV.

THE CHILDREN OF JOHN 3D AND REBECCA (KENDALL) SEATON (CONTINUED).

AMBROSE SEATON, son of John and Rebecca, was born at Amherst, New Hampshire, on September 27, 1804. He graduated from college in 1825, and was Town Clerk in Amherst in 1829. He was proficient in music, teaching it successfully and leading the choir in their church, as his father had done before him. But medicine was his chosen profession, and he practiced it with honor and profit in Amherst, New Hampshire, in Boston, Massachusetts, and in Maysville, Kentucky, while he lived in each city.

Mary Rand Goss was born in Amherst in the same year that Ambrose Seaton was, and more than likely they were schoolmates there. However that may be, they were married in Amherst on November 12, 1828, by Jeremiah Barnard.

Ambrose and Mary Seaton had the following children: 1. Mary Elizabeth; 2. John Ambrose; 3. Nathan Kendall; 4. Helen Augusta; 5. Ann Martha; 6. Sarah Frances; and 7. Charles Stewart. Of these children, Nathan K., Ann Martha and Sarah Frances died young.

While Ambrose lived at Amherst and led the choir in the Presbyterian Church he had an experience that has been reported to us by Miss Charlotte H. Abbott, of Andover. It appears that "when Rev. Silas Aiken was ordained, after Doctor Lord had resigned in 1828 at the close of his term, the choir had some kind of a misunderstanding, and struck, leaving young Ambrose in the singers' seats alone. A hymn was read, but there were no singers in the choir. The senior deacon, equal to the occasion, rose and led off with Saint Martin's, and, some of the congregation joining in, a good all-around service of song was enjoyed. Ambrose, in vexation, probably because the choir had failed him, rushed down the gallery stairs two steps at a time and off to his boarding-house."

Ambrose Seaton moved from Amherst to Boston in 1830, where he practiced his chosen profession. He also taught music and led the choir of the Unitarian Church on Purchase street while living there. From Boston he moved to Maysville, Kentucky, where he continued the healing art and led the choir in the Presbyterian Church. He died in Maysville on April 9, 1866. Mary R. (Goss) Seaton was born March 25, 1804, and died July 4, 1863.

THE CHILDREN OF ANDREW AND POLLY (BOWERS) SEATON.

MARY L. SEATON was born in Merrimack, August 14, 1790, and died on September 24 of that year.

JAMES SEATON, son of Andrew and Polly, was born in Nottingham West, March 31, 1792. He was a Clerk in the Navy Yard at Charlestown, Massachusetts, in the early part of the Nineteenth century, during the administrations of Jackson and Van Buren. While there he owned a metallic plate of the Seaton coat of arms that was brought from Scotland, from which many prints were struck off and distributed in the family. He is reported never to have known the happiness of married life, but to have died single at Charlestown, June 2, 1834.

ISMENIA SEATON, the third child of Andrew and Polly, was born in Nottingham West, on September 10, 1793, and died in 1870. There is a record of the fact that Ismenia Seaton was published to James Moore of Charlestown on December 19, 1815, and in "our intentions." Miss Charlotte H. Abbott of Andover writes: "I find James Moore, of Charlestown, published to Ismenia Seatown on January 7, 1816. A little later they were married here." Evidently here was a little tragedy in real life—a regular lovers' quarrel, that was made up after a short interval. They moved to Medina, Ohio, and it was through their efforts that Ismenia's father was persuaded to move his family to the same place some time later. They are said to have had no children.

JOHN SEATON, son of Andrew and Polly, was born at Hancock,

June 6, 1795. When old enough, in 1821, he went to sea, but the vessel in which he sailed was swallowed up by the insatiable ocean, and neither the ship nor he was ever heard of afterward.

ANDREW SEATON 3d died at three years and nine months old, having been born December 13, 1796, and died September 11, 1780.

MARY E. SEATON, the second daughter in the family, of the same name, was born at Hancock, December 9, 1798. She married Jesse Hawley, residing at Dunham, P. I., where he died, leaving one daughter. Second, Mary married Thomas R. Greenleaf, September 11, 1826, and lived at Salisbury, then at New Philadelphia, Ohio, where he died. Mary E. died at Lebanon, Missouri, May 3, 1873. Her children were: Elvira, Charles, and Andrew, born in Salisbury and died young. George Henry, born in Salisbury, November 5, 1833, was in the commission business in Chicago and in St. Louis for several years. He was also a banker for twenty years in Lebanon, Missouri. He married Eliza Harrison, and had three children.

As Mrs. Greenleaf, Mary had two children, George and Andrew Greenleaf. The family lived for a while in Mayslick, Mason county, Kentucky, where Mr. Greenleaf was a prosperous merchant. He visited relatives in Greenup, Kentucky, about 1840, since which time we have no mention of his family.

ANDREW SEATON, the second of that name in this family, was born August 18, 1800, and married Celinda Nabors. They had two children, Mary and Lucy. Andrew Seaton died in 1841, at Cleveland, Ohio. We have no further record of the children.

TYLER SEATON was born at Hancock, October 26, 1802. He was at New Orleans, Louisiana, and in Texas, but the last heard of him he was on Lake Ponchartrain, in Louisiana. It is supposed that he died of cholera in that State.

REED PAGE SEATON was born at Charlestown, Massachusetts, July 25, 1805, and died at Medina, Ohio, July 13, 1877. He married Frances Henrietta Abbott (who survived him), on November 27, 1834.

Their children were: James, born December 13, 1834, married Mary Wornack, and resides at Grayson, Carter county, Kentucky. Emma Ismenia, born April 1, 1839; married Nathan McClure, who died in Washington, leaving a son, who is a graduate of the Columbus (Ohio) Law School. Emma Ismenia married, second, Thomas H. Johnson, a resident of Medina, Ohio.

Isaac Bowers Seaton was born March 14, 1809. He lived in New Philadelphia, Ohio, from which place he moved to Fort Dodge, Iowa. He died August 21, 1866.

CHAPTER XLV.

THE CHILDREN OF GEORGE SEATON, SON OF KENNER.

CHARLES D. SEATON, son of George and grandson of Kenner, was born in Madison county, Kentucky, in October, 1803. He married Elizabeth Payne, in Jefferson county of the same State, in 1827. He is supposed to have continued to live in the State made famous by its beautiful women, fine horses, and good whisky, until in 1844, when he moved to Columbus, Adams county, Illinois, at which place he made his home up to the time of his death, on April 3d, 1872.

There were born to these good people eleven children, of whom only four were living in 1902. The names of the children were: 1. Apphia; 2. James Allen; 3. Jane; 4. George K.; 5. Sarah; 6. Mary Louise; 7. Lavina; 8. Herbert; 9. Maud. The names of the other two do not appear on our roster.

Charles D. Seaton was a Democrat in politics until his son, James Allen, was wounded by the Confederates while he was serving his country in the Union Army during the War of the Rebellion, after which time he was a staunch Republican during the rest of his days. When the rebels injured his son they touched the father in a tender place, and his sympathies were transferred from the Democrats to the Republicans. Not that it is to be understood that all Democrats were rebel sympathizers,—far from it,—but many were. As General John A. Logan said: "I do not say all Democrats were rebels, but I do say that all rebels were Democrats."

ALLEN ROSE SEATON, brother to Charles D., was born April 28, 1808, in Jefferson county, Kentucky, where he was married to Sarah Pound, who was born there on August 7, 1811. She died at Hall, Morgan county, Indiana, January 31, 1884; and Allen died at the same place on September 6, 1895, at 80.

The children of Allen and Sarah Seaton were: John P.; George W.; Charles; Richard, who died at four and a half years old; James P.; Grafton W.; Mary Elizabeth; Sarah Jane; and Apphia M.

JOHN SIMPSON SEATON, the next son, was probably born in Kentucky. He qualified himself as a physician, and lived at Louisville, Kentucky, the last heard of him. He married Mary Kellar, and had one daughter. Both mother and daughter died soon after the birth of the latter, and John S. married Mary Hicks some time later. There were four children: Blanch; Crittenden; Curran; and Eliza, of whom we have no further mention. John S. died in Louisville, aged seventy-four years.

JESSE D. SEATON, the youngest of the family, married Lucinda Hill, a widow, whose maiden name was Crump. They are reported not to have been blessed with children. Jesse D. served his county for four years as Sheriff. He died in Louisville, Kentucky; and further than that deponent saith not, and history is as silent as the grave.

MARY (POLLY) SEATON married John Miller. Their children were: Sarah Miller, who lives in Louisville, Kentucky; Peter Galt Miller; Henry C. Miller; Emory; and Selden.

Mrs. Mary Miller is said to be interested in genealogy and to delight in discoursing on the subject. It was of her son Peter Galt Miller, that Rev. James A. Seaton wrote: "He is one of the best men alive."

From *The Christian Companion*, of Louisville, Kentucky, of June 28, 1905, we learn that he was president of Bridgeford & Company, manufacturers of stoves and ranges, having worked his way up from messenger-boy by diligence and integrity. He was a director in the Louisville Water Company, and held official positions in other important business enterprises. He was a faithful member, an elder in the Broadway Christian Church, a regular attendant and worker in the Sunday-school and prayer-meeting. Although a busy man of affairs, he found time to do a great deal of preaching for churches within reach of Louisville.

He was unassuming and unpretentious in all that he did. He married Miss Kate Dodge, and the union was a most congenial and happy one. To this union five children were born. A little girl died many years ago; the other four, two young men and two young ladies, remain. We have not learned the names of the children, except that one daughter was Kate Galt Miller. A portrait and biographical sketch of him were printed in the *Christian Companion*.

ELIZABETH SEATON married Thomas M. S. Reynolds. Their children were: Simpson; George; Theodore; and eight others, whose names have not been mentioned to us. The family moved to Lincoln, Nebraska, from Kentucky. The eldest son, Simpson Reynolds, was a lumber dealer at Seward, Nebraska, the last we heard of him.

SARAH SEATON, the youngest child in the family and the only living representative in 1903, was born March 3, 1828, in Jefferson county, Kentucky, and was married to John Ward Jean, on February 11, 1847, by Joseph A. Sweeney. Mr. Jean was born in Henry county, Kentucky, on April 10, 1821, and died January 16, 1897. He was a saddler and harness-maker by trade, and he cultivated some land. For the last twenty years before his death he followed farming only.

There were born to these good people eleven children, all of whom were born in or near Jeffersontown, Kentucky.

1. George Noel Jean was born April 8, 1848. He was married to Nettie Berkele November 7, ——, by Elder Randolph. He learned his trade with his father, but when married he moved to Garrard county at the solicitation of his father-in-law, and engaged in farming; but after a few years he was appointed Government Storekeeper. He is now Deputy Internal Revenue Collector, and lives at Danville, Kentucky, but still owns his farm. There has been only one child raised by George and Nettie Jean, Dr. George William Jean, who was sent to the Philippine Islands as a Lieutenant Surgeon after that memorable first of May when Dewey surprised the whole world at Manila Bay. About one year in that climate, with the work he had to do, was too much for the

Doctor, and he was sent home for medical treatment. After his recovery, he was sent to Fort Adams, Long Island, where he was in the spring of 1904.

2. William Curtis Jean, born December 9, 1849, died April 4, 1852.

3. Jesse Simpson Jean was born December 25, 1851, and died August 17, 1864.

4. Myers Seaton Jean was born January 21, 1854. He was married to Eunice Welch, November 11, 1880, by Elder Peter Galt Miller, who is a son of Mrs. Sarah (Seaton) Jean's eldest sister, who lived to marry. Myers lives in Louisville, Kentucky, where he is employed in the hardware store of Bridgeford & Company. He has no heir apparent to his possessions, so far as we are informed.

5. Alice Medora Jean was born January 17, 1856, and has been persuaded to add the name Mills to those given her by her parents, and so Kenner Mills and Alice Medora Jean were married June 14, 1882, by Elder P. Galt Miller. They made their home within sight of Alice's mother, and were farmers. Their children are Guy Forrest, age seventeen, and Ethel, who is fifteen. It has been reported to us that Mrs. Nora Mills lived in Washington, D. C., her husband having some office with the Government.

6. Lucelia Hobbs Jean, born April 12, 1858, married George S. Mills, November 23, 1881, and lives six miles from Louisville, Kentucky. They have four children: Verna Malott is a successful school teacher; Nettie Jean, George Everett and Sarah Seaton Mills complete the number.

7. Lenora Marcia Jean, born July 8, 1860, has never married, but makes her home with her mother, each a great comfort to the other.

8. Clarence Pryor Jean, born October 2, 1862, married Elizabeth R. Porter October 9, 1889, Elder P. Galt Miller officiating. They make their home in Louisville, Kentucky, where Clarence is employed in the hardware business with his brother Myers. Clarence and Elizabeth have four children: Winnie Hays; John Porter; and the twins, Enid and Eaine.

9. John Miller Jean, born February 17, 1866, is practicing

medicine in Woodford county, Kentucky, his residence being at Pinchard, but his postoffice address is Fort Garrett. He is not married.

10. Foree Clay Jean was born April 22, 1869, and married Fannie Stout on March 28, - — . He is farming about two miles from his mother's home, and is said to be a born farmer. There are two children in the home: Sarah Charlotte, aged four, and Orville Rhea, two years old.

11. Frank Lowe Jean, born August 31, 1871, lives in Malott, where he runs a general merchandise store. He also manages his own and his mother's farms, they being partners in the store and the farms, and he is also the postmaster in Malott. Frank has one boy, four years old.

The whole family of Jean are very temperate, none of them using tobacco or spirituous liquors, and none of them have more than one living wife.

THE CHILDREN OF RICHARD AND ELEANOR (MUNDELL) SEATON.

KENNER SEATON, son of Richard and Eleanor Seaton, was born May 7, 1862, at Camp Point, Illinois. He was married to Hannah Margaret Hunsaker, daughter of Samuel Y. and Matilda Angeline Hunsaker, the ceremony taking place at the home of her birth, on September 11, 1884.

The children of Kenner and Hannah M. Seaton were as follows: Hattie Bailey Seaton, born December 19, 1888; Richard Wiley Seaton, born December 24, 1892; and Irene Maud Seaton, born November 24, 1898.

The family address at present is 807 North Eighth street, Quincy, Illinois, where Kenner has made his residence for eight years. In 1892 he moved to Kansas, but after four years' experience there, he returned to the State of his nativity. He is a railroad switchman, but the remainder of his life-story is not ours to give.

JOHN SEATON, a brother to Kenner 2d, was living at Camp Point, Illinois, in the year of our Lord 1902, where he followed the honorable calling of a farmer for many years, a man grown old in good works.

JAMES SEATON, M. D., died in the fifties, never having taken unto himself a helpmeet to divide his cares of life and multiply his comforts.

RICHARD SEATON, JR., was born December 19, 1835, in Adams county, Illinois, where his father's family had located, and where Richard 2d was married to Nancy Ellen Curry, on October 15, 1857. He was postmaster at Camp Point, Illinois, in 1902, having served the people of that city for many years in that capacity.

They had two daughters, Rebecca and Margaret, whose short biographies follow.

REBECCA SEATON, daughter of Richard, Jr., married Thomas Bailey, of Camp Point, Illinois. She died without issue, about 1882. Her sister, Margaret, married Joseph Wallace. They lived and died at Camp Point many years ago, leaving a large family, of whom we have no further mention, except that their eldest son, Richard Wallace, moved to California a long time ago, the exact date not being ours to give.

THE CHILDREN OF KENNER SEATON, SON OF RICHARD, JR.

CHARLES ALLEN SEATON, son of Kenner, was born in Jefferson county, Kentucky, January 8, 1836. He married Mary E. Kelley, January 24, 1856; and second, after Mary's death, he was married to Annie Feldhaus, on January 2, 1895. The father of the first wife was Captain Samuel Kelley, a soldier in the War of 1812, and of the second, Joseph Feldhaus, of Louisville, Kentucky.

Charles Allen Seaton built the first store and was the first person to sell merchandise at the point afterward called Seatonville, Kentucky. He was elected magistrate, and was reëlected four times, serving in that capacity for sixteen years. He was then elected Marshal of Jefferson county and the city of Louisville, and was later appointed Public Administrator and Guardian over the same territory. He is at this writing a notary public and postmaster at Buechel, Kentucky, having never made his home outside of the county in which he was born, and where he was a farmer a portion of the time. He says he never knew a Seaton who was a very bad fellow, and never heard of one of the name or blood who was executed or incarcerated in a penitentiary or even in a jail.

Charles Allen Seaton is a Democrat, and a member of the Christian Church. His children were: 1. Maximilian Sylvester, deceased; 2. Mallie Belle; 3. Eggleston Kimpton, deceased; 4. Leslie Clina; 5. Ardenia Capitolia; 6. Perlie Cleopatia,—all born at Seatonville, Jefferson county, Kentucky.

Mallie Belle married V. L. Ford. Ardenia C. is also married, the ceremony in both cases having been performed by Elder Peter G. Miller. Leslie C. married Miss Belle Steele, of Louisville, Kentucky, September 4, 1900, when he was about thirty-two years old, his birthday having been September 16, 1868. They have no offspring. Leslie C. is a commercial traveler for the Louisville Cider Vinegar Works, with headquarters at Thomasville, Georgia, during the winter and spring months, but he is on the road almost constantly. His home address is Buechel, Kentucky.

WILLIAM CHESLEY SEATON, son of Kenner, was born in Jefferson county, Kentucky, October 22, 1847. He is a single man; is an auctioneer and traveling salesman. His home is at Louisville, Kentucky, where he has lived for five years, having previously resided at Fairmount, in the same State. He was a Constable for several years and was then elected Sheriff, serving four years in that capacity.

CHAPTER XLVI.

THE CHILDREN OF SAMUEL AND HANNAH (EDDY) SEATON.

JUDGE JOHN SEATON.

JOHN SEATON, of Greenup, Kentucky, was born in the old Boone house near Greenup, on July 25, 1823. He attended school principally at home, but also attended the Boston and Hingham (Massachusetts) schools from 1836 to 1839. He was almost raised in his father's store in Greenup as a salesman and bookkeeper.

He voted for Henry Clay for President on November 7, 1844, and on the same day rode on horseback to Grayson, Carter county, Kentucky, and opened his stock of goods and began the business of merchandising on his own account, having previously shipped his goods to that place.

He was married to Mary Elizabeth Rice, daughter of John and Elizabeth Rice, on Thursday, Thanksgiving Day, November 20, 1845, the first Thanksgiving ever observed in Kentucky. Mary E. Rice was born in Greenup county, Kentucky, on October 26,

1825. They were married three miles below Greenup, at her uncle William Biggs's home, by the Rev. Abel A. Case, at nine o'clock A. M., and rode on horseback to Greenup, where they took luncheon, and continued their journey in the saddle to Grayson, twenty-seven miles in all, the same day, and took their supper in their own log house, built of round logs, thus beginning housekeeping on their wedding-day.

Their oldest two children were born at Grayson, Hannah Elizabeth on August 7, 1847, and Anna on February 16, 1849. While they lived in Grayson, John Seaton built a large frame dwelling and store building on the hill opposite the court-house square, which was afterward called the Gable house.

He quit business in Grayson in the fall of 1849, having lived there five years to a day. From Grayson he moved to his father's New Hampshire charcoal and iron furnace in Greenup county, arriving a few days after he quit at Grayson. At the furnace he assisted in the store and office until his father's death, which occurred at the furnace on March 29, 1850. In July of that year John moved his family to Greenup, where his eight other children were born, and where three died and the wife and three daughters still lived in 1903.

His father had bequeathed all his estate to his wife so that it could the more easily and cheaply be settled up, she having the power to sell or rent real estate without a decree of court. John then went to work to assist his mother in settling his father's business, attending to various tedious land and other suits, some of which caused great trouble and expense, being forty years, from 1852 to 1892, in court.

The heirs of Joshua Harlan, of Philadelphia, produced in 1852 and had recorded for the first time anywhere a deed dated October, 1794, purporting to have been made by the patentee, Thomas Keith, of Fauquier county, Virginia, for the same 20,626 acres of land that Samuel Seaton had bought in 1844 of the heirs of said Keith, and upon which he had erected his New Hampshire furnace. Suits were brought in Greenup and Lewis circuit courts in 1852 in the name of Harlan's heirs against the heirs of Samuel Seaton and others for the lands, upon which, in the Court of Ap-

—19

peals, the Harlans recovered the lands, but the Seatons were given a lien upon the property for their improvements. Harlans never paid the judgment to Seatons for the improvements, and the lands in both counties were sold, bringing only a small part of the claim, and leaving, with the interest, many thousand dollars behind. Harlan's deed was dated two years before his father's birth, and had never been recorded anywhere in Virginia or Kentucky until in 1852, two years after the death of Samuel Seaton, and fifty-eight years after it was dated till it was recorded, and still it took the land, though it cost a common lifetime and a fortune at law.

John Seaton is a practical accountant, and has been employed in writing up sets of books at various places in Kentucky and Ohio, and as expert in writing and straightening up tangled accounts for the Ashland Coal and Iron Railway Company and others. He opened in 1854 the books for the Kentucky Iron, Coal and Manufacturing Company.

He was Deputy Clerk, also Master Commissioner in Chancery several years. And he was licensed to practice law, the interesting document being signed by Judges L. W. Andrews and Richard Apperson, Jr.

He was "for the Union at all hazards" in the War of the Rebellion, and this in Kentucky, and was selected as a straight-out Union man in 1862 as County Judge and served as such to 1866. He received a certificate of qualification as Clerk of the Court of Appeals, and was an unconditional Union candidate for that office in 1866, but withdrew in favor of General Hobson, who ran and was defeated by Judge Alvin Dewal, a Democrat.

He was born during the presidential term of James Monroe, the same year of but before the proclamation of the lately much-talked-of Monroe Doctrine. He voted for Henry Clay and a protective tariff in 1844, and for William McKinley and a protective tariff in 1896 and again in 1900, having voted for President fifteen times and never for a Democratic President or their principles. He was a strong Whig of the Adams-Clay-Webster school as long as the party existed; he is still in favor of the principles of that party. He was always opposed to secession, nullification, repudiation and the so-called Democracy, "their parent," as he puts it. Though not in favor of slavery, and opposed to its extension, he did not see how it was to be gotten rid of, till the slaveholders solved the problem by declaring war against the Government and firing on Fort Sumter.

He admits his folly in supporting Bell and Everett in 1860 as a middle party, though he still thinks their platform, "The Union, the Constitution, and the Enforcement of the Laws," is good doctrine.

After President Lincoln's first inauguration and the firing on Fort Sumter, he became an ardent supporter of Lincoln's administration and in favor of coercion and any other proper means of putting down the Rebellion. His motto at that time was in substance the same as that of the family for hundreds of years, the only difference being in the wording. There is so little difference between Hazard yet Forward and The Union at all Hazards, that it is hardly worth mentioning.

In 1864 he warmly supported Lincoln's reëlection and upheld the Republican party, canvassing several counties for the cause. He favored, canvassed for and voted for the thirteenth, fourteenth and fifteenth amendments to the Federal Constitution, and feels proud that he was able to *see the right* and that he never supported the "so-called Democratic, Populist, Greenback, nor any other party in opposition to the old Whig and Republican parties," perhaps having inherited his opposition to them from his father and grandfather. He has voted for several individuals who were Democrats when there was no national issue at stake,—the best men for local office, but never for Democratic principles.

He received several copies of the coat of arms from his uncle, Nathan K. Seaton, and also has one very old copy that he has had for nearly seventy years, that tradition says was brought from Scotland to Ireland and thence to America. It was transmitted to him from his grandfather, Deacon John Seaton 3d.

The ten children of John and Mary E. Seaton were: 1. Hannah Elizabeth; 2. Anna; 3. Rebecca; 4. John; 5. William Biggs; 6. Nathaniel Eddy; 7. Edward Eddy; 8. Mary (Molly); 9. Dora Peck; and 10. Samuel, of whom more hereafter.

Rebecca Seaton, daughter of Samuel and Hannah Seaton, was

born near Marietta, Ohio, March 2, 1826, and married Dr. Alfred
Spaulding, on May 14, 1846. They had six children: 1. George
Atherton Spaulding, born January 14, 1849; married his cousin
Rebecca Atherton Davis, of Amherst, New Hampshire, September
4, 1878. They have two daughters, Honora and Mary Seaton
Spaulding, and live at 248 Lenox avenue, New York. Honora
Spaulding was born July 25, 1881. Mary Seaton Spaulding was
born July 8, 1883, and died February 24, 1897. George A. Spaul-
ding is a practicing physician in New York. 2. Hannah Eddy
Spaulding, born November 2, 1853, died July 28, 1854. 3. Alfred
Matthias Spaulding was born April 13, 1857. He lives at 419
West One Hundred Forty-fifth street, New York, and is a practicing physician. 4. Helen Hookaday Spaulding was born October 30, 1860. 5. Rebecca Wentworth Spaulding was born September 15, 1863. 6. Samuel Seaton Spaulding was born August
1, 1869. He is superintendent of safe deposit vaults at Mount
Morris Bank, in New York city.

Rebecca (Seaton) Spaulding died at the home of her son Alfred,
in New York, on September 6, 1896.

EMILY SEATON, daughter of Samuel and Hannah Seaton, was
born May 7, 1829, and died on August 10, 1831.

EMMA SEATON, the next daughter of Samuel and Hannah Seaton,
was born November 1, 1831, and died October 2, 1832.

SAMUEL SEATON, youngest son of Samuel and Hannah Seaton,
was born at Greenup, Kentucky, July 7, 1833. He was evidently
given a good education at home, and taught the moral law as well.
He describes himself as the "lightest weight Seaton" he ever
heard of, weighing only one hundred and five pounds; as being
over seventy years old, without ever having had toothache or
rheumatism, and was never "tight," which latter is something to
be proud of even in Kentucky, "and rich (in the Lord) and always happy." About five years after his father's death, or in
1855, he went to Comal county, Texas, to the family of George
Wilkins Kendall, a cousin to his father, and a native of Amherst,
New Hampshire. Mr. Kendall was the man who started the New
Orleans *Picayune*, and was then editor and part owner of the paper,

the firm being Lumsden, Kendall, Holbrook, and Brillet. After visiting the Kendalls a while Samuel Seaton went to Fort Worth, in Tarrant county, Texas, to his uncle Nathaniel Eddy's, who was a brother to Samuel's mother, then alive. He taught school in Fort Worth and Dallas for several years.

He married Lizzy Addington, in Fort Worth, and at the commencement of the Civil War, being a strong Union man, took his wife to Greenup, Kentucky, where he remained, teaching school, clerking, etc., to the close of the war, at which time, in 1865, while he was still in Kentucky, he was appointed by ex-Governor William Dennison, Postmaster-General, as Postmaster of Dallas, Texas. He immediately returned to Texas and entered upon his duties as distributor of Uncle Sam's mail. Some time after this he went to Fort Worth, where he bought a farm and built some business houses in the city, where he yet resides (1903). He had no children by his first wife, after whose death he married for second helpmeet, Jennie Pollard Johnson, of Fort Worth, by whom he was presented with one son, Samuel Seaton, of whom a very meager sketch later.

After ten years of married life together, his wife Jennie died, at Fort Worth; and on November 10, 1886, he was married to Miss Lavora Patton, of Senatobia, Mississippi. In 1887 they moved to New Decatur, Alabama, and from there to Anniston, and later to Mobile, the last three places being in the same State. Last of all they returned to Fort Worth, where they now reside, and from which city they made a visit to relatives in Greenup and Ashland, Kentucky, in 1901.

SAMUEL SEATON, only child of Samuel and Jennie P. Seaton, is reported to us to be a Christian gentleman, a druggist at Fort Worth, Texas. If we had further information it would be gladly given, for such as we have give we unto you, as was said by One of old.

MARY PECK SEATON, the youngest daughter in the family of Samuel and Hannah Seaton, was born at Greenup, Kentucky, on March 26, 1836. She was married to John Means, of Ashland, where they now reside, so far as we know.

CHAPTER XLVII.

THE CHILDREN OF AMBROSE AND MARY (GOSS) SEATON.

MARY ELIZABETH SEATON, daughter of Doctor Ambrose and Mary Rand (Goss) Seaton, was born at Amherst, New Hampshire, on November 3, 1829. She is living at Greenup, Kentucky, single.

JOHN AMROSE SEATON.

JOHN AMBROSE SEATON, the first son in the family, was born at Boston, Massachusetts, January 5, 1832. He was married to Margaret Arthur, at Maysville, Kentucky, on October 25, 1859. She was born in Cincinnati, Ohio, on February 5, 1840, and was a daughter of George Wiles Arthur and his wife Lydia (Hunt) Arthur.

After seven years in Boston, John went with his father's family to Maysville, Kentucky, leaving the former city in May, 1839. He lived for thirty years in Maysville, during which time he was engaged in the drug business for twenty-one years, and for the last thirty-four years he has lived in Cleveland, Ohio, where he is interested in the Seaton Manufacturing Company, and writes all kinds of insurance, with an office at 414 Cuyahoga Building, his home being at 103 Glen Park Place.

He is an elder and clerk of Calvary Presbyterian Church, trustee of Cleveland Presbyterian Union, secretary and treasurer of the Alumni Association Chautauqua C. L. S. C., president of the Class of 1896, Chautauqua C. L. S. C. of the United States of America.

He was a member of the "Home Guards" of Kentucky during the Civil War for a brief time, but never had any real service.

The children born into this family are: 1. Frances; 2. Sara; 3. Lillie; 4. George Ambrose; each of whom will receive further attention at the proper time and place.

NATHAN KENDALL SEATON, son of Ambrose and Mary R. Seaton, was born in Boston, Massachusetts, January 1, 1835, and died in the same city on October 12 of that year.

HELEN AUGUSTA SEATON, the second daughter, was born in Boston, on July 22, 1838. She was married to Alfred D. De Bard at Maysville, Kentucky, January 25, 1859. They lived in Greenup of that State, where they had eight children born to them, to wit:

1. Alfred 2d, who married Myrtle Haworth, in Kansas, where they are living and have four children, viz.: Helen; Mahlon, now deceased; Ambrose Seaton De Bard; and Alfred Jones De Bard.

2. Mary Seaton De Bard. Married Thomas N. Biggs, and has three children: Alfred De Bard Biggs; Naylor Bragg Biggs; and Seaton Humphrey Biggs,—all of whom are living at Greenup, Kentucky.

3. Harriet Eliza De Bard. Died young.

4. Helen Goss De Bard. Married James Burns. They have

had three children, as follows: Gordon, deceased; Helen Seaton Burns; and George W. Mead Burns.

5. Carrie Belle De Bard. Is deceased.

6. Harriet Davis De Bard. Is single.

7. Margaret De Bard. Married Samuel E. Peters, in Greenup, where they are now living. They have had three children: Henry William Peters; Alfred De Bard Peters, deceased; and Margaret De Bard Peters.

8. Eunice De Bard. Married W. B. Taylor, Jr., and they are living, at the present writing, in Gallipolis, Ohio. They have one child, Charles De Bard Taylor. William B. Taylor, Jr., was born in Greenup county, Kentucky, September 26, 1875, and died in Gallipolis, Ohio, October 23, 1893, and was buried at Greenup, Kentucky.

Ann Martha Seaton was born at Maysville, Kentucky, on August 23, 1840, and died there on April 30, 1848.

Sarah Frances Seaton was born at Maysville, Kentucky, August 2d, 1842, and died in the same city on the 13th of March six years later.

CHARLES STEWART SEATON was born at Maysville, Kentucky, May 29, 1849, and died at Cleveland, Ohio, October 16, 1898. He was married in Cleveland, May 18, 1871, to Sarah Hollenbeck, who was born December 13, 1843, and died at Cleveland in August, 1879. They had three children whose names follow, and who are living in Cleveland: Carrie; Charles Ambrose; and Elizabeth.

After the death of Sarah (Hollenbeck) Seaton, Charles took unto himself a second wife, who was a sister to his first, Lizzie Hollenbeck by name. The latter marriage took place December 30, 1880. Lizzie was born October 13, 1843. She is living at Cleveland, but has no children to cheer her heart.

THE CHILDREN OF CHARLES D. AND ELIZABETH (PAYNE) SEATON.

APPHIA SEATON, daughter of the above-named worthy people, married a Mr. Butler. She died in September, 1864, leaving three children, as follows: 1. Clinton Butler, who is somewhere in Kansas. 2. Ora Butler. Married a man named Welch. They live in Brookfield, Missouri, where he practices the honorable profession of the law. 3. Ella Butler. Married Sanford Heron. They live at Kirksville, Missouri, and are engaged in the most independent of all callings and live close to nature, being farmers.

JAMES ALLEN SEATON, the next child, was born in Jefferson county, Kentucky, on February 28, 1840. He moved with his father's family to Columbus, Adams county, Illinois, in 1844,

REV. JAMES ALLEN SEATON.

where he grew to manhood on a farm, fourteen miles east of Quincy. He attended the public school, and then a Presbyterian Academy at Clayton from 1859 to 1861. His time was divided between work on the farm, teaching school, and attending the academy, until in February, 1862, when he married Mary E. Bradley, of Columbus, Illinois.

He entered the Union Army on August 7, 1862, was wounded in the succeeding year, and mustered out of the service as a lieutenant on September 27, 1864. This contracted army record falls far short of doing the subject justice, but what is to be done about it? The Seatons are somewhat like the traditional woman, " When she will, she will, and you can depend on't; but when she won't [tell], she won't, and that's the end on't." The well-known modesty of the Seatons will seldom allow them to say much of their own doings and has doubled the work of securing the material for this book many times over, and has prevented its being anywhere near what the writer desired it to be.

Listening to sermons by the Reverend John Lindsey, of Eureka, Illinois, the subject of this sketch was convinced and was baptized by Reverend P. B. Garret, and became a minister himself in 1871, and has been faithful to his calling from that time. He was pastor at St. Augustine, Cambridge, Atlanta, and La Harpe, in Illinois; Watertown, Dakota; Corvallis and Bozeman, in Montana; and at Marion, Iowa, continuing at the latter place for nearly five years. The Marion *Sentinel* says of him: "During his stay with us he has made a host of friends among our citizens, who join in congratulating him on his success and wishing him many years of happiness and prosperity."

His last appointment was at Webster City, Iowa, from which place he resigned June 9, 1902, on account of the effect of a sunstroke which he received in 1864, and which troubles him very much every summer in the heated term. He has held many excellent meetings, and is in hearty sympathy with all evangelists who work after the New Testament model. He has taken part in several public debates: two with Adventists, one each with Baptists, Universalists, United Brethren, Methodists, and Mormons. In a busy life he has had his trials and triumphs, shared by his happy Christian family, all of whom have been added to the church between the ages of eight and fourteen years. The children are: Ossian Ellsworth; Juniata Jane; Frances E.; George W.; Clara Bell; Nellie M.; and Addie.

Elder Seaton has been a lecturer of considerable reputation. His principal subjects were: "Foundation and Formation of

Character." humorous, instructive, and very helpful; "The Castle of the Antilles," humorous, but instructive; "That Boy," needed in every community. "Not one in a hundred understands 'That Boy.' Humorous and instructive, helps the boys, their parents and teachers, makes better boys."

The Elder was engaged in the work of the ministry for thirty-two years, with very little rest during all those years. A hint of his character may be surmised from the following sentences from one of his letters to the writer:

"My face is perhaps too short, but I try to make people happy. The world has no time for a minister with a disordered liver who looks as if he was going to, or returning from a funeral, or who expects to have one of his own in an hour or two. Although this may be true, we have our share of sorrow, but the world does not want to hear of trouble,— it has its own. This is a true saying: 'Laugh, and the world laughs with you; weep, and you weep alone.' Give us plenty of sunshine in life."

The Elder says he is like his father was, except that his father was tall, bony, and dark of complexion, while he is stocky and fair. He further remarks: "I am a little proud of the Seaton tribe. I never heard of one of them being a drunkard, in jail, a Democrat, or running away with another man's wife."

In another letter Elder Seaton says: "I have never known of a Seaton being an inmate of the pen, a drunkard, a prize-fighter, or a scalawag; so I am very proud of the name, and claim all Seatons as my relatives. They are brave, but modest, full of sympathy, and generous almost to a fault. They cultivate lofty ideals, and feel that they are here in the world for some good purpose."

JANE SEATON, the next daughter in the family, married Joseph Kelly, in 1844, in Kentucky, where she was born. She now lives in Hutchinson, Kansas, with her daughter, Joan (Kelley) Stenbeck, wife of a gentleman of the latter name.

Jane (Seaton) Kelley was the mother of six children, three sons and as many daughters. One of her daughters, Mrs. Sarah (Kelley) Davis, has a farm near Sterling, Rice county, Kansas. Of the remaining four children of Jane Kelley we have no mention.

GEORGE K. SEATON was born August 16, 1828,—in Kentucky, no doubt. He died at Golden, Illinois, on July 24, 1901. He was a widower at the time of his death, and left four children, as follows: 1. William A.; 2. Charles D., for the boy's grandfather; 3. Herbert; and 4. Maud.

SARAH SEATON married W. R. Thomas. They live at Linneus, Missouri.

MARY LOUISE SEATON married Peter Felt. They live at La-Clede, Missouri.

LAVINA SEATON married William Nichols, of Saline County, Missouri. She died many years ago, leaving one son, Ellsworth Nichols.

HERBERT SEATON, I believe, was somewhere in Oklahoma the last heard from him.

MAUD SEATON is unknown to the writer, except by name; and there were two others of the family, whose names even are not known to him.

CHAPTER XLVIII.

JOHN P. SEATON, eldest son of Allen R., married Ruth M. Carder. Their children were: Joan, who married Frank Garrison; Galt; Indiana, married Frederick Wilhite; Georgia is now Mrs. Frank Shields; Vesta E. was united in marriage to Thomas Crews. He was the only one of the boys who did not enter the Federal army during the Rebellion, but, his father being old and his brothers all in the army, he decided to remain at home to look after their affairs, which he did well. He was a loyal citizen, and did what he could to keep the "Knights of the Golden Circle" and the "Butternuts" in check,—they being formidable enemies of the country in Indiana at that time. Further particulars remain to be learned.

GEORGE W. SEATON, with two of his brothers, enlisted in the Federal army in August, 1861. In the following winter he contracted typhoid fever at Crab Orchard, Kentucky, and, after being confined in the hospital there and at Lexington for four months, was discharged on account of what was thought to be permanent disability, and went home. While he was in the hospital his wife visited him and ministered to as many of the inmates as possible, until she finally succumbed to the same insatiable disease, and died as much a martyr to the cause of saving the Union as any soldier who was killed in battle. She spent her last days and all of her strength in waiting upon her husband and the other sufferers, and then gave up her life in a negro jail, then used as a hospital, at Lexington, Kentucky. She left a little girl about four years old, now Mrs. Olie Smith, wife of James S. Smith.

George returned home, as stated, and lingered between life and death for a long time, but finally, in the fall of 1863, being somewhat better, he reënlisted in the One Hundred and Seventeenth

Indiana Regiment, and was sent to East Tennessee with General Burnside, at Knoxville and Greenville. He belonged to the famous "Persimmon Brigade," commanded by General Wilcox. He served out his term of service, but returned home a physical wreck, and has been such to the present time, suffering from varicose veins, and lung and heart disease, contracted in the army.

George W. Seaton is a Republican, and a member of the Christian Church. He married Matilda Wellman, who died in the hospital during the War of the Rebellion. After her death he was married to Martha Rankin, by whom he had no children.

CHARLES SEATON was born March 21, 1835, near Hall, Morgan county, Indiana, on the Seaton farm. He grew to manhood there, and attended the common school until he was ready for a promotion to Belleville Academy, in Hendricks county. After his course at the academy he taught school during the winters and farmed with his father in the summers, until he had saved enough money to take him through the two courses of medical lectures then required, and in the spring of 1858 he took up the study of medicine in the office of his uncle, Doctor John Simpson Seaton, of Jefferson county, Kentucky, where he continued the good work for about a year. In the fall, after having studied a while with Doctor Samuel B. Mills, he attended the Kentucky School of Medicine at Louisville, Kentucky, until he graduated from that institution on the 28th day of February, 1860.

On May 4th of that year he began the practice of his chosen profession at Hall, Indiana, his home town. After Fort Sumter was fired on, April 12, 1861, by General Beauregard, and the Rebellion was in full swing, he closed his office, and, with two of his brothers, George W. and James P., enlisted for three years or during the war. They were assigned to Company A, Thirty-third Regiment, Indiana Volunteers. At the organization of the company he was elected First Lieutenant, and was afterward promoted to the captaincy of the same company. The regiment was sent to Kentucky, and finally attached to the Army of the Cumberland in Tennessee. He was at the post of duty on all the marches and in the battles of that army.

On March 5th, 1863, he was captured with the entire brigade at Thompson's Station, Tennessee, and sent to Richmond, Virginia, where he was confined in Libby Prison for about two months, when he was liberated, exchanged, and soon after rejoined General Rosecrans's army at Franklin, Tennessee, and remained in that army until after the surrender of Atlanta, Georgia, September 4th, 1864, when his health failed and he was compelled to resign

CHARLES SEATON, M. D.

his commission and go home. After about four months' rest he resumed the practice of medicine where he left off about three years before. He continued in the practice of his profession until in the fall of 1883, when he was elected to the office of County Treasurer, continuing to serve in that capacity until 1888.

When the artesian water was discovered at Martinsville, Indiana, he took charge of the medical department of the first sanitarium, and was successful in demonstrating the medical properties of the water and its adaptability to the treatment of various diseases, for which it has become noted. He has been connected with the sanitarium up to the present time, and is now in charge of the Hills-Cohn Sanitarium at Martinsville, Indiana.

In politics he has always been a Republican, and he is a member of the Christian Church, in which he has filled every position from usher to treasurer, deacon, and elder, and, but for his excessive modesty, might have been a preacher. He has taught the Bible class in the Sunday-school for many years. He has also served as Trustee in the school district, and is now President of the United States Board of Pension Examining Surgeons at his home town, which position he has held for eight years. He is a member of the Masonic order and of the Grand Army of the Republic, being Past Commander in the latter organization.

On the 14th day of April, 1864, while he was in the army, he was married to Miss Mary Genevieve Major, and to them were born two children, a son and a daughter, the latter of whom died at the age of nine days, unnamed. The son, Sims Major Seaton, lives at Camden, Ohio, where he is assistant manager of a large photograph and publishing house. He married Miss Katharine Birtsch of that place about twelve years ago. They have no children.

RICHARD SEATON, son of Allen R., died at four and a half years of age.

JAMES P. SEATON, son of Allen R., enlisted in the Federal army in August, 1861, remained with the regiment three years, and then reënlisted for three years more. He was severely wounded in the leg at the battle of Peach Tree Creek, Georgia, on July 20, 1864, and was in the hospitals at Chattanooga and Nashville, Tennessee. He was at the latter place when General Thomas defeated Hood there on the 15th and 16th of December, 1864, as his company was with Sherman on his march to the sea. He was then sent to New York, thence by steamer to Savannah, Georgia, where he joined his company and marched through the Carolinas to Washington, D. C., and was in the grand review. His terms of service covered all the time from August 15th, 1861, to September 21, 1865. He was captured with other members of his company, and served a time in Libby Prison. When exchanged he returned to the front, and was with the Cumberland Army to the end of the war.

After his discharge from the army, like a sensible young man he courted and married a nice young lady in the person of Miss Elvira Wilhite, and started out to make a home. They raised a respectable family. Their youngest son, O. R. Seaton, was in the Cuban War, and was sent to Porto Rico, where he served until his eyesight failed and he was discharged.

James P. Seaton was a Republican, a Mason, a G. A. R. man and a deacon in the Christian Church, and he died as he had lived, a Christian.

The children of James P. and Elvira Seaton are three: Edgar A., Olive O., and Vaugie Seaton. The latter married Verna Whitaker, but has no children.

MARY ELIZABETH SEATON, daughter of Allen R., married Elder Jesse B. Johnson, by whom she had six children, as follows: Lucile Johnson married Lafayette Wilhite, and has ten children; Charles Johnson married a Miss Dane. They have seven or eight children: Melvin Johnson married a Miss Allison, and has one child; Frank Johnson married another Miss Allison, and they also have one child; Carrie Johnson married Kellar Smith, but has no offspring; Cecil Johnson married a Miss Wiles, but is without heirs.

SARAH JANE SEATON, daughter of Allen R., married John T. Lewallen. Their children are Elmer, Oral, Pearl, and Etta.

APPHIA M. SEATON, daughter of Allen R., married R. M. J. Pound, and had one child; then she and the child both died.

GRAFTON WHITAKER SEATON, son of Allen R., was born March 5, 1846, at Hall, Morgan county, Indiana. He graduated from the Louisville (Ky.) Medical College in 1870, and was married to Sarah Elizabeth, daughter of Captain Andrew T. Wellman, March 2d, 1871, at the place of his birth. He is now a physician and surgeon in Indianapolis, Indiana, the family home being at 1117 Olive avenue, where they have lived less than a year, having formerly made their home at Hall from 1868 to 1874; at Oberlin, Ohio, about a year, then back to Hall again in 1888, besides five

—20

years in Cartersburg, Indiana, and Montezuma for a year, then back to Cartersburg, then to Indianapolis.

For a short time Mr. Seaton served in the Seventeenth Indiana Regiment in the Rebellion, and was later a member of the One Hundred and Seventeenth Indiana Regiment, in Company D. He was discharged in 1864, disabled for further service, the result of sickness and exposure; and still he says his life has been uneventful, running along as quietly as the brooks by which he sported in his youthful days, nothing worth reporting having occurred to him.

The children of these good people are as follows, all of whom are living at this date, and all were born at Hall, Indiana: Harry Alfred Seaton, born April 16, 1872; Guy Alfred, born September 8, 1873. He is a doctor, and is probably practicing medicine at Martinsville, Indiana. Edna Earl Seaton was born August 13, 1875; and Nellie Seaton was born July 3, 1880.

CHAPTER XLIX.

THE CHILDREN OF JOHN AND MARY E. SEATON.

HANNAH ELIZABETH SEATON, eldest child of John and Mary E. Seaton, was born in Grayson, Carter county, Kentucky, in her father's log house, on Saturday, August 7, 1847. She was married to Jerome B. Secrest, at her mother's house near Greenupsburg, Kentucky, on February 15, 1866, at 10 o'clock A. M.

Mr. Secrest was born in Lewis county, Kentucky, September 25, 1843.

They had eight children: 1. Lida Secrest, born at Concord, Kentucky, January 23, 1868, died young; 2. John Seaton Secrest, born November 13, 1869, at Concord; 3. Mary Secrest, born March 4, 1872, died young; 4. George Rice Secrest, born in his grandmother's house, on April 7, 1874; 5. William Arthur Secrest, born at Willard, Carter county, Kentucky, October 5, 1878, died at the same place, January 10, 1881; 6. Rebecca Hookaday Secrest, born at Grayson, April 16, 1883; 7. Sally Dorsey Secrest, born at Eminence, Kentucky, August 18, 1886; and one whose name is not in our possession.

John Seaton Secrest, above, married Emma Arnold, in Ashland, Kentucky, February 18, 1895. They have had two children. The first died young, perhaps unnamed; the second, Mary Elizabeth Secrest, was born at a place called Rush.

ANNA SEATON, daughter of John and Mary E. Seaton, was born at Grayson, Kentucky, February 16, 1849, and died at Greenup, September 24, 1852.

REBECCA SEATON, born February 13, 1851; died in September, 1896.

JOHN SEATON was born January 13, 1854, and died August 10 of the same year.

WILLIAM BIGGS SEATON was born July 18, 1855, in Greenup, Kentucky, on Forrest street, in his grandmother Hannah Eddy Seaton's home. He was given a good education, which probably occupied the most of his time till he went to the Bellefonte Iron Furnace, in the same county, about the middle of March, 1872, and began work for Means, Russell & Means, afterward incorporated as the Means-Russell Iron Company. At first he was their storekeeper, and later, furnace clerk, assistant manager, etc. He remained there till in 1882, when he went to the Mount Savage Iron Furnace, in Carter county, to manage the business there for Joseph S. Woolfolk, the owner, which he successfully operated something over two years. Then he took a trip south to the iron regions, where he with others contemplated starting a car-wheel works at Birmingham, Alabama, but on account of the death of one of his associates the project was given up. He then went to Ashland, Kentucky, and learned the banking business, after which he and Charles P. Mead went to Charleston, West Virginia, and with others, organized the Charleston National Bank, in September, 1884. He was made teller, and then cashier, of the bank.

On the 17th of September, 1885, he was married to Elizabeth Isabella, daughter of John Means, of Ashland, Kentucky. Their first child, Harriet Hildreth Seaton, was born at Charleston, on June 18, 1886, in which year he moved to Ashland, Kentucky, and took the position of bookkeeper and cashier of the Ashland Coal and Iron Railway Company, at their general office in Ashland. Afterward he moved to Bellefonte Iron Furnace, three miles from Ashland, and acted as manager until the furnace ceased to be operated, when he built a residence on Bath avenue and moved to Ashland.

After the death of John Russell, the president of the Russell & Means Iron Company, he was elected their President and General Manager, which position he still held in 1902.

With others he organized the Citizens Telephone Company of Ashland, and the Lawrence Telephone Company of Ironton, Ohio. He was elected President of both companies, and he is Secretary and Treasurer of the People's Telephone Company of Catlettsburg. He was elected Secretary and General Manager of the old Kentucky Iron, Coal and Manufacturing Company, and was appointed assignee of the Ashland Improvement Company, which latter concern has since been closed. Besides the above, he was elected one of the Directors of the Ashland Coal and Iron Railway.

Elizabeth Isabella (Means) Seaton was born August 8, 1855, and has five children: Harriet Hildreth, already mentioned; Isabella Seaton was born at Bellefonte, Kentucky, May 17, 1888; John Means Seaton was born April 15, 1891, at Bellefonte; Kendall Seaton was born February 26, 1893, at Bellefonte; and Edward William Seaton was born at Ashland, April 26, 1894.

NATHANIEL EDDY SEATON was born October 11, 1857, and died about eleven months later. Edward Eddy Seaton was born August 2, 1860, and, as far as we know, is still making history.

MARY (MOLLY) SEATON was born July 15, 1862, and lives at Greenup; and Dora Peck Seaton was born June 7, 1865.

SAMUEL SEATON was born November 24, 1867. He married Belle McNeal October 7, 1899. They have one son, Vernon Seaton.

THE CHILDREN OF JOHN AMBROSE AND MARGARET (ARTHUR) SEATON.

FRANCES SEATON, the first-born of these estimable people, was born at Maysville, Kentucky, on September 27, 1860. She is a disciple of celibacy, at least she practices that theory, evidently not agreeing with Boyle, where he says: "He that said it is not good for man to be alone placed the celibate amongst the inferior states of perfection." She is a graduate of Wellesley College, of Massachusetts, and is a teacher in the Cleveland (Ohio) High School, in which city she makes her home. She also has an "M. A." from Cornell University, and, if we are not mistaken, she is the author of "A Study of Birds and Animals."

SARA SEATON was born at Maysville, Kentucky, February 13, 1863. She is a graduate of Wellesley College, in Massachusetts, and is a teacher in the Cleveland (Ohio) High School, where she lives a life of single-blessedness, too busy preparing lessons and grading papers to waste any of her valuable time in being married or other trivial affairs.

LILLIE SEATON was born at Maysville, Kentucky, on May 6, 1867, and died at Cleveland, Ohio, on the 13th of October, 1874, a sweet bud transplanted from an earthly to a heavenly home.

GEORGE AMBROSE SEATON was born August 7, 1878, at Cleveland, Ohio, where he secured his education, having graduated from Adelbert College, Cleveland, with "B A.," and from Case School of Applied Science of the same city with "B. S." He is unmarried, and lives at Glen Park Place, Cleveland, Ohio.

THE CHILDREN OF CHARLES STUART AND SARAH (HOLLENBECK) SEATON.

CARRIE SEATON was born August 19, 1872, in Cleveland, Ohio, where she resides as the wife of Fred Stewart Hodges, their marriage having taken place on September 19, 1894, in the city of her birth. They have the following-named children, all of whom are living in Cleveland: Wayne Stewart Hodges, born in Cleveland, July 3, 1896; Forest Seaton Hodges, born as above, on May 28, 1898; and Clyde LeRoy Hodges, born July 31, 1900.

CHARLES AMBROSE SEATON was born February 23, 1875. He lives in Cleveland, Ohio, unmarried.

ELIZABETH SEATON, daughter of Charles Stuart and Sarah Seaton, was born on the 8th of October, 1877. She was married to Henry Van Bolt on June 12, 1901. Mr. Van Bolt was born September 29, 1875. They have no children to cheer their lives. Their home is at Cleveland, Ohio, at the time of this writing.

THE CHILDREN OF JAMES ALLEN AND MARY E. (BRADLEY) SEATON.

OSSIAN ELLSWORTH SEATON, the first child, was born at Camp Point, Illinois, on November 12, 1863. We have not been favored with a detailed account of his boyhood as was desired, but he married Eva Russell on the last day of June, in the year of our Lord 1900, in Minneapolis, Minnesota. Only a short year after his marriage he started for the Klondike, to make his fortune in the gold mines, evidently, and nothing has been heard from him since that unfortunate twelfth day of July, 1901. He had considerable money with him when he departed, and fears are entertained by his friends that he was either drowned or foully dealt with on the journey.

JUNIATA JANE SEATON, with a great many others whose names are mentioned in this book, is entitled to the same apology as is given above as to the meager account of their youth, and in fact their whole life. However, she was married to Shelly Horton, of Stuartsville, Minnesota, on October 20, 1886, by Elder A. D. Traveller, of the Methodist Episcopal Church. Their children are three, as follows: 1. Roy S. Horton, age fourteen at the present writing; 2. Homer Horton, twelve years old; and 3. Mary Horton, a ten-year-old maiden. Charles D. Horton died at twelve months of age.

FRANCES E. SEATON was married at Estelline, South Dakota, on September 5, 1888, to H. H. Reeves, who is the cashier of the Bank of Brookings, in the South State. They have two sons: Edwin Allen Reeves, thirteen years old, and Walter Seaton Reeves, a youth of ten years.

GEORGE W. SEATON died at two years old.

CLARA BELL SEATON is a clerk in the Bank of Brookings.

NELLIE M. SEATON is a bookkeeper and cashier in C. A. Skinner's dry-goods store in Brookings, South Dakota.

ADDIE SEATON, the baby of the family, died at twelve months of age, in December, 1882.

THE CHILDREN OF GEORGE K. SEATON.

WILLIAM A. SEATON is a carpenter by training, and lives at Quincy, Illinois, where he is foreman of the bridge-builders of the Chicago, Burlington & Quincy Railroad. He is another "fellow that looks like me," and if the truth, the whole truth, and nothing but the truth has been told of him, there is no danger of our friend ever getting into trouble on account of his beauty, for it is said he resemble the writer so closely that the portrait of either might be mistaken for that of the other by intimate friends.

CHARLES D. SEATON 2D is a professor in the Deaf and Dumb School at Devil's Lake, North Dakota, himself having been educated at the Deaf and Dumb Asylum in Washington, D. C.

HERBERT SEATON is said to live somewhere in Oklahoma.

MAUD SEATON, "a fine young lady," lives at Golden, Illinois, unmarried. She was attending the Gem City Business College at Quincy, Illinois, in September, 1903.

CHAPTER L.

A VIRGINIAN.

DOWN in Virginia there lived a Seaton, whose name we have been unable to learn, but the family tradition says that he was a captain of a company in the Revolutionary War, so it is probable that he must have been born not very far from 1730. This soldier left a Bible to his descendants, on the fly-leaf of which was written this prayer:

"From Doctors, Lawyers, Preachers and the Devil, good Lord, deliver us."

The last seen of that ancient Bible by George Warren Seaton, a descendant of the former owner, it was in the possession of his grandfather's sister, Mrs. Lucy Cox, of Mead county, Kentucky, who is long since dead, but her grandson, Gus. Cox by name, lives at Wichita, Kansas.

The Revolutionary soldier, above, had three sons, George, James and William, who, very early in the nineteenth century, settled in Kentucky. Of William Seaton nothing definite is known, but George and James made their home in Breckinridge county, Kentucky, James moving from Fauquier county, Virginia, or possibly, according to Booker Seaton, another of this branch, from Westmoreland county.

GEORGE SEATON was a Revolutionary soldier, and drew a pension as such. He went to Kentucky from Pennsylvania. His name is found on the "Pension Roll of Revolutionary Soldiers" as a private and sergeant in the Virginia Militia. His place of residence was at that time Breckinridge county, Kentucky, and he drew $78.33 per year, his name having been put on the roll October 21, 1833, at the age of seventy-nine years; so he must have been born in 1754.

George Seaton had a son, William Kinnel Seaton, and perhaps

others. The son was born in Pennsylvania, and moved with his father, while quite young, to Kentucky, where he died in 1852 or 1853, aged sixty-five years. He was married to Mary Anna Reeder, and had seven children, as follows:

1. William Seaton 2d; died in infancy.

2. Thomas Holt Seaton; died in 1901 in Breckinridge county, Kentucky, aged seventy-four years; unmarried.

3. Richard Stevens Seaton lives somewhere in Texas. He must have been born about 1831.

4. James Reeder Seaton is dead. He left quite a family in Breckinridge county, Kentucky, among them John Seaton, of Hardinsburg, in that State; Laura Seaton, who married a Mr. Compton, a cashier in a bank in the last-named place; and Emma Seaton, of the same village.

5. Mary Seaton married James Barnes. They have had five children. The family lives at Hardinsburg, Kentucky.

6. Martha Seaton is single, and lives at the village last named.

7. Booker Seaton was born December 25, 1834, in Breckinridge county, Kentucky, where he lived until in May, 1870, when he moved to Linn county, Kansas. He has been a farmer until recently, when he moved to Lacygne, Kansas, to take his ease for the rest of his days. On May 23, 1877, he married Eleanor Elizabeth Dalton, at Sedgwick, Harvey county, Kansas, and they lived happily until her death March 18, 1899, at Lacygne, Kansas. Booker Seaton's second wife was Dillie Mitchell, a widow at the time of their marriage, she having previously married a man named Ellis.

JAMES SEATON, the other brother of the three, among other children had a son, James D. Seaton, who was born in Fauquier county, Virginia, January 1, 1804. He moved to Breckinridge county, Kentucky, and married Harriet Greenwell, who was born in 1812. They had children as follows:

1. Wilfred Seaton died unmarried, in Kentucky.

2. Eleanor Ellen Seaton married, first, Franklin Dalton, and after his death she was married to Booker Seaton, on May 26,

1877, at Sedgwick City, Harvey county, Kansas, and died on March 18, 1899, at Lacygne, Kansas, without issue by either husband.

3. Luella Seaton married Luther Hendricks, whose present address is Cloverport, Kentucky. They have not been blessed with offspring.

4. Sarah Jane Seaton married Peterson Roff, whose address is State Reform School, Topeka, Kansas. They have five children.

5. George Warren Seaton married Annie, daughter of Elder William Head, of Linn county, Kansas, in 1865. They moved to what is now Harvey county, Kansas, in 1869, and located a homestead, to which the family moved in the next year. He managed the farm until in 1887, when he established a drug business in that county, where he continued to operate until in 1893. Then he moved to Lacygne, and conducted the same business until in November, 1903.

At the breaking-out of the War of the Rebellion he enlisted in Company K, Third Kentucky Cavalry, and served three and a half years in the Federal army. He took part in the battles of Bowling Green, Shiloh, Nashville, Stone River, Jonesboro, Wainsboro (where General Joe Wheeler went after them), Atlanta, Kenesaw, and others. At Stone River he was badly injured by his horse falling on him, and in the same battle a shell bursting close to his head destroyed the hearing in one of his ears.

Annie (Head) Seaton died in 1876 in Harvey county, Kansas, and was buried at Sedgwick City in that county. They had children as follows: 1. Harriet Seaton was born June 12, 1866, at Cloverport, Breckinridge county, Kentucky, and finally married Jefferson Miller at that place. They have four children. 2. Anna Theresa Seaton, born October 18, 1868, married William Urton, and has two children. They live at Wichita, Kansas. 3. Ellen Dalton Seaton, born April 18, 1870, married John B. Saunders at Lacygne, Kansas, who is a merchant at Fort Worth, Texas. They have two children. 4. Clora Seaton, born April 7, 1872; married Frederick Judson at Lacygne, and died October 23, 1902, at Knoxville, Tennessee, childless. Mr. Judson was agent and manager for the Swift Packing Company. 5. James Davis Seaton, born in October, 1873, lives at Cloverport, Kentucky, a family man. 6. Benjamin Harned Seaton lives at Guthrie, Oklahoma. 7. John P. Seaton died young and unmarried. 8. Albert Seaton, son of George Warren, is among the deceased. His widow and two children live at Elmdale, Kansas. 9. James H. Seaton is located at Newton, Harvey county, Kansas. He graduated from the Kentucky School of Medicine at Louisville, in 1866, and practices his profession at Newton. 10. Jefferson D. Seaton died without issue.

George Warren Seaton, the father, married for his second wife Mrs. Edith A. Clute at Lacygne, Kansas, July 20, 1896. No children have been born to the latter union.

SOME VIRGINIA AND TENNESSEE IMMIGRANTS TO KANSAS.

JOHN M. SEATON is supposed to have been born in Tennessee or Virginia. He was the youngest son of his father's family, and had at least one brother. He enlisted from Virginia in the United States Army for service in Mexico; was at the battle of Vera Cruz, and, on the march toward the city of Mexico, lost his life at the battle of Cerro Gordo, a mountain-pass in the Cofre de Puerto, in southern Mexico, about sixty miles from Vera Cruz. Here, on the 18th of April, 1847, General Scott with an army of 6000 men, following up his successes at Vera Cruz, found General Santa Anna with 3000 Mexicans awaiting him and blocking the pass. After several unsuccessful attempts to find another route, General Scott decided to assault the army in the pass. He succeeded in routing the Mexicans, capturing about 3000 prisoners, between four thousand and five thousand stands of arms and over forty pieces of artillery; but among the sixty-three Americans killed in the battle, our kinsman, John M. Seaton, died in a blaze of glory.

Long before this time he had married Elizabeth Jones, daughter of a Vermont farmer, who later moved to New York State; Elizabeth being a daughter of a first marriage. Her mother died about 1801, when Elizabeth was born. There were several children born to this union, and Mr. Jones married again and raised numerous other children. Both sets of children were raised together, the wives having been sisters.

John M. Seaton also served the Republic of Texas, and his wife received a land warrant (three sections) in Hardeman county, Texas, through which two railroads now run, and in which Beaumont is located.

There was recently published in a Clarksville, Tennessee, paper a notice which states that Sheriff Stafford has received from J. Q. Lillard, of Amity, Louisiana, a letter asking information concerning people by the name of Seaton. The letter states that there is valuable land in Texas for the heirs of John M. Seaton, who went to Texas previous to 1837.

Elizabeth Seaton, widow of John M. Seaton, drew a pension up to the date of her death, in 1865, on account of the services of her husband in the United States Army.

JOHN SEATON, son of John M. and Elizabeth Seaton, was born June 11, 1834, in Ohio. He spent his boyhood and learned his trade of coppersmith and heavy iron work in Louisville, Kentucky, where he received his education, except the last season, which was spent at Cincinnati, Ohio. He served his apprenticeship without indenture, and soon after that worked as journeyman in St. Louis, Missouri, from which city he went to Alton, Illinois, and began business on his own account. He ran a shop with from twelve to twenty men until Fort Sumter was fired upon, when he secured a drummer and fifer and started around to secure recruits, raised a company, and went into camp May 11, 1861, and was made Captain of Company B, Twenty-second Regiment, Illinois Infantry.

He served until the 19th of July, 1862, when he resigned, like many others, thinking their services were no longer needed, as they thought the war was practically ended, and being anxious to return to their business, which they had left at something of a sacrifice. He was drilling, scouting, fortifying, skirmishing, and was in the battle of New Madrid in the spring of 1862. From there, after lying around a month, they crossed the river as advance guard of General Pope's Army at Island No. 10, which had been evacuated. They followed up to Tiptonville, where 6000 surrendered to the Twenty-second regiment, thinking all of Pope's army was there. They returned to New Madrid, then went to Fort Pillow after two days' delay on account of high water, then went up the Tennessee and took part in the siege of Corinth. They were a month approaching Corinth, expecting battle. May 31st they found Beauregard had evacuated; then John sent in his resignation and went back to Alton and started up his business again.

He continued in business at Alton until in 1872, when he removed to Atchison, Kansas, where he established his present business, which has made a healthy growth. He was Councilman in Alton, and Chief Engineer of the Volunteer City Fire Department. In Atchison he served three terms (six years) on the School Board, after which he went to the Legislature in 1879, and was almost continuously there until 1902. He was a candidate for nomination for Governor of Kansas with six others, and received more votes than any other except W. E. Stanley, and was next to him in each ballot, gaining on each ballot.

The Atchison Foundry Company, of which John Seaton is President, is employing upwards of 200 men. The company was incorporated on January 1, 1903, taking in several of the former employés, among whom are John C. and Leroy George Seaton, sons of the former proprietor. John Seaton owns the Atchison Theater, has numerous real-estate investments in St. Louis, Kansas City, Camden county, Missouri, Eldorado Springs, Cedar county, Missouri, Fort Smith, Arkansas, and Topeka, Kansas.

John Seaton was married to Charlotte E. Tuthill, on the 9th of April, 1857, at Alton, Illinois. Pardon T. Tuthill, the father of Mrs. Seaton, is a descendant of a Tuthill who came over in the Mayflower, and his descendants have lived at Orient, Long Island, where dozens of families of the name now reside, not far from New London, Connecticut, across the Sound.

There have been born into the family of John and Charlotte Seaton three girls and two boys, as follows: Lillie M. Seaton; married a Mr. Moore and after his death, George W. Hendrickson. 2. Mary Elizabeth Seaton; married Dr. W. H. Conditt. 3. John

Charles Seaton; married Lillian Burtis, of Waterville. He is a a member of the Atchison Foundry Company, being vice-president and general manager. 4. Nellie Tabor Seaton; married Theodore Byram, of Atchison. She died in Kansas City, Missouri, in the fall of 1902, of peritonitis, and the body was taken to Atchison for burial. 5. Leroy George Seaton is single, and lives at the home of his father. He is a bookkeeper at the foundry.

Mrs. Lillie M. Hendrickson lives at Effingham, Atchison county, Kansas; and Mrs. Mary E. Conditt at Kansas City, Missouri.

John Seaton prepared and read a paper on "The Battle of Belmont" before the Kansas Commandery of the Military Order of the Loyal Legion of the United States, that is said to be the best account of that battle ever written.

The residence of the family, 520 South Fourth street, Atchison, is beautifully located, high up on the bank of the Missouri river, and the wife and mother is a beautiful lady, lovely beyond the art of society.

There is a short biography of Captain John Seaton of Atchison in "Eminent Men of Kansas," page 185.

He was a member of the Board of Directors of the Kansas Penitentiary, and was elected as president of the Board.

SOME VIRGINIA-PENNSYLVANIA SEATONS.

JAMES CARMICHAEL SEATON and his wife, Elizabeth, went from Virginia to Nebraska with his father in 1854, locating at Bellevue, Sarpy county. They appear to have lived at one time at Uniontown, Fayette county, Pennsylvania, but whether before or after their residence in Virginia it is impossible to say with certainty.

The children of J. C. and Elizabeth Seaton were: 1. Hiram. 2. Susan, who married a Collier. 3. Sallie, who became Mrs. Crawford. 4. Merchant. 5. Mary; became Mrs. Ingraham. 6. Frank. 7. Rebecca; married a Martin. 8. James 2d. 9. Juliet; married Robert Bony. 10. John Swan.

A daughter of the Bonys lives at Kansas City, Kansas, their address being 732 Nebraska avenue, and her married name is Lallie B. Crawley.

JOHN SWAN SEATON went to Baltimore, Maryland, and there

met and married a Miss Ellen Rowler, daughter of William and
Harriet (Donaldson) Rowler. J. S. was born at Uniontown, Fayette county, Pennsylvania, where relatives are reported to reside
at the present writing. He was a member of the First Nebraska
Veteran Volunteers; went into the army as a private in 1861,
enlisting at Syracuse, Missouri. After serving out the two years
for which he first enlisted, he reënlisted in a cavalry company as a
second lieutenant, continuing in the service until July 1, 1866,
when he was honorably discharged. The command to which he
belonged was stationed at Fort Kearney, Nebraska, at the time of
the muster-out. He died in 1874, but his wife is still awaiting
the summons to meet him on the other shore. She is seventy-six
years old, and is sojourning on the Pacific coast.

The children of John S. and Mary Ellen Seaton were: 1. William
De V. Seaton, who died in Omaha, Nebraska, June 1, 1873. 2.
Charles Fuller Seaton; lives in California with his second wife.
He had one daughter, Edith Seaton, by his first wife, but none
by the second, neither of whose names has been given us. 3.
John Hamilton Seaton, the only other child reported to us, was
born at Bellevue, Nebraska, on July 26, 1857. He was married
at Omaha, Nebraska, October 2, 1884, to Agnes Virginia Russell,
daughter of Newell and Paulina (Blachley) Russell.

John H. Seaton is a carpenter and builder at Omaha, where
he has made his home since July 19, 1876, when he moved from
Bellevue, except that he was in Seattle, Washington, from May 2,
1902, until September 29, 1903. He is, and always has been, a
Republican, and is a member of the Baptist Church.

The children who have come to them are: 1. Elizabeth B., who
was born at Omaha, August 18, 1885. 2. John Russell, born
November 25, 1888, where all the children were born, Omaha,
Nebraska. 3. Ernest Lawrence, born April 4, 1891. 4. Earl
Millard, April 30, 1894. 5. Ruth Allen, March 1, 1897; and 6.
Lola Agnes, born July 11, 1901.

CHAPTER LI.

JOHN SEATON was born at Whitby, England, in 1734, and was married to Hannah Gallilee at the same place in 1763. Miss Gallilee was also born at Whitby, in the selfsame year. John died in the year 1789, and Hannah in 1811.

Their son, Thomas Seaton, was born at the Whitby home in 1777. He married Mary Littlefair in 1807, who died the next year, leaving a son, Thomas L. Seaton, who was born at Whitby in 1808. He was married to Mary Longford in 1840, at Padstow, Cornwall, Mary having been born at that place in 1818. She died at Kingston-upon-Hull in 1896. Thomas L. having preceded her to his rest in 1870, dying at Padstow.

Their son, Albert Edward Seaton, was born September 3, 1848, at Padstow, Cornwall, England. He was united in the holy bonds of wedlock to Mary Hellyar Spettigue in January, 1873, at Whitstow, Cornwall. Mary was the daughter of Joseph Spettigue, of Whitstow. She died at Kingston-upon-Hull, Yorkshire, on May 16, 1876, where she was buried.

Albert Edward Seaton was again married, on August 22, 1889, this time to Edith Gertrude, daughter of George Stephenson, a merchant of Hull, at the home of the bride's father.

The only child by the first marriage was Mary Catharine Seaton, born in 1874; and to the second union, Edith Jane Seaton, born in 1891; Edward Lancelot, born in 1892; Sylvia May, 1895; Reginald Ethelbert, 1899; and Gilbert Christopher Scoresby in 1901.

Albert Edward is a civil engineer, shipbuilder and marine engineer. He is the author of a "Manual of Marine Engineering," published by D. Van Norstrand, which was revised in 1890. The "Thermodynamics of the Steam Engine," by Cecil H. Pea-

— 21

body, mentions and quotes from the above work, and in "Mechanical Drawing and Elementary Machine Design" mention is made of the same author and his work as authority on the subject. Kent's "Mechanical Engineer's Pocket Book" mentions and gives quotations from the same book in several places.

Mr. Seaton was consulting engineer for some years. He has held the office of Justice of the Peace, or Magistrate, for Hull. For eight years he was in the naval service of his country. His present address is Wilton House, Kingston-upon-Hull, and his office at No. 32 Victoria street, London, S. W.

A letter from Mr. Seaton sets forth a different theory of the origin of the family from that generally entertained on this side of the ocean. He claims that the family was originally English, and that some of the members first went to Scotland with Robert Bruce.

OTHER ENGLISH SEATONS.

JOHN SEATON, of England, was born May 27, 1744, his parents having evidently emigrated from Scotland. He had, according to the record in the old family Bible, five sisters and one brother, to wit: Sarah Seaton, born June 26, 1742; Ann Seaton, born June 27, 1746; Edward Seaton, born October 25, 1747; Rachel Seaton, born July 6, 1750; another Ann Seaton, born February 7, 1752; and Mary Seaton, born in August, 1754. All these lived in England.

John called his wife Mary, but further than that we are not informed as to her name. Their only child, so far as the record shows, was Joseph Seaton, who was born in England August 3, 1781. He married Elizabeth Walker, on June 18, 1806, in St. Mary's Church, in Beverly, England.

JOSEPH and ELIZABETH SEATON came to this country with their family in June, 1830, and settled in Utica, New York, where he worked at his trade, being a wheelwright. Of his children we know comparatively little, but his death and burial in Utica Cemetery are attested by a tombstone close to the west fence and not far from the one on the south. The inscription on the headstone is as follows:

"Sacred to the memory of Joseph Seaton, who died November 19, 1848, aged sixty-eight years. 'Mark the perfect man, and behold the upright; for the end of that man is peace.'"

Elizabeth Walker was born March 27, 1783, in England. She died February 15, 1855, in Utica, New York, and was buried beside her husband. This is a copy of the statement on her burial tablet:

"At rest, Elizabeth, wife of Joseph Seaton, who departed this life February 15, 1855, aged seventy-three years. 'Then shall the dust return to earth as it was; and the spirit shall return to God who gave it.'"

There were born to Joseph and Elizabeth Seaton thirteen children, as follows:

JOHN WALKER SEATON was born March 22, 1807, in England. He married Harriet Nightingale July 4, 1831, and died August 10, 1869, aged sixty-two years, four months and eighteen days.

JOSEPH SEATON 2D was born June 4, 1808, in England. When grown to manhood he married a lady named Hellen Kelly. He passed over the dark river to his reward December 30, 1880, after seventy-two years, six months and twenty-six days of the joys and sorrows of this life.

BENJAMIN SEATON, the third son, was welcomed into the family circle on November 10, 1809, in England, and departed this life September 18, 1817, while only a small boy, and is happy, "for of such is the kingdom of Heaven."

EDWARD SEATON was born in England, on August 4, 1811, and died before he had attained his first birthday, on April 19, 1812.

EDWARD SEATON 2D was born on February 15, 1813, about ten months after his brother of the same name had died, and was given the same name. He married Mary B. Whiffen on April 30, 1849, dying on March 22, 1872.

MARY ANN SEATON, the first daughter born into this family, was born September 10, 1814, and died within a year.

MARY ANN SEATON 2D was born on October 29, 1815, in England.

In the course of some few years she was married to David Nightingale, probably a brother to Harriet Nightingale, who espoused John Walker Seaton, Mary's brother. This happy event took place on November 21, 1832, and Mary Nightingale died on the 15th of February, 1882.

RACHEL HELEN SEATON was born in England, on the second of May, 1817, and died about a year later, on May 12, 1818.

RACHEL HELEN SEATON 2D was born March 19, 1819, in England. She married Carrol M. Steele April 30, 1837, and died on the 20th of February, 1855.

SARAH SEATON was born October 25, 1820, in England. She was married July 21st, 1838, to John Whiffen, who was more than likely a brother to Mary B. Whiffen, who married Edward Seaton 2d. Sarah Seaton Whiffen died February 23, 1854.

ELIZABETH SEATON was born March 25, 1822, in England. She married, on November 21, 1841, Isaac Whiffen, the third of the family to unite their destinies with the Whiffens. From the fact that Elizabeth Seaton's death was not recorded with the others of the family, it is supposed that she was still among the living when the record was made, in January, 1892.

SUSANNAH SEATON was born in England, November 27, 1823, and died about a month later, on December 30, 1823.

We have no account of any children having been born to any of the children of Joseph and Elizabeth Seaton thus far, even if they had any, which they may have had.

BENJAMIN WELBON SEATON, the only one of this large family with whose posterity we will have to do at present, was born January 13, 1825, in England. He married Julia E. Bond, December 30, 1849. They were the parents of ten children, viz.: 1. Elbert; 2. Franklin B.; 3. Clarence H.; 4. Mary; 5. Morris; 6. Helen; 7. Hiram Johnson; 8. Clara Elizabeth; 9. John Hervey; and 10. Charles A.

Julia Elizabeth Bond, wife of Benjamin Welbon Seaton, was born August 30, 1822, in Philadelphia. Her father, Mulford R.

Bond, who was born on October 26, 1798, married Julia A. Johnson, who was born January 18, 1800, the wedding taking place on the 20th of October, 1821. Mr. Bond died January 11, 1879, and his wife on March 13, 1847, both in Chicago, Illinois.

Julia Seaton's grandfather was Elisha Johnson, of Long Island. He was a Revolutionary soldier, who served five years and eight months in the patriot army, and was one of the three soldiers who, on September 25, 1785, while under orders, rowed Benedict Arnold to the ship Vulture when he escaped after his treachery. Mr. Johnson was an agent for a colony of French refugees who attempted a settlement, but failed on account of the Frenchmen not being used to laboring, and the first winter being severe, with heavy snows. Many of the colonists starved and froze to death.

Elisha Johnson married Mary Reeves, a Rhode Island lady, who was married at fifteen years of age and bore thirteen children, nine of whom grew to maturity. She made with her own hands all of their clothing, except shoes, from the raw material,—wool and flax,—carding, spinning and weaving and afterward making up the cloth into clothes. She also knit their stockings and plaited their summer hats. She died May, 1860, at the age of ninety-four.

THE CHILDREN OF BENJAMIN W. AND JULIA E. (BOND) SEATON.

ELBERT J. SEATON was born October 20, 1850, in Chicago, Illinois. He died August 10, 1851, without having known much of either the joys or sorrows of life.

FRANKLIN B. SEATON was born September 14, 1852, in Chicago, and died at Cambridge, Illinois, January 2, 1870.

CLARENCE H. SEATON, son of Benjamin W. and Julia E. Seaton, was born December 18, 1853, in Chicago, and died July 5, 1854.

MARY SEATON was born in Chicago, on February 7, 1855. She was married to William A. Worthington, on April 8, 1875. Mr. Worthington died March 28, 1881, and she was again married, on October 14, 1885, this time to Chauncey Clapham. Her only child by Mr. Worthington was Elizabeth Worthington, born September 24, 1870, in Nebraska, and died December 5, 1881, at

Cambridge, Illinois. Her children by Mr. Clapham were: Benjamin Clapham, born April 13, 1887, in South Dakota; Robert Clapham, born June 13, 1889, in the same State as his brother; and Julia Candence Clapham, born August 31, 1891, also in Dakota. The Clapham children are still among the living, so far as we have been advised.

MORRIS SEATON was born October 18, 1855, in Chicago, and died November 17 of that year.

HELEN SEATON was born November 1, 1857, at Prairie City, Illinois.

HIRAM JOHNSON SEATON was born May 9, 1860, at Kewanee, Illinois. He was publisher of a newspaper at Comanche, Iowa, the last heard of him by the writer.

CLARA ELIZABETH SEATON was born July 2, 1863, at Kewanee, Illinois, and married George M. Leathers July 6, 1881. Their only child, Harvey Leathers, was born April 22, 1882, in Chicago.

JOHN HERVEY SEATON was born September 13, 1865, at Wethersfield, Illinois.

CHARLES A. SEATON was born April 21, 1868, at Wethersfield, Illinois. He was publishing a newspaper at Clarence, Iowa, at the date of our last information.

Another British Seaton is OSCAR MAUSCAUS SEATON, of 1524 Fifth street, Washington, D. C., being a native-born citizen of the Island of Jamaica, B. W. I. He was born August 9, 1874, and came to this country in 1902 to study dentistry. His father resides on the island and is a Justice of the Peace and Clerk of the Municipal Board for the Parish of Westmoreland. He was born in 1844, and is a widower.

Oscar was a volunteer in the Jamaica Militia, but resigned, as the hours of drill clashed with his official duties as a second-class clerk in the General Postoffice in Kingston, Jamaica, where he served four years, and as a second-class clerk in the Internal Revenue department at Morant Bay and Chapelton for six years. He is an Episcopalian, Church of England.

MARTIN ALEXANDER SEATON, father to Oscar, was born in 1840, at Manchester, Jamaica, British West Indies, and was married in 1865 to Ophelia Isabella Munroe, who was born in 1845, at Savanna, Lamar, Jamaica, B. W. I. He is Inspector of the Poor in addition to his other official duties. His other children besides Oscar are: Martin Alexander Seaton, Jr., who is married and has three children, one boy and two girls. He is Clerk to Messrs. Nathan Sherlocks and Company, General Merchants, 96-98-100 Itarban street, Kingston, Jamaica, County of Saney; David Taraies Seaton is a second-class clerk in the Collector-General's office in Kingston, Jamaica; Reginald Emanuel Seaton is Deputy Clerk of the Court, Parish of St. Mary, his postoffice being Port Maria. This family has relatives in England and Scotland, but we are not informed as to their names and addresses.

WILLIAM SEATON lived and died at Elm Tree Inn, Intake, Sheffield, England. He married Mary Driver, of the same address. Their son, William Newbould Seaton, was born about 1834, at Sheffield, Yorkshire, England, where he married Harriet Walker, who was born in the year above mentioned. They came to America, and he died somewhere "out West" in the United States, his wife living until February 17, 1890.

Their son, Charles Seaton, born December 14, 1859, at Sheffield, England, must have come to America with his parents. He married Emma Susan Rupley, June 9, 1866, at Poughkeepsie, New York. This Mrs. Seaton died December 20, 1892, at Brooklyn, New York, and was buried at the Evergreen Cemetery. The children of this union were: Bessie Rupley Seaton, born April 10, 1887; Edward Newbould Seaton, born February 26, 1889; Nellie Walker Seaton, born October 22, 1892; and Donald Charles Seaton, born March 16, 1891, died August 4 of the same year.

For his second wife, Charles Seaton married Mary Adams, on October 29, 1895, in New York city. They have one daughter, Ida Adams Seaton, born February 7, 1897. Mr. Seaton is assistant manager in a drug house at No. 20 Schenck avenue, Brooklyn, New York, where he has made his home for fifteen years, having previously lived in New York city. He mentions the crest in England as being a deer *en rampant*.

LIEUTENANT JOHN SEATON, of the Royal Navy of England, was also in the service of the King of Spain at one time, and was knighted by him for services in the field during the Peninsular War, receiving the Order of the Tower and Sword. He married Esther Saunders, and made their home in Yorkshire, England.

The children of John and Esther Seaton were three, as reported to us: Their son Henry Francis Seaton married Mary Compton, and lives at Cadborough Bay, Victoria, B. C. They have one son, Arthur Henry Seaton, who was born December 19, 1872, at Enfield, Middlesex, England, and it appears he is a single man, a draughtsman by profession. At our latest advices he was transiently located at 1328 Melleville street, Vancouver, British Columbia, but his home has been at San Francisco, California, and at Seattle, Washington.

The late William Arthur Seaton, son of John and Esther, was born at North Cave, Yorkshire, in 1834. He married Pauline Corbet, in January, 1866. Pauline was the daughter of Philip and Jane Corbet, of Shrewsbury. William Arthur was a Lieutenant in the Royal Navy and Commander in the Peninsular and Oriental Company. The present address of the family is Old Charlton, Kent, England, and has been for the last five years, they having formerly resided at Westcombe Park, Blackheath, from 1831 to 1899, and in the neighborhood of Southampton before.

In politics William Arthur Seaton was a Conservative, and in religion, Church of England.

The children of William Arthur and Pauline Seaton were five: 1. William Roseland, born at Southampton, in 1870, was a civil engineer in the Royal Navy, and was drowned from Her Majesty's Ship "Victoria," in 1893. 2. Esther Jane Seaton was born in 1873, at Woolston, Southampton. 3. John Francis Seaton, born in 1876, was a clerk in the National Bank of India; is now in Karachio, India. 4. Archie Corbet Seaton, born in 1879, at Kitterae, near Southampton, is an electric engineer at the Electric Harbor Works, Durban, South Africa. 5. Cyril Gervas, born in 1879, at Kitterae, near Southampton, is a clerk in the postoffice at No. 122 Leadenhall street, London, England.

Frederick Seaton, son of Lieutenant John and Esther Seaton was drowned.

ALEXANDER SEATON, OF ENGLAND OR SCOTLAND.

ALEXANDER SEATON was born in one of the above countries. He came to America and bought land in Westmoreland county, Pennsylvania. He died on March 7, 1822, leaving his land to Thomas Seaton, who was probably his brother. Thomas held the land until his death, July 21, 1831. when it passed to his brothers, John and James, and his sister Harriet, who had intermarried with one Berry.

THOMAS SEATON, above, had a son, George Washington Seaton, who died in Ligonier Valley, Westmoreland county, Pennsylvania, somewhere about 1874, at the age of eighty-five years. This George Washington Seaton married Jane Menhirter, who lived to be eighty-seven years old. They had a son, Thomas A. Seaton, born at Ligonier in 1825, who married Ann Matilda Cole, who was born at the same place and in the same year as her husband. They had four sons and one daughter:

1. BURNERD COLE SEATON, born in 1848, at Ligonier, practiced medicine for thirty-one years, and died October 9, 1903, at Bolivar, where he was buried. He married Sarah Adelaid Miller, at Bolivar, in 1874. She was born in West Virginia, in 1857, and died in August, 1901. They had children as follows: Leander Miller Seaton, born in 1875, at Bolivar, is an M. D.; Carrie; Rebecca; Edna; Lillian; Charles Forrest; and Ethel Maud Seaton.

2. JOHN SEATON, born in 1852, at Ligonier, married Ida Patterson, in Bolivar, in 1888. Their present address is Bolivar, Pennsylvania. They have three children: Frank, Wilbur, and Hazel.

3. THOMAS SEATON, born in 1854, at Ligonier, died in 1885, at Pittsburg, but was buried at Bolivar. At the time of his death he was attending a medical college in Pittsburg. He married, in 1878, Amanda Luilleger, but had no children.

4. LEANDER SEATON was born December 25, 1858, at Ligonier. He never married, but died at Pittsburg, and was buried at Bolivar. He was practicing medicine before his death.

5. AUGUSTA SEATON, born in 1860, at Ligonier, married Daniel Brown, in 1879, at the home of her youth. She died at Derry Station, Pennsylvania. They had three children: Edna Brown married Allen Culp. They lived at Wilkesbarre, Pennsylvania. Blanch and Olive Brown reside at Derry Station.

ENGLISH-MASSACHUSETTS SEATONS.

WILLIAM SEATON, of Bristol, England, must have been born not very far from 1770, for his son Robert was born October 13, 1792. When William died the flags in Bristol were hung at half-mast; so, presumably, he was a public officer.

ROBERT SEATON, son of William, was born at Bristol, and came to America with his family about 1846. His son, Worthington Winton Seaton, was born in Bristol, September 16, 1842, and was about four years old when he came across the Atlantic. He is located at No. 61 South street, Boston, Massachusetts, where he is engaged in the leather business, according to the Boston 1903 Directory. His home is at No. 16 Davis avenue, Brookline, Massachusetts, from which place a letter was received from his wife, Mrs. Sarah M. Seaton.

ENGLISH-OHIO SEATONS.

JAMES SEATON, of England, married Margaret Dickson. Their son, Robert Seaton, was born at Charnlockhead, Thornhill, Dumfries, Scotland, and married Dorothy Struthers, who was also born in Scotland, at Falkirk, their marriage taking place at Niagara Falls, Canada, on December 11, 1850. Their children were: William T. (now dead), and James Walter Seaton of 866 Rockdale avenue, Avondale, Cincinnati, Ohio. William T. Seaton left a daughter, Gertrude Dorothy Seaton, who lives at Grand Lodge, Michigan.

JAMES WALTER SEATON, born at London, Canada, December 7, 1854, was married to Bertha Newberry, at Buffalo, New York, April 11, 1883. Miss Newberry's ancestors were born at Somersetshire, England. James W. is a solicitor of Bradstreet's Mercantile Agency, his present address being 866 Rockdale, as above, where he has lived over twenty years, having formerly made his home at Detroit, Michigan, and at London, Canada. He is a Republican and a Presbyterian. His only child, Ethel Seaton, born February 26, 1844, at Cincinnati, Ohio, is unmarried, heart-whole and fancy-free, a devout Methodist.

CHAPTER LII.

ENGLISH SEATONS.

FRANCIS SEATON was born at Goole, England, about 1794. He had one sister, Mary Frances Seaton, who was married at Goole about 1814. His wife was also born in England, as were at least some of their children. Francis and his wife both died at Walden, New York, the former in 1861 and the latter in 1884 or 1885. The names of their children follow:

1. DANIEL SEATON came to this country with his parents, and settled at Walden, New York. He was a soldier on the Federal side during the Rebellion, and is now an inmate of the Soldiers' Home at Bath, New York. With his brother Mark he enlisted as a nine-months man in Hawkins's Zouaves, from Newburg, New York, served his time out, reënlisted for three years, and at the expiration of two and a half years took a thirty-days furlough and again reënlisted, and was mustered out at the close of the war, having done his whole duty from beginning to the close of his term of service.

His only son was John Francis Seaton, whose widow, Mrs. Eva B. Seaton, resides at No. 311 Seventh avenue, Newark, New Jersey. Their son, Howard Brierley Seaton, was born in 1890.

2. MARK SEATON had the same experience in the war as his brother Daniel, both enlisting at the same time, in the same command, serving together through the war and being discharged at the same time and place, having served through the whole of the terrible struggle. Mark is supposed to have died in the West. He had a son living in Oklahoma or in the Indian Territory about 1894.

3. WILLIAM SEATON was a sailor. He served on an English man-of-war, and later sailed as a minor officer on the steamer

"Scotland," in the White Star Line between New York and Liverpool, for some years. Still more recently he was in the British army in India, and died in a London hospital from a disease contracted while serving there.

4. JOHN SEATON, born June 7, 1817, in Leeds, England, was twice married. His first wife was Frances Law, who died at Glenham, New York, about 1844, their marriage having taken place in England. They had no issue. For his second wife he wooed and won Susannah Bray, who was born June 11, 1816, near Manchester, England. She had been previously married to Joseph Wharam, who died in England before Susannah came to America, a widow with one daughter, then five years old, who is now in Torrington, Connecticut, as Mrs. Edward Capel. John and Susannah Seaton were married October 17, 1846, at Newberg, New York. John died at Walden, New York, December 23, 1868, from an accident. Susannah died in Ansonia, Connecticut, March 27, 1880.

The children of John and Susannah Seaton were: 1. Francis W., born July 22, 1848, now resides at Goshen, Connecticut. He was married at Walden, New York, April 9, 1873, to Mary Boothroyd. 2. John T. Seaton, born September 25, 1853; married at Thomaston, Connecticut, April 22, 1880, to Elizabeth Capel. They reside at James street, Torrington, Connecticut. 3. Martha A. Seaton, born August 25, 1850; married at Walden, New York, April 15, 1872, to George S. Burden. Their present address is 364 North Main street, Torrington, Connecticut. 4. Ann Jane Seaton, born July 25, 1847; died in infancy. 5. Sabina R. Seaton, born July 15, 1855, at Walden, New York; died September 25, of the same year. 6. Charles W. Seaton, born July 31, 1856, at Walden; was married to Sarah E. Summer, April 12, 1882, at Ansonia, Connecticut. Miss Summer was born in Birmingham, England, February 16, 1861. Her father was Charles Summer and her mother, Hepzibah (Coxson) Summer. Both died in Birmingham, England. She had eleven brothers and sisters, all of whom, except two sisters and one brother who live in California, are now dead. Charles W. Seaton is foreman in a

wire-mill in Ansonia, Connecticut, where he has resided since 1874.
The first seventeen years of his life were spent at Walden, New
York; then he lived at Torrington, Connecticut, about eleven
years. He is a Republican in politics and is a member of the
Episcopal Church, having been baptized in the Methodist Church.
The children of Charles W. and Sarah E. Seaton are: Ruby E.,
born January 16, 1883, at Ansonia, Connecticut, and Charles A.,
born November 18, 1886, at the same place. Both are single.

5. HANNAH MARSTON, daughter of Francis Seaton, died in
Vineland, New Jersey, in 1902, aged about eighty years.

6. MARY HOLMES, born in 1824; lives at Walden, New York.

7. JANE SEATON was born about 1826. She was married to
Joseph Hartley, September 12, 1847, at Leeds, England, where
Mr. Hartley was a cloth-finisher. They came to America soon
after their marriage. They have lived at their present address,
Pittsfield, Pennsylvania, for thirty years, and before that, at
Titusville, near Poughkeepsie, New York, for twenty-four years.
They are retired farmers.

The children of Joseph and Jane Hartley were: Elizabeth
Hartley, who married Frank Allen, in 1875; Martha Jane Hartley
married James N. Young, in 1872; and Richard Seaton Hartley
married Mary I. Giles, in 1876.

Richard S. and Mary I. Hartley live at Youngsville, Pennsylvania, R. F. D. No. 2, where they own and operate the "Smith
Hill Stock Farm," breeding high-class cattle and poultry, making
choice butter and selling the Omega Jr. cream separators. Richard S. Hartley reports that William Seaton served in the army
during our Civil War, then went back to England, enlisted in the
British army, and died in India.

The last heard of Mark Seaton he took up a soldier's claim in
Kansas to make himself a home. He had a son who went to
Kansas about 1874.

Mrs. Martha Jane (Hartley) Young lives at 108 Howard avenue, Utica, New York.

INDIANA AND ILLINOIS SEATONS.

GEORGE WASHINGTON SEATON lived in Posey county, Indiana from which section he moved to Canton, Illinois, where he died on February 21, 1904. His children were William Pitt, Charles, Catharine, Annie, and Richard. We have no particulars regarding the lives of any of the children, except William Pitt, who also moved from Posey county, Indiana, to Canton, Illinois, possibly at the same time his father did. From Canton he removed to Farmington, in 1884, and in 1889, to Peoria, Illinois. He married Miss Hannah Petrie, daughter of P. W. Petrie of Farmington, and two children have blessed the union.

ROSS PETRIE SEATON was born at Canton, Illinois, on the 25th of October, 1882. He attended the public schools in Peoria until in 1896, when, on account of poor health, he spent about a year in California, finishing his education after his return to Peoria, in the public schools and Bradley Polytechnic Institute of that city. Since 1889 he has been engaged in the brokerage business. He is senior member of the firm of Seaton & Field, at No. 12, Chamber of Commerce.

ERMA LOISE SEATON was born November 6, 1884, but whether before or after her father moved to Farmington we are not informed.

JOHN SEATON, OF HUNTINGTON, INDIANA.

JOHN SEATON was born February 20, 1828, in Crawford county, Indiana. His father was born in Tennessee, in 1802, and his mother in Indiana, Crawford county, in 1803. They were married in 1821 by a Methodist minister, Mr. Seaton being a preacher of that denomination. Mrs. Seaton's ancestors are said to have come from Caucasia.

John Seaton was married to Mary Catharine Ott, at Mifflin, Indiana, by the Rev. John Hughes, in the Methodist Church, October 16, 1856. Mary Catharine was a daughter of Malachi Ott, who married a lady by the name of Ware, her mother being a Burr.

John is a retired blacksmith, being too old to perform such

strenuous labor as is required of artists in his business. He has lived in Huntington, Dubois county, Indiana, for about eight years, having formerly made his residence near Grantsburg, in 1865, from which locality he moved to Mifflin in 1872, and to St. Anthony in 1896, thence to Huntington.

He enlisted in the Union Army July 13, 1861, and was not discharged until May 31, 1865, at Washington, D. C. In politics he is a Republican and in religion a Methodist.

The children vouchsafed to this family were: John Wesley Gordon Seaton, born at Mifflin, Indiana, June 4, 1860; married C. E. Tillman July 13, 1884, at Banta, Indiana. He is a Republican, and a member of the Friends' Church. His business is carpentry. For ten years last past his home has been at West Newton, Indiana. From 1860 to 1893 he lived at the home of his birth, then at Banta from 1893 to 1894.

The children of J. W. G. and C. E. Seaton are Nellie Alra, born at Mifflin, July 20, 1885, and Ward Tillman, whose birthday was November 21, 1891.

OLIVER PRESTON MORTON SEATON, son of John and Mary, was born at Grantsburg August 19, 1862. He lives at Taswell, Crawford county, Indiana. He married Alice Benham, at Mifflin, March 24, 1887.

EMMA LOU ALICE SEATON was born at Grantsburg, March 24, 1866. She married "Rile" Robertson, at Taswell, October 30, 1887, Rev. Mr. Brock performing the interesting ceremony. They reside at English, Crawford county, Indiana.

MARY LUARCIA SEATON, born at Grantsburg in the year 1868, September 8, was married to Elias Stolk Beard, February 14, 1898, at St. Anthony, by Esquire Ray. They are domiciled at Huntingburg, Dubois county, Indiana.

WALTER SEATON was born May 1, 1871, at Mifflin, and his brother, Charles T. Seaton, July 6, 1874, at the above home.

MAUD E. SEATON was born August 12, 1877, at Mifflin. She was united in marriage with Hugh H. McConnel, at Huntingburg, June 21, 1904, by Rev. Mr. Priest. Their home is at Evansville, Indiana, 1103 South Governor street.

A REAL REFORMER.

GEORGE G. SEATON, a farmer and pioneer settler of Rockford, Illinois, was a very devout man, and smoking and drinking he held to be sins that could not be condoned by any religion. He had a deep-rooted horror of the cigarette habit, and never lost an opportunity to wage war against it, either in public or among his friends and relatives.

He left an estate worth $50,000. The principal legatees under his will were his daughters, Mrs. Alice Crunke, and his son, Arthur Seaton. To four nieces and six nephews he bequeathed sums ranging from one hundred to two hundred dollars each, with the proviso that if any of the legatees should use to excess either cigarettes or alcoholic liquors, that portion which was to go to them should go to some charitable institution, to be determined by the executors. All of the heirs are said to have been of the same opinion as Mr. Seaton, on this question.

CHAPTER LIII.

ROBERT SEATON.

Robert Seaton was born in Scotland or Ireland, probably the latter, about 1775 or 1780. He married Jane McCabe, of County Down, Ireland, whose ancestors were among the early settlers of the latter country, coming from Scotland. In 1806 Robert and his family set sail for America, but, sad to relate, he died on the voyage, and was doubtless buried in the hungry ocean that has so often bereaved those who have trusted their lives upon its restless bosom, hoping to better their condition by leaving the Old World for a home in the New.

Mrs. Seaton settled in Cumberland county, Pennsylvania, and six months after the death of her husband, gave birth to a son, to whom she gave his father's name, Robert Seaton. Some time after locating at the above place, Jane Seaton was married, to Robert Crawford, an Irish school teacher. She is said to have been a Protestant, a seceder, now called United Presbyterians, in faith.

Robert Crawford died in 1843, aged seventy-six years, and his wife Jane in 1841, aged seventy-four years. Both died and were buried in Fayette county, in western Pennsylvania.

The children of Robert and Jane (McCabe) Seaton, as far as known to us, were: 1. Matthew; 2. James; and 3. the Robert 2d whose birth is noted above.

THE CHILDREN OF ROBERT AND JANE (McCABE) SEATON.

Matthew and James Seaton, sons of the above worthy people, are among the altogether too large number of those whose life history remains to be traced, although every means at hand, or within the grasp of our mind, has been employed to do these persons, and all others, full justice.

ROBERT SEATON, JR., we have already learned was born on this side of "the big pond," about six months after the death of his father, or in the year of our Lord 1806, in Cumberland county Pennsylvania. He was married to a Pennsylvania Dutch lady by the name of Anna Seachrist on Independence Day, 1826. They had seven children, all of whom were born in Fayette county, Pennsylvania, viz.: 1. James; 2. Jain Martha; 3. Anna; 4. Joseph Crawford; 5. Mary; 6. Frances Elizabeth; and 7. Matthew Alexander Seaton. Robert Seaton, Jr., died in 1846, aged forty years.

THE CHILDREN OF ROBERT, JR., AND ANN (SEACHRIST) SEATON.

JAMES SEATON, son of the above parents, has no attainable personal history, except that he was born in Fayette county, Pennsylvania, on January 6th, 1828.

JAIN MARTHA SEATON was born in Fayette county, Pennsylvania, July 11, 1830, and died in the same county on November 26, 1833.

ANNA SEATON was born at the same place as the above-mentioned members of the family, on March 31, 1833. She was married to George Glendenning, a blacksmith, sailor, and soldier, and now lives at Abilene, Dickinson county, Kansas.

JOSEPH CRAWFORD SEATON was born July 20, 1835, in North Union township, Fayette county, Pennsylvania, two miles from Uniontown, the county seat. He learned the profession of a printer at Galesburg, Illinois, on the *Free Democrat*. It was providentially his good fortune to work for two years at his trade in Conneautville, Crawford county, Pennsylvania, on the *Courier*, owned by G. W. Brown, who afterward became famous by publishing *The Herald of Freedom* at Lawrence, Kansas, of which publication Preston B. Plumb, afterward United States Senator from Kansas, and Thomas A. Osborn, at one time Governor of Kansas, were at different times the foremen.

The whole outfit of the *Herald* office was thrown into the Kansas river and everything about the office destroyed by the pro-slavery advocates in the early political troubles of Bloody Kansas. The only crime charged against the proprietor of the paper was that he upheld the doctrines of the Free-Soil party, or the anti-slavery element.

Mr. Seaton also worked two years in Pittsburg, Pennsylvania, in a book- and job-office, from which position he enlisted into the Union Army, after having worked at his profession for nine years in all. While he was in the army all of his surplus wages were sent home to assist his sisters in completing their education. After his return from the war, he was appointed Census Enumerator for the townships of Dunbar, North Union, Menallen, and Stuart, in Fayette county, Pennsylvania, being a strip of territory twelve by twenty-four miles in extent.

It was on May 4, 1861, that he enlisted in Company G, Ninth Pennsylvania Reserve Corps, under Colonel Jackson, afterward Brigadier-General, who was killed at Fredericksburg, the regiment being under the immediate command of General George B. McClellan. It was not until May 12, 1864, that he was mustered out of the United States' service, having served all of the time in the same company and regiment in which he first enlisted, and never having been wounded, or been in a hospital. He took an active part in all of the battles in which his regiment participated during his term of enlistment, as follows: Drainsville, Virginia, December 20, 1861; a skirmish at Meadow Bridge on the Chickahominy river, June 23, 1862; Mechanicsville, Virginia, June 26, 1862; the latter being first day of the famous seven days' fight; Gaines Hill, Virginia, June 27, 1862; Glendale, or Charles City, Cross-roads, June 30, 1862; Malvern Hill, on the James river, July 1, 1862; Groveton, Virginia, August 29, 1862; Manassas, Virginia, August 30, 1862; South Mountain, Maryland, September 14, 1862; Antietam, Maryland, September 17, 1862; Fredericksburg, Virginia, December 13, 1862; Gettysburg, Pennsylvania, July 2 and 3, 1863; Rappahannock, Virginia, November 15, 1863; and Mine Run, Virginia, November 30, 1863.

Mr. Seaton came to Kansas in 1870, and took up a homestead, but worked most of his time in the Abilene *Chronicle* office until in 1872, when he went back to Pennsylvania and was married to

Mary Bianca Carson. The all-important ceremony was performed by Reverend Mr. Axtell, an uncle to Miss Carson. Miss Carson was born at Uniontown, Fayette county, Pennsylvania, April 16, 1845, where she attended school, and finally taught in the schools of her native county, where she was well known and where her many good qualities were appreciated. She proved herself a successful business manager and had saved her wages until, when she was married, she had quite a snug sum laid by with which to begin housekeeping.

The newly married couple arrived at Abilene, Kansas, on August 2, 1872, near which city they have since made their home, and where they have a fine farm consisting of two hundred acres of creek-bottom land and two hundred and forty of upland prairie, in Garfield township, Dickinson county, Kansas. They keep a dairy and raise stock in connection with grain-farming, have a fine home, a liberal supply of this world's goods, and four bright children, to say nothing of the grandchildren, which we must agree with them are as sweet and smart as live anywhere.

They have quite an extensive library for farmers, and are students as well as farmers, taking great delight in their books.

Mr. Seaton is a Republican in politics, and is a member of the Methodist Episcopal Church.

The children born to these estimable people are: Lena Bianca; William Carson; Frances Elizabeth; and Robert Lincoln.

MARY SEATON, a sister to the subject of the foregoing sketch, was born March 14, 1839, in Fayette county, Pennsylvania, where she received her education. She was a school teacher in and around Abilene, Kansas, for several years, where she married a German Reformed preacher, John A. Nicolai by name. Mr. Nicolai was a real-estate dealer as well as a preacher, and secured for himself a liberal amount of property. He died before they had any children, leaving his widow well provided for in land, besides a fine residence in Abilene, and some other property in California. The date of the demise of Mr. Nicolai was March 4, 1893.

Mrs. Nicolai chose her brother, Joseph Crawford Seaton, for her executor, and he has in his possession the deeds and other legal papers belonging to the estate.

FRANCES ELIZABETH SEATON, daughter of Robert, was born December 10, 1840, at Connellsville, Fayette county, Pennsylvania, where she received her education at the select school in her native town. On October 8, 1868, she was married to Joseph Taylor, by Reverend B. F. Woodburn. Mr. Taylor was a citizen of Ligonier village, in Westmoreland county, Pennsylvania, where they made their home for nine years; then they came to Kansas, and settled near Abilene, arriving in January, 1878. They have raised only one child, a son, Harry Seaton Taylor.

Harry Taylor is still single, and was living with his parents when I visited them in the summer of 1902. He is a graduate of the High School of Abilene and of the Atchison Commercial College, and is an expert bookkeeper, stenographer and typewriter by profession, having had good positions in Kansas City, Missouri, for several years.

At one time he was in the hardware business, in partnership with Herbert Landis in Ralston, Pawnee county, Oklahoma, but not being suited with that branch of business, and finding an advantageous opportunity to dispose of his interest in the business, he did so, and returned to the home of his youth.

MATTHEW ALEXANDER SEATON was born August 4, 1843, in Fayette county, Pennsylvania.

THE CHILDREN OF JOSEPH CRAWFORD AND MARY BIANCA (CARSON) SEATON.

LENA BIANCA SEATON was born at the beautiful site of the Seaton homestead near Abilene, Kansas, on October 20, 1873. She attended the Dickinson County High School at Chapman, Kansas, after she was through the district school, and has added to her education by some travel, and attending the Columbian Exposition at Chicago, Illinois, in 1893. She was united in marriage to Thomas Erskine Robson by the Reverend J. H. Kuhn. Mr. Robson is of English descent on his father's side and Scotch on his mother's.

There have been born to Mr. and Mrs. Robson three children, as follows: Erskine Seaton Robson, born October 20, 1896; Earl Lincoln Robson, born September 5, 1898; and Jane Ann Robson, who was born July 29, 1901. Each of these children was born in Wheatland township, Dickinson county, Kansas, on the Robson farm, which consists of three hundred acres of choice land, about one-half of which is in cultivation and the remainder in meadow and pasture. The farm is principally devoted to dairying and raising grain, the greater part of which is fed to livestock on the farm.

The Robsons were married at the home of the bride's parents, by the pastor of the Sunnyside Methodist Church.

WILLIAM CARSON SEATON was born near Abilene, Kansas, on May 11, 1876. He attended the Dickinson County High School at Chapman, Kansas, taught school in his home county, and finally enlisted about May 1, 1898, in the since famous Twentieth Kansas Regiment, Infantry, for the Philippine War, serving under Frederick Funston, the captor of Aguinaldo, the leader of the Filipinos. Young Seaton had the misfortune to contract that loathsome disease, smallpox, soon after arriving at the Philippines, thus missing the first two battles in which his regiment participated; after which he was engaged in fifteen battles, besides numerous skirmishes. He was fortunate enough never to have been wounded, but had a siege of measles and some other diseases.

When his term of enlistment had expired he came home with the regiment; then attended the Kansas City Business College for about six months, to finish his education.

He was Census Enumerator for Wheatland and Garfield townships, in Dickinson county, Kansas, for the twelfth census; then entered the postoffice in Abilene as general-delivery clerk, where he was still employed in September, 1902.

William Carson Seaton married Nellie Lesley Lowry, daughter of Obed Lowry, of Abilene, Kansas, on June 11, 1902. Rev. F. S. Blaney, pastor of the Presbyterian Church in Abilene, officiating.

Miss Lowry was born September 16, 1876, in Franklin county, Pennsylvania. She taught school in the home county in Kansas for several terms before she was married. She is a lovely lady, well informed, and a splendid housekeeper and home-maker, as the writer can testify from a personal acquaintance with the lady herself and her tasty cottage home.

FRANCES ELIZABETH SEATON was born December 24, 1878, at the Seaton home near Abilene Kansas. She lives with her parents, a beautiful and bright young lady, something of a musician, and, best of all, an efficient helper in the home of her youth.

ROBERT LINCOLN SEATON was born November 4, 1883, at the homestead on the hill near Sunnyside Church, in Dickinson county, Kansas. He is fitting himself by practical experience to manage a farm of his own at some future time, by assisting his father in the operation of the home farm and livestock. He also attends the Kansas State Agricultural College, at Manhattan, Kansas, taking the farmers' course. Robert is a bright young man, and there is no doubt that he will make a creditable showing in whatever line of work he may undertake.

CHAPTER LIV.

JAMES SEATON and his wife Martha lived in County Tyrone, Ireland, at a place called Dranity. He was a man of some wealth, and had twelve children, all boys: 1. George; 2. Thomas; 3. Alexander; 4. William; 5. James, Jr.; 6. Robert; 7. David; 8. Jared; 9. John; 10. Hezekiah; 11. Joel; and 12. Nathaniel.

GEORGE SEATON was born in County Tyrone, Ireland. He married Nancy Amberson in the old country, and came to America about 1778, settling in the Ligonier Valley, near Greensburg, and not far from Pittsburgh. Nancy's people were Lutherans, while George's were Church of England; so both young people were disinherited and disowned by their parents.

George was a Captain, his brother Thomas a Lieutenant, and another brother, Alexander, a First Sergeant in the same company during the Revolutionary War; all having come to America together, or at about the same time, and the company to which they belonged served in Lafayette's division.

After the Revolution, George and his brothers, Thomas and Alexander, settled down in Westmoreland county, Penn., George in the Ligonier Valley and the other brothers in Johnstown.

George and Nancy became "well to do," and had twelve children:

1. John Seaton; a doctor; married, and died in Washington, D. C.

2. William; a preacher of the Methodist Episcopal Church; married Jane Huston.

3. Robert; a tanner; had two sons. He died in the West.

4. Elizabeth; died at twelve years of age.

5. Thomas; married Betsy Mavis. They had three children: Margaret, who married Robert Lamberson, by whom she had six

sons and two daughters, from whom there is a very large connection in Franklin, Penn. Margaret is now, 1903, in her 88th year, and is the mother of Mrs. George P. Hukill, of Franklin, Penn., widow.

6. Jackson; has a large family, all married, and living in Franklin and other places in the Keystone State.

7. George, Jr.; became a hatter, and married a Miss Maher. They have seven children, only one of whom appears in our notes. Jane Seaton, who in 1816 married a Morrow, of Altoona, Penn., and had eight children.

8. Amberson; learned the tailor trade. He married, but died without issue in Steubenville, Ohio, his wife dying within a few minutes after her husband.

9. Jane; married Robert Jackson. They had two daughters, Eliza, who married a Little, and Nancy, who became Mrs. Sloan, and had four sons.

10. Mary (Polly); married an Alexander, and had one daughter. Polly Alexander died at Steubenville, Ohio.

11. Nancy; married a McClellan, and had eight children, in Franklin, Penn., and has descendants in large and wealthy families in that commonwealth among the Plumers, Dales and Snowdens, in Franklin, and in the person of Judge Bredin, of Butler.

12. Martha; married John Ausstraw, and had four children: Joseph, Alexander, Nancy, and Theresa Ausstraw.

After the death of Nancy (Amberson) Seaton, George married for his second wife Martha Ausstraw, a widow, whose maiden name was Martha James, daughter of Henry James, of County Derry, where Martha was born. By her George Seaton had two sons—David, born in 1802, and Alexander White Seaton, born in 1804.

One of our correspondents gives the name of James Seaton as a son of George, stating that he went to Kentucky when a young man. Possibly he was one of the other boys having a double name that has become separated.

ALEXANDER SEATON, brother to George, finally located in Washington, D. C. There is nothing known of his descendants for sure.

Thomas, the other brother who came over with George, was married and had six sons, two of whom married, but none are now living.

One record says that Nancy Seaton, daughter of George and Nancy (Amberson) Seaton married first an Ogden, by whom she had a son, William Ogden, who, on account of being nicknamed "Hog-den" by his school-mates, took his mother's surname, Seaton, by which he is known. He was last heard of at Greensburg, Penn. He was partly raised by Alexander White Seaton.

By this record, Nancy Seaton is said to have married, secondly, a McFarland, but lived only a short time after this latter marriage.

ALEXANDER WHITE SEATON, son of George and Martha, was born May 23, 1804, in Westmoreland county, Pennsylvania. He married Phœbe Griffin, March 3, 1835, in the same county, where Phœbe was also born, August 12, 1818. Their children were: 1. George, born December 4, 1835; 2. Amberson, born October 8, 1837; 3. Wright J., born February 1, 1840; 4. Catharine, born February 19, 1842; 5. Mary Jane, born August 4, 1844; 6. Ann Eliza, born October 22, 1846; 7. Alexander White 2d, born April 4, 1850; 8. William F., born November 2, 1852. We have the card of a W. F. Seaton, of St. Louis, Missouri, who is general manager and secretary of the Metropolitan Electric Company, with an office at 917-919 Market street; whether the same as above or not, we are unable to say.

Alexander White Seaton, father of the above children, died in Wayne county, Ohio, November 16, 1855. His wife, Phœbe, died in Van Wert county, Ohio, October 16, 1875.

DAVID SEATON, son of George and Martha, was born February 22, 1802, and is said by some to have come to this country from Scotland and settled in Ohio. He married Catharine Piper, on November 9, 1826. They were living in Westmoreland county, Pennsylvania, on August 23, 1834. Their children were as follows: 1. Uriah C., born October 9, 1828, and died in Denver, Colorado, leaving a widow and one daughter, neither of whose names we have learned. 2. Peter Piper, born January 20, 1831; enlisted in the army during the Civil War, and was never heard from afterward by his friends. 3. George Washington, born August 11. 1833, in Westmoreland county, Pennsylvania. He married Martha Purcell, and had issue as follows: John Henry Calaway Seaton, who lives at Day, Taney county, Missouri; Elizabeth Jane; Mary Ellen; Nancy Catharine. (These three girls were named for three of their father's aunts.) Then comes William Ernest Seaton, who lives at Kansas City, Kansas. He says that David Seaton, his grandfather, was the eleventh son of George and Martha Seaton. Jonathan Seaton, born September 23, 1836; Washington Seaton, born August 16, 1839, remain to be traced, as do his brother and two sisters to follow: Martha, born May 30, 1841, and Mary Catharine, who was born February 7, 1844. William Henry Seaton was born May 2, 1847, in the Buckeye State. His widow, Mrs. Georgia Seaton, our informant for this line of Seatons, and her four children, live at Crane, Stone county, Missouri, the husband and father having died on the 19th of June, 1901.

The children of William Henry and Georgia Seaton are these: Della Alvina, born January 6, 1884; Howard Mortimer, born exactly two years after his sister; Iva Ethel Frances, born December 27, 1889; and Floyd Washington, born February 11, 1892.

AMBERSON SEATON, second son of Alexander W. and Phœbe, born at Carna, Oklahoma, has resided there for thirteen years. He volunteered in 1861, and served three years in Company H, Sixteenth Ohio, in the Civil War. On December 25, 1880, he was married to Sarah Ann Still, in Benton county, Arkansas. Of this marriage three sons have been born: George, born December 12, 1881, died February 12, 1882; Samuel A., born in 1883; and Alexander Wright Jackson Seaton, who was born in 1887.

Alexander Wright J. Seaton and his son are among those for whom we are seeking.

A REAL SCOTCH FAMILY.

GEORGE SEATON, born about 1700, lived in the pass of Kilikrankie, Blair Athol, Perthshire, Scotland. He was a soldier, and followed his chief to the Highlands, being his target- or shield-bearer. He spelled the name Seton, and was a wearer of the Athol tartan. He had three children: Duncan, James, and John.

JAMES SEATON was a very handsome youth, and a lady took him to her home in Edinburgh and educated him because of her admiration for his beauty; but finally he disappeared from Edinburgh, and it was supposed that he went to Virginia or South Carolina, in America.

JOHN SEATON, son of George of Blair Athol, seems to have so far escaped our search.

DUNCAN SEATON, son of George, was born in Perthshire, about 1745, and a year or two later Margaret Cameron was born in the same settlement. These two people were made one flesh, became husband and wife, in the course of time, and had two sons, John and Robert, and three daughters, Margaret, Jeanet, and Elizabeth.

One of our correspondents claims that Duncan Seaton was a soldier, and was at the battle of Culloden. We have no doubt that every able-bodied adult male was a soldier at that time, but it must have been Duncan's father, George Seaton, who was at Culloden, April 16, 1746.

JOHN SEATON, son of Duncan, was born at the Blair Athol home, March 28, 1795, and was married to Christian Seaton, his second cousin, on March 15, 1826. Christian was born January 10, 1800, at Blair Athol. John and Christian Seaton brought their family to America, the land of promise to them, in 1843, arriving in Pennsylvania in the summer or fall, and remained in Juniata county for about two years; then moved to Illinois in 1845, where Christian died on December 20, 1878, and John on July 21, 1881, at Sunbeam, Mercer county. For about two years they lived in Warren county, but in 1848 they returned to Ohio Grove township, where they spent the remainder of their days.

The children of John and Christian Seaton were George and John J. Seaton.

ROBERT SEATON, son of Duncan, was born in 1793. He married Marjorie Douglas. To them were born eight children, as follows: Robert, John, Daniel, James, Duncan, Margaret, Elizabeth, and Jessie.

Robert, son of Duncan Seaton, died in 1852. His family, except Robert and John, whose families live at Blair Athol, Scotland, came to Illinois in 1853.

DANIEL SEATON, son of Robert, was born in London, in 1822, and married Mary Cameron in 1856, having emigrated to America in 1852, locating in Illinois. To Daniel and Mary Seaton were born four children: Allen, Ellen, Roderick, and George A. Allen resides at Sunbeam, Illinois; Roderick at Grand Island, Nebraska; and George A. at Seaton, Illinois.

JAMES SEATON, son of Robert, made his way to Illinois from Scotland, and married Elizabeth Saunders, of Ontario. To them were born seven children, as follows: Stewart, George, Elizabeth, Marjorie, Mary, Isabella, and Robert.

James Seaton died July 2, 1903, at Little York, Illinois, where the family resides.

DUNCAN SEATON, son of Robert, was born at Perthshire, Scotland, in 1834, and removed to Illinois in 1853. He espoused Elizabeth Crabtree in 1859, enlisted in the One Hundred and Second Regiment of Illinois Volunteers, September 21, 1862; served his adopted country through the war, and was discharged June 16, 1865, when there was no further need of his services. He died at Sunbeam, Illinois, in 1898, leaving three sons: Robert B., who lives in Onawa, Iowa; Douglas, who lives in Peoria, Illinois; and John, who is deceased.

GEORGE SEATON, son of John and Christian, a farmer, owning five hundred acres of land, and founder of the village of Seaton, in Mercer county, Illinois, was born February 14, 1839, at Blair Athol, Perthshire, Scotland. He came to the United States in July, 1843, and, after residing two years in Juniata county, Pennsylvania, went by way of the Ohio and Mississippi rivers to Mercer county, Illinois, arriving there in November, 1845. The family moved to Warren county in 1846, but returned to Ohio Grove township, Mercer county, in 1848.

George lived with his parents until they died, as set forth in the sketch of their lives. In 1883 he formed a partnership with R. J. Cabeen in buying and selling grain and lumber, continuing that business until in 1898, when the partnership was dissolved. In 1882 he built the first house in what is now the village of Seaton, which was named in his honor, and in March, 1883, platted the original town, to which he has subsequently made six additions.

In 1894 he built the Seaton Block, which is the finest in the village, and in 1903 the Opera House Block. On August 15, 1903, the principal business street of the village was burned, and it was largely through Mr. Seaton's efforts that a substantial class of buildings has been erected in place of those destroyed by the fire.

In conjunction with R. J. and Thomas B. Cabeen, he was instrumental in securing the railroad that now runs through that section of the country. In 1891 he started a private bank in Seaton, which was reorganized into the State Bank of Seaton, and of which he is now president. Mr. Seaton was one of the organizers of the Abington Mutual Insurance Insurance Company, and is president of that organization, which is in a very prosperous condition.

On February 26, 1884, he was married to Mary Jane, daughter of James and Janet (Semple) Brown, of Kirkwood, Illinois, and they are the parents of five children : Cora May, born December 9, 1874, died December 19, 1891, in Monmouth, Illinois. John Charles Seaton is cashier of the State Bank of Seaton. He was born September 27, 1876. Robert James Seaton, hardware merchant in Seaton, was born January 16, 1879. George Frederick Seaton, born February 10, 1881, is in college; and Boyd Blaine Seaton, born March 28, 1889, is still in school.

Mr. Seaton, his wife, brother John J., and his niece, Miss Elizabeth Seaton, visited Ireland, England and Scotland in 1889.

The children of George and Mary Jane (Brown) Seaton are all at home, none of them having married. The wife and mother of this family was born in Larne, County Antrim, Ireland, on July 26, 1851. She came to Illinois, in the United States of America, when a child ; went back to Ireland in 1858 ; and, when her mother died, in 1865, she returned to Illinois. She is a descendant of the Campbells in Argyle, of Scotland.

The children of Duncan and Elizabeth (Crabtree) Seaton were:

1. Robert Bruce Seaton, who was born in Mercer county, Illinois, and married, December 30, 1883, Sarah, daughter of Joseph Rader, who married a Miss Sellers.

Robert Bruce is a farmer, and has made his home at Onawa, Monona county, Iowa, for four years, having previously lived at Seaton, Illinois. His children are: Clarence, born in 1886; James, born in 1888; Warren, born in 1892; and Boyd, who was born in 1896.

2. Douglas Seaton makes his home at No. 3017 North Madison street, Peoria, Illinois. He was married in December, 1903.

3. John Seaton is deceased. Of the five daughters, Mary, Eva and Melissa are single; Hattie married a Mr. Harrison, and sojourns at Keithsburg, Illinois; and Elizabeth married a Mr. Atchison, and resides at Fort Madison, Iowa.

JOHN J. SEATON, son of John and Christian, was born January 8, 1830, at Kilikrankie, Blair Athol, Scotland. He was married November 16, 1850, to his cousin, Elizabeth, daughter of Robert and Majorie (Douglas) Seaton. John J. is a farmer and merchant at Seaton, Illinois, where he has lived since 1883. He is a Republican in politics, and a Presbyterian.

The children of John J. and Elizabeth Seaton are as follows: John H. Seaton, born about 1864, lives near Lyons, Nebraska. Majorie Seaton married a Mr. Vance, and resides on the old homestead, one and a half miles northwest of Seaton. She was born about 1867. Elizabeth Seaton is single, and makes her home with her uncle George Seaton, in Seaton, Illinois. She was born in 1873.

CHAPTER LV.

WILLIAM SEATON is supposed to have been a native of Scotland, from which country he is said to have come to America. The date of his death is set at about 1808 or 1810, and the place in the State of Pennsylvania, where he was living about 1802. He is given credit with having two sons, Myers and Samuel Clark Seaton, both of whom are deceased. Samuel Clark Seaton is said by one of our correspondents to have died at Centerville, Indiana, at about forty.

MYERS SEATON was born in Greene county, Pennsylvania, in 1802. He married Elizabeth C. Dill, by whom he had the following children: George Myers Seaton, of Oakland, California; James Alexander Seaton, of Richmond, Indiana; Leroy W. Seaton, deceased; Joseph Henry Seaton, of San Luis Obispo, California; Mary, deceased; Samuel Clark Seaton, of Burlington, Iowa; William Dill Seaton, of Indianapolis, Indiana; and Adeline Russell Stilson, wife of Rev. A. C. Stilson, of Los Angeles, California.

Myers Seaton moved to Indiana about 1840. He died at Keokuk, Iowa, April 10, 1863, and his relict, Elizabeth, in March, 1894, at Indianapolis, Indiana. Myers was a merchant and postmaster at Centerville, Indiana, for many years, having lived there about twenty-five years.

JOSEPH HENRY SEATON, son of Myers, is a physician at San Luis Obispo, California, having graduated from Louisville (Ky.) Medical College, in 1857. He was born July 29, 1836, at Centerville, Indiana. He was married to Josephine Blount, on January 7, 1879, at Colusa, California. Their only child is Joseph Henry Seaton, Jr., born July 23, 1883, at the present place of residence of the family. Joseph Henry Seaton has lived at San Luis Obispo since 1877, to which city he moved from Keokuk, Iowa, where he had made his home for about twenty years, leaving there in Au-

—23

gust, 1875. He was Surgeon of the Twenty-first Missouri Infantry, Volunteers, for about three years, 1862–3–4, during the War of the Rebellion.

GEORGE MYERS SEATON, of Oakland, California, son of Myers Seaton, was born August 5. 1830. at Carmichael. Greene county, Pennsylvania. He married Mary S. Anderson, at Keokuk, Iowa, September 16, 1861. They have no children. He is a retired merchant, and has resided at Oakland for thirty years.

WILLIAM DILL SEATON, son of Myers and Elizabeth C. Seaton, was born October 28, 1845. at Centerville, Indiana. In 1872 he married Alice M. Howland, at Indianapolis, Indiana, who traces her family back to the Mayflower. They have four children: William H., born in 1873; Helen, born in 1876; Albert C., born in 1884; and Mary, born in 1890.

William Dill Seaton is in the hat business in Indianapolis, Indiana, where he has resided for thirty-nine years, having formerly lived in Keokuk, Iowa, and in Colorado.

JOHN SEATON, OF SCOTLAND.

JOHN SEATON was born in the south of Scotland, in 1798. He married Mary Cook, who was born in 1795. The family came to the United States in 1828, leaving some married sisters of John's in the country of their nativity. For a while after their arrival in this land of the free, where the rich held slaves, they made their home in New York. then they moved West. for at that early date, at well as later, people went West to better their fortunes. After the fatigues of a long, rough journey in a wagon, they finally landed at Battle Creek. Michigan, and some time later continued their weary way westward to Peoria, Illinois, where they made their home.

John Seaton, Sr.. died at the hospitable home of his son, John L. Seaton, in the year of our Lord 1850. and the partner of all his joys and sorrows followed him to their eternal rest six years later.

The children of John and Mary (Cook) Seaton were as follows: John L. Seaton, born at Mauchline, Ayrshire, Scotland. March 16,

1826. He was well educated, a scholar and a gentleman, and especially an affectionate son and brother. He taught school at Peoria, Illinois, when old enough, and finally bought a farm near that city, where his parents, and in all probability his sister, lived with him, and where he was married, but to whom we are unable to say.

John L. Seaton was a Captain and Provost Marshal in the Union Army, where, like all of the name, so far as heard from, he cheerfully and faithfully performed all of the duties of his responsible position.

As stated, we have no word as to whom he first gave his name and fealty; but for his second wife he chose Mrs. Lucy J. McAfee, daughter of Bishop Forsyth, a noted Presbyterian divine, and they were married in 1866. But before this time he had moved from Peoria to Paducah, Kentucky, after his discharge from the army, and it was at the latter place that his first wife died.

Mr. Seaton was a Mason of high degree, and was extensively engaged in handling Shorthorn cattle, beside conducting a dry-goods business. He died in 1866, and his wife, Lucy Seaton, in 1877.

Catharine Seaton, sister of John L., was born at Mauchline, Scotland, in 1824, and died in 1851.

W. H. FORSYTH SEATON, a son of John L. and Lucy J. Seaton, was born in Cincinnati, Ohio, on May 27, 1868, and his sister, whose given name is unknown to the writer, in 1870. Neither of of these good people has married, but live together on the fine farm formerly owned by their grandfather at Cynthiana, Kentucky, where they raise fine Shorthorn cattle and large numbers of choice Poland-China hogs, in addition to the usual farm crops of that section of the country.

Mr. Seaton received the finishing touches to his education at Central University, in Richmond, Kentucky, and it is likely that his sister did the same.

SCOTCH-VIRGINIA SEATONS.

JOHN KNOX SEATON was related to John Knox, the Scotch reformer, on his mother's side of the house. He had three brothers:

James Carson, Adam Maxwell, and Wilson Seaton. The family seat of his ancestors near Edinburgh, Scotland, was called "Seaton Hall."

The family was banished from Scotland, and went to the north of Ireland after the fall of Mary Queen of Scots. The family came to America before the Revolution, and lived in and around Richmond, Virginia.

JOHN KNOX SEATON was born in Virginia, U. S. A., and his wife, whose name we have not learned, in England. Their children were John Knox Walker Seaton and a brother, who lives in Keokuk, Iowa, whose name was not given.

JOHN KNOX WALKER SEATON was born in Allegheny county, Pennsylvania. He married Mary Elizabeth Allen, daughter of William and Eliza Muir, in Kentucky, in 1862. His home has been in Louisville, Kentucky, for forty-six years, where he is a druggist. There is an only child, a daughter, Allene Seaton, who is single, and lives at home. J. K. W. Seaton is a Democrat and a Presbyterian. He claims that the Seaton girl who was a Maid of Honor to Mary Queen of Scots married the "Black Douglas"; that George Seaton was the founder of Washington, D. C.; and that his name and that of William Wirt are on the Continental scrip that was used in Virginia in 1776.

SCOTCH-ENGLISH SEATONS.

ABRAHAM SEATON, born at Eglington, had a brother John in London, and a sister, Mrs. John Twiggs, in Leicester. John had but one child, a son, Fred Seaton, who was with the Vanderbilts in New York city. Before engaging with the Vanderbilts, Fred Seaton was the private secretary to a Mr. Carrol, a rich gentleman who traveled most of the time, visiting Asia, Africa, Alaska, and other places. Fred is married, since which time his friends in the West have heard little of him.

The children of Abraham Seaton were George and Henry, who lived at 218 Lexington avenue, San Francisco, California, having once cultivated a farm two miles from Jewell Center, Kansas, where their sister, Sara E. Seaton, visited them. George was married in Red Cloud, Nebraska. Henry and Sara are still single. Abraham 2d, the eldest child, died a number of years ago, as did the youngest.

Abraham, Sr., died June 19, 1899, and his wife on the 17th of April, 1903.

The eldest daughter, Rose, is in Lansing, Iowa, at the present time, where some, if not all of the children were born. The second daughter, Lizzie (Seaton) McNeal, is with her husband and two children at their home at Custer, Washington State. Sara E. is at Emmetsburg, Palo Alto county, Iowa, where she has been, for almost twelve years, a bookkeeper in the Palo Alto County Bank. Rose and Sara E. intend to change their place of residence to the State of Washington in the near future, as 32 degrees below zero in Iowa is not exactly to their liking.

Abraham Seaton's grandfather went from Scotland to England, settling at Oakham, Rutland county, where Abraham and his father were both born, and where some members of the family still reside.

SCOTCH-CANADIANS.

JAMES SEATON, of Thornhill, Dumfriesshire, Scotland, was born and died in that locality; dates unknown. His wife was Barbara Smith, who is said to have been born, married and deceased there. Their son, John Smith Seaton, born in 1813 at Thornhill, married Margaret Nicholson (who was born in 1816, at Peebles), the interesting ceremony taking place at place of her nativity. Margaret died at St. John, New Brunswick, Canada, in 1854, and John in 1867.

The children of John S. and Margaret Seaton were: John S. 2d, named for his father; James, so called for his grandfather; and two daughters, Barbara, for her grandmother, and Sarah.

John Smith Seaton, Jr., came to America in 1850, with his family, and two years later went to St. Johns, New Brunswick, where he yet resides.

James Seaton, son of John S. and Margaret, was born August 7, 1843, at Thornhill, and married Eliza Macintyre on December 15, 1863, at St. Johns. Her father was Scotch and her mother

English. James and Eliza Seaton have one child. Archibald Thornhill Seaton, born at St. Johns. New Brunswick, June 16, 1878. James is a painter, his present address being 19 Prospect street, St. Johns, where he has lived for fifty-two years. He has held city offices and served in the Volunteer Militia over thirty years.

CHAPTER LVI.

SCOTCH-IRISH SEATONS.

JEREMIAH SEATON and his two brothers, William and Thomas, lived in Ireland, possibly at Castlederg, where some of the family made their home for a great many years, and where there is a castle and family burying-ground, with a vault and many tablets.

William Seaton is said to have come to America, made a fortune, returned to Ireland, bought a farm near Stanolar, County Donegal, and died there without issue.

Although the early Seatons are said to have been Catholics, Jeremiah and William were Presbyterians, and so far as we know, all of their descendants have been Protestants.

Jeremiah Seaton married Nancy Neal, in Ireland, where both were born. They had six sons and two daughters. Five of the sons came to America, probably encouraged by the experience of their uncle William, and it is said that two of William's brothers also come over the sea, in 1818.

The children of Jeremiah and Nancy Seaton, as we have the names, were: John, Thomas, Robert, William, and Samuel.

JOHN SEATON, son of Jeremiah, went to Washington county, Iowa, where some of his descendants still live. Thomas made his home at Lawrence, Kansas. He died there about 1888. William located in Carroll county, Ohio, and died there in 1882.

ROBERT SEATON, son of Jeremiah, was born near Antrim, County Tyrone, Ireland, in October, 1800. His wife was a native-born American, having first discovered America in Cecil county, Maryland, in 1803. They were married at Lancaster, Pennsylvania, in the fall of 1826. Robert died at Fort Wayne, Indiana, in 1879, and was buried there.

ROBERT LESLIE SEATON, son of Robert, was born at Amsterdam,

Jefferson county, Ohio, June 2, 1843. He lives at Fort Wayne, Indiana, and has two sons and one daughter, all of whom are at home with their loving parents.

Robert Leslie Seaton married Martha Jane Bell, at Zanesville, Wells county, Indiana, March 13, 1873. Her parents were Evan and Eliza (Johnston) Bell. Robert has been with the Fort Wayne Traction Company for the last fourteen years, having lived on a farm in Carroll county, Ohio, until 1866, when he went with his father to a farm in Allen county, where they remained till in 1874, when they settled at Ossian, Wells county, Indiana, from which community they removed to Fort Wayne, December 1, 1887.

Robert Leslie Seaton did not enter the army during the Civil War, but remained at home to attend to affairs there while his brother John, and brother-in-law, Stine, enlisted in 1862, and served until the close of the war in the Army of the Cumberland.

JOHN SEATON, son of Robert, was severely wounded at the battle of Kenesaw Mountain, and was never afterward well, and he died in August, 1894.

Robert Leslie Seaton was postmaster for two years, then resigned. He is a Democrat, and an Old School Presbyterian.

The children born of Robert Leslie and Martha Seaton were: William Deloss, born at Ossian, Indiana, May 11, 1874; John Edgar, born February 28, 1877; Mary Bell, born April 2, 1880; and Rolla Floyd Seaton, born April 24, 1884,—all of them having been born in the same town. The home address of the family is 201 East Butler street, Fort Wayne, Indiana.

SAMUEL SEATON, son of Jeremiah, was born in County Donegal, Ireland, in 1803; came to America in 1835. He resided in Carroll county, Ohio, where he died May 11, 1851. He married Nancy Jackson, who lived in Jefferson county, Ohio, and he built the "Seaton House," in the county above named, in 1848. It is a fine, large brick structure, built after the ancient Irish fashion, and still remains with "Samuel Seeton" cut in the stone lintel.

The children of Samuel and Nancy Seaton were: Margaret A., Thomas, Elizabeth, and probably others.

MARGARET A. SEATON, daughter of Samuel, was born and has

lived all of her days in Carroll county, Ohio, except four years
that she spent in Kansas. She was born September 27, 1844
and was married to Robert Kellar December 4, 1872. They reside at Wellsville, Ohio, where they have made their home for
two years. They left Kansas and returned to Ohio in the "grass-
hopper year," having endured four years of Kansas experience.
The Kellars are Presbyterians and Democrats.

Their children are: Mary P. Kellar, born September 4, 1873,
at Olathe, Kansas; Samuel Edmund Kellar, born July 14, 1876;
Leray Kellar, born October 3, 1879; Charles Kellar, born November 29, 1882; Joseph Kellar, born July 1, 1885; and John Kellar,
born July 20, 1888.

Mary P. Kellar was married to H. L. Miller. They live in
Lytton, Iowa. Samuel Edmund Kellar is in Colorado, on a railway bridge crew. The other Kellar children work in a rolling-
mill with their father at Wellsville, Ohio.

THOMAS SEATON, son of Samuel and Nancy, is a carpenter, and
lives with his wife at Olathe, Kansas, in a two-story double house,
their son and his family occupying a part of the dwelling. Mrs.
Seaton was born October 15, 1833. She is supposed to be a third
cousin of Grover Cleveland, the twenty-second President of
these United States. Her grandmother's maiden name was
Nancy Neal, who was from County Londonderry, or County Antrim, Ireland. She married Mrs. Seaton's grandfather, Alexander
Liggett, in the old country. This Nancy (Neal) Liggett had a
brother and a sister, who married a man by the name of Trainer,
and whose descendants are living in Steubenville, Ohio. Nancy
came to America with her husband and her brother, about 1795.
They settled on a farm near Harper's Ferry, Maryland. The
brother located in Baltimore, where he "kept store." Nancy had
six daughters. Two of them married Seatons,--Robert and William. Jane Liggett married Thomas McComb, a manufacturer
of cotton goods at Lancaster, Pennsylvania. "Uncle Neal," the
Baltimore merchant, had a daughter, Anna Neal; also a daughter
Elizabeth, who died before reaching womanhood. It is believed
there was a son Thomas. Looking into Grover Cleveland's biog-

raphy, we find that his mother was Anna Neal, daughter of a Baltimore merchant, or merchant and bookseller, and book-publisher, of Irish birth; and the fact that Grover had a sister Elizabeth may point to a maternal sister of that name.

The son of Jeremiah Seaton, who remained in Ireland, was Joseph. He left a family of two sons, Samuel and Thomas, and three daughters. One of the daughters never married, but Jane Seaton married Mr. Rule. They live at Indianapolis, Indiana, I believe. Mary Seaton married a Patterson. They have descendants in Ireland and in this country.

SAMUEL SEATON, son of Joseph, is a press agent in his locality in Ireland, and he writes interesting stories for several different periodicals.

ELIZABETH SEATON, daughter of Samuel, married her cousin, and lives at Lawrence, Kansas.

The founder of this branch of the family in Ireland originally went from Scotland, whence he fled when Mary Queen of Scots was overthrown, and settled at Castlederg, in County Tyrone.

Several grandsons of Samuel Seaton have been located, but their parents' names and life-stories have eluded us so far in the search.

EDWARD SEATON, a grandson of Samuel, was crushed to death in a mine accident at Farmington, West Virginia, on September 24, 1903.

There is also a grandson, possibly a son of Elizabeth, who lives at Osawatomie, Kansas.

Another grandson of Samuel is named Robert Liggett Seaton. He resides at Fort Wayne, Indiana. He says that W. D. Seaton, of Indianapolis, Indiana, told him that Robert and one of W. D.'s brothers looked enough alike to have been twins.

OLIVER SEATON, of What Cheer, Iowa, is another grandson of Samuel.

SAMUEL T. SEATON, son of Thomas and grandson of Samuel, was born in Carroll county, Ohio, November 14, 1861. He has lived in Olathe, Kansas, since 1873. He was educated mostly in

private schools and at the Kansas State University; was admitted
to practice law in 1885, and followed that business exclusively
until 1898, when he went into the newspaper business. He is the
local attorney of the Frisco and Santa Fe railroads, and has such
ability as a lawyer that the companies allow him to try cases
alone and prepare the briefs in them when they go to the Supreme
Court. He was editor and publisher of the Olathe *Register*, a
Democratic newspaper, the only one of that persuasion in Johnson county, until November 27, 1905, when he sold out the
business for $4,000, having in seven years brought the subscription
list from eighty to 1463, and the value of the plant from $375 to
the amount for which it was sold.

SAMUEL T. SEATON.

Samuel T. wields a trenchant pen, which is dipped in gall when
he is assailed by political enemies. He is a wideawake, well-read
man, an indefatigable worker in whatever occupies his time, and
has dug up a long array of items for this book (many of which he
has neglected to turn over), having an intuitive scent for facts
pertaining to the subject under consideration, whether it is law,
news items, or family history.

His library is more extensive and varied than any other in the family that is known to the writer. He has a lovely wife, who is well educated and able to run the *Register* in time of need; a leader of advanced thought in the club to which she belongs, and for which she writes and reads articles on timely topics. They were married about 1887, and have two daughters: Nellie, born in 1888, and Grace, who was born in 1893; and they had one son, Glen Miller Seaton, who died in infancy, about 1890.

It was the wish of the writer that Samuel's name should appear on the title-page hereof as one of the editors, authors, or whatever you may call it; but no, that could not be agreed to. He was writing a book treating of "Greek Politics, Utopian and Practical, before the time of Plato."

Samuel T. reports that he saw at a Kansas City bookstore some books containing the armorial book-plates of a Major R. S. Seaton. The plates were done in Chippendale style, and the arms were those of the Seatons. He also saw in some encyclopædia an account of a General Seaton, who died about 1886, and who at one time had command of the English troops in Ireland.

A PENNSYLVANIA FAMILY OF SEATONS.

John A. Seaton was born in Greene county, Pennsylvania, October 30, 1840. He married at Newton, Iowa, Emma, daughter of Stacy and Jane Bevan, on April 4, 1864. Emma was born in Ohio, in 1841. John A. is now a farmer and fine-stock dealer at Vernon, Kansas, where he has made his home for the six years last past, having formerly lived at Newton, Iowa, from March, 1857, until the same month in 1898.

He was a private in Company B, Thirteenth Iowa Volunteers, from October, 1861, to the same month two years later; was wounded May 12, 1863, at the battle of Raymond, Mississippi, in consequence of which his left leg was amputated below the knee.

He was elected Clerk of the Court in Jasper county, Iowa, in 1864, and reëlected in 1868, serving two terms. He is a Hoch Republican, and has been a member of the Methodist Episcopal Church since 1864.

The children of John and Emma Seaton are as follows: 1. Elvin R. Seaton, born January 27, 1868; 2. C. D. Seaton, born No-

vember 6, 1869; 3. Sarah Seaton, born April 1, 1875; 4. R. K.
Seaton, born November 13, 1878; 5. Arthur G. Seaton, born
May 28, 1880; 6. Mary Elma Seaton, born May 4, 1883; 7.
J. E. Seaton, born March 15, 1886.

The father and mother of John A. Seaton were born and married in Washington county, Pennsylvania. Their names have
not been made known to us.

Elvin R. Seaton, number two above, was married at Newton,
Iowa, March 28, 1897, to Mary Tilton, daughter of Hon. Elvin
Tilton and his wife Mary, of Iowa county, Iowa.

Elvin R. is a lawyer by profession, and practices his calling at
Hubbard, Iowa, where he has made his place of abode for the last
ten years, having previously resided at Newton for six years and
on a farm in Iowa county for twelve years, besides two at Des.
Moines, and at Iowa City three years. He is a Republican in
politics, and belongs to the Methodist Episcopal Church.

The children born to Elvin and Mary Seaton, all of whom were
born at Hubbard, Iowa, are as follows: John A. Seaton, Jr.,
born January 11, 1888; Elvin T. Seaton, born April 27, 1900; and
Elma B. Seaton, born November 22, 1904.

CHAPTER LVII.

GREENE COUNTY, PENNSYLVANIA, SEATONS.

J. D. SEATON was born in Greene county, Pennsylvania. He had an only sister, Charlotte Seaton, who married a Mr. Riggs. They moved to Ottawa, Kansas, several years ago, and he died there some ten years later. Mrs. Riggs lived with her son, J. D. Seaton Riggs, who was named for his uncle, and who has been Principal of Ottawa University for a number of years.

J. D. Seaton had eight children—six girls and two boys. One son died while quite young, and the other, Walter L. Seaton, lives at Duluth, Minnesota, where he is engaged in electrical work. He has been married eleven years, but has no children.

Mrs. Charlotte Riggs is said to have kept a record of her branch of the family.

In Volume XXV, Pennsylvania Archives, under "Warranties of Land in Greene County," there is to be found the name of one John D. Seaton, who had taken ten acres August 5, 1785. Possibly this man may have been an ancestor of the J. D. Seaton mentioned above.

TENNESSEE SEATONS.

BENJAMIN SEATON, a Scotchman by birth, came to America and settled in one of the Eastern States, from which locality he moved to Virginia, thence to eastern Tennessee, at the settling of that country, locating in Greene county. He married Elizabeth Bird and had twelve children, ten boys and two girls, as follows: 1. John; 2. James; 3. Solomon; 4. Moses; 5. Ira; 6. George Washington; 7. Philip; 8. Jacob; 9. David; 10. Sally; 11. Jackson; and 12, a girl, name not given.

JOHN SEATON, the eldest son, was a noted preacher, and was chosen by his bishop to go to Mississippi as a missionary, about

1816. He was married, but we have not been told the name of his wife, nor whether they had issue.

JAMES SEATON married Jincy Hiser, and had at least two boys, Anderson and Henry, who are remembered by Barton Seaton, son of Jacob. Anderson Seaton married Clara Broyles. They live in Sevier county, Tennessee.

James Seaton was a soldier in the War of 1812, and his widow wrote to his brother Jacob asking him to send her proof of her marriage to James, to assist her in securing a pension for his services in that war,—which she succeeded in getting. He is said to have moved from Tennessee to Missouri many years ago, with three or four of his brothers.

SOLOMON SEATON married a Miss Trotter. He lived not far from Nashville, Tennessee, from which State he moved to Missouri many years ago. He had four sons and three daughters, as follows:

1. John R. Seaton, of Turney Station, Clinton county, Missouri, who is a man of about seventy years, at this writing, and has five sons and two daughters: Thomas, Monroe, James McClellan, Eugene, John R., Jr., Margaret, who married Dudley Walker, and Carrie, who is the wife of Marion Campbell.

2. William Seaton, of Lathrop, Missouri. He has children as follows: Thomas Jefferson, Francis Marion, who is deceased, Henry, Solomon, Ira, Charles Graham, Nannie, Adelia, and Lulu.

3. Thomas Seaton, son of Solomon, died at Lathrop, Missouri. His children were: Perry W., who lives at No. 20 Westport avenue, Kansas City, Missouri. He travels for Nelson Baker & Company, of 816 Broadway, Kansas City. Minnie, who married a Mr. McKenzie, and lives at the address above. Nellie, now Mrs. Samuel Beatty, of Parsons, Kansas.

4. Margaret Seaton married J. G. Rand, of Lathrop, Missouri. Their children: Lucy Rand married H. E. Page; Gussie Rand took a Mr. Dustman for her husband; Ella Rand is Mrs. William Ellidge; Clara Rand is Mrs. Barlow, of Kansas City, Missouri; and Ralph Seaton Rand is probably single.

5. Carrie Seaton married William Holland, of King City, Missouri. They have one daughter, Lora Holland.

6. Belle Seaton, of Turney Station, Missouri, is single.

7. James Wesley Seaton, of Lathrop, Missouri, married Mary Samantha Herriot. Their children are: George Milton Seaton, of 527 Stewart avenue, Kansas City, Kansas, who was born February 7, 1875, in Clinton county, Missouri. He is unmarried, is a conductor on the Metropolitan Street Railway, and is studying osteopathy during his leisure moments. He is said to very much resemble his cousin, Perry W. Seaton, mentioned above. And Edward Nathaniel Seaton, who was born in the same county as his brother, on November 20, 1873.

MOSES SEATON, son of Benjamin and Elizabeth (Bird) Seaton, married a Barnhart. He was one of the brothers who moved to Missouri, since which time we have lost trace of him.

IRA SEATON, son of Benjamin, leaves no data with us for a sketch of his life.

GEORGE WASHINGTON SEATON, son of Benjamin, married a Miss Losson. He is reported to have moved to Missouri with his brothers, but he has escaped our search thus far, though one of our correspondents reports that he died in Sevier county, Tennessee.

PHILIP SEATON, son of Benjamin, married Mary Barnhart, in 1820. He was born on Horse creek, in Greene county, Tennessee, in 1800, he being twenty and Mary nineteen years of age when they were married.

A son of Philip and Mary Seaton, named James Benet Seaton, was born in Sevier county, Tenn., on the 28th day of December, 1831. He was married in his home county, on the 22d of September, 1852, to Sarah M. Andes, daughter of John and Lettie Andes, who were of Dutch descent.

JAMES BENET SEATON is living on a farm near Bank, Blount county, Tenn., where for thirty-eight years he has continued to make his home, having removed to that place from Sevier county in 1866. He served in the Union Army in the Rebellion as a Second Lieutenant in Company M, Second Tennessee Cavalry, Volunteers. He was a Justice of the Peace in Sevier county, but resigned upon removing to Blount county. He was a Whig, when

Whigs were in existence, and served as a circuit-rider in the Methodist Church for thirty years as a member of the Hilston Conference. He has no children.

WILLIAM BRUCE SEATON, son of Philip and Mary, was born at Sevierville, Sevier county, Tenn., December 15, 1843, and married at Pigeon Forge, June 2, 1870, Sarah Virginia Trotter; and, after her death, Harriet Angeline McGhee, on October 28, 1875, at Loveville, Knox county, Tenn. He is a farmer near Maryville, Tenn., where he has lived for eighteen years, having removed from Sevierville in 1866. He was a First Sergeant of Company E, Ninth Tennessee Cavalry, Volunteers, from October 1, 1863, to September 11, 1865. In politics he is a Republican, and is a Methodist. His children by the first marriage are: Mattie Bell, born March 22, 1871; William Mitchell, born July 9, 1872; James Trotter, born August 24, 1874, at Sevierville. And by his second wife: Edgar Otto, born October 28, 1876; Lena, born April 12, 1878; Philip Axley, born February 21, 1883; and Nora May, born January 28, 1887, at Maryville, Tenn.

MATTIE BELL SEATON was married at Saticoy, Ventura county, California, October 21, 1900, to James W. Hitch. William Mitchell was married at Bank, Blount county, Tenn., to Dellie Hall. Edgar Otto was married at Maryville, Tenn., to Marjorie Fitch, October 2, 1902.

JACOB SEATON, son of Benjamin, married Sally Reymel, who died in 1877. Jacob died of cholera, July 17, 1873. Mrs. Seaton had four brothers—Isaac, Jacob, John, and George Reymel. She had ten children by Jacob: Ira, Isaac, William, Elizabeth, Rebecca, Moses, Barton, John, Eliza, and Mary Ann,—all of whom, except Barton, are deceased.

ELIZABETH SEATON, daughter of Jacob and Sarah, was born in 1824 and died in 1884. She married Ozy Broyles Williamson, who was born in the First Civil District of Greene county, Tennessee, the marriage taking place in 1841, at the home of the bride's father, in the aforesaid district. The Williamsons were farmers in early life, but Mr. W. has worked at carpentry later. They

—24

reside on Horse creek, where they have lived for sixty-two years, never having lived more than a mile from their present home. Mr. W. was a captain of a militia company at their spring and fall musters, and was a Justice of the Peace for twenty-one years. He is a Republican and a Methodist.

Their children are: 1. Frances Marion Williamson, married to Elizabeth Caroline Broyles; 2. Smith Reeves Williamson, married to Frances Walker; 3. Sarah Elizabeth Williamson, married John Maise Broyles; and 4. Kittie Williamson, married Enons Newton Reeves. All the children were born in the First District of Greene county, Tennessee, where they now reside.

BARTON SEATON, son of Jacob and Sally, was born in Greene county, Tennessee, in the year 1832. He married Mary J. Willis in 1858. They lived in Tennessee until in 1882, when they moved to Arkansas, and from there went to the Cherokee Nation, where Mary died. Barton was raised on a farm. He was a Union man during the Rebellion, but was conscripted into the army of the Confederacy, arrested and marched into camp, but he did not fight for Jeff. Davis. One of his brothers served three and a half years in the Federal Army.

Barton is a Republican, and is a member of the Methodist Church. The children of Barton and Mary are: 1. Moses; 2. Sarah Ann; 3. Elizabeth; 4. Melissa; 5. Victoria; 6. Emory; and 7. Rosa. Melissa and Rosa are deceased. Rose died single; Moses married Martha Kilgore; Sarah Ann married Henry Collier. "Betty" became Mrs. Lafayette Elder. Melissa became Mrs. John Henson. Victoria married John Girder; and Emory, Hattie Cox.

Barton Seaton lives with his daughter, a widow, near Weir City, Kansas. Mrs. Sarah Collier has three boys: Moses, born in 1883; Edgar, born in 1886; and Garland, born in 1884. The boys are well called colliers, for they work in the coal-mines.

DAVID SEATON, son of Benjamin, was born in Greene county, Tennessee, March 1, 1799, and died exactly sixty years later. He married Alice Green, of Washington county.

JACOB M. SEATON, son of David and Alice, was born August 26,

1832, in Washington county, Tennessee. He married Rebecca Marks, on November 8, 1859, who is deceased. He is a farmer at Chucky City, Tennessee, and has lived where he was born. He was in the Confederate service during the War of the Rebellion. And he has been a Justice of the Peace and Notary Public for thirty-six years; is a Democrat and a Methodist.

The children of Jacob M. and Rebecca (Marks) Seaton are: James W.; Jerusha E.; Martha A.; Melinda J.; Jacob Roswell; Sarah L.; and May. James W. Seaton was killed by lightning in Nebraska in 1894. Jacob Roswell Seaton, son of Jacob M., was born in the First District of Washington county, Tennessee, July 2, 1874. He is a rural free delivery mail-carrier, Route No. 4, from Chucky City; is single, a Democrat, and a Methodist.

MARK L. SEATON, another son of David and Alice, was born in the First District of Washington county, Tennessee, July 5, 1841. He married Elizabeth Painter in 1866. They are farmers at the place of his birth, where he has lived all of his life thus far. He served in the Confederate Army during the "late unpleasantness"; is a Democrat and a Methodist.

The children of Mark L. and Elizabeth Seaton are: D. M. Seaton, who married Effie Bailey; R. C. Seaton, was married to Eddie Broyles by J. M. Seaton, Esquire. The other children, who are not reported to us as having been married, are Fred and Annie Seaton. The address of Mark L. Seaton is Chucky City, Tennessee, R. F. D. No. 4.

JACKSON SEATON, son of Benjamin, married Susan Wilhite.

Here our information ends. What became of the other children of Benjamin Seaton we are unable to report at present. Nor can we tell where Benjamin's brother, Moses, who came to America with him, located, though he is said to have gone West, and some of his descendants are supposed to reside near Knoxville, Tennessee.

MORE TENNESSEE SEATONS.

WILLIAM HENRY SEATON was born July 15, 1809, in Tennessee; Elizabeth Hester Kennedy, born December 22, 1804. They were married January 26, 1832.   Elizabeth died in Kentucky, November 15, 1868; and William H. in Blair, Nebraska, September 22, 1877.

They had children as follows: 1. Susan Hester, born November 5, 1832, died in June, 1869, the wife of Hans Gittings; their marriage having taken place on February 27, 1851.   2. John Willard, born February 27, 1834; died July 15, 1852.   3. Charles Henry, born December 9, 1835; married Mary E. Burgiss January 30, 1865, and died July 25, 1901.   4. Mary Elizabeth, born March 12, 1837; married Polac Browner, on October 12, 1865; and George Dawson after the death of her first companion.   5. Ann Eliza, born October 30, 1839; married David A. Kemp, October 12, 1865, and died June 9, 1875.   6. Sarah Matilda, born January 30, 1841; married Kendrick O. Stanfield, November 9, 1865, and died February 14, 1889.   7. Loisa Adeline, born December 27, 1843. 8. William Cole Seaton, born July 27, 1846; married Sarah E. Lamb, November 6, 1867, and died January 22, 1899; his wife preceding him, dying January 14, 1893.   William Cole Seaton was born in the great State of Kentucky, where his wife also first saw the light of day, and where they were married; but he died in St. Louis, Missouri, and she in the thriving city on the other side of the State, Kansas City.

Their children were as follows: 1. Annie Laura, born August 27, 1869, to whom we are indebted for the record of their branch of the family, and who signs her name Annie L. Maher and gives her address at 143 East Center street, Butte, Montana; 2. John William, born April 4, 1871; 3. Edward Seaton, born March 26, 1873; 4. Clyde Seaton, born March 2, 1875, and died August 13, 1876; 5. Robert Seaton, born March 27, 1877; 6. Maud Seaton, born January 22, 1879; 7. Mattie Seaton, born January 5, 1881; 8. Peter Seaton, born March 14, 1883; and 9. Grace Seaton, who was born August 3, 1888.

CHAPTER LVIII.

NEW-YORK-WISCONSIN SEATONS.

JAMES WILSON SEATON, a native of the State of New York, was born May 28, 1824, Queen Victoria's birthday, of full Scotch parents, in the town of New Hartford, New York, about four miles south of Utica. The family resided in Utica while Governor De Witt Clinton was digging the Erie Canal, but in 1829 removed to Sanquoit, seven miles south of the city, on Sanquoit creek, which flows into the Mohawk river. He first attended the "Methodist School House" when he was seven years old, and ten years later was the school-master in the same school, and later taught in the West Exeter, Otsego county, and Talberg, Oneida county, schools.

In 1841-42-43 he attended Oneida Conference Seminary, at Cazenovia, Madison county, New York, and had for classmates General Joseph R. Hawley, Senator from Connecticut; Bishop Edward G. Andrews, of the Methodist Episcopal Church, and his brother, Charles Andrews, now one of the judges of the Supreme Court of New York; Leland Stanford, the millionaire Senator from California; General Slocum; and other distinguished members and ministers of the Methodist Church. In 1845-6 he taught select school at Lee Center, and studied law with E. G. Parkhurst in Rome, New York. In 1847, being then twenty-three years old, he took Greeley's advice and went West to grow up with the country.

In company with ex-Chief Justice Cole after voyaging around the lakes and landing at Milwaukee, he made a trip in hacks to Potosi, Wisconsin, arriving in July. Here he entered the law office of Cole & Biddlecome for two months, and was admitted to the bar of Grant county in October of the same year. Judge Charles Dunn was upon the bench, and Samuel Crawford, Judge Cole and George W. Larkin were the examining committee.

After getting his diploma he opened a select school in Potosi.

The next year he bought out Lucien B. Leach in the Potosi *Republican*, which he edited and published until 1855, when the paper was sold to E. R. Paul, who moved it to Duluth.

He was elected first Town Clerk when the State was admitted, in 1849, and served ten years in that capacity, also as Justice of the Peace and Town Superintendent of Schools at various times. He was elected to the State Senate in May, 1853, and served during the impeachment trial of Judge Hubbell. He also served the Assembly in the years 1859 and 1860, and was for a number of years a member of the Town and County Board, and one term as Chairman of the Board. He was on the committee with Hon. George W. Ryland when the present court-house and jail and county poorhouse were built, and served two or three terms on the Financial Committee of the County Board.

In 1855 he engaged in the mercantile business at Potosi with his brother, T. R. Seaton, and continued the business till 1879, when he resumed the practice of law and insurance business, which he continued to manage up to the time of his death.

He said the most important occurrence in his life was his marriage at Cassville, June 15, 1850, to Amanda F. Bushee, daughter of Barton Bushee, one of the early merchants and smelters of Cassville.

He was a contributor to newspapers, especially obituary articles, and was a regular local correspondent of "matchless versatility" for more than fifty years, writing for recreation, a labor that was a pleasure.

He was always reading or writing when not engaged with other duties. His home was on a high hill in Potosi, Wisconsin, and the last thing he did was to read the nineteenth chapter of Ivanhoe, spread the book, open, face down, on the table as if intending to resume the reading; then he stepped out of the door, fell on the walk, and died Friday morning, February 12, 1904. The funeral was held on Sunday, the 14th, conducted by the Masonic fraternity at the cemetery.

He was a church-going man, singing in the choir, and serving as trustee and treasurer for a great many years.

His wife and two daughters, Mrs. Mary B. Husted and Mrs.

Mabel Cochrane, preceded him to that bourne whence no traveler returns.

There were born to James W. and Amanda F. Seaton three sons and three daughters. One daughter and the three sons remain to mourn the loss of a father whose delight was to make them happy.

James W. Seaton was a member of Warren Lodge No. 4, of Potosi, over which he presided as Worshipful Master for many years. He was a lover of the Bible, and was always to be found with one within reach, either at home or in his office.

The interment was in the Van Buren cemetery, beside the grave of his wife, whose death occurred three years before, her funeral taking place on the day that would have been their golden-wedding day.

OTHER SEATONS.

JOHN SEATON was a farmer at Fayetteville, Tennessee. His children were: Benjamin Copeland Seaton; Henry, who resides at Houston, Texas; Massey; Sarah, who married G. G. Gilbert; George, who died; and Annie. There was also said to be a Benjamin Franklin Seaton, son of either John or Benjamin Copeland Seaton, who married Rebecca Jane Gilbert. Their children were: 1. Charles Tribble Seaton, who married Mrs. Nebill, of St. Louis, Missouri. They had no offspring. 2. William Franklin Seaton married Miss Mattie Hunter, of Lamar, Tennessee, and has three children: Jessie May; George Edward; and Benjamin Copeland. 3. Hattie Bee married at Nashville, Tennessee, to George T. Blake, but has no issue. 4. Katie Copeland married W. J. Boomer, of Springfield, Missouri, but has no children. 5. Warren Seaton, 6. Eddie Seaton, and 7. Ollie Lee Seaton, are children at home with their doting parents.

A NEW-YORKER WHO WENT TO MICHIGAN.

WILLIAM L. SEATON was born in Oneida county, New York, August 19, 1823. He was married at McConnellsville, New York, January 17, 1849, to Roxanna Parker, daughter of Abraham and Julia A. Parker. Mr. Seaton has made his home at Jackson, Michigan, for fifty years, and before moving to Jackson lived at Sanquoin, New York. He was Warden of the Michigan Penitentiary for six years and Postmaster in Jackson for twenty-four years. Since 1854 he has been a Republican.

The only child of William L. and Roxanna Seaton is Walter Scott Seaton, who is an express agent with the Wells-Fargo Company in New York city. He was born at Jackson, Michigan, May 26, 1866.

William L. Seaton's parents were born in Ayrshire, Scotland, about 1800, and married in 1818, but their names have not been made known to us. He gives the name and address of Oscar Seaton, of Potosi, Wisconsin, and Thomas R. Seaton, of the same place, who are probably relatives of his.

MORE NEW-YORKERS.

WILLIAM HARCOURT SEATON was born November 2, 1876, at No. 66 Herkimer street, Albany, New York. He is single; is in the shoe business, and is an expert sign artist; is a Democrat and a Baptist. He has lived all of his life, so far, in Albany, as has his brother John Rhodes Seaton, both residing at 123 Central avenue in 1904.

Their father, William C. Seaton, and their mother, Anna (Rhodes) Seaton, were both born in Albany, and were married there. Their grandfather and grandmother were both born in England, but their fore-names are not known to us. The great-grandfather and great-grandmother died in England, leaving extensive estates.

PENNSYLVANIA SEATONS.

ROBERT M. SEATON married Mary Lock, both dying in 1903. They lived in Pennsylvania, where Lamberton Seaton, their son, was born. They had another son, George Seaton, who resides at St. Clere, Kansas.

Lamberton Seaton married Sophia Harrison, of Hope, Illinois, the marriage ceremony having been performed at Danville, near by, in 1874.

George Robert Seaton, son of Lamberton, was born at Ogden, Champaign county, Illinois, August 8, 1875. He has a brother, Edward Seaton, in the Philippine Islands. George Robert married Sylvia Parsons, May 18, 1899. They have been farmers at

Anness, Kansas, since January 17, 1905, George having formerly made his home at Hope, Vermilion county, Illinois, up to 1878, when he went to Sharpsburg, Pennsylvania, where he resided until 1882; then he removed to Armstrong, Illinois, and remained there till 1904, when he quitted that place. He finally located at Anness. George is a Republican in politics.

The children are: William Leslie, born January 29, 1900, at Armstrong, Illinois; and Winnie Ruth, born June 2, 1903, at the same place as her brother.

ROBERT SEATON was born in Huntingdon county, Pennsylvania, of Irish parentage, in 1763, and went to Butler county with his family in 1800. He settled in what is now Marion township, and at once set to work and erected a log cabin, in which his daughter Eliza was born four days after the family arrived at their destination. Mr. Seaton was a millwright, and built nearly all the mills in that section of the country, in his day, furnishing the lumber for the same, in payment for which he received a certain per cent. of the profits for a term of seven years. About 1815 he built a fulling-mill on the South branch of Slippery Rock creek, and subsequently a tannery. These he carried on until his death, in 1852. He married Mary Davis, of Huntingdon county, and their children were as follows: Polly, who married Robert Shaw; Alexander; Eliza, who married Stephen Vanderlin; Ann, who married Robert Hutchinson; Margaret; Thomas; Robert; William; James; and John.

ALEXANDER, eldest son of Robert and Mary Seaton, was born in Huntingdon county in 1790, and went to Butler county with his parents when about ten years old. On attaining his majority he purchased a farm on what is now the line of Mercer and Marion townships, his residence being in the former. He was a millwright and farmer, and erected a saw, grist and cloth mill, which he operated for many years.

Mr. Seaton married Isabella, daughter of Andrew Donaldson, and reared a family of eight children, namely: Margaret, who married James Bailey; Robert F.; Andrew; Mary A., who married John Buchanan; John; Thomas; William A.; and Abner.

Mr. Seaton was a member of the United Presbyterian Church. In politics he was a Democrat, and held the office of Justice of the Peace for many years.

Robert F. Seaton, eldest son of Alexander, was born upon the Seaton homestead, in Marion township, in 1821. He learned the stone-mason's trade, and subsequently engaged in farming. He married Mary A., daughter of Alexander McMurray, and their children were as follows: Samuel M.; Eva J., wife of John Ray; Matilda, deceased; Samantha; Seretta, wife of John Murrin; and Scott A.

William A., fifth son of Alexander and Isabella Seaton, was reared on the homestead farm, and acquired a common-school education. When eighteen years of age he began learning the blacksmith trade with James McDowell, of Harrisonville, Butler county, and served an apprenticeship of two years, for which he received fifty dollars in store goods. He next worked one year at Clintonville, Venango county, for which he was paid seventy-five dollars. In 1851–2 he followed lumbering, at Irwinsburg, on the Conawango river, and in the spring of 1853 he located at Mercer, Pennsylvania, where he worked at his trade until the summer of 1854. He then entered Westminster College, at New Wilmington, in that State, where he spent the fall term of 1854 and the winter and summer terms of 1855. In the fall of the latter year he went to California and worked at his trade in the mining regions until the spring of 1857. He then purchased a claim and embarked in mining, which he followed two years. In the spring of 1859 he sold his claim and engaged in farming in Feather river valley, which he continued until April, 1861, and then started for the old home in Butler county, where he arrived in safety. On September 16, 1861, Mr. Seaton enlisted in Company L, Fourth Pennsylvania Cavalry, and participated with his command in the seven-days fight before Richmond, Gaines Hill, Mechanicsville, Glendale, Malvern Hill, Antietam, Fredericksburg, Gettysburg, Shepherdstown, and many other engagements, and was honorably discharged September 17, 1864.

After his return from the army he worked at his trade in Grove

City for eight years, and then purchased his present farm, upon which he has since resided. Mr. Seaton married Ann E., daughter of Robert Hutchison, of Marion township, on August 6, 1863, and has two daughters, Anna B. and Ella M. He is a member of the United Presbyterian Church, also of the Grand Army of the Republic, and is a man of upright character and strict integrity.

SAMUEL M. SEATON, eldest son of Robert F. and Mary Seaton, was born March 9, 1847, on the Seaton homestead in Marion township. He received a common-school education, and was reared upon his father's farm. In 1864 he enlisted in Company G, Fourth Pennsylvania Cavalry, and served with his regiment until the battle of Amelia Springs, where he was taken prisoner and held until the surrender of General Lee. When the war was closed he returned to his home and engaged in the lumber business, but subsequently located upon the homestead, where he remained until 1888. In that year he removed to his father-in-law's farm in Marion township, but in 1892 he settled upon his present farm, which he had purchased some years previous. In 1893 Mr. Seaton was elected on the Republican ticket as Prothonotary of Butler county, and began his official duties in January, 1894. He served for some time as Deputy Prothonotary under Prothonotary Thompson, and also three years as deputy for Prothonotary Mc-Collough. He has always been an active participant in local politics, and has filled the offices of Collector and Secretary of the School Board of Marion township. He was married in 1872 to Juliann, daughter of William Black. Five children have been born of this marriage, as follows: Cora B., deceased, who married V. W. Parker; E. Tillie; Robert W.; and two that died in infancy. Mrs. Seaton died May 28, 1903.

Samuel M. Seaton is a member of the Butler United Presbyterian Church, of Z. C. McZuillen Post, G. A. R., and Mylert Lodge I. O. O. F., of Centerville.

WILLIAM SEATON, son of Robert, was born in Butler county, in February, 1804. He was reared on the old Seaton homestead, and resided there until his death, in 1886. He married Rebecca Vanderlin, a daughter of John Vanderlin, of Venago township, to whom were born the following children: Kate; Margaret, who married Thomas Hovis; Caroline, who married James Jack; John; William G.; Hettie, who married Stephen Cooper; Amos; Elias; and Lewis.

Amos Seaton, son of William and Rebecca, was born in Venango township, Butler county, August 23, 1838. He was educated in the common schools, and learned the blacksmith trade, which he followed four years. In May, 1861, he enlisted in Company C, Eleventh Pennsylvania Reserves, and participated in the first battle of Richmond, Malvern Hill, Charles City Cross Roads, Gettysburg, the Wilderness, and other engagements, and was wounded in the battle of Charles City Cross Roads. He was honorably discharged on June 20, 1864, and reënlisted on August 24, following, in Company D, Fifteenth Pennsylvania Regiment. He was mustered out of the service June 20, 1865, and returned to his home, where he resumed his life upon the farm. He has devoted his entire attention to agriculture, with the exception of four years' residence in Butler.

Mr. Seaton married Mary, daughter of Samuel Laughlin, of Marion township, who has borne him seven children, viz.: Hettie; Delphina; Ada; Ersie; Homer; and Darley M. Politically Mr. Seaton is a Republican, and has served one term as Treasurer of Butler county. He is a member of the G. A. R. and the U. V. L., and is connected with the Methodist Episcopal Church.

CHAPTER LIX.

A SEETON FAMILY.

JAMES SEETON, who was of Scotch descent, was born in County Donegal, Londonderry, Ireland. He married Martha Crawford, of County Tyrone. He had a brother Thomas and a sister Mary.

About 1822 he, with his wife and three children, sailed from Belfast, Ireland, on June 24. His children were Mary Ann, aged twelve; Andrew, ten; and James, six years old. He landed at St. Johns, New Brunswick, on the 24th of July, and remained there a month, then went to Londonderry, Nova Scotia. There they had four additional children: John, William, Joseph, and Robert. James Seaton died in 1858.

Mary Ann, the first child, married James Boyce, of County Armaigh, Ireland, in 1830, and resided in Nova Scotia. They had five children: Elizabeth, James, Andrew, Sarah, and Martha. Of these children, Elizabeth married William Fletcher, of Folly Village, N. S., and had nine children: James, Margery, Arnold, Everett, Bertha, Gertrude, Margaret, Emma, and one unnamed.

Sarah married Joseph Foss, and lives in Goffstown, N. H.; Martha married Thomas Moore, of Economy, N. S. They had eight children: James, Andrew, Mary, Herbert, George, Rachel, Howard, and Mabel. They now reside in Waltham, Massachusetts.

Andrew leaves two children, Harold and Jennie, who live in Bennington, New York.

Mary Moore married Oscar Watts, of Waterbury Center, Vermont. They have three children: Almira, Jennie, and Loring.

Rachel Moore married George Gale, of Canton, Ohio. They have one child, Irene Gale.

ANDREW SEETON, the second child of James and Martha, was born May 11, 1809, probably at Londonderry, Ireland. He was married to Matilda Porter, at St. Johns, New Brunswick, October 4, 1838, by Rev. R. Wilson, of St. Andrew's. Miss Porter was born at the St. Johns home, February 2, 1821. Andrew had four brothers: James, born in Ireland; John William; Joseph; and Robert Beatie; and two sisters, Elizabeth and Martha.

ROBERT BEATIE SEETON, son of James and Martha, was born May 2, 1849, at Meagher's Grant, Nova Scotia, and was married to Alice L. Bullis, at Lawrence, Massachusetts, in 1871. Alice was of Holland Dutch descent, her ancestors having come over to New York several generations ago.

Robert B. was a brass-finisher, having worked at one place for over thirty years, where he came to his death in December, 1903. He was a straight Republican, having served as chairman of the Republican City Committee. Both Robert and his wife were Protestants among Catholics.

The children of Robert and Alice Seeton were Alice Frances R. and Charles Robert Worrell Seeton, both of whom were born in Lowell, Massachusetts, the former in 1872 and the latter in 1873. Neither of these young people was married at the time of our last information.

James Seeton had twelve other children, besides Robert Beatie: Margaret Jane, born 28th February, 1840, was married to Hodgett F. Worrall, May 21, 1857, at Londonderry, Nova Scotia, by the Rev. J. Forsythe, of Trinity Church, Truro. They had seven children: Sarah, Annie, Louise, James, William, Florence, and Thomas. Of these children, Sarah married Ed. Peters, of St. Johns, New Brunswick. They have two children, Mary and Shirley. Annie married Whitmore Merritt, of St. Johns, and has two children.

Louise married a Lithcoe, of Halifax. They are credited with two children.

Florence married Thomas Gilbert, and resides at 24 Leroy street, Lowell, Massachusetts.

Martha Ann, born January 14th, 1842, was married to Joseph E. Richards, on January 5, 1860, at Londonderry, N. S., by the Rev. A. L. Willy. They had five children: Hattie, Minnie, Clifford, Andrew, and Charley,—all living except Andrew.

Mr. and Mrs. Richards reside in Londonderry, Nova Scotia, and have some married children.

ELIZABETH SEETON, born February 17, 1844, was married in Musquodobit, Nova Scotia, to Michael Brown. They are both deceased, leaving one child, Fannie, of Newark, New Jersey.

SARAH SEETON, born December 25, 1845, died soon after.

DAVID, born February 28, 1847, was married in Portland, Maine, in 1874, by the Rev. Mr. Carruthers. He now works in Readville, Massachusetts, in a car-shop; has two sons, Leonard and Edward, residing in West Newton, Massachusetts.

ROBERT SEETON, born May 2, 1849, was married in Methuen, Massachusetts. He died about a year ago, leaving two children, Alice, of Lowell, and Charley, of Lawrence. His work was brass-finishing.

ALVIN, born March 14, 1851, was married in Goffstown, N. H., by the Rev. Mr. Pollard. He has three children: Gertrude, Edith, and Ross. He still resides in town, his occupation being a tinsmith.

EDWARD, born February 8, 1853, was married in Maitland, Nova Scotia. He has three children: Stanley, George, and Helen. He lives in Chelmsford Center, Massachusetts, and is by trade a wheelwright.

ESTHER, born May 8, 1855, was married to Henry Merrill, at East Weare, North Dakota, by the Rev. Mr. Warren, August 14, 1875. They have three children: Archie, Willey, and Annie. They reside in Goffstown, N. H., keeping a summer hotel.

JAMES, born June 12, 1857, was married in Wilton, N. H. He was killed on an elevator in Lowell. His widow and two children, Margaret and Marion, reside at No. 30 Third avenue, Lowell, Massachusetts. He was a blacksmith.

SARAH, born January 1, 1859, was married in Goffstown, by the Rev. Mr. Remick, to Stanley Loche. They lived in Locheport,

Nova Scotia. Sarah died several years ago, leaving three children: Meta, Russell, and Harold.

LOUISE, born May 9, 1861, was married in Meagher's Grant, Nova Scotia, to Charlie Armond, of Halifax. By occupation an editor. Louise afterward married Thomas Hartnoll, of Milford, New Hampshire, where they now live.

WILLIAM, born February 3, 1867, is deceased.

ELIZABETH, third child of James and Martha, married James Johnson, of Halifax. They had eight children: James, Sarah, George, William, Andrew, Edward, Martha, and one who died.

JAMES SEETON, the fourth child of James and Martha, married Sophia Wright, and they had six children: John, James, Emma, Martha, Louise, and Alden. He afterward married Miss Mythias, of Musquodobit. Their children were: Hattie, Maud, Fannie, Bessie, Ida, and James.

JOHN WILLIAM SEETON, fifth child of James and Martha, married Elizabeth McDonald, of Pictou, Nova Scotia. He died in 1848, leaving two children, Margaret and John William 2d, the latter of whom was born June 7, 1853, at Londonderry, Colchester county, Nova Scotia. He was married at Elmfield, Nova Scotia, June 21, 1877, to Annie Munroe, daughter of George Munroe, who was born in Scotland, in 1816, and who was a son of Robert Munroe and Anna (Mathewson) Munroe. Annie's mother, Margaret McIntosh, daughter of Alexander and Janet (Murry) McIntosh, was born in Pictou, Nova Scotia, in 1819.

John William Seeton 2d is a driver, and resides at 47 Highland avenue, Lynn, Massachusetts, where he has made his home since May 1st, 1890, having formerly lived at Lisbon Falls, Maine, from August 13, 1888, to May 1, 1890, at Springhill, Cumberland county, Nova Scotia, from 1873 to 1888, and previous to that time at his birthplace. He was brought up a Presbyterian, but the family now worships with the Congregationalists.

The children of John William and Elizabeth Seeton, all except one of whom were born at Springhill, Nova Scotia, are: George Wimburn, born May 19, 1878; was married December 24, 1903, in Springfield. Massachusetts. to Miss Ethel May Tufts of Lynn, of that State. They live in Waterbury, Connecticut. Edith Elizabeth Seeton, born June 25, 1880; Margaret Wilhelmina, born July 26, 1882; Anna Ovetta, born August 28, 1884; Jessie Thorburn, born June 20. 1888. and Grace Purington, born at Lynn, Massachusetts, June 19, 1891. live at the last-mentioned city.

JOSEPH SEETON, the sixth child of James and Martha, married Emma Metsler, of Halifax. They have four children: Louise, Gertrude, Isabella. and Adolphus. the latter of whom died November 18, 1901.

ROBERT, seventh child of James and Martha Seeton. married Isabella Anderson, of Musquodobit Harbor, Nova Scotia. They have had four children: Hattie, Edward. Bert. and Ella.

Robert was a merchant in Halifax. He died a short time ago, at the age of eighty-eight.

CHAPTER LX.

NEGROES WHO ARE NAMED SEATON.

JOSEPH HENRY SEATON, a negro, lives at Springfield, Massachusetts, No. 19 Lombard street. He was born in Richmond, Virginia, in 1884, and is single, a hotel man, and a druggist. He has lived at Springfield for nine years, having moved to that city from his birthplace in 1894. He belonged to Company B, Tenth Massachusetts Regiment, Boys' Brigade: is a Republican and a Baptist. His father, William Seaton, was born in Richmond, Virginia, in 1861; married Rebecca Allen, who was also born in Richmond during that first year of the Civil War. They were married in the Confederate Capital City, in 1882.

William Seaton's parents. Moses and Matilda Seaton, were slaves, the one in Kentucky and the other in Virginia, but were emancipated by their owners, whose surnames they retained after they were freed. Matilda Seaton was born in Kentucky, in slavery; was set free before the War of the Rebellion, and went over into Virginia, where she was married to Moses Seaton, who was a slave to another family of the name, who also gave Moses his freedom.

Moses and Matilda Seaton had another son, Cæsar Seaton, whose whereabouts are unknown, but inquired for.

The writer has been told there are other negroes who support our family name, in Atchison, Kansas, Lawrence, Kansas; and there is one Joseph Seaton, a colored man, who works at the Grand Central Hotel in Wheeling, West Virginia, who secured his honorable patronymic in the same way.

In this connection it may not be out of place to recall the statement, made elsewhere in this book, that William Winston Seaton, of his own accord, emancipated more of his own slaves than all of the Abolitionists in the North had ever liberated before the war. And it appears from the above that he was not the only member of our family who gave freedom to his bondsmen.

SEATON HOSPITAL FOR CONSUMPTIVES, SPUYTEN DUYVIL, N. Y.

CHAPTER LXI.

MISCELLANEOUS MENTION.

IN Volume II. of Sidney Lee's Dictionary of National Biography, are numerous biographies of Seatons and Setons. On page 177 of "An Old Family," last paragraph, only one son is named to George Seton of Cariston, and the names of the other issue are omitted. Burke gives the names of two other sons, one of whom, David, married and settled in Yorkshire and had issue. Burke says: "There is reason to believe that this David Seton was the ancestor of the Seatons residing at Gottenburg, Sweden, who trace their descent from Robert Seaton of Grimethorp Hall, County of York, who died 1716, aged 78, who may have been David's son. Robert's great-grandson was John Fox Seaton of Pontefroct, who besides other children, had two sons, General Sir Thomas Seaton, K. C. B., born 1806. His life is given in the Dictionary of National Biography.

ALEXANDER SETON, a Scotch Friar and Reformer, took a prominent part in the Reformation "of which Erasmus laid the egg which Luther hatched." The above Dictionary says he was a brother to Ninian Seton of Touch, mentioned elsewhere.

Burke and the Dictionary of National Biography say that Alexander Seton, the defender of Berwick, was probably a brother of Christopher Seton, brother-in-law to King Robert Bruce.

In the Pennsylvania Archives, third series, Volume XX, page 551, is reprinted a Transcript of Taxables of Cumberland county for 1782, where one JAMES SEATON is listed as having one cow liable for taxation.

In the eighth volume of the Virginia Historical Magazine, page 361, under "Extracts from Register of St. Paul's Parish," Stafford county, is a notation of the marriage of Burdett Clifton to GRACE SEATON, May 18, 1745.

WILLIAM SETON.

From Heitman's Register we learn that William Seton, born at Washington, D. C., was appointed Second Lieutenant in the First United States Infantry, in February, 1818; was First Lieutenant January 1. 1819. His name was dropped July 26, 1819.

Henry Seton, born in New York, was a Captain in the Fifty-fourth New York Infantry, April 16, 1864; was honorably mustered out April 14, 1866. He was a Second Lieutenant of the Fourth U. S. Infantry on May 11, 1866; First Lieutenant on the 17th May, 1872; Captain January 3, 1885; Major in Twelfth U. S. Infantry December 23, 1898. Retired October 10, 1899.

Under date of October 1, 1903, the writer received a letter from Major Henry Seton from Phœnix, Arizona, from which it appears that he was again in the army, and that he is a brother to Archbishop Robert Seton.

A Genealogy by Pierce, of Chicago, on page 396, gives the career of General John Gray Foster, born in Whitefield, New Hampshire, in 1823, married Mary Moale and Anna Johnson, died in Nashua, New Hampshire, in 1874. He was a Mexican war veteran under Scott—Grad. U. S. Military Lead—Coast Survey—Professor of Engineering at West Point—at Charleston, South Carolina, in Civil War—Defended Fort Sumter, and did other service during the war. His only daughter, Anne Moale Foster, married Captain Henry Seton of the Regular Army, at Fort Sheridan; no dates given.

Samuel Seton, of Virginia, a Lieutenant of Artisans and Engineers February 16, 1801, was honorably discharged June 1, 1802.

Algernon S. Seaton, born New York, a Sergeant in First Wisconsin Cavalry August 14, 1861, a Captain in December, 1861; honorably mustered out October 31, 1864; again a Captain in March, 1865; Brevet Major of Volunteers July 17, 1865, for efficient and meritorious service; honorably mustered out 19th July, 1865.

In Vol. XXIII. Pennsylvania Archives, is reprinted the Rolls of Pennsylvania "Rangers on the Frontier, 1778–1783." The following Seatons' names appear:

On pages 287, 318, Benjamin Seaton, Westmoreland county, in

Samuel Shannon's Company. On page 215. Richard Seaton,
Northumberland county, and Isaac Seaton, of the same county.
On page 290, Thomas Seaton, Westmoreland county, and on page
339 the same name from Northumberland county. On pages
222 and 263, William Seaton, of Northumberland county.

In Vol. XXIII, on page 480, in the List of Pennsylvania Pension-
ers appears the name of George Seaton, of Greene county, as Sergeant, at 2 p. m., January 3, 1816.

In Vol. XXV, under head of " Warranties of Land," there is
found the following: Bedford county, page 631, Ebenezer Seaton,
400 acres, February 10, 1794; Ezekias Seaton, 400 acres, same
date; Greene county, page 632, Reason Seaton, 400 acres, Feb.
10, 1794.

In Vol. XXVI, under same head, Washington county, Francis
Seaton, 400 acres, May 26, 1785; James Seaton, 300 acres, April
4, 1786.

From the Encyclopædia Britannica Biographical Dictionary we
learn William Winston Seaton was born in 1785, and died in 1866;
E. A. Seton, born 1774, died 1821; Robert was born 1839; Samuel Waddington Seton, an American educator and banker, born
1789, died 1869; and William Seton, an American soldier and
author, was born in 1835.

A James Seton appears to have been in the city of New York
in 1758, for there is on record there a power of attorney, dated
January 11, 1758, given by Harry Roe to his trusty and loving
friend, William Seton, of the city of New York, merchant, which
was signed by James Seton and another gentleman as witnesses.

Major Henry James Seton, of the Royal Irish Rifles, was among
the English officers dangerously wounded in an encounter with the
Boers in South Africa.

A Lieutenant Seaton is reported as having served in Colonel
Clinton's American Regiment, in one of the early wars of the
country.

A Lieutenant John Seaton was in Colonel Graham's American
Regiment in the year 1776, War of the Revolution.

An Ensign Seaton was enrolled in one of the patriot regiments
commanded in the Revolution by Killian Van Rensselaer.

In volume 32 of the California Law Reports mention is made of a G. W. Seaton, who died in San Francisco in 1865, and left D. M. W. Seaton and Phœbe Seaton as executors of his last will and testament.

There are Seatons mentioned in J. E. Jackson's History of St. George's Church, Doncaster; in Bridge's Northamptonshire; and in C. W. Hatfield's Historical Notices of Doncaster.

Seyton is named in Metcalf's Visitations of Northamptonshire. Seton in Arnot's Brief Notices of Families, and in Walter Pringle's Memoirs, by Rev. Walter Wood.

R. C. Seaton was the author of "Sir Hudson Lowe and Napoleon," published by Scribners.

Sir T. Seaton was the author of "From Cadet to Colonel," which was published by Rutledge, 1876.

Henry Seton Merriman, the author, and English novelist, is Hugh Seton Scott, in fact, the former name being only a pseudonym. He has written a long list of popular stories.

In Smith's Leading Cases. Alexander Seaton, a lawyer, is mentioned.

A Grant Seaton was hanged by a mob in Missouri on a charge of having killed a man, but it later appeared that he did not commit the crime, preferring to suffer death rather than accuse a woman who did the deed, and who afterward confessed the crime. This information comes through Samuel Eugene Seaton, of Center, Colorado, who was acquainted with Grant Seaton. This Samuel Seaton is said to be a son of Richard Aliph, descendant of Kenner Seaton.

Charles H. Seaton, of the Census Department of the United States, was appointed from the Eleventh Massachusetts Congressional District.

Charles W. Seaton, of New York, is listed as a Superintendent of Census. It is possible that he is the same man mentioned on page 394 as living at Newark, New Jersey.

There is a "Seton Infirmary" at Austin, Texas, presided over by the Sisters of Charity, and evidently named for Mother Elizabeth Ann Seton, the founder of the first society of the Sisters of

Charity in the United States. So says The National Magazine
for August. 1904.

A very nicely written letter was received from Mr. James Seaton,
of 248 South Clinton street, Baltimore, Maryland, acknowledging
the receipt of our letter of inquiry. He thinks he is the only
Seaton of his branch living, and gives no further particulars.

In the story "The Duke Decides," by Headon Hill, a Mr. Seaton
is mentioned as purser of the ocean steamship "Campania."

We have account of a John Seaton who married Mary Murdock.
They had a son, Robert Seaton, who was born in Union county.
New Jersey, in 1815, and married Anna E. Kelly at New Orleans,
Louisiana in 1849. Miss Kelly was born at Charleston, South
Carolina, in 1831. Their son, Walter Seaton, was born July 27,
1850, at New Orleans. He married Margaret Harrold Gill, at
Philadelphia, Pennsylvania, January 7, 1900. Miss Gill's parents
were English and Swede. She died childless some time ago.

Walter Seaton is a dentist, and has lived at Philadelphia about
twenty-seven years last past, having made his home at Pass
Christian, Mississippi, from 1851 to 1877.

CHAPTER LXII.

INTERESTING COINCIDENCES.

In the county of Haddington, in Scotland, there was at a very early date a monument of some pretensions to Robert Ferguson, and at the same time a collegiate church of Seton, which latter was built before 1390. These people being of the nobility, they were doubtless well acquainted. About four hundred and fifty years later Andrew P. Seaton, of Henderson, New York, was married to Laura A. Ferguson, of Watertown, in the same county. Thus the church and monument of the ancestors of these people were located in the same county in the old country and their descendants both lived in the same county in the New World and were made one by law and gospel. For a fact, there seems to be "a divinity that shapes our ends, rough hew them as we may."

From the study of the records we learn that in the year 1741 Elizabeth Seaton was married to John West, of York River, in Virginia, a scion of a noble British house, being a direct descendant from father to son of Lord De la Warre, the gorgeous Governor of Virginia, the Wests being a family of great historical distinction. About one hundred and thirty-seven years later the writer, a Seaton and a blood relation of the said Elizabeth, married a direct descendant of the Virginia Wests in the person of Sadie Bartley, whose grandfather, Joseph Bartley, married Sarah West, of the distinguished Virginia family. However, neither of the contracting parties to the later marriage was aware that the other was related to the earlier couple until some time after their wedding had taken place.

Among the interesting facts that have developed in the study of the Genealogy of our family, of which there have been several different works published, may be mentioned the fact that among the children of Joseph Seaton and his wife Elizabeth there was a

son born on August 4, 1811, who was given the name Edward
Seaton. He died on April 19, 1812, and another son was born on
the 15th of February, 1813, who was likewise named Edward
Seaton. On the tenth of September of the next year a daughter
was born to the same parents, who was named Mary Ann Seaton.
She died before she was a year old, and another daughter, born
October 29, 1815, was also given the name Mary Ann Seaton.
Again, on May 2, 1817, a daughter was born, who was named
Rachel Helen Seaton. She lived only about a year and a week,
and a later daughter, born on March 19, 1819, was likewise given
the name Rachel Helen Seaton.

It may be considered as something of a curiosity that the son
of Philip de Saytoun shou... have been called Setoun instead of
Saytoun.

Alan de Winton married Margaret, heiress of Seton, and assumed
his wife's name instead of using his own.

Alexander Seton married Elizabeth, heiress of Sir Adam Gordon. He was created a lord, and entered Parliament as Lord
of Gordon. Some of his descendants took the name Gordon,
while others retained that of Seton.

CHAPTER LXIII.

The following names and addresses have come into our possession, but for some reason no answer has been received to letters sent them, unless we have mixed matters. If removed, please send new address and biography.

Seaton, Adelaid, Portland, Oregon.
- A. C., Cleveland, Ohio.
- A. H., San Francisco, Calif
- Alberta, Newark, N. J.
- Albert P., New Hartford, N. Y.
- Alice, Charlton, Canada.
  - - F., Lowell, Mass.
  - - (Mrs.) San Francisco, Calif.
- Ann, New York city.
- Arthur H Seattle, Wash.
  - - L, Washington, D. C.
  - - R., New York city.
- Augusta, Chicago, Ills.
- B. C. (M.D.), Bolivar, Penn.
- Benjamin, Worcester, Mass.
  - - C., New York city.
  - - F., Washington, D. C.
- Bessie E., Quincy, Ills.
- Blanch B., Indianapolis Ind.
  - - H., Louisville, Ky.
- Carrie J. Grand Gulf, Miss.
- Catharine, Washington, D. C.
- C. E., Louisville, Ky.
- Charles, Ansonia, Conn.
  - - Washington, D. C.
  - - C., Washington, D. C.
  - - D., Portland, Maine.
  - - F., Seattle, Washington.
  - - F., Minot, S. D.
  - - F., Washington, D. C.
  - - H., Newark, N. J.
- Charlotte C., Washington, D.C.
  - - F., Washington, D. C.
- Clarence, Richmond, Va.
- Cora Hawley, Jacksonville, Fla.
- Daniel T., Baltimore, Md.
- David, Troy, New York.
  - - M., New York city.

Seaton, Donald, New York city.
- Dorothy, Cincinnati, Ohio.
- Earl L., Chicago, Ills.
- E. A., Lacygne, Kan.
- Edgar, Maryville, Tenn.
- Edith M., Peoria, Ills.
- Edward, Baltimore, Md.
  - - 2d, Washington, D. C.
- Eli V., Louisville, Ky.
- Eliza, Quincy, Ills.
- Elizabeth, Seattle, Wash.
- Emma, Louisville, Ky.
  - - San Francisco, Calif.
- Ernest, Chicago, Ills.
- E. R., Hubbard, Iowa.
- Esther, New York city.
- Eva R., Minneapolis, Minn.
- Everett, Detroit, Mich.
- Frances J., Toronto, Can.
- Frank H., Seattle, Wash.
  - - T., Louisville, Ky.
  - - W., Glenburn, N. D.
- Frederick A., Chicago, Ills.
- Frederick, Buffalo, N. Y.
  - - Butte, Mont.
  - - Indianapolis, Ind.
  - - A., Chicago, Ills.
- George C., Chicago, Ills.
  - - C., Ladd, Ills.
  - - D., Chicago, Ills.
  - - M., Richmond, Ky.
  - - W., Lacygne, Kan.
  - - W., Hall, Indiana.
  - - W., Quincy, Ills.
  - - W., Washington, D. C.
  - - R., Minneapolis, Minn.
  - - New York city.
- Georgiana, Baltimore, Md.
- Guy Hillard, Spokane, Wash.
- Hamilton, Washington, D. C.

Seaton, Hannah P., Peoria, Ills.
  Harry A., Chicago, Ills.
  - B., Denver, Colo.
  Henry C., San Francisco, Calif.
    D., Indianapolis, Ind.
    Baltimore, Md.
  Herbert A., Toronto, Can.
  H. E., Cambridge, Mass.
  H. F., Victoria, B. C.
  Howard E., Richmond, Va.
  - Washington, D. C.
  Hugh, Arbuckle, Calif.
  H. Y., New York city.
  Isabel D., Chicago, Ills.
  - Jackson M., Chucky, Tenn.
  Jacob A., Baltimore, Md.
  - - Galesburg, Ills.
  - James E., Baltimore, Md.
    - H.(cashier), Plainview,Tex.
    - H., Detroit, Mich.
    - K. W., Louisville, Ky.
    - M., Brooklyn, N. Y.
    R., Turney, Mo.
    Walker, Cincinnati, Ohio.
  - Grayson, Ky.
  - New York city.
  - St. Johns, N. B.
  - Jane K., Minneapolis, Minn.
  - Jeremiah L., Chicago, Ills.
  Jesse, Columbus, Ohio.
  John J. Portland, Oregon.
  - R., Chicago, Ills.
  - John R., Richmond, Va.
    - W., Detroit, Mich.
    Brooklyn, N. Y.
    Day, Missouri.
  - (M. D.), Louisville Ky.
  Julia A., Denver, Colo.
  Juliet, Chicago, Ills.
  - Larson, Seattle, Wash.
  Lawrence, Denver, Colo.
  Lawson, Indianapolis, Ind.
  Lawyer, Clinton, Mo.
  Lenora, Seattle, Wash.
  - Leonard W., Rochester, N. Y
  L. E., Cabella, Kan.
  - Letitia C., Denver, Colo.
  - Lillian A., Atchison, Kan.
  - - Washington, D. C.
  - Lizzie, Hotchkiss, Col.
  - Lottie F., Washington, D. C.
  - Louise A., Pueblo, Colo.
  - - M., Denver, Colo.

Seaton, Louise, Brooklyn, N. Y.
  - Troy, N. Y.
  Lulu P., Quincy, Ills.
  Lycurgus, Louisville, Ky.
  Mamie, Washington, D. C.
  Margaret, Columbus, Ohio.
  - Lowell, Mass.
  Martha J., Winamic, Ind.
  Mary B., Washington, D. C.
  - J., Columbus, Ohio.
    San Francisco, Calif.
    Washington, D. C.
  May, Toledo, Ohio.
  M. D., Belgrade, Neb.
  Minerva A., Newark, N. J.
  Minnie, Louisville, Ky.
  Mollie A., Seattle, Wash.
  - Nellie, Rockford, Ills.
  - Interbay, Wash.
  N. G., Maryville, Tenn.
  Olive O., Cleveland, Ohio.
  - Brooklyn, N. Y.
  Oscar, Atlanta, Ga.
  - Chicago, Ills.
  Pauline (Mrs.), Kent, Eng.
  Perry M., Richmond, Va.
  Peter, Butte, Montana.
  R. Frank, Richmond, Va.
  Robert B., Lowell, Mass.
  - - H., New York city.
  - (Capt.) Chicago, Ills.
    Colorado Springs, Colo.
    Baltimore, Md.
    Troy, N. Y.
  Rufus S., Rochester, N. Y.
  Ruth, Wheeling, West Va.
  Sadie, Chicago, Ills.
  - Chucky Tenn.
  Samuel B., Rochester, N. Y.
  - Washington, D. C.
  - Burlington Iowa.
  - Louisville, Ky.
  - New York city.
  - Peoria, Ills.
  Sarah, Longmeadow, Mass.
  - Washington, D. C.
  Solomon, Nashville, Tenn.
  Stanley, Lowell, Mass.
  Stephen, Chicago, Ills.
  - Seattle, Wash.
  Strobridge, Chicago, Ills.
  Stuart, Little York, Ills.
  Thaddeus K., Denver, Colo.
  Theresa, San Francisco, Calif.

INDEX.